Latinos and the U.S. South

Latinos and the U.S. South

José María Mantero

Westport, Connecticut
London

Library of Congress Cataloging-in-Publication Data

Mantero, José María, 1964–
    Latinos and the U.S. South / José María Mantero.
        p. cm.
    Includes bibliographical references and index.
    ISBN 978–0–313–34510–4 (alk. paper)
1. Hispanic Americans—Southern States. 2. Latin Americans—Southern States. 3.
Hispanic Americans—Southern States—Social conditions. 4. Latin Americans—Southern
States—Social conditions. 5. Latin America—Emigration and immigration. 6. Southern
States—Emigration and immigration. 7. Immigrants—Southern States—Social conditions.
8. Alien labor, Latin American—Southern States. I. Title. II. Title: Latinos and the
US South.
F220.S75M36 2008
304.8'7508—dc22   2008000205

British Library Cataloguing in Publication Data is available.

Library of Congress Catalog Card Number: 2008000205
ISBN: 978–0–313–34510–4

First published in 2008

Praeger Publishers, 88 Post Road West, Westport, CT 06881
An imprint of Greenwood Publishing Group, Inc.
www.praeger.com

Printed in the United States of America

The paper used in this book complies with the
Permanent Paper Standard issued by the National
Information Standards Organization (Z39.48–1984).

10 9 8 7 6 5 4 3 2 1

For Mila and Daniel

Contents

Preface

The current phenomenon of transnational immigration and displacement affecting countless individuals around the world poses a very real set of challenges to law enforcement organizations, schools, hospitals, courts, and businesses that are looking to adapt to the arrival of their most recent residents. As citizens from developing countries are relocating to developed nations in search of economic opportunities and political stability unavailable to them in their homeland, communities in the United States, Spain, Germany, France, and England, for example, are reexamining their current priorities and choosing to reallocate social, political, and economic resources in response to the demographic changes.

Currently, the United States is witnessing the growing and relatively uninterrupted influx of Latin American nationals to states such as Arizona, New Mexico, California, Texas, Florida, and New York, which have maintained a historically significant Latino population, and to areas of nontraditional Hispanic migration and presence such as central Tennessee, rural North Carolina, and southern Ohio, which have been historically unaccustomed to receiving Spanish-speaking immigration. In the summer of 2000, I journeyed to Kentucky, Tennessee, Mississippi, Louisiana, Alabama, and Georgia in order to get a better idea of the impact Hispanic immigrants were having on communities in both the urban and rural South and to begin to research the possible parallels between the varieties of Southern and Latin American cultures. In my travels, I encountered the richness and extraordinary complexity of the Latin American immigrant population in this country, meeting citizens from Colombia, Cuba, Mexico, and Nicaragua, among many others, who had been here for generations, who spanned all socioeconomic strata, and who found themselves here either by choice or by inertia. Some were eager to share their experiences, while others were understandably reticent to open themselves up and reveal what had possibly been, up to that point, a rather intimate and unspoken part of their life.

While I had always suspected some general similarities between the emblematic versions of what we understand to be the U.S. Southern and Latin American cultures, this book is partly a result of these discussions, due to the fact that they brought to life what had been, up to that point, undefined hints of equivalencies and resemblances. For that, for their confidence and willingness to speak to me, I am deeply and especially indebted to those who took time to share their experiences, particularly Norma Antillón, Elsa Baughman, Miguel Calvo, Luis Cartagena, Pablo Garzon, Jerry Gonzalez, Ted Henken, and Terry Horgan. Their willingness to talk with and frequently open their home or business to a complete stranger and discuss their relocation, decisions, family history, and impressions of their communities speaks volumes about their generosity. I am thankful and appreciative of their strength, and this book owes a debt of gratitude to the generations of Latin American immigrants that preceded them and to those that will certainly follow.

In the process, there have also been a number of people who consistently encouraged me. Elizabeth Demers first believed in this idea and was exceptionally helpful in the process. I am also thankful to José Luis Gómez-Martínez, who provided valuable suggestions after an early reading of the manuscript. I consider Jo Ann Recker and David Knutson both departmental colleagues and unrelenting friends who supported this project enthusiastically from the beginning. My parents Nieves and Manuel Mantero, my sister Laura, and my brothers Miguel, Francisco, and Vicente have always been a source of inspiration as I grappled with this work and, along the way, with my own hybrid identity.

Finally, I have nothing but appreciation and love for my wife Mila and our son Daniel, whose recent arrival and presence in our life has brought an anticipated yet unimagined joy. The presence of both of them has been a constant source of encouragement. Over the course of these years, Mila endured the falls, winters, and springs of Cincinnati, Ohio, and spent the summers in Madrid, Spain, traveling with me in both countries and listening to my brainstorms as I would read and gather material for this book and disappear for hours in an attempt to organize the year's material and write. It was for them that this was written, *siempre*.

Introduction

Over the last 30 years, the United States has undergone a series of social, political, and economic changes that has transformed the country from within and marked a "before" and an "after" in the history of this nation: September 11, the Iran hostage crisis, the Reagan presidency, the rise of technological stocks, and the flight of manufacturing to other countries, for example, have cast long shadows whose effects are still being evaluated. But few events have transformed communities as much as the recent influx of Latino immigrants who have brought the limitless varieties of Latin American cultures to the United States. As Jerome R. Adams has written, "News articles lump together *all* Hispanics, whose presence is described in breathless terms like 'rising' and 'growing' and 'increasing.' Rarely are Hispanics portrayed as contributing to housing booms, providing needed services, or improving efficiencies."[1] As demonstrated by the 2006 marches in over 140 cities against proposed immigration legislation and the participation in these demonstrations of approximately 500,000 people in Washington, D.C., 500,000 in Dallas, another 500,000 in Los Angeles, 300,000 in Chicago, and 200,000 in Phoenix, for example, the substantial Latino minority is gradually realizing its political and economic clout and advancing transformations across the country. Many of the changes undergone by educational systems, hospitals, police departments, businesses, and government offices are due, in part, to the growing presence of Latin American immigrants in nontraditional areas of migration, as these changes are deeply affecting the present and are forecasting the adaptability of this country to the presence of a not-so-new

Latino population that is multilingual, politically active, and economically robust.

In her short story "The Displaced Person" (1954), Georgia writer Flannery O'Connor characterized the struggle between whites, blacks, and new immigrants in the rural South of the 1950's as a battle waged between ethnocentrism and economic necessity, calling attention to the relationship between African Americans, whites, and new immigrant populations, the paucity of labor, and, as the title implies, displaced identities. In the narrative, the landowner, Mrs. McIntyre, expresses mixed passions and attitudes that may very well be true not only for the U.S. South of the 1950s but for the rest of the country as well, both yesterday and today: " 'One fellow's misery is the other fellow's gain. That man there,' and she pointed to where the Displaced Person had disappeared, '—he has to work! He wants to work!' She turned to Mrs. Shortley with her bright wrinkled face. 'That man is my salvation!' she said."[2] While at present Latinos may not necessarily be saving the U.S. South, they are deeply influencing the social, political, and economic fabric of communities that have for decades existed rather naïvely between the racial poles of Black and White Americans and their respective communities. The presence of Latinos in the Deep South today has transformed much of the region into an unanticipated grouping of cultures that, based more on their atypical commonalities, may speak more directly and intensely to how future generations of immigrants will affect change in this country and to what degree this country will change to accommodate those new populations. Over the next sixty years, "Latinos will account for more than 40% of all U.S. population growth."[3] What will this expansion mean for cultural and civic organizations, business ventures, public service programs, school districts, and government institutions? As Luis Fraga et al. have noted, the relationship between the new Latino populations and those individuals living in the United States must be urgently and unavoidably mutual if we are to forge a broader, more inclusive version of this nation: "Broadening America's vision of itself ultimately means getting many powerful groups to abandon the (often unconscious) fact that their sensibilities speak to everyone's needs and aspirations. At the same time, a willingness to chart a course for all people in the United States means getting Latinos to abandon the (often unconscious) assumption that politics can never be anything but a battle of raw self-interest."[4]

This comprehensiveness should be mutually inclusive on the part of both Latinos and non-Latinos. In this respect, perhaps the manner in which Latinos are or are not assimilating into the South's towns and cities and how Southerners are adapting to the changing circumstances brought about by the recent immigrants may shed light on a once and possible future United States. Writing in the late 1940s, the historian V. O. Key noted, "In its shortcomings the South has all the failings common to the American states."[5] These "failings" have today given way to learning experiences that, in many areas of the U.S. South, are still being assimilated and processed and that have touched on a number of difficult issues traditionally viewed as the exclusive domain of the Southerner, yet today have proven to be the property of much of the nation. "The South, different in so many ways for so much of its history, now offers lessons to the rest of the country."[6]

The U.S. Census Bureau divides the South into the following three regions: South Atlantic (Delaware, District of Columbia, Florida, Georgia, Maryland, North Carolina, South Carolina, Virginia, and West Virginia), East South Central (Alabama, Kentucky, Mississippi, and Tennessee), and West South Central (Arkansas, Louisiana, Oklahoma and Texas). For the purposes of the study I will focus primarily on the southeastern portion of the country, including states bordering the Gulf of Mexico. In his book *Democracy Heading South: National Politics in the Shadow of Dixie* (2001), Augustus B. Cochran defines the South as the 11 states that seceded from the Union and further divides these into two groups: the Deep South (Alabama, Georgia, Mississippi, South Carolina, and Louisiana) and the Rim South (Tennessee, North Carolina, Virginia, Florida, Arkansas, and Texas). Although Florida's and Texas's Hispanic populations warrant studies in their own right, they do not generally enter into the parameters of this book due to the historical and cultural differences evident between them and the vast majority of the states of the U.S. South. For the rest of the Southern states, the presence of Latino immigrants has led to a repositioning of Southern identity and, consequently, of the role that the region will play in the nation's future.

In my own case, my family moved from Kalamazoo, Michigan, to Athens, Georgia, in August of 1973. As we had arrived in the United States some four years earlier, my impression as an eight-year-old was that we were, once more, leaving for another country, that "Georgia" was as distinct a nation as "Michigan," and that we were moving to a different place, one where the language would, again, be mysterious and new. I was only off a bit. Initially, our integration into the Athens community was uncomplicated, as our arrival to the United States had dispensed with the culture shock of a transcontinental move (more for my parents than for us five children, since none of us were yet six years old), and the Latin American immigrants from places such as Puerto Rico, Venezuela, and Cuba who were then living in Athens provided a more than welcoming atmosphere for us in our new environment. As the months passed in Georgia, I recall becoming aware of differences between the two newest places in my mind: people spoke another way, slurred gently, half-sang or lazed their words along, and at times my parents had difficulty understanding them (as they still do today); during the Georgia winters, the snow that fell—if at all—was generally a light dusting, enough to send the local Department of Transportation into an unanticipated yet loudly declared state of emergency; summers in Georgia seemed inexhaustible, as temperatures began to rise noticeably in March, topped off in August, and frequently stayed warm and muggy well into October; and the talkativeness and energy of many African Americans we met at our schools, grocery stores, and bank reminded me of some of the warmth that we had left behind in Spain.

From June to September we would usually return to our homeland, but as adolescents there were years when, due to circumstances, we remained in Athens and took our first summer jobs or just revelled in living life by the side of the neighborhood pool, next door to our house, on the other side of a now-disappeared thicket. During those summer months when we were unable to travel to Madrid and Sevilla, our parents made sure to take us on at least one trip, to one destination that was relatively close but still far enough away that it retained an element of that anticipated brightness that envelops a vacation. I recall the beaches and crocodile farms of St. Augustine, Florida, the long coastline of Isle of Palms and the aircraft carrier Independence of Charleston, South Carolina, the variety of kitsch, colors, and tourist shops of Cherokee, North Carolina, the quiet squares and smoothed cobblestones of River Road in Savannah, and the tranquility of Tybee Island, Georgia. Over the course of every year we would make periodic visits to Atlanta, to places such as the now-defunct Oxford Books and to shopping centers such as Lenox Square Mall (before its postmodern transformation into a McMall some years ago), when the city was, in the 1970s and 1980s, a barren urban blight along a landscape that was looking to reinvent itself (an opportunity subsequently served on a silver platter by the 1996 Olympics). I also travelled with my youth and teenage soccer teams throughout the state and into South Carolina, Tennessee, and Alabama, almost always playing under a relentless sun that, coupled with the humidity, made me feel as if I were wearing a warm, wet blanket over my head and shoulders.

As I journey today through parts of the South, I want to believe that I am aware of the distinctness of my surroundings, of the differences between cities and regions that, though they may share the same name—Athens, Georgia, Athens, Tennessee, and Athens, Alabama, for example—they are, in essence, discretely diverse communities. That is today, as an adult. As a child, was I aware of these regional differences, of the variations within what has been termed a "Southern identity"? I think not. I believe I was aware that I was in a place unlike Michigan, but I do not believe I was noticing the slight yet significant dissimilarities between Athens and Augusta, Georgia, or between Savannah and Charleston. At the time, I was merely living there, submerging myself in an atmosphere in which I was in a constant state of flux: always belonging, always unbelonging. The South was, I imagine, my place to be, a land that, within its uniqueness and its omnivorous variety, came to be that point called home and that land which, with its Georgia pine trees, red clay, and ingrained regional distinctiveness, automatically—and perhaps subconsciously—lent itself to the development of an identity within an identity: I was a multilingual individual, living between two countries, firmly rooted in both, experiencing Southern variations on that "American way of life." (As well as all the possibilities offered by our regional understanding of Madrid and Sevilla in Spain.) To paraphrase Richard Rodriguez, "biculturalness happens." (Even in the South, perhaps especially in the South.)

When my family came to settle into our new residence some 800 miles south of Michigan, we also continued to return to Spain every possible summer. There we managed to divide our time between my mother's family in Madrid and my father's family in Sevilla, once more experiencing and turning into unwitting evidence of the regional differences existent between the two cities. If in each place we were commonly chided about how "American" and non-Spanish we were in our speech, dress, mannerisms, or accents, the prolonged time spent in both areas of Spain made us soak in the customs or speech patterns of each region, as if we were hungry for a set of cultural touchstones. Upon returning to Madrid from a prolonged summer stay in the town of Sanlúcar la Mayor, I recall my cousins in Madrid, for example, teasing me about my (once-again) recent Andalusian accent, particularly taking notice of how many final consonants simply disappeared from words (particularly the *s*).

The regional differences between the regions of Castilla and Andalucía have their roots in events that happened over 1,000 years ago, yet still affect a profound influence on daily life there. Since much of what is to-day Andalucía remained under the control of Arab sultans from the eighth to the end of the fifteenth century, the presence of North African or Middle Eastern cultures is visible today in the architecture of the Alhambra palace in Granada or the *mezquita* church in Córdoba, in the white, thick-walled houses found in towns such as Vejer and Ronda, in the etymology of words like *algebra, alacrán* (scorpion), or *algodón* (cotton), and in the green eyes and dark complexion of many of its inhabitants. For all of its uniqueness, Andalucía has regularly maintained a tense relationship with the rest of Spain, particularly with the central government in Madrid. It has been the region that has witnessed the highest percentage of its people emigrate to other countries and regions of Spain, and has also consistently suffered the highest unemployment in the country, as the region attempts to cease its dependence on agriculture and diversify technologically and industrially. Andalucía also continues to bear the brunt of a number of linguistic and cultural stereotypes that range from the insulting (that the region is the educational backwater of Spain) to the romantic (all Andalusians are charming).

Differences between northern and southern regions of a country are not unique to Spain or the United States. Disparities that transcend the merely geographical exist in Mexico, Nicaragua, Colombia, and Argentina, among others. In Mexico, for example, the northern states are frequently marked by the presence of the *maquiladoras* on the border with the United States, and daily life is inextricably linked to circumstances directly linked to their northern neighbor. The southern states, however, are geographically and politically distanced from the central government in Mexico City and find themselves pursuing policies that approach the concepts of autonomy found in Canada, France, or Spain. In Argentina, the south-central pampas are home to the gaucho and the distinctly non–Buenos Aires life that he has historically led, while the northern region shares more cultural affinities with the highland cultures of Bolivia or Chile than with the colder climates of the south. And in Nicaragua, the cool northern mountains that gave refuge to the Sandinista rebels during the 1960s and 1970s are a world away from the southern border with Costa Rica and the protracted desire to build a transoceanic canal through the San Juan River and over the San Juan isthmus. Instead of simply distinguishing each of these nations from the other, these differences between northern and southern regions illustrate the commonalities that these countries share and may offer possible opportunities for transnational cooperation that looks to both develop sound domestic policies and improve continental alliances.

Throughout my life, bouncing between the United States and Spain has allowed me to better understand the mechanisms at work in both of my countries; but it has been while living in distinct regions of each nation that I have come to appreciate the complex set of historical mechanics at work in the construction of nationhood. In travels throughout the U.S. South, in conversations with Latinos, in the emerging cities, and from within the misleading isolation of the countryside, there emerges a sense of Latino or Hispanic ownership of place that manifests itself in two separate ways: 1) a pride in one's country of origin; and 2) a pride in one's community of residence, whether it includes other Latinos, Anglos, African Americans, Asians, Europeans, or all of the above. Regrettably, this dual pride may be difficult to reconcile, as an allegiance to both one's small and large homelands may lead to the fragmentation of a possible unified Latino or Hispanic population and may actually transfer and transport some of the social, political, and economic issues from home here to the United States. According to Latin American residents, for example, Baton Rouge in the 1970s witnessed the continuation of the ideological conflicts that had existed in Nicaragua for years between Somocistas and Sandinistas, the two sides of the Nicaraguan Revolution (1977–1979).

While it seems logical that Nicaraguans at opposite ends of the political spectrum, for example, would not automatically find common ground upon emigrating to the same community within the United States, conflicts between individuals of the same nationality are a reality often ignored in the generalizations and research on individual national (im)migrant populations. If anything, these transdomestic conflicts may in the future intensify due to a sense that one's new existence abroad has been reduced to its essence, and, when residing outside of one's native soil, one's political or social convictions may be magnified and may perhaps be paramount to other concerns. When living outside one's large or small homeland there may exist a sense of representativeness: that I embody a certain part of the population that remains in my country and must, therefore, put additional effort into expressing and supporting the imagined ideals of that population. The geographical, psychological, and emotional distance from home may lead to the immediate idealization or demonization of one's adopted country, creating a set of circumstances defined by the extremes: the nostalgic pining for one's past place and/or the profound rejection of the new community. It is in the intersection between these that notions of "pride" and "honor" are forged, both of them subservient and connected to a set of immediate circumstances: "pride" represents not only where the individual has been, but also what he is accomplishing in the immediate present (ensconced in the cultural geography of the United States); "honor" reflects that connection between the individual and the community, the realization that one is much more than oneself: one is, as a member of a myriad of groups, an extension of these groups. Either pride or honor by itself is precarious, as, in the case of the first, it can lead to an exaggerated sense of egocentrism and self-worth, disconnected from one's circles; in the case of the second, to the complete neglect of the individual for the sake of the community.

Recent Latino immigrants to the United States appear to have balanced both extremes, as they frequently arrive with a preestablished connection to other family members or to other immigrants from their country that are already living in the United States, taking an immense pride in the difficulties they are enduring and in what is being accomplished on a daily basis. Perhaps this presence will also serve as a reminder to others in the United States of the importance of balancing individual pride with a sense of honor, of belonging to something larger than oneself.

Encounters and conversations with Latinos throughout the U.S. South have reinforced the presence of conflicts and interests existing both within a national group of immigrants, between those different nationalities, and between Latinos and non-Latinos. The interviews that began in May of 2000 and are included in this work are by no means intended to be exclusive nor to provide a scientific sampling of a heterogeneous immigrant phenomenon. Quite the opposite: they are set down in order to provide initial—albeit anecdotal—evidence of the diversity inherent in the words "Latino" or "Hispanic," of the extent to which immigrant populations have assimilated their experience in Southern cultures, and of the richness that any individual life possesses.

If the Latino communities in the U.S. South are particularly and potentially fragmented along lines that transcend the merely national or patriotic, what is the future of terms such as "Latino" or "Hispanic"? On one hand, it is clear that entities like the United States Federal Government are frequently in need of such terminology in order to effectively disburse federal monies to the states and to track the qualitative and quantitative changes in the population. On the other hand, the all-encompassing terms "Latino" and "Hispanic" continue to mislead and misrepresent the diversity (or lack thereof) of the Latin American population whose first language is not English.

As a nation, the future United States will move beyond ethnic and racial classifications that may only serve to muddy the cultural waters and promote the perhaps simplistic classification of individuals according to country of origin (not unlike what the Bureau of Citizenship and Immigration Services—formerly known as the Immigration and Naturalization Service—has been doing for years). One possibility is to clarify the distinctions between "Latino" and "Hispanic" by specifying that "Latinos" are the individuals and descendants of individuals from Spanish-speaking countries living within the borders of the United States, while the word "Hispanic" would refer primarily to those residing in Spanish-speaking countries. The terms, therefore, would be descriptions of a geographical nature instead of distinctions centered merely on dangerously subjective ethnic or racial considerations. Not unlike European immigrants today, Mexican citizens would then be regarded first and foremost as Mexicans, and secondly either "Latinos" or "Hispanics" depending on their place of residence. Considering all permutations and the series of issues and circumstances that fashion a sense of identity, it is foreseeable that problems will arise and individuals will justifiably rebel against these classifications. Would indigenous inhabitants of Chiapas, Mexico, for example, choose to be known as Mexicans? Do those individuals from the English-speaking Caribbean coast of Nicaragua wish to be known simply as Nicaraguans outside their land? The potential for divergence is unending, as each of us determines our individual identity through the conscious and unconscious combination and recombination of personal, social, economic, and political factors that affect our daily existence.

An important component of identity has traditionally been the manner in which racial and ethnic groups have been defined, particularly by those outside who have simply looked to impose simple classifications upon a minority population. Such is the case, for example, with the terms "Hispanic" and "Latino."[7] If the labeling of transnational immigrant population groups has proven to be an understandably challenging process, the Census Bureau term "Hispanic" has been soundly criticized recently for its apparent insensitivity to the ethnic origins of recent Latin American immigrants. Suzanne Oboler, for example, writes that "the ethnic label 'Hispanic' obscures rather than clarifies the varied social and political experiences in U.S. society of more than 23 million citizens, residents, refugees, and immigrants with ties to the Caribbean and Central and South

American countries"; Angel Oquendo declares that "Hispanic" "is linked to the brutal Spanish colonization of America"; and Marta E. Gimenez asserts that "Hispanic" "is a politically distasteful label, yielding nothing but a bogus identity that blurs the differences between Latin Americans, Spaniards, and people of Spanish, Mexican, Cuban, and Puerto Rican descent who have lived in the United States for generations."[8] The term "Latino," on the other hand, distinguishes itself from "Hispanic" by distancing itself from Spanish colonial history in Latin America, recognizing the historical plurality of nations whose inhabitants speak Spanish, Portuguese, or French, and forging an identity based on the autonomous variety of ethnic experience on the American continent. Yet there are also problems with this expression, as it seem to ignore indigenous peoples and immigrant populations such as the Chinese in Cuba or Peru that have made a significant impact on their adopted countries. As language is principally of a denotative nature and inflicts meaning rather than releasing it, what seems to be at stake is that marginalized and minority populations have a voice in their own characterization. As Eduardo Mendieta has indicated, both terms are ultimately problematic: "To be a 'Hispanic' or 'Latino' is to be signified upon rather than to be the one who signifies."[9]

Latin American immigrants to the U.S. South have traditionally not been party to the distinctions and debates centering on cultural nomenclature, preferring instead to carve out their patch of identity by combining aspects of their small and large homelands. Born in Peru, Miguel Calvo, for example, has lived in Florence, Alabama, and Covington, Tennessee, and has served as Executive Director of Latino Memphis Conexion, witnessing both the growth and the divergence of interests of Latino communities in the area. Although there exists in Memphis a Hispanic Business Alliance, that, as their Web site explains, "Envisions a Greater Memphis area recognized for equal Hispanic participation and contribution to its economic and political infrastructure with mutual respect for all languages, cultures, and traditions," in Calvo's opinion, in Memphis "there is no cohesion between [Hispanic] groups."[10] Now living in Jackson, Mississippi, Elsa Baughman arrived in Hattiesburg, Mississippi, in 1976, after reading an advertisement for Mississippi State University in Venezuela. As she states, she raised her daughters "with the Hispanic culture" and in 1995 co-founded the Mississippi Hispanic Association. Throughout her years of living in the state, she admits that "it is difficult to maintain a Latino identity here," partly because "I thought that it was very important to absorb the American atmosphere." In Jackson she helps to organize the Latino Festival every year, acknowledging that it can be a difficult chore, primarily because of Latinos themselves and the cultural differences that exist between them and the U.S. Anglo culture: "The Latino is not accustomed to belonging to groups. The first thing that a Hispanic asks me is 'What will the organization do for me?' Every year we have an annual meeting, and no one comes, absolutely *no one.*"[11] Does the declaration that "no one comes" have any connection to Elsa's statement that "it is difficult to maintain a Latino identity here" and her implicit wish to assimilate into "the American atmosphere"? Many immigrants may feel more Mexican, Colombian, or Bolivian than "Latino" or "Hispanic," and it has traditionally been the case that organizations exist specifically to aid those recently arriving in large cities such as Los Angeles, Houston, Chicago, or New York.

The recent Latin American immigrants to the United States may be unaware of the bureaucratic and cultural nomenclature surrounding ethnic and racial populations in the United States and may perhaps even be justifiably cautious about entering a cultural landscape mapped by the name game—about renaming themselves "Latino" or "Hispanic" and being obliged to disconnect themselves from their homeland—or, quite possibly, they simply may not be familiar with what is meant by these terms in the first place. Before our presence in the United States, immigrants may have felt more allegiance to a small homeland—a town, city, or province—rather than any large homeland, their country of origin. Upon entry into the United States, a "Latino" or "Hispanic" identity is imprinted upon a web of other identities that, due to the weighty decision to leave one's country, has been relegated to secondary importance. In the United States, for example, being from the Caribbean coast of Nicaragua instead of the capital city of Managua makes little administrative difference and carries little—if any—cultural cachet, as immigrants are recorded simply according to country of origin. In Nicaragua, the linguistic, cultural, and historical differences between the Managuan and the person born in Bluefields on the Caribbean coast are vast, as they both come from exceptionally diverse sociopolitical regions that look to coexist beneath the banner of the Nicaraguan flag (not unlike what occurs to a U.S. citizen abroad: within the borders of the United States, there is an implicit understanding that someone from Louisiana and someone from Massachusetts will be different; yet to many of those who live outside the country and may be unfamiliar with regional differences in the United States, both are simply citizens of the United States, all localisms aside). An immigrant's identity has shifted upon arriving in this country, as we, like all who reside here, are classified and categorized according to gender, race, age, educational level attained, and religious affiliation, among other banners and column headings. Was none of this significant back in the country of origin? Was there no need to keep track of this information, of these statistics? Quite possibly someone did, but upon arriving in the United States, Latino immigrants—as other immigrants—are subtly expected and instructed to recompose themselves, to reconstruct their personae based on patterns that fit the history, language, and design of their adopted government. Such, perhaps, is part of the price paid for emigrating.

While language may be the principal factor in influencing one's sense of integration or assimilation into a community in the United States, our profession also plays an important role in affecting the degree to which we may adapt to the country and our children's reaction to their adopted community and to their home culture. What does exist is a diversification on all levels of the Latino experience, an experience that is dependent on country of origin, socioeconomic level, education, gender, age, and race, among other factors. These factors are distinct determinants that both unite and separate, making identity a fluid game of shifting categories and correspondences. Say you are a single, 30-year-old woman of modest means from Mexico, belonging to an indigenous blood line, and a manual laborer. Perhaps you have more in common with a 32-year-old Bolivian mother of three, whose husband left her nothing when he died in the tin mines at the age of 40 after laboring under inhuman conditions for 20 years. Or do you have more in common with a compatriot, say a 50-year-old Mexican woman whose family claims descent from Spain and who "married well," as befits someone of her social class? In many countries, patriotism is often only expressed as a last resort, in what may be described as national emergencies or celebrations. Purportedly patriotic symbols such as flags or national anthems are often associated with conservative ideologies that look to preserve a utopian national past. Consequently, patriotism is rarely flaunted to the extent found in the United States. There must be a logic regarding why this nation insists upon shaping the contemporary immigrant experience to its own particular history and its own patriotic image, instead of allowing this and every generation of immigrants to construct their own fluency and pace of assimilation. The United States is a product, in large part, of difficult immigrant experiences, and today many U.S. voters and elected officials run the risk of homogenizing the contributions of new immigrant populations through legislation and laws that look to either rapidly integrate the new arrivals into society or shut them out completely. (Or perhaps both, as the second may be a direct consequence of the first.)

Although "there is little evidence that the gains for Latinos were accompanied by losses for non-Latinos,"[12] recent anti-immigrant attitudes expressed by political figures and laws written and approved by communities across the United States reflect the extent to which society is threatened by the local impact of Latino immigration and serve as reminders of the enduring effects of September 11, 2001. When CNN reported that Newt Gingrich, for example, remarked in a speech to the National Federation of Republican Women in 2007 that "We should replace bilingual education with immersion in English so people learn the common language of the country and they learn the language of prosperity, not the language of living in a ghetto," his observation earned him both accolades from the more conservative press and harsh criticism from Hispanics and Hispanic organizations across the country: some understood his words as only defending the very practical reality that immigrants learn the language of the nation that takes them in, while others criticized the negative connotations implicit in his unspoken statement on the Spanish language and Spanish-speaking immigrants. Yet his misspoken opinion simply reflects the impression that many across the United States have of Latin American immigrants arriving in this country, particularly of those who choose to have little or no interaction with the English-speaking community, of the federal government's inability to resolve the apparently unceasing immigration of undocumented citizens from Latin American countries to the United States, and of continuing local efforts to take matters into their own hands. As Stephen Yale-Loehr and Ted Chiappari have written regarding the continuing congressional dialogue on immigration, "many states and cities have jumped into the fray with their own immigration laws. Most of the measures attempt to encourage foreign nationals to leave by making life and work within their states and communities effectively impossible without proper documentation."[13] Gingrich's apology a few days later—broadcast in both Spanish and English—did little to change opinions on either side of the issue, as those who agreed with him continue to be convinced of the increasing ghettoization of Spanish-speaking immigrants in their towns and cities, while those in disagreement understood his original statement to be an honest albeit tactless representation of the tensions and misperceptions lurking just beneath the surface of those same communities.

Due to the changing circumstances, the federal government post-9/11 began to play a more active role in immigration reform and border control. The Clear Law Enforcement for Criminal Alien (CLEAR) Act of 2005 represented the government's intention to articulate a more cohesive immigration policy, specifically in regards to law enforcement. Section 8, for example, increased federal detention space for undocumented immigrants and immigrants found to be breaking the law, and Section 11 provided broad immunity to law enforcement personnel and agencies "from claims of money damages based on any incident arising out of enforcement of any immigration law, except for any violation of criminal law." On its Web site, the National Council of La Raza (NCLR), an organization that defends Latino interests, criticizes the fact that the CLEAR Act "gives state and local police officers the right to enforce all federal immigration laws, gives financial incentives to states and localities to comply [with the Act], and criminalizes all immigration law violations."

On its Web site, the NCLR also describes a number of distinct acts that look to follow in the footsteps of the CLEAR Act. Passed by a vote of 328 to 95, the Community Protection Act of 2006 (H.R. 6094) "expand[s] expedited removal of anyone immigration officers believe to be a noncitizen," and, in the opinion of the NCLR, "severely limits due process" as it provides for the rapid deportation of individuals and may cause the expatriation of people who are actually United States citizens. The Immigration Law Enforcement Act of 2006 (H.R. 6095) "contains language from the CLEAR Act reaffirming the 'inherent authority of state and local police to enforce federal immigration laws.'" And, in a surreal piece of legislation, the Border Tunnel Prevention Act (H.R. 4830) "prohibits the unauthorized construction, financing or reckless permitting (on one's land) of a tunnel or subterranean passageway between the United States and another country."

Ironically, the all-encompassing CLEAR Act moved many communities to conclude that the federal government was simply not doing enough to stop illegal immigration and that local citizens must take an active role in writing legislation appropriate for their community. One of the more notorious examples was the Hazleton, Pennsylvania, Illegal Immigrant Relief Act of 2006: "Landlords would be fined for providing housing to undocumented immigrants. Businesses or organizations known to employ or provide job assistance to undocumented immigrants would be denied permits and contracts. The ordinance would also make English the city's official language and generally require all city documents to be in English only."[14] Although suspended in September of 2006, the law took the incentive from the federal government and paved the way for other communities across the nation. In Colorado, for example, House Bill 06-1343 took effect in January 2007, compelling state employers to confirm the legal work status of all employees and to "sign an attestation confirming under penalty of perjury that the employer has not knowingly hired an illegal worker,"[15] with a $5,000 fine being levied for the first incident and $25,000 for subsequent violations. In Oklahoma, the first session of the 51st state legislature introduced the Oklahoma Taxpayer and Citizen Protection Act of 2007, giving law enforcement authorities the ability to confiscate and shut down the property of anyone found to be giving any type of assistance to undocumented immigrants. English-only ordinances passed in Taneytown, Maryland, Shenandoah, Pennsylvania, and Hazel Park, Michigan, and Riverside, New Jersey, voted in favor of laws that monitor the housing and employment of immigrants. A zealous example of nativist sentiment occurred in Pahrump, Nevada, where, as the Puerto Rican Legal Defense and Education Fund announced on their Web site, the English Language and Patriot Reaffirmation Ordinance "would make English Pahrump's official language [and] prohibit flying a foreign flag by itself." The U.S. South has also been witness to this renewed current of xenophobic patriotism, as local voters and city councils in communities such as Gadsden, Alabama, Canton, Georgia, Pickens Co., South Carolina, and Gaston, South Carolina, approved a number of similar laws that look to keep a check on employment practices, immigrant housing, and/or the exclusive use of the English language, including the Georgia Security and Immigration Compliance Act.

Although in the short term these measures are frequently justified as actions that look to simply preserve a community from unwarranted lawlessness and are often defended in the name of national security, they frequently occur as a result of perceived threats that take the form of cultural transformations and may actually transpire alongside other changes that are taking place along the opposite side of the rhetorical fence (such as the restaurant chain Pizza Patron's decision to accept Mexican pesos as well as United States dollars at its establishments in Colorado, Texas, Arizona, and New Mexico). Billboards advertising in Spanish, Spanish-language radio programs, groups of non-English speaking individuals, and the presence of children who have not yet learned to speak English, among others, present the very visible face of a community in transition from a monocultural grouping of those traditionally known as Blacks and Whites to a more diverse grouping of races and ethnicities. In the opinion of some, these immigrants also pose serious challenges to the social, political, and economic stability of a community, as it is unprepared for the sudden alterations in its fabric and races to make the necessary adjustments. In the process, the most popular solution these days has commonly been to approve stopgap measures that, for example, look to control the number of immigrants living in an apartment or make companies accountable for the hiring of the same undocumented workers who have been building homes in the area or tending to the landscapes of a town. The long run, however, will show that these radical measures will serve to further close a community off from the rest of the country and impede the formulation of laws that will look to both supervise the application of practical regulations and assimilate those new immigrants that are making positive contributions to a community.

This work intends to offer a panoramic perspective of parallels between the U.S. South and the Latino cultures, including past and present Latin American nations and the varieties of immigration to the United States. The first six chapters look to contextualize the current demographic changes within a broader historical, political, and economic context that serves to establish connections between the seemingly sudden alterations in Hispanic immigration and the transformation of Southern communities. Chapters 7, 8, and 9 delve into more humanistic correlations, specifically with regard to literature, music, land, and religion. And Chapter 10 explores linguistic and ethnic tensions that present very specific challenges to both long-term residents and more recent immigrants to the region. To the extent that this work limits its scope to the subjects listed here and looks to establish more specific points of departure for future studies, it is my opinion that the unanticipated transformations that towns and cities across the U.S. South are currently undergoing due to the influx of domestic and international Latin American immigration may aid other communities across the country that are facing similar issues.

I

Histories

൜ൖൖൖൖൖൖൖൖൖൖൖൖൖൖൖൖൖൖൖൖൖൖൖൖൖൖൖൖൖൖൖ

FIRST CONFLUENCES: TOWARD DISTINCT SHARED HISTORIES AND COLONIALISMS

History is not destined to repeat itself. While events in time commonly compel us to find parallels in an effort to understand the motivations and consequences of the moment, each event is singular in its causality. The roots of the historical confluences between the varieties of U.S. Southern culture and the Hispanic presence in the same region lie in the Spanish and British colonizations of the Americas, which looked to divide the unconquered territories between European powers. The differences between both colonial projects actually found their battle ground in the U.S. South, as the Spanish, British, and French fought for the coastline from South Carolina to Louisiana in an effort to gain the strategic upper hand. It is no coincidence, then, that today's Latin American immigrants to the U.S. South may actually find themselves walking in familiar territory.

Grand generalizations abound regarding the conquest of the American continent by colonial powers, yet it is in the apparently minute national and regional details that true comparisons can be made. In the case of Mexico, for example, their independence from Spain in 1810 had little in common with the French occupation of the country toward the middle part of the nineteenth century and with the prominent role that U.S. politics and enterprise would play during the presidency of Porfirio Díaz at the end of the nineteenth and beginning of the twentieth century. Yet, all three periods in the history of Mexico have come to inform national identity in ways that avoid those facile comparisons that seem to emerge almost inevitably whenever it is deemed that History is taking place. Over the course of debating a more active U.S. role in the Balkan wars of the 1980s, for example, voices against intervention frequently expressed a fear that an armed presence there would only get the country into another Vietnam. And currently, the cultural and political hostilities in Spain are reminding many of the chaotic origins of the Spanish Civil War in the early 1930s. Each example certainly offers sadly enduring parallels between a nation's present and past history; but the foundations and identity of a contemporary nation-state are established nominally during unique times of expansion and collapse, of colonization, and of the marginalization and subjugation of populations.

Latino and Hispanic populations have had an enduring presence in the southeastern region of the United States since the sixteenth century, when Spanish exploration of the region began in earnest. In 1513, Ponce de León arrived in what is today the state of Florida, with other explorers soon to follow: Diego Mirvelo (1516), Francisco Hernández de Córdoba (1517), Pánfilo Narváez and Álvar Núñez Cabeza de Vaca (1528), and Pedro Menéndez de Avilés (1554), founder of St. Augustine, Florida, the first city of what would become the United States of America. While most of these expeditions took place in the region of present-day Florida, there were a number of journeys into other areas of the U.S. South. In 1520, for example, an expedition led by Lucas Vásquez de Ayllón founded a settlement on the coast of Georgia, giving the "youngest" colony of what would be the thirteen English colonies "the distinction of being the site of the earliest European settlement."[1] Unfortunately for the Spanish, when Ayllón died in 1526 the soldiers decided to abandon the site due to a lack of food and the constant threat of attack by the indigenous population.[2] By 1521, Spaniards had also landed on the South Carolina coast and led various expeditions into the area, chief among them being Hernando de Soto's explorations of what would become the Carolinas, Georgia, Alabama, and Louisiana between 1538 and 1540. During that time, there were also a total of sixteen Spanish missions in the state of Georgia, and in 1569 one of the Jesuit brothers, Brother Báez, wrote the first book in what would be the United States.[3]

Spanish presence in the U.S. South over the course of the seventeenth century increased due to the development of its economic interests in the region and the growing allure that the area presented to a Spanish empire on the decline. During this time, the territory possessed by the Spanish was still considerable, as the land between Florida and the

Chesapeake Bay was known as "Tierras de Ayllón" ("Lands of Ayllón") in honor of the explorer Lucas Vásquez de Ayllón, who had reached this part of the New World in 1504. In the seventeenth century, Spanish missionaries were not long in disembarking at the new territories in the U.S. South. Between 1635 and 1675, "the Franciscans operated between forty and seventy missions, catering for perhaps 26,000 Hispanicized natives, who were organized in four provinces: Timicua in Central Florida, Guale along the Georgia coast, Apalachee on the northeastern edge of the gulf; and Apalachicola to the west."[4] Along the panhandle of what would become the state of Florida, explorations were being regularly carried out, engaging the inhabitants and embarking on social and economic relations that frequently turned violent. In his report dated March 14, 1686, the explorer Alonso de Posada noted the geographical advantages and available food supply in the territory around the Bay of Espíritu Santo (on the coast, between present-day Tampico and Apalachee):

> [F]ood resources are already assured since it is known that wild cows called buffalos are so many and so infinite in number all along the frontier lands of the coast and in the interior that however great the number of nations kill to nourish themselves, there still remains a large number in spite of the fact that animals such as lions, tigers, wolves, bears, mountain dogs which they call coyotes cause a great deal of slaughter among them.[5]

Posada's principal motivation in writing his letter was to justify his extended explorations and incursions into hostile territory, lands that in reality may not have produced enough food to sustain both his men and the inhabitants. In his correspondence, Posada addresses any objection that the Spanish Crown and his superiors may have had to his continued presence in the region by emphasizing, for example, the "infinite" number of buffalo found in the region and the general abundance of the land. Colonialist as his perspective may be—an "infinite" number implicitly provided by God for the nourishment of his men—Posada manages to connect the sheer natural wealth of the southern coast that he has been surveying to Spain's continued dreams of empire.

In the eighteenth century the Spanish government remained strongly committed to its presence on the American continent in spite of difficulties at home and the growing British interest in expanding its colonies both southward and westward. During what may be considered the pinnacle of colonial presence in the American territories, a number of distinct powers vied for land and the riches that this land possessed. Due to the growing British influence in the Spanish possessions, in 1739 the conflict known as the War of Jenkins's Ear broke out between these two nations.[6] During the eighteenth century in the territory of Mississippi, skirmishes and battles occurred between the Spanish and British forces that fought for control of the region, as Natchez became a key point in Spanish-North American relations.[7] With the expulsion of the French in 1763 and the British recognition in 1783 of the independence of its former colonies, "the new United States and Spain found themselves face to face in a territory that was practically empty,"[8] and decided to focus their efforts primarily on the southern region of the new country. In 1764, before the thirteen colonies became independent, Antonio de Ulloa was named the first governor of Louisiana; and until 1793, Louisiana was part of the diocese of Cuba.[9]

Tensions between Spanish and British forces, between the indigenous populations and the new immigrants of the land, would come to a boil in the U.S. South toward the latter part of the eighteenth century, as pioneers would use the different powers against each other in search of guarantees and protection from "Indians." In August 1788, Tennessee pioneer James Robinson played to Spanish interests and convinced the newly formed state of North Carolina that the region of Cumberland "should henceforth be called the Miró District" in order to distinguish them from the rest of the state.[10] Sadly for Mr. Robertson, the Treaty of San Lorenzo (1795) would "mark the end of Spanish ambitions in the region" and reincorporate the area back into the state of North Carolina.[11]

In 1779, in the northeast corner of what is now Tennessee but was then North Carolina, the state of Franklin was formed—separately, again, from the state of North Carolina—in order to reunite itself with Spain because of the political difficulties that the new governor, John Sevier, had faced. On September 17, 1788, Sevier wrote to Diego de Gardoqui, the Spanish diplomatic representative to the United States in New York, justifying his interest in allying with the Spanish crown: "The people of this region have come to truly realize upon what part of the world and upon which nation their future happiness and security depend and they immediately infer that their interest and prosperity entirely depend upon the protection and liberality of your Government."[12] Tensions continued to build, as Spain at the time did not possess the economic strength or military fortitude to gain another smaller colony, and the federal and state governments of the incipient United States did not want to relinquish control over the area and give Spain a potential foothold in the southern Appalachians. On February 27, 1788, fighting erupted between Sevier's supporters and other citizens of North Carolina over "the continued refusal of the federal Congress and that of North Carolina to recognize [the region's] independence."[13] On June 21, 1788, New Hampshire became the ninth state to ratify the Constitution, "thereby consolidating the power of the central government. The State of Franklin required the protection of a superior power, and Spanish assistance was inadequate."[14] The Spanish adventure in the area was over before it began, as a new authority had asserted itself in the shadow of a weaker one whose scope of influence was dwindling with each passing day.

After recognizing the independence of the United States in 1779, Spain continued holding claim to the vast Florida territory and in 1783 signed the Treaty of Paris, formally placing the area once again under Spanish control. Political, economic, and geographical chaos followed, as "the Alabama region was the source of constant machinations as the Spanish, British and Americans vied for the loyalty of the Creek [population]."[15] The eighteenth century began to witness the wane of Spanish influence in the U.S. South, but Spanish imperial presence in the area was remarkably notable. The nation's first Spanish-language newspaper, *El Misisipi*, was founded in New Orleans in 1808, reflecting the economic forces at play there and the amalgam of cultures that was shaping the city, something that was due in part to the arrival in cities such as New Orleans, Philadelphia, and Baltimore of refugees and exiles from the Spanish provinces in the South, particularly from Texas.[16] This territory, which was a Spanish possession at the time, began to suffer a number of attempts to unite it with the budding United States. In 1811, for example, a North American invasion of the Texas territory was led by the Mexican Gutiérrez de Lara. And in San Antonio in 1814, the Spanish agent Juan Mariano Picornell declared the Republic of Texas—with the help of North American mercenaries—which dissolved almost immediately. Many of these initial efforts at establishing Texan independence at the beginning of the nineteenth century originated in New Orleans, "a center of espionage and arms trafficking, where a powerful society of Businessmen promoted the attempts at Mexican insurgency."[17] Over the course of 1809 and 1810, for example, in the New Orleans area the colonists in western Florida rebelled and took advantage of the French invasion of Spain, requesting their incorporation into the United States.[18] Curiously, on September 26, 1810, a group of rebels declared the Republic of West Florida and swore allegiance to Spain. By October 27, 1810, William Claiborne, the Governor of the Territory of New Orleans, "received orders to take the sectionist district," essentially ending the rebellion on the same day and quashing the designs of the insurgents.[19]

The war between Mexico and the United States from approximately 1846 to 1848 was the first war motivated by Manifest Destiny and represented the culmination of years of border tension and devices between the two nations. As Thomas J. Davis has written, "In confronting Mexico, the United States faced what it might have been as a darker version of itself. It faced another new American nation that had thrown off European colonial rule and established independence. It also faced another multicultural society composed like itself mostly of Indians, Europeans, and Africans."[20] Although tensions began around approximately 1835, when Texas revolted against the central authority of a Mexican government that rejected an offer by the United States to buy the region of California, the origins are somewhat scattered over a period of two decades. During this time, the gradual incorporation of an independent Texas to the United States and the enthusiasm of President Polk's support for a conflict with Mexico precipitated an already tense situation and provided the sparks necessary for war to break out in 1846. It would only be later that the Mexican-American War came to be directly connected to the subsequent Civil War in the United States, as the anti-war movement in the 1840s was associated with the anti-slavery movement and future Civil War soldiers at this time were to have their first battlefield experiences. According to Jerome R. Adams, "The war crystallized points of contention between two cultures, exaggerating their differences and deepening their prejudices."[21]

During the Civil War between the Union and the Confederacy, more than 100,000 Mexican-Americans fought for both sides,[22] the vast majority of them participating on the side of the Confederacy or supporting the Confederacy's efforts in a direct manner. The politician-soldier Santiago Vidaurri, for example, proposed breaking away Northern Mexico so that the region could join the Confederacy; and Santos Benavides, a former Texas Ranger and the only Mexican colonel in the army of the seceded states, headed the Confederate 33rd Texas Cavalry, a Mexican-American unit that participated in the 1864 Battle of Laredo and helped defeat the Union forces there. Cubans who aided the Confederate side during the war included José Agustín Quintero (Confederate States Commissioner to Northern Mexico), Ambrosio José González (artillery officer under the command of General P. G. T. Beauregard in Charleston) and Lola Sánchez, a woman who had her sisters serve meals to visiting Federals while she went out at night and warned a Confederate encampment nearby.[23]

Slavery was an issue that came to be one of the principal pillars in the construction of a U.S. Southern identity during the nineteenth century and ultimately resulted in armed conflict between the states. As British and Spanish exploration and exploitation of the U.S. South during the sixteenth and seventeenth centuries produced substantial revenue for both the Spanish Crown and the British colonials, both nations also began to diversify their interests, introducing slavery into their respective colonies and gradually constructing an unforgiving economic enterprise that would have long-lasting effects upon the future Latin America and United States, particularly the Deep South states. Although the legal and practical origins of contemporary slavery in European countries such as Portugal and Italy can be traced back to the thirteenth and fourteenth centuries, when the Italians were using African slaves to work on sugar plantations in Cyprus and the Portuguese began their incursions into West Africa,[24] in thirteenth-century Spain King Alfonso the Wise enacted his *Siete Partidas* (Seven Laws) to define the status and the rights of slaves in Castile and "[endowing] the slave with a legal personality."[25] Once the Spanish had arrived in the Americas at the end of the fifteenth century, King Alonso's *Siete Partidas* and the *Leyes de Burgos* (Laws of Burgos) defined the condition of the continent's indigenous peoples and recognized these populations to be "free beings possessing reason [that] should not nor could not...be submitted to slavery, excepting those rebelling against the monarchical authority,"[26] without making any direct reference to the business of importing slaves from West Africa or other Spanish colonies.

The importance of the Laws of Burgos resides in the fact that, instead of attempting to write new laws for the first Spanish possessions in the Caribbean, this new legislation employed preexisting Spanish rulings and was intended to be simply an extension of Spanish law, something that was to be "of extreme importance for Cuban slavery, because the colonials were presented *ab initio* with a complete and historic slave legislation, which had already been applied to the African Negro for at least a century before."[27] Coupled with the ambiguous position of the Catholic Church regarding the possession of slaves in the new Spanish colonies,[28] the presence of preexisting slave legislation in the Latin America of the sixteenth century often allowed the African population more autonomy than they would receive in the future southern United States and would prove over time to be a reference point for those who advocated a more humane treatment of slaves.

As groups of émigrés began to settle in the British colonies at the beginning of the seventeenth century, the presence of slaves would make itself known initially in three areas: Chesapeake Bay (Virginia and Maryland), the coastal Carolinas, and later Georgia.[29] Although documentation of the first slaves in the Virginia colonies places their arrival circa 1612, "The first evidence as to the actual status of Negroes does not appear until about 1640. Then it becomes clear that *some* were serving for life and some children inheriting the same obligation."[30] The forced arrival of these first West Africans made to travel from their homeland to the eastern coast of what would become the United States was rapidly followed by acts and laws that looked to define the condition of the slave in the British colonies, setting limits to his activities and limiting the interaction between races. In the same year of 1640, "Virginia law set Negroes apart…by denying them the important right and obligation to bear arms,"[31] legislation that would be directly connected to the 1680 Virginia Act for Preventing Negroes [sic] Insurrections that declared that "it shall not be lawful for any negroe or other slave to carry or arme himselfe with any club, staffe, gunne, sword or any other weapon of defence or offence."[32] During this time, different pieces of legislation were enacted that looked to control the social impact of the African population. In the 1660s, legislation was written in the British colonies against miscegenation; in 1664, the colony of Maryland "prohibited interracial marriages," and in 1691, "Virginia finally prohibited all interracial liaisons."[33] Since many of these acts were written principally in order to prevent the assimilation of the African race and to deny the slaves the weapons necessary for an insurrection, it was clear that the integration of the slave into the social fabric of the colonies and, ironically, the possibility of slave rebellions and revolts were concrete facts from the moment that the British expatriates began to participate in the slave trade. Such legislation represented a sort of emergency measure and was commonly written after the fact, making local laws essentially moot in the face of sustained relations between British colonialists and the West African slaves and servants. In contrast to the Spanish colonies in the Americas, slavery became a local issue in the British colonies, as "local economic needs [in the British colonies] would tend to be the dominant force in defining the legal structure of Negro slavery and social attitudes toward the slave."[34]

Over the course of the eighteenth century, the institution of slavery in the British colonies would continue to leave its mark through a variety of factors that combined the altered social dynamics with the lasting economic and demographic impact of the slave trade. Between 1732 and 1754, for example, 35 percent of immigrants entering New York City were slaves.[35] With the purchase of slaves by families who lived in both urban and rural areas, urban slavery in the British colonies began to acquire characteristics distinct from rural slavery, as many of the slaves of the city were principally "domestic servants, distributed in ones, twos, and threes throughout the larger houses of the town."[36] The urban slave was "mobile, often skilled, and occasionally literate."[37] The institution of slavery, then, evolved from being a principally rural fact to a phenomenon that included practically all social strata and labor responsibilities of the burgeoning colonies.

At a time when the effect of slavery could be sensed in the new United States in the countryside and the city, both the *educated* urban objections against the continued assimilation of African Americans into a mainstream society that was dominated by white, Anglo-Saxon, property-holding males and the legislation and proclamations against their potential liberation also increased in number over the course of the nineteenth century. Thomas Jefferson's generalizations on the African race merit attention, for example, as they reflect a majority of the attitudes of the leading classes present in the newly independent nation: "They seem to require less sleep," "Their griefs are transient," "his imagination is wild and extravagant," "they are inferior to the whites in the endowments both of body and mind."[38] The Petition Against Emancipation written by the inhabitants of Halifax County, Virginia, in 1785, is also a compelling sample of the variety of arguments employed against the freeing of the slaves, maintaining that emancipation "involves in it, and is Productive of Want, Poverty, Distress, and Ruin to the Free Citizen; Neglect, Famine, and Death to the helpless Black Infant and superannuated Parent; the Horrors of all the Rapes, Murders, and Outrages... inevitable Bankruptcy to the Revenue, and consequently Breach of Public Faith, and loss of Credit with Foreign Nations; and lastly Ruin to this now free and flourishing Country," and ultimately declaring that "Slavery was permitted by the Deity himself."[39]

The Northwest Ordinance of 1787 "kept slavery out of the vast territory to the north of the Ohio river,"[40] and represented the first step toward eradicating slavery on the soil of the fledgling United States. It was a matter of time before the U.S. South took a more active defense of the "institution." Some may have argued, for example, that the presence of slaves in a community founded by Lucas Vasquez de Ayllón at or near the mouth of the Peedee river in 1526 in present-day South Carolina represented evidence that the South was historically positioned to maintain an active slave culture, and "By the 1720s, blacks outnumbered whites by more than two to one" in South Carolina.[41] Curiously, "Slavery in colonial South Carolina...had more in common with slavery in the West Indies than either had with the institution in Virginia and Maryland."[42] Yet the reasons why slavery flourished in the U.S. South were less connected to technological advancements or to some intrinsic historical design than to daily economic reality, particularly the proliferation of cotton west of Virginia and into Kentucky and Tennessee and, in areas such as the South Carolina low country, to the geographic, climactic, and topographical parallels between the region and the West African landscape.[43] In the region, then, slavery began to acquire characteristics that distinguished its practice from the North, as it was in the Southern states that it "showed qualities of flexibility, adaptability, mobility, and expansiveness which were largely unsuspected at the time when U.S. independence was achieved,"[44] a fact that would come to define relations between slaveholding states and the rest of the nation.

As had been the case in the British colonies and, after independence, in Northern states, Southern communities also began to write their own slave legislation. Enacted in 1824, for example, the Louisiana slave code looked to further objectify the slave by integrating slaves and their property to everything else the master owned, stating that "All that a slave possesses belongs to the master."[45] The more complete Alabama slave code of 1852 distinguished between slaves, "free persons of color," and "free colored mariners," curiously proclaiming that "no slave can, under any circumstances, keep a dog."[46] The sheer number of laws defining the condition of a slave would actually come to confirm the constant interaction in the U.S. South between master and slave in the eighteenth and nineteenth centuries, something that actually contributed to the "erosion of African heritage"[47] and played a significant part in the North American slave's gradual disengagement from his or her culture of origin.

At the brink of the Civil War in 1860, the slave population in the fifteen slave states did not reach 4 percent, as out of a total population of 123 million, approximately 4 million were slaves.[48] This varied, however, depending on the state, as in Maryland, Missouri, and Delaware, 13 percent, 10 percent, and 1.5 percent respectively of the population were slaves; whereas in South Carolina and Mississippi, more than half the population were slaves.[49] Some 75 percent of Southern white families owned no slaves whatsoever,[50] while in western Virginia and North Carolina and eastern Kentucky and Tennessee, "there were few, if any, slaves."[51] For states such as South Carolina and Mississippi, the issue became a litmus test for state's rights and further identified the economic arguments at stake. (Although limiting the discussion to simply viewing slavery in economic terms is both naïve and impertinent due to what Peter

J. Parish has termed "the centrality of slavery in the whole Southern way of life."[52]) As with the distribution of the slave population, the economics of slavery "differed between the upper South and the lower South, or between the Atlantic seaboard and the lower Mississippi valley, or between cotton and sugar plantations."[53] Ironically, the relative economic success of slavery plantations would come to hold the Southern economy back, as "plantation slavery cotton cultivation removed any incentive to switch from agriculture to industrial and urban development."[54] The emancipation of slaves, then, took on the characteristics of regional distinctiveness, as freedom came at different times to different regions, often representing "a piecemeal process taking place over months or even years—not a single glorious day of jubilee," and introducing the slave into self-determination "amid all the suffering, misery, dislocation, and confusion which have commonly been the fate of the refugees, the homeless, and other defenseless victims of warfare throughout history."[55]

This marginalization of slaves in the United States allows us to identify a number of legislative, economic, and/or cultural parallels and differences between slavery policies in Spain, Latin American nations, and the United States, principally with respect to the U.S. South and the ascendancy of slave culture in the region. During the times of Spanish imperialism, "the Crown of Castile found it expedient and profitable to allow individuals to carry out at their own expense the conquest of the New World in the name of the Crown,"[56] whereas British authorities ruled over a state of affairs where "Every colonizing enterprise was given complete freedom over its undertaking, with little or no interference from the Crown and its administrative organization."[57] Slavery in the Spanish colonies would distinguish itself from slavery in the British colonies by "the physical proximity [in the Spanish colonies] between slave and master," the capacity of the city slave to "move about freely in public spaces," and by the fact that "between the master and the slave there were at least two intermediaries: the Church and, above all, the judicial system."[58]

Locations such as Cuba and Virginia also allow us to better understand the initial attempts at legislating the African presence in the Spanish and British colonies, as the political and economic importance of slaves to the mother country and their strategic location for the importation of human beings placed each in a position unlike that of other colonies on the continent. The Cuban slave codes, for example, focused on slaves instead of masters or non-slaves and "never forgot the legal personality of the Negro," while "the Virginia codes ultimately reduced the Negro to chattel slavery" and centered primarily "on the master and his rights."[59] The laws regarding a slave's private life were not as intrusive in the Spanish colonies as those written in the British colonies during the seventeenth and eighteenth centuries. In the Spanish and Portuguese colonies, for example, slaves could buy and hold property,[60] and those "owned by different masters were not to be hindered from marrying, nor could they be kept separate after marriage."[61]

Within the context of slavery's inhumanity, the evidence suggests that the lives of those slaves living in the Spanish colonies and newly founded Latin American nations may not have been as harsh as that of their counterparts to the north. As David Brion Davis has written, "Numerous accounts from the late eighteenth and nineteenth centuries tell us that the Latin American slave enjoyed frequent hours of leisure and was seldom subjected to the factory-like regimentation that characterized the capitalistic plantations in the north; that he faced no legal bars to marriage, education, or eventual freedom; that he was legally protected from cruelty and oppression, and was not stigmatized on account of his race."[62] Conversely, the situation of the African American in the United States is in part a direct consequence of racial policies enacted by distinct administrations. Writing in 1969, Davis noted that "the Negro in the United States today has far more economic and educational opportunities than the Negro in Latin America, [but] he also suffers from more overt discrimination from whites who feel superior but are unsure of their own status."[63]

The supposed relative absence in Latin American nations of an imported historical shame founded on one's race or ethnicity came to only superficially characterize race relations in these countries, as slaves, free descendants of African immigrants and indigenous peoples would continue to be marginalized throughout the course of the nineteenth and twentieth centuries. In contrast to the United States—where "anyone with the slightest trace of Negro blood was classified as black"[64]—societies in Latin America acknowledged "various subtle [racial] gradations"[65] and elegantly—albeit colonially—gave voice to the racial and ethnic variety of peoples present in a society according to the degree to which the distinct elements were present in an individual. These distinctions, however, would frequently prove to be both superficial and academic, as the dominant classes continued to be those who were either European or directly descended from European colonists, and the gradations represented what would be recognized as the mere racist mirroring of European norms, values, and taxonomies. More recently, the migration of indigenous, ethnic, and racial minorities to Latin American cities has continued to increasingly racialize the economies of most major urban areas and intensify the structural problems found therein, bringing the moment's historical circle to a close. As Jacques Poloni-Simard has written, "At the beginning of the twenty-first century Latin America has turned into the privileged laboratory of the liberal economy, as in the sixteenth century it was of westernization."[66]

Upon the arrival of the Europeans to the American continent, the groups that suffered the most from slavery, warfare, and disease were the virtually incalculable variety of indigenous populations. In the Spanish Americas, individuals such as Antonio Montesinos and Fray Bartolomé de las Casas in the sixteenth century were the first "to recognize that the black cause and the indigenous cause were the same," leading to a gradual deconstruction of exactly who constituted an "Indian" and to a determination of the differences between "Indigenist" and "Indianist" discourses.[67] Fray Montesino's speech in 1511 in favor of the indigenous of Santo Domingo, for example, and de las Casa's work decades later, would have a lasting impact upon reforming relations between the Spanish Crown and indigenous populations of the Americas.

In the wake of warfare and struggles against the Spanish empire at the beginning of the nineteenth century, "the nations born from independence were built upon the exclusion of the indigenous from citizenship, redirecting him, in this way, toward his indianness, beyond the inability to write, which was the condition to vote, without truly integrating them into the nation according to the principle of equal rights."[68] Today in Latin America resentments and tensions remain between indigenous and non-indigenous groups that have witnessed their rights fade away, their lands confiscated by governments eager to please national and international investors, and, as Marie-Chantal Barre noted, the continued colonization of their indigenous regions.[69] Barre herself distinguishes between the terms "Indian" and "indigenous," noting that the word "Indian" "is born with the colonization of America," while the more contemporary term "indigenous" "runs the risk of eliminating the colonial connotation."[70] In a number of nations, the considerable percentage of indigenous peoples constitutes a true challenge for the future. Mexico, for example, is 30 percent Amerindian, with "more than 200 distinct tribes or ethnic groups who speak more than 50 languages or dialects"; the 44 percent of Guatemala's population who are Amerindian "remain largely outside of national culture, do not speak Spanish, and are not integrated into the national economy"; the Bolivian population is 30 percent Quechua Indian and 25 percent Aymara Indian; Peru is 45 percent Indian, and Ecuador 25 percent Indian.[71]

In the United States, the presence of indigenous populations through-out the eastern coast did not deter British colonists from steadily claiming indigenous lands through forced expropriations, inequitable treaties or open warfare. As settlements were founded, the flames of conflict between indigenous groups and nonnative Africans were frequently fanned by British colonials, who often hired members of the Cherokee, Catawba, and Chickasaw tribes to track down runaway slaves.[72] Writing in the nineteenth century, Cherokee Chief John Ross expressed to Arkansas Governor Henry M. Rector the anti-abolitionist position of the Cherokee people: "As I am sure that the laborers will be greatly dis-appointed if they shall expect in the Cherokee country 'fruitful fields ripe for the harvest of abolitionism,' &c., you may rest assured that the Cherokee people will never tolerate the propagation of any such obnoxious fruit upon their soil."[73]

When the contemporary United States was created upon its independ-ence from Great Britain in 1776, nineteenth-century explorers set out to chart the geographical possibilities of the new country, regardless of the indigenous groups that they would find along the way. The Indian Removal Act of 1829, obligating all Indians to move west of the Missis-sippi River, was a consequence of these explorations and of the express desire to conquer lands from the Atlantic to the Pacific. A number of tribes such as the Creek and the Choctaw signed treaties that gave up their land to the United States government,[74] while others such as the Cherokee continued to fight the state of Georgia and federal government in the courts. Ultimately, the occupation of the lands of American indige-nous tribes and the displacement of these groups would culminate in 1838 in the mandatory march known as the Trail of Tears, when sixteen thousand members of the Cherokee tribe were forced on a one thousand mile journey to established "Indian territories" in Kansas, Oklahoma, Southern Nebraska, and eastern Colorado, with an estimated four thou-sand dying along the way.

Today, after centuries of marginalization, many indigenous popula-tions in the United States and Latin America have been separated further from their environment by being placed in reservations and territories that confer a certain degree of political and economic autonomy while, at the same time, making them responsible to a federal government that chooses the precise degree of self-rule. One remarkable example of more current tensions between indigenous peoples and the United States government occurred off the coast of San Francisco in 1969, when a group of individuals occupied Alcatraz island and reclaimed the land for the original indigenous inhabitants for twenty-four dollars in glass beads and red cloth, the same price paid for Manhattan island in the seventeenth century. In Latin American countries, however, the situation is markedly different due to the number of nations that are home to a considerably high percentage of people that consider themselves indigenous peoples. A number of indigenous movements in Ecuador, Bolivia, Peru, and Mexico, among others, have experienced a political revival of sorts in the last ten years, defending the renewed centrality of indigenous interests on the national agenda and calling for increased opportunities for indigenous populations that will be forced to leave lands which can no longer sustain them and migrate to urban centers.

Throughout the twentieth century, Latin American citizens began to recognize the economic attraction and political stability of the United States and continued to immigrate. Although the vast majority settled in the Southwestern area of the country and in cities such as Miami, New York, or Chicago, historical events such as the Spanish-American War, the Mexican Revolution, and the Cuban Revolution have also contributed to the contemporary diffusion of the Hispanic populations to both large cities such as Atlanta, Charlotte, New Orleans, and Memphis, and to smaller, more rural communities in the area such as Fairhope, Alabama. In the U.S. South, "Immigrants from Mexico and Central America have transformed some small towns, but the great majority has settled in job-laden metropolitan areas. No longer are Latino workers only migrants, picking crops when ripe and then moving on; now they are staying, with a disproportionate clustering in low-wage occupations."[75] Underscoring these findings, W. Thomas Smith Jr. has written that, in today's South, "A new and fast-growing Hispanic population is adding a new ethnic dimension to the U.S. South and altering the region's traditional face of grits, Confederate flags, and civil rights marches."[76] The recent populations of Latin American immigrants to the U.S. South are continuing to chart their own distinctive course in the region, living the history of the continent and incorporating elements of past generations into a contemporary fusion of cultures that utilizes in its construction both the tools of the past and the technological innovations of today.

IDENTITY, THE U.S. SOUTH, AND LATIN AMERICA: MYTH, CONSTRUCTION, IMPOSITION

Due in part to a series of historic social, political, and economic conflicts arising within its own ambiguous borders, the U.S. South as a cultural construction is a historical product of Southerners and non-Southerners, as both of these populations have had a direct interest in the evolution of the Southern persona and in the political, social, and economic infrastructure of the region. Many general and often stereotypical elements of the South—its diverse food, its rich literary traditions, its distinct musical expressions, its individual and evocative inflections—have been conveniently lionized, eulogized, and, above all, mythologized in an attempt to link the cultural landscape to political and ideological changes. Above all, the mythification of a particular event, individual, or any other manifestation of a historical person or moment leads to the reinforced marginalization and subjugation of those same populations by those residing in the area where the myth originated, as the (new) powers search for and create a bridge that will link their (new) authority to the historical current of the conquered people. Myths such as the cutting of the cherry tree by a young George Washington, the "saving" of the Spanish people by the battlefield ghost of St. James riding his steed against the Moors, or the alleged incorruptibility of Eva Peron's body serve to grant firmness to the new powers (in these cases, respectively, to authenticate the figure of George Washington as an honest individual, to corroborate the link between Francisco Franco's dictatorship and a Christian/Roman Catholic Spain, and to verify the permanence of President Juan Domingo Peron's ideas among the Argentine people).

The French writer Roland Barthes has researched the power of myths to subjugate a people and hypnotize them into willing acceptance of the new authorities vis-à-vis the "discovery" of these historical bridges. In his writings, he highlights, for example, the fact that the myth "is a type of speech chosen by history" that "cannot possibly evolve from the 'nature' of things,"[77] as its principal aim is to persuade and conquer. Since myths are therefore human compositions that emerge from shifting individual constructs and contexts, "there is no fixity in mythical concepts: they can come into being, alter, disintegrate, disappear completely."[78] Additionally, the myth "gives [things] a natural and eternal justification, it gives them a clarity which is not that of an explanation but that of a statement of fact."[79] To these ends, we may appreciate that myths are consistently being manipulated for the purpose of "occupying" a historical figure who transcends the mere moment in order to win the allegiance of a population through the appropriation of that figure's history and appeal, subtly integrating it into the fabric of the nation's speech and altering the previous message (i.e., the discourse of the vanquished). In this way, history appears to be a series of battles that exchange one discourse for another and substitute one myth for another in a surreptitious attempt to proclaim, above all, an allegedly transparently just and righteous victory.

The U.S. South has had no shortage of mythic figures and moments that speak to the constant flux present in the forces of transformation; but is there such a thing as a mythical South, or is the region simply one more variation of a United States conceptualized from both within and outside its borders? The South is eminently American—in a national and continental sense—to the extreme that strains of the national character may be found delicately amplified in the region, a product of the area's own particular takes on history. As Steven A. Channing has written regarding the South in the nineteenth century, "Two and a half centuries of contact between whites and blacks, masters and slaves, planters and non-slaveholders had exerted a profound influence on the Southern people. Distinctive regional variations on American attitudes toward sexuality and family, land and work, politics and the realm of God had evolved in the special context of the presence of plantations and African slaves."[80] These roots of Southern particularity and injustice may be traced back to its own land and to a time that, as Channing alludes, witnessed the rise of the phantom of slavery; but it is also evident that the non-South popularly known as the North has also had a hand in mythifying the region and creating for it an identity that would best serve its own interests.

Although Northern manipulation of Southern identity is best evidenced immediately after the Civil War—during the period generally known as Reconstruction—Northern efforts at determining Southern cultural autonomy are apparent as early as 1815. At that time, "because Southerners failed to develop marketing and transport facilities of their own, including banking, credit, and insurance resources, shipping companies, marketing connections and other middleman activities, they turned perforce to the North for these services."[81] The relative underdevelopment of the South and its profound rural, agrarian nature led many inhabitants to initiate a relationship of economic dependency with the North, establishing themselves as the needy ones. Gradually, Northern businesses fomented this association, as many were interested in keeping the South on the economic margins of the North and in extending the image of a Southern region dependent upon commerce with those outside the borders of Dixie. Many Southern businesses in turn accepted the secondary role assigned them by Northern interests, and the creation of the South from outside had begun.

In the region, the relationship between distinct racial, ethnic, and indigenous groups and the local communities also shares a number of commonalities with the rapport that the region has had with the rest of the United States. As Jonathan Daniels stated rather ethnocentrically in 1938, "For good or for ill, being a Southerner is like being a Jew. And indeed, more needs to be written about the similarity of the minds and the emotions of the Jew, the Irishman, the Southerner, and, perhaps, the Pole, as a basis for the better understanding of each of them and of them all."[82] Published some seventy years ago, Daniels's racially tinged and somewhat paternalistic observations do not hide the fact that, in his opinion, the Southerner may be included among other populations that have been colonized and systematically marginalized from positions of power and authority on their own land. In his dated opinion, it would appear that learning from these marginalized populations paradoxically precedes acknowledging their existence and simply valuing and respecting diverse customs and traditions without sensing the need to encapsulate and comprehend them. The Southerner is linked to the Jewish culture, the Irish people, and, "perhaps," the Poles through the shared epic of displacement. What is unique is that, after the Civil War and during Reconstruction, Southerners were displaced within their own land, suffering what Bertram Wyatt Brown has termed an internal colonialism that was imposed principally by the Northern states.[83] This, in turn, led not only to an affirmation of regional identities within the South but also, ironically, to a crisis that the South still suffers: Is it the Antebellum South that is firmly anchored in its traditions, a New South that is leading the nation in employment, economic diversification, and demographic growth, or that No-South that is witnessing the disappearance of its alleged time-honored traditions and whose population and customs are becoming more indistinguishable from the rest of the nation? The answer may be all three, as the region struggles to forge a link between the past and present and to be inclusive of an ever-diversifying population.

Whatever the process may be that the region is going through in its own reification, the U.S. South today remains a locus of the whirlwind of history, suffering from the pressures and pleasures created by the extremes: by an exaggerated nostalgia for the apparently existential clarity that existed for white Southerners before, during, and immediately after the Civil War, and by an unbridled desire to move beyond what it was, to find its own identity through what Walter Hines Page described in 1902 as "training that brings economic dependence [and] sets the strongest and most natural forces of life at play."[84] The South is, as Richard Gray maintains, "a site of struggle,"[85] but this is true at a number of levels: the history of the region gives witness to and commonly triggers the scuffles between social, economic, and political poles within its own region, between historically diverse customs, traditions, and perceptions on its own land (as Katherine DuPre Lumpkin wrote, "to be a Georgian in South Carolina was not to feel immediately at home,")[86] between national and international populations resettling in the area, between the distinct elements of those immigrant populations, and, among others, between tradition and change.

One historical difference between the role that religion has had in the development of the archetypal Southern way of life and those customs that developed from religious life in Latin American society is the Roman Catholic Church hierarchy's general support and participation in the fifteenth- and sixteenth-century Spanish colonial project meant to subjugate the population and derive economic benefits from occupied lands. In this sense, both the South and Latin America are distinct yet share a unique record of oppression, each possessing a separate set of historical circumstances that have defined their contemporary societies. While regions of Latin America were Spanish or Portuguese colonies for over 300 years, calculating the chronology of the Northern colonial impact upon the Southern population and classifying the South as a colony of the North becomes more problematic as both the "North" and the "South" run the danger of becoming relative geographical expanses that were located within the borders of an industrializing country and whose supposedly salient characteristics may disappear in the blink of an eye. If we examine Southern history, however, plentiful examples abound that reveal the extent to which the U.S. South has been an internal colony of the North.

Past attitudes regarding the fate of the U.S. South and the various possible solutions to what has been frequently termed "the Southern problem" have often and seemingly inevitably employed a language not unlike that employed by empires when referring to their colonies. Specific comments before or during the Civil War—such as New York Senator Hamilton Fish's declaration in 1860 that "the South was or would be splendid colonies to the North,"[87] or Lincoln's stated intention to colonize the nation of Haiti and the Colombian province of Panama with emancipated blacks[88]—reflect behaviors and attitudes that had been latent in the country as early as the beginning of the nineteenth century. As I. A. Newby has stated, at this time "The South was rich in natural resources, and since the North had a head start in manufacturing, the extracting and processing of raw materials for Northern industries were the readiest roads to economic development."[89] As is the case today in the global relationship that exists between developed and developing nations, at that time, Northern entrepreneurs who were interested primarily in economic profits took advantage of the raw materials readily available in the U.S. South and used these resources principally for their own economic advancement. Over the course of the nineteenth century, the South may have developed economically, but the region was at a consistent disadvantage in regard to Northern businesses that looked to exploit Southern goods like cotton and tobacco.

Curiously, over the course of time, a number of Southerners have actually contributed to this colonization of the spirit and to a blind acceptance of a totemic pre–Civil War identity. While the writer W.J. Cash, for example, looked to demythify that all-too-familiar South of white columns and fragrant magnolia trees, in the process he frequently employed a language that replicated a colonizer's mentality. His classical work, *The Mind of the South*, sought to offer an apparently exhaustive psychological analysis of the region and its peoples, of its dilemmas, and its challenging relationship with the north. Constituting one of the first systematic attempts at understanding the roots of Southern social dynamics, *The Mind of the South* was far from inclusive or conclusive. Often his remarks regarding African Americans, agriculture, and political customs reflected generalizations that were assumed by the majority of the white Anglo population and that sustained a number of Southern stereotypes. At the beginning of his work, for example, Cash notes how "[p]rior to the close of the Revolutionary period the great South, as such, has little history."[90] While, in this case, his comments are contextualized within a pre–Civil War "Great South" framework that implicitly includes the plantation and the agrarian tradition, Cash's comment ostensibly ignores the history and presence of those who lived in the U.S. South before it was colonized by the British, French, and Spanish and delicately credits these European cultures with having brought "history" to the "Great South." Cash himself even acknowledges the colonial condition of the South, stating that "Even the Old South had been pretty much in the position of a European colony set down in a nation side by side with, and faced by the tariff to buy everything it needed from, an economy with a much higher and continually mounting standard of living."[91] Unfortunately, his generalizations commonly emulated the conqueror's language and may have contributed to pseudo-colonial attitudes that non-Southerners had of the South. When he writes of "the men of the South,"[92] for example, it is implicit that this represents the white Anglo men of the South and, therefore, unconditionally excludes the African American, the Hispanic, and the indigenous populations; when he notes that, in his racist attitudes, Louisiana governor Huey Long was "[a] completely normal Southerner toward the Negro,"[93] he does more than implicitly criticize or merely describe the prevailing attitudes of white men in the 1930s South: by utilizing the word "normal," Cash implicitly justifies the marginalization of the African American culture in the South and, as is evidenced by his choice of words, speaks from the position of the colonialist. His remarks regarding the movie "Gone With the Wind"—that it was "a sort of new confession of Southern faith" and that "attendance at the [Southern] theaters took on the definite character of a patriotic act"[94]—limit the scope of what may be considered a "Southerner" to those individuals in the vast minority who could, at the time, afford to attend a screening of the film. The point here is not to be overly reductionist in our detailing some of Cash's observations, but rather to demonstrate how even Southerners and Southern intellectuals echoed opinions that perhaps involuntarily promoted the presence and the existence in the South of a colonial spirit promoted by the north. In this manner, the origins of some of the very problems suffered by a majority of Deep South states regarding poor education, low income, and poor health care may be partly traced back to northern attitudes that expressed a desired colonialist exploitation of the South that began long before the irruption of the War Between the States in 1861.

The post–Civil War South was a land torn apart not only by war but by the existential angst that follows defeat, by the sense that their side had lost, that their ideals were to be buried under an avalanche of Northern intentions altruistically labeled as a "Reconstruction" meant to right the wrongs of the region. As profoundly necessary as the changes were, they began with seemingly simple premises that originated with an economic transformation of the region and soon spread to the social and political arenas. As Joseph S. Himes has written,

> The Civil War imposed at least three lasting changes on the structure of the region: 1) It abolished the legal institution of black slavery and thereby in a single stroke altered the work structure and swept away a major portion of wealth in the region; 2) It necessitated creation of a new labor system of free workers that was based on several credit patterns—sharecropping, the company store, and the advancement of seeds, tools and supplies to tenants; 3) These changes alienated poor whites and blacks, made them competitors for economic and political values, and established the structure of inter-group competition and controversy.[95]

Through a transformation of the work structure, of the distribution of wealth, of the labor system and, ultimately, of the social, political, and economic dynamics between races—again, crucial and necessary—the North appeared to impose their values from an ethically and morally superior colonizing position that was, in fact, directly linked to the economic benefits resulting from these changes.

Even the indispensable writings of the abolitionist Frederick Douglass took on a colonialist and moralizing tone as he understandably wrote in favor of post–Civil War Northern intervention in the South. In his 1866 article "Reconstruction," Douglass argues from a morally superior standpoint that is, in effect, directly related to the economic expansion of Northern interests: "[The people] want a reconstruction as will protect loyal men, black and white, in their persons and property; such a one as will cause Northern industry, Northern capital, and *Northern civilization to flow into the South*....The South must be opened to the light of law and liberty."[96] Interestingly enough, Douglass associated the South's potential moral progress with the advancement of the Northern way of life, from their economic customs to their "civilization" and to the implicit notion that "law" and "liberty" were nonexistent in the South before the North "saved" the region from itself.

The next year, Douglass published "An Appeal to Congress for Impartial Suffrage," another essay in the *Atlantic Monthly* that once again underlines the errant ways of the South. In the article, he outlines the work ahead for suffragists and examines the role of the American people and, by extension, of the Senate and the House of Representatives: "What then is the work before Congress? It is to save the people of the South from themselves, and the nation from detriment on their account. Congress must supplant the evident sectional tendencies of the South by national dispositions and tendencies. It must cause national ideas and objects to take the lead and control the politics of these states."[97] Notwithstanding the response and attention that the issue warranted, the tone of Douglass's declarations resembles the writings of some of the Spanish, British, Dutch, or German colonizers and sympathizers within these colonial systems. His distinction between those "saved" (and, implicitly, those "lost"), his advancement of the complete substitution of one lifestyle by another, and the prominence of "Northern" (or "Union") ideals as apparently universal "national" principles speak to an underlying colonial discourse that, at least until the withdrawal of Federal troops from the South in 1877, continued to suppress the Southern populations. As crucial as the elimination of slavery and a set of political, social, and economic transformations was to the South, the manner in which these were carried out by Northern authorities may in fact have contributed to the attitudes and to the desire to construct a Southern identity drastically distinct from the rest of the nation. Due, in part, to the attitudes expressed by Northern industrialists and politicians and to the greediness of Southern businessmen who frequently looked to profit from Northern commerce at the expense of their communities, the South during Reconstruction became, in effect, an exploited country within a country —a region that sometimes had more in common with other conquered nations than with their own United States—and found its own *raison d´etre* in a hatred of the occupiers. As Cash wrote in 1941,

> Not Ireland nor Poland nor Finland nor Bohemia, not one of the countries which prove the truth that there is no more sure way to make a nation than the brutal oppression of an honorably defeated and disarmed people—not one of these, for all the massacres, the pillage, and the rapes to which they have so often been subjected, was ever so pointedly taken in the very core of its being as was the South. And so not one ever developed so much of fear, of rage, of indignation and resentment, of self-consciousness and patriotic passion.[98]

The great resentment evident among Southerners immediately following the conclusion of the Civil War in 1865 was due not only to the fact that they lost the war but also that the victors intended to reshape Southern society according to Northern standards and mores. The South was not historically alone in this resentment, as other peoples and nations throughout history have, rightfully or wrongfully, begrudged the occupation of their land and the consequent remapping of their identity by conquering forces, creating unexpected parallels between the South and other cultures. As Deborah Cohn has stated, for example, "Cuba's struggle for social, political, and economic independence from Spain bore more than a passing resemblance to the South's embattled relationship with the North."[99] In his article "The South Has Risen Again. Everywhere," published October 19, 1997 in *The New York Times*, David Galef quotes Bill Ferriss, Director of the Center for the Study of Southern Culture at the University of Mississippi, as recognizing not only the commonalities between the South and other colonized peoples but also the cultural consequences suffered by the vanquished: "The South is to New York as Ireland is to London. We are the colony, and we export art and literature and music." Often a colony's autonomous identity is appropriated by the colonizer and converted into a consumer product, a simple commodity to be traded or exploited in the open cultural market. In the case of the South, cultural icons and regional identities began to be subsumed as early as Reconstruction.

The effects of Reconstruction on the identity of the post–Civil War South should not be underestimated by those looking today to understand the relationship of the region to the rest of the nation and its impact on recent immigrant populations. Its programs and laws reached far into the community, for it touched and looked to cut the social, political, and economic fabric of the region into a pattern resembling Northern society. Essentially, the Reconstruction Acts of 1867 set up the following: separation of the Confederacy into five military districts (all but Tennessee), "procedures for creating new governments," the naming by President Johnson of military governors who would "[conduct] a new voter registration in which blacks as well as whites participated," and the proposing of new state constitutions "to the new electorate for approval."[100] While these changes were noble and indispensable to the integration of the region into the political fabric of the country, they also represented the imposition of a Northern vision that looked to recalibrate life in the Confederacy. The South after the Civil War was "too agricultural, its urban middle class too small, its social services too underdeveloped, its hostility to liberal attitudes too pronounced, its poverty too widespread to fall into the northern pattern of development."[101]

The time immediately following Reconstruction became known as Radical Reconstruction due to the extent and magnitude of the reform measures: military occupation from one to three years, "new and more liberal state governments, the 14th and 15th Amendments, a series of civil rights laws, and certain efforts to promote interracialism in politics and integration with some public accommodations."[102] What occurred at this time characterized the battle between reality and perception: the supposed actuality represented and necessitated a reformulation of Southern laws and a recreation of Southern society in accord with a more virtuous set of social standards. Its perception by Southerners was what I. A. Newby has called a "loss of political control,"[103] the fact that Georgians, Alabamians, or Mississippians, for example, were no longer able to manage their own destinies. In effect, "This was the real significance of Reconstruction. By placing [Southern] whites in a position they considered menacing and ignominious, it brought to the surface a hidden dimension of their deepest nature."[104]

In offering a Southern perspective, Newby aligns himself with a colonial discourse that reflects not the voice of the conquered but of the conqueror. Even from the outside, though, he does note a few of the negative consequences of Reconstruction. In his opinion, these originated principally in attitudes already present and latent in the Southern spirit: "Certainly there was damage to the section's mind, spirit, and culture, by Reconstruction, but the damage came not from Radicalism, but from the extremism of whites themselves....[The Radical Reconstruction] program brought to the surface prejudices and hates already there."[105] These "prejudices and hates already there" in the South may have already existed before Reconstruction, but being conquered and occupied by the North did not ameliorate nor modify these. As he states, Reconstruction fell short in many ways, as it "was in effect 'radical' enough to arouse whites but not to safeguard blacks."[106]

Writing in the 1930s, W.J. Cash would possibly have agreed with Newby's appraisal of the negative consequences of Reconstruction, but not with his desire to place the blame squarely on the shoulders of the white Southerner. In *The Mind of the South*, Cash declares that the "Yankee" made the Southern mind "one of the least *reconstructible* ever developed."[107] Reconstruction was "simply an extension of that [Civil] war, on lines yet more terrible and exigent,"[108] threatening to turn the Southern people into the image of that Shakespearean character, Prospero's Caliban. At this time, "[t]olerance, in sum, was pretty well extinguished all along the line, and conformity made a nearly universal law. Criticism, analysis, detachment, all those activities and attitudes so necessary to the healthy development of any civilization, every one of them took on the aspect of high and aggravated treason."[109] During Reconstruction, the North and Northern business interests imposed upon the South more than simply new sets of laws and a short-term military occupation: they attempted to mold the region into the mirror image of Northern society without considering the significant historical differences that demanded a more balanced approach to a power and an authority imposed from outside the region. Notwithstanding the crucial issue of slavery, its necessary eradication, and the emancipation of slaves, many Southern institutions reflected a complex set of cultural customs distinctly different from the North that were, in the end, held in contempt by the majority of the Northern population.

For these and other reasons, the first sector to suffer the impact of Reconstruction was the Southern economy, as Northern capture, occupation, or recovery of Southern industries and agriculture continued unabated into the twentieth century. Between 1860 and 1870, for example, the South's portion of the nation's wealth declined from 30 to 12 percent.[110] A decade later, from 1880 to 1900, the political and economic circumstances surrounding Reconstruction and post-Reconstruction in the South had produced "a semi-colonial economic dependency on the North and had a direct negative impact on the region's long-term development: in the 1920s the South's standard of living had dropped to the lowest in the nation, its illiteracy rate the highest."[111] To refuse to view the South as a partial consequence of Northern policies and laws is to accept the dualistic perspective that *only* white Southerners were responsible for their fate. The "institution" of slavery had washed away any of the childlike innocence that the region could claim, but the imposition and aggression of Northern institutions soon made them full partners in the present and future situation. As I. A. Newby writes,

> Northern investment was responsible for much of the [Southern] growth after 1880, but the growth masked the detrimental effects of outside ownership. As major segments of the economy came under northern control, economic decision-making was removed from the South and profits were drained away (In 1868, for example, northerners controlled only a negligible portion of Southern railroads. Only 11 of the 280 directors of twenty-five major railroad companies at that time were northerners. By 1900, however, fully 90% of the section's mileage was in the hands of northern-owned companies, and it was Southern influence that was now almost negligible).[112]

The situation continued well into the twentieth century, as many Northern businesses took advantage of the position afforded them by their circumstances and proceeded to exploit the Southern economy. At the beginning of the twentieth century, for example, approximately half the large sugar plantations in Louisiana were in Northern hands and vast amounts of acreage and timber were owned by either Europeans or Northerners.[113] In 1907, J.P. Morgan and his U.S. Steel Corporation bought the main steel producer in Alabama, Tennessee Coal, Iron, and Railroad Company, controlling assets that, in part, consisted of iron and coal deposits in northern Alabama and southern Tennessee, paying a price of $35 million for them when their worth was estimated at over one billion dollars.[114] In the South, "the Morgan holdings were so vast that their decisions became a significant factor in the South's economic development, serving to increase and perpetuate colonialism."[115] During that time, "the process of colonialization accelerated," as a number of Southern oil, natural gas, sulphur, and textile industries were bought by northerners.[116] As is evident, the colonial projects of the North and the economic impact of Reconstruction turned the South into little more than a dependency of Northern business and political authorities.

In the opinion of some, the South consequently turned into nothing more than uncivilized patch of land, a cultural black hole from which very little escaped and even less was produced. The irascible H. L. Mencken, for example, took full advantage of this reputation. In his essay "The Sahara of the Bozart," published November 13, 1917, in the New York *Evening Mail*, Mencken parodied the expression "beaux arts" and offered a view of a South void of any cultural contextualization. His views, in essence, reflected many national (read "Northern") opinions of the South and were informed by the subtle yet prevailing colonial discourse of the times. Interestingly, his points of reference for many of the comparisons he offers of the South are not necessarily the non-Southern United States but rather other lands and peoples that had been exploited and marginalized by Europe and the United States. Throughout the essay, a number of times Mencken mentions Southern culture in the same breath as other semi-industrial or developing societies: "It is as if the Civil War stamped out every last bearer of the torch, and left only a mob of peasants in the field. One thinks of Asia Minor, resigned to Armenians, Greeks and wild swine, of Poland abandoned to the Poles." With regard to the state of Virginia, Mencken says it is "an intellectual Gobi or Lapland," and compares the lack of intellectual stimulation in Georgia at the time to the Balkans or the coast of China.[117] His references are not by chance, as Mencken looks to construct a South that, in his opinion, has much more in common with areas such as Armenia, Greece, Poland, Lapland, the Balkans, or the coast of China than with states like New York or Massachusetts or cities such as Boston, Washington, Philadelphia, or Baltimore. Interestingly, his choice of international locations as points of reference speaks more to his own mindset and the dominant ideology existing throughout the northeastern United States, reflecting distinct sets of colonial and neocolonial positions that looked to underestimate and wipe away the potential cultural contributions of Southern societies. As he himself indicates regarding Virginia, "one could no more imagine a Lee or a Washington in the Virginia of today than one could imagine a [Thomas] Huxley in Nicaragua."[118] In the nineteenth century, Nicaragua—a nation colonized by the Spanish crown whose Caribbean coast was controlled by English piracy—was also habitually controlled by United States business interests such as those of Cornelius Vanderbilt and the Louisiana interloper William Walker, and decidedly fits much better into Mencken's rhetorical designs.

In the essay, Mencken's use of unambiguous language to describe the South also deserves a closer look, as it provides examples of vocabulary that is used allegedly transparently but is, in effect, an ingenious way to influence and inculcate a population. When he hypothesizes, for example, that "[i]f the whole of the late Confederacy were to be engulfed by a tidal wave tomorrow, the effect upon the civilized minority of men in the world would be but little greater than that of a flood on the Yang-tse-Kiang [river],"[119] we must recognize the historical context yet question the implications of the term "civilized" and conclude that they stem from a principally colonialist position of dominance and superiority. As he writes of Southern contributions to science, theology, and philosophy and declares that "[i]n all these fields the South is an awe-inspiring blank—a brother to Portugal, Serbia and Albania,"[120] care must be exercised not to restrict our denotation of "knowledge" to European or North American empirical or canonical specifications that narrowly value written expressions of language—at the expense of oral traditions and cultures—and that Mencken attempts to convey through his choice of language. Similarly, when he declares that "[i]t is highly probable that some of the worst blood of Western Europe flows in the veins of the Southern poor whites, now poor no longer,"[121] not only should we take his extremism with a grain of humor and a dose of satirical salt, but we must also recognize his rhetoric and his implicit distinction between "best" and "worst" blood for what they are: colonially tinted ruminations of one who, with a quick pen and a measure of good fortune, wrote of the U.S. South from the outside, disguising both his privileged economic position and his subsequent prejudices. The region may indeed have been in dire need of a cultural and even a humanitarian reawakenening at the time, but, as with all things, the supposed truth of our ideas depends on the denotative consequences of our speech, on the connotations inherent in our language, and on the manner in which these are perceived.

During this period in history, many of the nations that both Cash and Mencken mention constituted satellite countries and territories that other imperial powers such as England and Russia were looking to exploit. In this sense, the South as a region opened by Northerners for economic exploitation during and after Reconstruction does not seem to be such an abstract comparison. According to Pete Daniel, as the South entered the twentieth century, "the capitalists of Northern states regarded the South as their colony."[122] Although the South has been criticized for maintaining an exaggerated nostalgia for the Civil War, it is redundant to state that this conflict remains an integral part of the region's historical identity. As I.A. Newby, among others, has indicated, after the Civil War, Southerners learned "the meaning of defeat."[123] The memory of loss and upheaval on their own land has given Southern states a reason for fighting for their own cultural survival and growth. If the institutions of many of these states have not progressed in time with the rest of the nation, may we trace the roots of this abatement to Reconstruction, when Northern industry entered the South and appropriated many of its lands, farms, and fields for its own economic gain? Taken in context with the war rhetoric that this country has continuously and very recently been subjected to, it is interesting to note that the South is the only territory of the continental United States that has lost a war on its own soil, that has seen itself in the position of the vanquished. Conceivably, Southerners may possess a distinct appreciation for the nuances of peace and the consequences of war, as they were not only defeated: they were defeated on their own territory, with their own soldiers dying in their fields and their homes burning before their eyes. Defeat, to the Southerner, may simply be a part of a life that escaped them but that, in the end, is always nearby as a distinct and viable possibility, not unlike what V.S. Naipaul referred to as the presence in the South of "the past as a wound."[124]

Perhaps that is part of what is missing in the contemporary arguments for national armed conflict: the recollection of loss. This remains present today, as the United States has recently been involved in a series of wars and conflicts on foreign soil and looks to either mythify some portion of a nation's past or obliterate it from the annals of global history. In Iraq, for example, the administration of George W. Bush at one point proposed to demolish the prison of Abu Ghraib in light of the torture that Iraqi prisoners endured there at the hands of United States soldiers, officers, and subcontracted security personnel. In the aftermath of justifying its activities and passing the blame between commanders and enlisted men, the military command and the Bush administration took what appeared to be a logical step in recommending the flattening of the prison. As much debate and conflict as the episode generated, the solution seemed to be a frighteningly simple one: if the penitentiary would be demolished and the physical evidence would no longer be present, the accusations surrounding the detention center and the treatment of Iraqis would dangerously acquire an intangible abstract character, and, as in many examples occurring throughout the history of Latin American nations, it would now be up to the victims themselves to prove that they had been cruelly and maliciously mistreated and to defend the truth of their experiences.

In Latin America, the importance of historical memory in the renovation and reinvention of national and autonomous cultures is partly due to an increased emphasis on the recuperation of lost stories—stories belonging to individuals whose apparent anonymity made their suffering initially appear to vanish from the history of the country or seem less tangible. Much like the current research on slave narrative in the nineteenth-century U.S. South, in recent times Latin American testimonial writers such as Rigoberta Menchú, Omar Cabezas, and Ana Guadalupe Martínez have served as representative voices that have exposed the suffering of a certain people or race marginalized by institutional power structures inherent to their nation. The discursive foundations of these voices may be traced back to the sixteenth century, when Spanish priests such as Bartolomé de las Casas and Guamán Poma de Ayala witnessed the atrocities committed by the Europeans in their efforts to enslave the inhabitants of the "New World." From that point on, first-person narratives that related and described historical events, distant populations or unjust living conditions formed part of the cultural and literary landscape in Latin America.

Latin American independence in the early part of the nineteenth century was a political reality that concealed the popular illusion of universal suffrage, as the infrastructure that Spain and Portugal had put into place was essentially maintained in every newly founded country due to the fact that the Creole or *mestizo* elite that rebelled against Spanish occupation sought to continue its hegemony in economic and political matters under the rhetorical umbrella of sovereignty and self-determination. Throughout that period, European colonial powers such as Germany and England maintained a presence in Chile, Peru, Argentina, Mexico, Nicaragua, and Colombia, for example, dividing up between the various foreign conglomerates natural resources such as tin, copper, and nitrates. By the middle of the century, the United States had entered the scene and projected itself as an economic force to be reckoned with and a military power to be feared, formulating the Monroe Doctrine (1823) in order to justify incursions into Caribbean nations and defend the area from European interests, in the process occupying and taking control of one-third of Mexican territory in 1848 with the rationale that these interventions promoted political stability in the region. The depth and frequency of these military movements and occupations reached their zenith in the first half of the twentieth century, as the United States directly or indirectly intervened in events in Nicaragua, Guatemala, Cuba, the Dominican Republic, Chile, El Salvador, and Panama, among others, and implicitly or explicitly supported the monopolizing efforts of corporations such as United Fruit or International Telephone and Telegraph.

In order to recover the history overlooked since the arrival of Europeans to the continent at the end of the fifteenth century, a number of

Latin American political figures and artists today accentuate the importance and persistence of historical memory through either a sound admiration or blind hatred of the United States. The Western Hemisphere in the last one hundred years has been dominated by U.S. interests and, much like the U.S. South, has suffered through continuous interventions (incursions that were publicly defended by presidential administrations but that occurred principally due to the fact that U.S. economic interests and government policies were inextricably linked). After the Civil War, for example, the U.S. South beheld the North maintaining its economic interests alive through rhetoric (much as Abraham Lincoln declared war on the Confederacy under the moral guise of eradicating slavery) and saw how these economic interests, once located and positioned in the South, began to operate distinct transformations throughout the community.

Presently, these two populations—the U.S. Southern and the Latin American—are coinciding and using their shared distinct histories of marginalization and oppression to forge ties that would perhaps be more difficult if not impossible in other regions of the world. What will emerge from this renewed contact in nontraditional locations of the United States between immigrant and non-immigrant? How will the U.S. South continue to remember itself as the numbers of immigrants increase, and how will Latin Americans in the U.S. South recall and shape their own individual stories? Is the Hispanic culture and economy in the U.S. South substantial enough to be considered a developing nation within a developed nation? The connections are being established and the communities in the U.S. South are reacting by using—and sometimes exploiting—the labor and talents that Latin American immigrants offer the region. And while complete assimilation is neither desirable nor plausible, what will emerge is something akin to Ilan Stavans's bilateral notion regarding the Hispanization of the United States and the Anglicization of Hispanics. U.S. Southerners and Latin American immigrants have already come into contact, and it is a distinct inevitability that the experience of colonialism will form a bridge between the varieties of cultures.

The step from economic infrastructure to cultural construction is perhaps difficult to detect, as institutions from both sectors rarely transparently commerced with each other in the process of mythifying a particular individual or a moment in history. In the nineteenth century, however, the relationship between economics and culture was quite possibly as distinguishable as it is today in the United States, where "infotainment," programs such as "Larry King Live," Hollywood gossip shows, and best-selling authors all coexist within the framework of profit. In the nineteenth century, the North had a vested interest in creating the Southern myth, as it justified the extension of Northern dominion over the region in a time of a vacuum of Northern identity. Efforts to pigeonhole the South, to make its identity unambiguous to all outside, spoke to a Northern search for stability within their own borders and, by extension, to the continuous (re)designation of what the nation was and would be. Regardless of a Northern disdain for Southern customs and trappings, the Northerner was indeed frequently looking to Dixie, searching for clarity in the nationalistic fog that enveloped the United States and Europe in this period. At that time, "Many Northerners began to cast their eyes southward because it appeared that an Old World aristocracy there had somehow discovered a way of assuring stability and cultivating a sense of gentility and decorum while maintaining a commitment to the public good under a republican form of government."[125] What was this Northern perception of "the public good"? In all probability, it signified social contentment, status quo, the permanence of structures, and the optimism of individuals who lived within them (including slavery, institutional prejudices, and oppression). Moreover, this sense of a supposedly stable "public good" was more than likely envied by a North that had witnessed the continuous interruption of its social fabric by industrialization and by unbroken waves of immigration from Europe (later, during Reconstruction, the South would equally take offense, and those coming to the region to take advantage of regional losses would be known as "carpetbaggers," and Southerners traitors to their own cause as "scalawags").

As much as Northerners expressed a desire to do away with slavery and, theoretically, to equate all human beings in the face of God and government, Northern creation and support of the Southern plantation myth reveals the extent to which many in the North coveted Southern culture's underpinnings, expressing righteous indignation at the existence of slavery and, at the same time, enjoying the economic fruits of sectional antipathy. After the Civil War, industrialism and the rise of factories was transforming the North and creating a class of individuals newly enriched by their circumstances. At the time, even the growing middle class began to enjoy some of the comforts provided by relative economic success, as these people began to vacation, to read during their leisure time, or to simply relax with their families. This northern industrialization and *bourgeoization* also brought with it a nostalgia for simpler times, for a life lived in the countryside, reaping the harvest or tending to the farm animals. At the time, "As America came to cherish the notion that agriculture was the most basic of industries and the agriculturalist the most virtuous of men both the North and the South could mutually agree to the plantation legend because of their mutual admiration for the plantation myth."[126] This plantation myth involved a clear, hierarchical order, the benevolent presence of authority, and the omnipresent thanks received by the workers and laborers. Curiously, "Though a titled aristocracy had long since been declared at odds with the American Creed, some apparently harbored the desire for such a class in the shadows of their minds. The Yankee, despite his stated though often superficial differences, liked to fancy himself a Cavalier at heart."[127] Gradually, the South paradoxically became both the repository of Northern (i.e. American) dreams and an example of a nation's worst vices. To this end, the mythification of the region served the purposes of the north, as it represented its past aspirations to a more solid and transparent cultural identity untouched by industrialization and all its materialistic trappings.

Mythification of the South through Northern efforts also occurred through the creation and appropriation of cultural symbols. As Henry Steele Commager has indicated, "The most familiar of Southern symbols came from the North: Harriet Beecher Stowe of New England gave us Uncle Tom and little Eva and Topsy and Eliza, and it was Stephen Foster of Pittsburgh who sentimentalized the Old South, while even 'Dixie' had northern origins."[128] Curiously, "no evidence exists that Foster ever visited the state [of Kentucky, where he allegedly composed "My Old Kentucky Home"], much less that he wrote his famous song there."[129] Also, the song "Dixie" was written by an Ohioan, Daniel Decature Emmett, in New York City in 1859.[130] The most inveterate of Southern symbols have frequently been Northern creations. Due in part to aesthetic and economic factors, Northern—non-Southern—writers and artists in general were embarking on a search for a cultural utopia of sorts in the face of the industrial upheaval suffered by the North. In effect, Northern artists began to territorialize Southern cultural commodities and to appropriate them for use "abroad," selling Southern mystique to those who had little—if any—idea what this meant, if it meant anything at all. (Not unlike today, when the South is still being packaged via the movies—"Sweet Home Alabama," "The Ladykillers"—sports—the growing national popularity of NASCAR racing—music—the "Nashville sound" and the "universally regional" songs of popular groups such as REM, the Indigo Girls, and Widespread Panic—and best-selling authors such as Pat Conroy, John Grisham, and Celestine Sibley, for example.)

To this end, the South has, in essence, also participated in the mythification of its own customs, culture, and territory. As Cash noted in *The Mind of the South,* after Northerners had been defining and exploiting Southern symbols for a number of generations, "Southerners themselves fully got around to adorning every knoll in the Old South with a great white manorhouse."[131] While Cash's seminal work on Southern identity has been gradually deconstructed since its publication, his perspective begs the question: What could Southerners possibly gain from commodifying their own culture and allowing themselves to be defined from outside its borders? On the one hand, after the Civil War and Reconstruction, the region was in dire need of an identity and purpose, which it found in songs and stories. On the other hand, it benefited them economically, as the South became a fashionable destination thanks, in part, to the messages of gentility, tranquility, and decorum expressed by its songs, art, and literature. Aside from the possible aesthetic attraction of cities like Savannah, Charleston, New Orleans, Mobile, Asheville, or Memphis, these places—regardless of their poverty, social unrest, degree of racial tension, educational underdevelopment, poor infrastructure, and/or economic difficulties—were infused (from the outside, of course) with the grace and charm they supposedly and historically deserved, attracting visitors who wanted nothing more than to revel in the gracious mystery and gothic elegance of the Spanish moss and fragrant magnolias. That is also part of the reason why today, in the face of decades of social transformation undergone by the South, the region and many of its inhabitants still help fabricate and cling to images of white-columned houses and azaleas in perpetual bloom: because these are interlocked with their historical identity and, simply put, because it is regularly profitable.

Throughout the nineteenth and twentieth centuries, there also occurred a demythification of the South, as intellectuals in the region began talk of a New South. Circa 1880, individuals such as Henry Grady, Richard H. Edmonds, Francis W. Dawson, Henry Watterson, and Daniel A. Tompkins "envisioned a new South characterized by industrial growth, economic diversity, and other 'attributes' of progress, especially prosperity, liberal social change, national reconciliation, and racial paternalism."[132] One of the leading champions of the New South was Henry Grady, a graduate of the Universities of Georgia and Virginia and a renowned journalist whose speeches in 1887 ("The South and Her Problem)" and 1889 ("The Farmer and the Cities") would come to define the identity of a post–Civil War South that made use of its forgotten natural resources and "diversified its agriculture," advanced relations between blacks and whites, and sought out "sectional reconciliation."[133] In Grady's words, "The new South presents a perfect democracy, the oligarchs leading in the popular movement—a social system compact and closely knitted, less splendid on the surface, but stronger at the core—a hundred farms for every plantation, fifty homes for every palace—and a diversified industry that meets the complex needs of this complex age."[134] His ideas portrayed a U.S. South that had come to terms with its defeat at the hands of the Union forces over twenty years earlier, reinventing itself through close collaboration with Northern investors. And although his ideas clearly looked to open the region to economic investment and encourage much-needed transformations in its sociopolitical dynamics, the trouble was that they fashioned a romanticized likeness of the South by contributing to the view that Southerners were principally genteel and generous in nature.

The New South creed of diversifying its economy and encouraging industry, surrendering agrarian ideals, welcoming Northern investment, and absorbing the virtues of the Northern work ethic, was basically "a formula for colonializing the southern economy and inveigling the southern people to accommodate themselves to the needs of the colonizers."[135] Writers such as Cash would also express their concern that at the center of the talk about the New South was the distribution of power and the preservation of the status quo. For Cash, "The New South meant and boasted of was mainly a South which would be new in this: that it would be so rich and powerful that it might rest serene in its ancient positions, forever impregnable."[136] In effect, this New South began to be constructed once the region was at the forefront of social changes (the civil rights movement, for example), economic productivity and employment (during the 1980s and 1990s), and cultural expressions that soon figured prominently on the national stage (blues, jazz, and, ultimately, rock and roll), developing into what George Washington Cable termed a "No South," a region "fully assimilated and essentially indistinguishable from the rest of American society."[137] Perhaps Cable was correct, and the future will witness an even greater degree of diversity in the region that will gradually render moot the alleged Southernization of United States, and perhaps the U.S. South will be the one of the first regions of the country in which its Americanization will supersede our national borders and acquire a bold continental connotation.

Traditionally, the South and its inhabitants have also been pariahs for much of the country's ills: it was the principal area of the country where the right to own slaves was defended; it seceded from the United States; it has been perceived as insular, backwards, and provincial; and many

states in the region have consistently been at the bottom of national rank-
ings of education spending, health care, and per capita income. Curiously,
these unhealthy differences that distinguish it from the rest of the country
also unite it with the Americas. As Jon Smith and Deborah Cohn have
written, "The very factors that allegedly make the South exceptional
within the context of the United States thus make it acutely familiar
within broader categories of Americanness and postcoloniality."[138] The
emergence in the eighteenth century, for example, of a Southern culture
and ideology distinct from those of its northern neighbors "was due to
the fact that racial demography and economic interest led Southern elites
to try to resist the ideological and social changes then transforming
the North Atlantic community. These changes included enlightenment
liberalism, the industrial revolution, liberal capitalism, political democracy, individualism, urbanization, and nationalism."[139] These institutional differences—rooted as they were in historical processes—were
evident as late as the twentieth century, when the idea of a supposedly
Solid South was born onto the national political scene. As Augustus
B. Cochran has pointed out, part of the country seems to have bought into
the worst aspects of this exclusivist Solid South and made these their own
national standards, including:

> [E]lections that ignored or blurred issues; weak, elitist, and even demagogic
> leaders; a proclivity to avoid problems and coast along with the status quo;
> rampant corruption and policymaking by deals; voters who were confused
> and apathetic; an appallingly low electoral base, including low turnout
> among even those lucky enough to be enfranchised; a resulting tilt toward
> the elites, while the have-not majority got taken for a ride; and a tendency
> to centralize decision-making in the federal system in the face of Southern
> state default.[140]

That the U.S. South is unique and that a self-proclaimed Southern
aristocracy is part of its mythology remain sensitive issues, as the region
has constructed itself in the face of an Other who has traditionally been
militarily stronger and economically better prepared to face the future;
but the relationship between the South and the non-South has not only
been continuous: the border between the two has been porous, and the
influences have been reciprocal. Moreover, the South has been the base-
ment and the attic of this place called Nation. As Peter Applebome has
written, "The South has been a lightning rod for our fondest hopes and
worst fears—a shadow theater for national guilt—a place to stow the
bloody rags we didn't want to see; a scapegoat for our worst failings;

a model for an imagined, perfect past; a hypothesis for a nation redeemed or a nation damned."[141] The surprise is not that the South reflected what may be perceived as national characteristics or trends, but that the rest of the country would attempt to portray events in the South as isolated exceptions to the national character. "If there is such a thing as a U.S. Southern identity, white or black, it consists neither in those traits that have historically been identified as 'Southern' and oppressed by an imperial North, nor in those traits that make it clearly part of the hegemonic United States, an oppressor of those further South."[142] As enthusiastically as the South has been constructing its own identity, the rest of the country has been assembling their own version of Dixie, a version that fit neatly into preconceived notions of time and place—of culture and authority—that allowed the non-South to play off of these negative representations of Southern institutions and fashion themselves as a counterpoint to them. As Gerster and Cords have affirmed in addressing Northern attitudes to slavery, for example, the South was viewed by the North as the exception which allowed them to live in relative tranquility: "The revered notion that race prejudice was a condition to be found exclusively in the prewar South allowed the North to escape its social guilt over the continued existence of discrimination."[143]

Interestingly, the negative distinctions and impressions labeling the South were perhaps already present at the creation of the United States. In a well-known letter to the Marquise de Chastellux , François Jean de Beauvoir, dated September 2, 1785, Thomas Jefferson distinguishes the character of the Northerner from that of the Southerner and offers a list of attributes: Where the Northerner is "cool, sober, laborious, persevering, jealous of their own liberties and just to those of others," Jefferson perceived the Southerner of the time to be "fiery, voluptuary, indolent, unsteady, zealous for their own liberties but trampling on those of others."[144] Was Jefferson's opinion of Southern people a way of detaching himself from his region, a way to honor and express admiration for that Northern spirit (whatever that may have been), or an initial attempt to isolate the more "fiery" politicians from the South? Although himself a Southerner, Jefferson would unmistakably not list these as his own characteristics, distinguishing further the genteel, cosmopolitan, and educated Southerner from the rural farmer who was not willing to see past his property line. Jefferson's characterization of the Southerner is especially interesting when noted alongside that of the Northerner, and the intention appears to be to lionize the (Northern) U.S. spirit in the face of a growing European examination of the United States and its politics.

If the Southerner is "indolent" and "unsteady," the Northerner—the individual truly at charge in Washington and Philadelphia, Jefferson seems to suggest—is "laborious" and "persevering," the epitome of how the United States wished to be viewed abroad.

More recently, general observations of the South have been mitigated by the role that the region has played in the social, political, and economic development of the country. In his seminal work *Southern Regions of the United States* (1936), Howard W. Odum's general description and alleged characteristics of Southerners contributed toward a romantic perception of the area and its inhabitants. According to him, Southerners possess "a certain distinctiveness in manners and customs; a certain poignancy and power of cultural tradition; evidences of capacity for romantic realism; and a certain reserve of social resources as well as physical wealth."[145] More recently, in a *New York Times* article titled "The South Has Risen Again. Everywhere," and published October 19, 1997, David Galef speaks to a Southern mystique that, in spite of—or perhaps because of—popular culture, remains present today: "The South is simply one of the last bastions of an earlier era, its mysteries and manners dating back to a time long before Colonel Sanders." The positive and negative characterizations have historically grown together, shaping the region's most salient characteristics: "To what extent, for example, did the hospitality, personalism, and social graciousness [Southerners] admired grow out of the social and racial inequality they [Southern liberals] deprecated? To what extent did the poverty and racism and undereducation they wanted to eliminate help pressure the ethos of rural and small-town society they often praised?"[146]

While these attitudes appear to justify the "customs" of that disappearing South, these and other descriptions written over the course of the years have been a double-edged sword for the region, as many Southerners have worked to promote and even exaggerate the sideshow imagery that centers on magnolias, columned porches, closeted skeletons, and a taste for the gothic and tragic. By advancing this representation, many in the South have laid the foundation for a very familiar and comfortable definition of themselves, one that timelessly delineates and emphasizes the South's static nature, one that would allegedly remain tried and true in the face of national trials and tribulations. Unfortunately, that same representation has also pigeon-holed the region and made difficult any cultural, political, or economic separation from a norm that has been in existence for over two hundred years, threatening to turn parts of the U.S. South—River Road in Savannah, Bourbon Street in New Orleans,

Beale Street in Memphis, or Main Street in downtown Nashville, for example—into parodies of themselves, hyperreal theme parks full of prepackaged authenticity and charm.

In a study published in 1996, Diane Roberts analyzed the culture of Southern myth-building and continuation and cited the prescriptive power of the magazine *Southern Living*, extending her critique to the South as a region and taking to task the role that the magazine plays in the region's projection of self-obsession and subtle romanticization: "*Southern Living* is still a part of the South's 'performance,' representing itself as special, chosen, a favoured region congratulating itself on not having the problems associated with the rest of the country."[147] This duplicitous part of its history is evident throughout the South in monuments, parks, or plaques that commemorate morally questionable events or memorialize dubious individuals in what may be a problematic manner. In Memphis, for example, on the shores of the Mississippi, there is a smallish, obelisk-type monument dedicated to Tom Lee, "a very worthy negro." Upon examining the sculpture, it is unfortunate, but one has the impression that the mere absence of the adjective "worthy" would communicate its exact opposite: that, at the time, to simply be an unmodified "negro"—a term that in and of itself carries a considerable amount of excess historical baggage—was enough of a burden upon an individual and necessitated a lexical boost. Other examples of problematic memorials across the South include monuments in Colleton Co., South Carolina, or Athens, Georgia, for example, which memorialize the Confederate effort during the Civil War and have raised community tensions—as citizens have asked for their permanent removal—or Monument Avenue in Richmond, Virginia, which includes memorials to Confederate figures such as Robert E. Lee, J.E.B. Stuart, Jefferson Davis, and "Stonewall" Jackson, among others.

While the cruelty suffered by African Americans in the U.S. South has surely differed from other parts of the country, events certainly and sadly prove that racial tension and violence are not unique to this frequently disparaged region of the nation. International populations are and have been making a significant impact on the region and the nation, transforming the dynamics of identity across the country and forcing us to look into the mirror and characterize for ourselves our own small and large homelands. Today, as Gregory Stephens has noted, "moving toward a bilingual, transnational South will also involve a reorientation of what it means to be a southerner, as well as what it means to be an American."

U.S. SOUTHERN "DISTINCTIVENESS" AND THE OTHER

The economic development of the U.S. South and the history, statistics, anecdotes, and existing stereotypes surrounding the region may hide the fact that the South has not only had more in common with the rest of the nation than was previously thought, but that frequently, communities in the South have been forced to face concerns that the rest of the country had swept aside, issues that may be gently broadcasting the social, political, and economic future of the United States. As Peter Coclanis has stated, "The South has already experienced many of the problems and throes of economic adjustment the United States as a whole has been going through in the past decade. What is happening to manufacturers and services today [nationally] happened to Southern agriculture one hundred and thirty years ago."[148] Without ignoring the region's present and past, it is evident that the South has had to contend with racial unrest and organized disturbances that began as early as 1866 in New Orleans and Memphis—in which many African Americans died at the hands of "rioting whites"[149]—and with issues such as civil rights and the perpetual conflict between local, regional, and national authorities and identities sooner, differently, and more extensively than the rest of the country.

In the wake of the national imperial project and cultural expansion that followed independence from England and the signing of the Treaty of Paris in 1783, the South became one of the first starting points for westward expansion and the "proving ground" for Manifest Destiny: the city of Baton Rouge was founded in 1794; in 1813, Mobile, Alabama, was captured by General Wilkerson; and in 1814 and 1818, the city of Penzacola [sic], Florida, was established.[150] According to Coclanis, "the South was integrated into world markets far earlier than the North was."[151] While the northern section of the national territory was also expanding westward at a surprisingly rapid pace, the geographical advantages of the South's waterways and coasts proved to be more than enough incentive for sustained efforts at colonization and development. As George Brown Tindall has studied, this growth included considerable numbers of immigrant populations who were different from individuals that had entered the areas north of Kentucky and Virginia. By 1860, "Southern cities had larger concentrations of foreign-language groups, such as French, Spanish, Italians, and Germans. [Conversely,] [t]he immigrants in northern cities were chiefly English-speaking groups, mainly British, Irish, and Canadian in origin."[152] During this time, "Southerners [also] assumed a decisive cultural affinity with aristocratic

European ruling classes in opposition to the aggressive, contentious northern democracy,"[153] extending and reinforcing cultural and economic transatlantic ties that, in their Southern opinion, had strengthened and supported the aristocratic notion of a culture far more "civilized" than their neighbors to the north. That this idea of Southern "culture" was based principally on Eurocentric ideals and only embraced white, property-owning males was, for the minority of the population in positions of power, a dubious point at best, regardless of Southern cultural claims to the contrary.

The authorities and infrastructures in the South, however, have remained generally monolingual, a linguistically monolithic totem representative of the first governors installed in the region by the central government. As has been the case in other circumstances, this apparent Southern characteristic reflected a trait that was present at the national level, one that remained hidden behind lines of defense and mirrored the extent to which "the American has been distinctly of the Southern persuasion."[154] In today's national party politics, some perceive the presence of what was known as a politics of the Solid South: enfeebled party competition, a narrow electorate, racialized politics,[155] and a political system that benefited from and grew out of greed, corruption, malfeasance, and a parlay of local interests over national ones. Augustus B. Cochran, for example, underlines the "decidedly undemocratic" nature of the Democratic Solid South and how these arrangements "threaten the vitality of our [national] institutions now."[156] Interestingly enough, this threat to "our institutions" has put the nation on virtually square political footing with the South: "Partly because of the new influence of Southern politicians, but more as a consequence of how issues of class, race, and gender have interacted with partisan politics in the last political generation, the South has liberalized while the nation has moved sharply to the right. This dual movement in contradictory directions has left region and nation comprehensively aligned."[157] This alignment is not necessarily beneficial to the country, according to Cochran, as the nation stands to inherit "the perversions of democracy" and the "chaotic politics" that permeated the Solid South and its political system.[158] The South may in fact be a political bellwether, and "an examination of Southern politics in the past might provide a timely warning about future directions in American politics."[159]

Historically, ethnic and economic diversity in the South distinguishes itself from that of the rest of the nation primarily due to the force and the omnipresence of the past, a past that has consistently been witness to the cultural and ethnic varieties of experience, buried beneath years of rhetoric and self-indulgence that have originated from both within and outside the South and have made problematic a regional identification with the rest of the nation. As Richard Gray wrote in 1996, "the transformation of the Southerner into the American has not really occurred or, at the very least, not been contemplated yet."[160] The balance between national identity and regional affections has at times been a delicate struggle in the United States, but if the South as a region is to integrate itself into a larger national and global community that welcomes heterogeneity and views ethnic differences as strengths, a middle ground must be found between an obsession with all things Southern and the persistent drive toward economic success.

Currently, Southern communities are looking to offer more opportunities to immigrants and to integrate themselves into a larger picture that searches to maintain its cultural uniqueness: "Even as it grows in people and jobs, even as it develops its own megametros and megabanks, even as it competes in a global economy, the South holds onto a fascinating distinctiveness."[161] Will this observed "distinctiveness" prove to be an albatross around the neck of the South? Will the South embrace the advantages that this "distinctiveness" may bring in the twenty-first century? If the alleged Southern uniqueness must be questioned in order to improve the region's overall economic performance, then will we see the ultimate fragmentation of the South and be witness to how every community will have to fight for itself without what has been the historical support of traditions of power (albeit white, Anglo-Saxon Protestant structures of power)? Dixie is globalizing, leaving in its gradual wake the apparent clarity of Southern customs and continuing to blend its cultural waters with those of other regions and nations.

In the opinion of James C. Cobb, events that truly shaped the destiny of the post-Reconstruction South occurred during "the turning period": from the Great Migration and World War I through the boll weevil invasion, the Great Depression, the New Deal, and World War II.[162] During this time, Southerners suffered a number of changes imposed from outside that would contribute to creating the aura of uniqueness and understated clout that most easily and dramatically characterizes the region. This New South had actually been forged some years earlier during the 1880s, when Southern identity was still reeling from the effects of Reconstruction and individuals such as Henry Grady were looking to reshape the South in light of industrial and social developments. Some such as W.J. Cash criticized the agenda of the New Southerners, alleging that it was simply a wistful search for an evaporated past: "The New South meant and boasted of was mainly a South which would be new in this: that it would be so rich and powerful that it might rest serene in its ancient position, forever impregnable."[163] The more society changed around them, the more many in the South tried to remain anchored to a fossilized past, one that was in direct opposition to the political, economic, and social advancements of many communities in the region in the twenty-first century. As Cobb has written regarding today's Dixie, "Questions about the South's cultural identity should move beyond a narrowly focused obsession with the issue of Southern distinctiveness relative to the rest of the nation. Instead, we should explore larger global commonalities, such as the influence of historical memory or the cultural consequences of modernization in other societies that have shared some of the historical experiences that seemed to set southerners apart from other Americans."[164] Without sacrificing "distinctiveness"—indeed, by using it as a point of departure—Southerners should explore the greater political, economic, or cultural commonalities shared with other global communities such as Andalucía, Spain, Sicily in Southern Italy, Scotland, Chiapas, Mexico, or Kashmir, India, where—differences notwithstanding—ethnic diversity has also been a constant point of tension and an integral part of daily life. These and other regions share a variety of broad characteristics: a generally polemical, marginalized, or nonexistent relationship with a central national government, economic impediments to progress (when compared with the rest of the nation), and an exaggerated cultural dependence on folklore (many times imported from outside). While it is unwise and impossible to ignore the historical differences between these regions, there have been moments in their respective histories when they shared more with other exploited areas across the globe than with regions within the boundaries of their own nation-state.

The initial racial and linguistic diversity of the South has been preserved throughout its history and into the twenty-first century, allowing the region to contribute to the continuous diversification of the United States and reaffirm its own regional identity. In today's world, "As globalization threatens to undermine the significance of national boundaries and institutions, the ongoing efforts of the [European Union] to shape Europe into what is effectively a single nation (and, some think, a single culture) make the South's relative success in avoiding total immersion in the American mainstream seem particularly relevant, as the European academic community's burgeoning interest in Southern literature and culture appear to suggest."[165] As it personifies the essence of the search for an evolving regional and national identity, the South showcases the influences that pass through any permeable border. According to Cochran, this exchange is mutual: "One prong of the forces at work has 'Northernized' the South, mainstreaming the once distinct region into a section that closely resembles the rest of the country on most indicators. The other prong of the dual transformation has produced a 'Southerniza-tion' of the North, paving the way for Southern politicians to assume national leadership roles and for traditionally Southern concerns and patterns increasingly to dominate American politics."[166] As George Tindall Brown has also noted, "It was less in some mythical racial 'purity' than in the diversity of their backgrounds that Southerners were the most American. Despite the melting pots that had bubbled away for two centuries, major elements of the colonial population remained visible in the white, black, Indian, and Hispanic elements of the twentieth-century South."[167] Throughout the years, the diversity of those "elements," their continued interaction, and the "unprecedented ethnic diversity"[168] existing today speak directly to the creation of a truly heterogeneous population in the region; unfortunately, they have also created tensions, with roots located firmly within a set of very specific geographical and cultural circumstances and that were, therefore, initially perceived to be unique to the South.

In the Deep Southern United States, the African American population has been the most historically marginalized. As Steven A. Channing has observed, "Between the founding of the Republic and secession—the life-time of a man—the white population of the South had multiplied five times and had expanded westward and southward across the Mississippi delta into Texas. But blacks had multiplied nearly as rapidly, an unparal-leled New World phenomenon."[169] Over the years, the historical presence of the African American population and the experience of displacement and disenfranchisement have evolved into fight, flight, or remain: to actively rebel against the marginalization maintained by the powers that be, to emigrate to other cities and regions in the United States, or to do nothing. Today, the cultural climate has improved and opportunities to prosper and coexist alongside other ethnicities have expanded as "[m]ore black Americans now move to the South [more] than to any other region of the nation."[170]

Over the course of moments crucial in the contemporary history of the South, African American voices have justifiably been among the most vociferous and most critical in expressing the need for a more just and inclusive Southern society, one that takes into consideration all of its population. As Cobb has written,

> Many of the most energetic and purposeful participants in the process of constructing a new southern identity are black southerners whose spirited attacks on the Confederate flag, "Dixie," and other symbols of the New South's racial order complement their efforts to establish monuments to their own crusade to overturn that order. Meanwhile, finding little else of substance in which to ground their claim to a distinctive identity, many white southerners continue to cling to "Dixie" and the Confederate banner, insisting that they represent more than a sordid history of slavery and racial repression.[171]

Narrow perspectives that refuse to understand Southern diversity as an asset to the region's future hold wistfully to a time when life was quite literally black and white, when the Stars and Bars was only a military banner instead of a symbol appropriated by racist groups and organizations. The danger is that once that symbol—whether it be a song or a flag—has been usurped, heed should be paid to those individuals belonging to populations targeted by a racist group's discriminatory rhetoric and bigotry. The voices of history are polyphonic and multichromatic— and marginalized populations have historically possessed superior memories (unlike those historical amnesiacs who have traditionally held to privileged positions of power).

The same Southern diversity that will drive the region to "explore [those] larger global commonalities" has been typically ignored due to the perception that the racial profile of the South may be easily divided into the traditional black and white poles of (un)attraction. According to Carole E. Hill, "From a national perspective, the South has traditionally been thought of as a region made up of whites and blacks, and since most social science studies have concentrated on local levels, regional complexity and diversity have been overlooked. Regional generalizations are often simplistic and sometimes diversity is ignored completely."[172]

In order to acknowledge and understand the advantages of Southern diversity, the next step would be to compare and contrast the demographic studies performed at local levels across the region, offering a broader analytical cross-section of the resources that are available and prepared to bring about substantial changes. In this manner, potential cooperation between diverse populations would have a quantifiable base of action and would include members of these disenfranchised communities, regardless of their ethnicity.

The battle over civil rights and the launch of the Civil Rights movement has, in the past, spotlighted the South's pro-slavery history and the region's inability to be genuinely inclusive of the African American population; but it may be argued that this inability reflected a national crisis that was all too easily regionalized. As Cochran has written, "With Watts, Detroit, and the cores of hundreds of other American cities smoldering in the wake of violent disturbances, it was hard to imagine that the problems of racism and inequality were merely residual or peculiar to the backward South."[173] Did many of the civil rights milestones—such as Rosa Parks's denial in 1955 to move to the back of the bus and the Little Rock crisis of 1957—occur in the South because of the region's prolonged history of objectifying, marginalizing, and dehumanizing the African American population, or did the South serve as a convenient wading pool for the national oligarchy, simply and sadly reflecting many of the "values" and beliefs present in the country at a specific moment? Even before the Civil Rights revolution, the establishment of a racist organization like the Ku Klux Klan reflected some inherently national prejudices, as, according to Cash, "the Klan summed up within itself, with precise completeness and exactness, the whole body of the fears and hates of the time, including, of course, those which were shared with the rest of America and the Western world."[174] Other moments in time have replicated the close relationship between "national" characteristics, customs, or trends, and ostensibly exclusively Southern ones. In 1968, for example, "the presidential campaign of former vice-president Richard M. Nixon denied what became known as the Republican 'Southern Strategy'—the use of racial wedge issues such as affirmative action and crime to drive white traditional democratic voters in the region to the GOP."[175] Given the supposed economic, cultural, and geographic differences between the territory and the rest of the nation, it has been historically painless for those outside the region to consign a secondary status to the South. But an overview of these specific examples and conflicts reveals otherwise, speaking more to the representative and national nature of regional circumstances rather than to the traditionally believed unique backwardness of the area.

While it is difficult to define a singular and exact moment of conception, it can certainly be argued that the Civil Rights movement had its organizational origins in a series of events that can be dated back beyond the independence of this country—to the establishment and commerce of the slave trade, for example—and passed through events such as the Plessy vs. Ferguson decision in 1896, Jackie Robinson's breaking of the color barrier in professional baseball in 1947, President Harry Truman's ten-point program in 1948, and the passage of the Civil Rights Bill in 1964. For the South, "race must be acknowledged as an important component of any definition of the South and its culture; it must be reinscribed into the region's past and present, rather than dismissed as relevant to African-Americans alone."[176] The prominence of seemingly isolated events in Selma, Birmingham, and Montgomery in the 1950s was later evident across the rest of the nation when non-Southern cities such as Los Angeles (1965), Detroit (1967), Newark (1967), and Cleveland (1968), among others, began to suffer the unrest that Southern towns and metropolitan areas had witnessed years earlier and had started to polarize public opinion across the country. During the decade of the sixties, "steamy little Selma [for example] was transformed into a mythic place that defined a rare moment in American race relations when who was right and who was wrong, which tactics made sense and which did not, had a moral clarity as transcendent as scripture."[177] As Applebome has stated, "What had conveniently been cast as a Southern issue in 1965 was now clearly and unavoidably the racial agony of the nation."[178] The events in the South in the fifties and sixties proved to be representative and prophetic of the tensions present throughout much of the land. Accordingly, "the notion that many of us grew up with of the South as a place apart when it comes to attitudes about race is hopelessly naïve."[179]

In the South there has also existed a certain romanticization and even a convenient fetishization of race relations between blacks and whites that can be traced to the colonization and objectification of the African American in the South and, by extension, in the rest of the country. In his work *The Mind of the South,* the language that Cash employs reflects his historical period and portrays the African American race as a homogeneous group that is far closer to the "savage ideal" of nature espoused by Jean-Jacques Rousseau in the eighteenth century than to the supposedly cosmopolitan civilization exemplified by the urban centers of the United States. Cash's comments in 1941 depict the Negro [sic] as "one of the world's greatest romantics and one of the world's greatest hedonists," "a creature of grandiloquent imagination, of facile enjoyment,"[180] and refer us directly to the appropriation of African American identity through generalizations and stereotypes that ultimately serve to subtly and paternalistically lay claim to the race in a more contemporary context. In other sections of the work, he identifies "the all-complaisant Negro woman," underlines the Negro's [sic] "remarkable talents as a mime," and identifies "the Southern Negro population [as] one of the most suggestible on earth."[181] In *The Negro and His Songs* (1925), a volume co-authored with Gary Johnson, Howard Odum—another well-known scholar of all things Southern—described Negro [sic] spirituals as "beautiful, childlike, simple and plaintive," and asserted that "their natures demand...some expression of their emotions."[182] Even the Cuban patriot José Martí, defender of human rights and individual freedoms—especially for the poorest of society—wrote from Charleston, South Carolina, in September 1886 that "[t]he Negro has great native goodness, which neither the martyrdom of slavery has perverted nor his virile fierceness obscured. But he, more than the men of any other race, lives in such intimate communion with nature, that he seems more capable than other men of shuddering and rejoicing with her changes."[183]

While the observations of Martí, Odum, and Cash may strike us as subjective generalizations that romanticize the African American and reflect popular (read "White Anglo-Protestant") culture and its categorization and commodification of African Americans more than any quasi-objective study of historical circumstances, their comments speak to their non–African American background and context and to justifications that may lie concealed beneath the veneer of time. On the surface there persists an apparent paternalism that looks to "care for" the African American because he cannot care for himself and, therefore, cannot project himself (at least, supposedly, in a white context in which cultural representation is manipulated in order to protect the interests of the dominant culture). Beneath that paternalism and the paternalistic tone there may lay a thin layer of guilt regarding the manner in which African Americans in both the United States and Cuba—Martí's homeland—have been treated by the dominant ethnicities. Cash's statements regarding the imagination, the capacity for enjoyment of the "Negro," and his supposedly innate hedonism; Odum's remarks regarding the "Negro" spiritual as "beautiful, childlike, simple and plaintive"; and Martí's assertion that the "Negro" rejoices in tune to the changes of Nature, paint a cheery image of the African American, one that may perhaps look to portray the African American race as joyful and innocent, happily oblivious to human suffering. Beyond the paternalism and a probable personal sense of guilt that serve to inform their comments, there may also exist a sense that the world—the modern, contemporary world, with its roots in Europe and North America and with its advances in transportation, medicine, commerce, and technology—was a frightening place to live (especially considering the period between 1886 and 1945) and that the search for a simpler and "purer" way of life was the answer to the wars, economic turmoil, and social unrest that cast a hungry shadow over those times. Unfortunately, and not surprisingly, the portrayal of the African American race was a superficial categorization, one that—without denying the joy or the grief that, for example, an African American spiritual may express and inspire—was imposed on black Americans from the outside and ultimately exported as a valuable profit commodity.

Located in Memphis in the old Lorraine Motel—the site where Martin Luther King Jr. was assassinated—the National Civil Rights Museum is found in a city that has received a large influx of Hispanic immigrants in the last ten years. As a cultural place of remembrance, the Lorraine Motel is frozen in time by both its own architecture and the images it displays. It is a museum in the strictest sense of the word in that it places and catalogues the distinct displays so that there may be a historical memory of events, a record of individuals who found their cause in the prolonged struggle against racism and marginalization. As you stroll through the halls, you may be bombarded by conflicting perceptions: how do I, as a non–African American, confront any personal or racial guilt and, at the same time, emotionally surrender myself to the likenesses captured by time? Perhaps personal and communal growth is ultimately achieved through a balancing of these two extremes. Confronting both one's own latent or implicit prejudices and the very explicit consequences that such prejudices may have may be more difficult than releasing yourself to the attraction of the extremes. National paintings, sculptures, music, and literature, for example, have represented these extremes and have searched for an exchange of ideas along and between the edges. By entering into dialogue with one's generation, with those that preceded it, and those that will follow, the art leaves a mark by which an era will be considered in the time to come.

In one of the exhibition rooms of the National Civil Rights Museum, there is a painting approximately seven feet wide by three feet tall by the New York artist Clarissa T. Sligh that is insightful in its simplicity. In black letters on a white background it reads "Mississippi is America," and echoes Malcolm X's declaration that "As far as I am concerned, Mississippi is anywhere south of the Canadian border."[184] Housed in what has become a national monument to the life and death of Martin Luther King Jr., the museum's displays are impressive as they trace the development of the Civil Rights movement through the history of the United States. The looping audiovisual exhibitions, the restaurant counter, the replicas of a burned school bus and of King's Birmingham jail cell, the preservation of his hotel room as he left it when he stepped out onto the breezeway, the hyperreal qualities of the museum-within-a-hotel-within-a-museum: it all goes toward bringing alive the efforts of the Movement through the sights and sounds of the struggle.

Some of the exhibits highlight the inclusive nature of the fight and the plight of different ethnic and racial groups and embrace them as part of the same difficulties faced by African Americans. In an exhibit marked "Organizations," for example, there is an undated black and white cutout photograph of two white women carrying a banner that portrays a bald white man extending his hand, palm out, "stopping" another man, who has brown skin. Beneath the caricature of the white man, the text reads, "Stop discrimination in hiring and firing negroes and Puerto Ricans," reflecting the problems faced by Puerto Ricans who in the 1950s came upon signs in restaurant doors that read "No dogs or Puerto Ricans allowed." While the situation may be more complex than the prejudices suffered by more than one ethnic or racial group, the caricature in the museum demonstrates an awareness of the Other that rings familiar in times of social fragmentation and vitriolic rhetoric. Apparently regional issues such as the birth of the Civil Rights movement and the treatment of racial and ethnic minorities struck a national cord, as other individuals across the country found commonalities within their own particular communities and proceeded to add their voices to the debates rising from the South. Unfortunately, it would appear that the most negative attributes of the Southern character have frequently been exported and usurped by radical organizations. As Applebome has written, "The varied groups of the extremist right fringe, from the armed militias to the white-supremacist right, have taken the worst elements of the South's past, its racism and blind hatred of central government, tied them together with old and new strains of the frontier ethic and the antitax movement, and created new variations on old, dark American themes."[185] It is no coincidence, then, that these "old, dark American themes" refer us back to Dixie's history and are habitually viewed as new examples of the South's unwillingness to change, instead of being perceived as what they may very well be: a litmus tests of national behaviors and attitudes.

George E. Pozzetta has written of how the South "has assumed something of a leadership role" regarding the new nativism and the impact that recent immigrant populations have had on the inhabitants of a community: "Large Asian and Latin American immigrations have often placed longer-settled residents in new and disturbing relationships with newcomers. Working-class Southerners, for example, have resented the job competition generated by Latin American immigrants in farm work and unskilled labor, while middle-class individuals have felt pressure from upwardly mobile Cuban exiles."[186]

Given what we have seen, the different and distinct possibilities of resentment expressed against new populations of immigrants reflect to a degree the attitudinal changes that occur across the rest of the nation. While the impact of recent immigration can be readily measured in other regions of the United States, the continuously growing populations that are being attracted to the South more than any other area of this country make the impact difficult to discern. As Pozzetta has stated, "As more Latin American, Asian, Middle Eastern, and African immigrants look toward the United States as a new home, the South will likely remain a focal point for issues centered on foreign immigration. National questions of how many immigrants should be allowed to enter and from where have assumed a new intensity in the region."[187] In a time of shifting immigration policies, the South's ability to embrace ethnic and cultural diversity in the twenty-first century will be manifest in the degree to which the diverse populations set down roots and reside in their respective communities. And it is in these processes that the region has been ahead of the rest of the nation, reflecting and shaping national tastes regarding politics, music, sports, and literature, and showing the effects of unexpected foreign-born immigrants upon both large and small communities.

The U.S. South today remains a place in a constant state of historical flux, as the residents keep a keen watch on the future and move between the present and the past, between the inherent racial and ethnic diversity found within, and still struggling to consider both tradition and change. As Richard Gray has written, "The South, and many Southerners, still manage to inhabit two separate moral territories: the one not quite dead, the other not yet fully born. For that matter, both the South and Southerners are now more than ever before a site of struggle between conflicting interests and voices, each one of them demanding recognition and power."[188] This, in essence, is the current legacy of the U.S. South: the presence of a very real collaboration and tension between various racial and ethnic groups, as these vie to have their voices heard. Latin American nations have also been witness to the struggle against History and continue to behold the communities that have arisen from the skirmishes for power and authority. How the arriving citizens from these nations are impacting the South and how the South's legacy will affect the nation's future remains to be seen in a region where the social, political, and cultural exchanges, collaborations, and hostilities between distinct ethnicities were first forecast centuries ago.

The United States, the U.S. South, Latinos, and Beyond
Current Initial Confluences

It is indeed a transparent fact that the Latino populations in the U.S. South are part of the South's heritage and part of the increasingly heterogeneous nature of the region today. As they have maintained a centuries-long historical presence and have chosen to invest in businesses, participate actively in schools, and actively contribute to the multiple varieties of progress, the majority of Latinos have a vested interest in the social, political, and economic infrastructure of their communities in the South. And while a great many members of the new populations of immigrants choose to work under demanding conditions—principally in construction, poultry, or agriculture—many Latinos are demonstrating a capacity to live a life that shifts easily between the new responsibilities shrouded in the culture of their work and the small homeland exemplified by their household.

In his work *Latinos Unidos: From Cultural Diversity to the Politics of Solidarity,* Enrique (Henry) T. Trueba has underscored the contributions that Latinos are making in the United States and how this country is able to better gauge its own development through the availability of opportunities for recent immigrants: "Latinos clearly occupy the most strategic position among immigrants as we approach the twenty-first century; the success of Latinos can easily become the success of America's democracy, as well as influence its economic, technological, and military survival."[1] As Trueba infers, the sheer numbers of Latinos will help to set the course for this country in the years to come, channeling resources and spotlighting issues that will gauge national transformations as demographics change across the country. Latinos work a variety of jobs, have children, send these children to schools and to the doctor, contribute to local charities, and earn money that is funneled into both the local economy in their place of residence and remitted back to the national economy in their country of origin. For many Latinos, the daily reality of shifting constantly between a life with non-Latinos and a life among those who are from their own heritage cultures contributes to the creation of a multifaceted existence that is consistently enriched by the interplay between languages, customs, responsibilities, and other ethnic groups (an interplay that some may view as disruptive to their community). As Trueba has suggested, "the instability in the lives of many Latino immigrants is compensated by the stability of their networks and relationships as well as by their ability to adapt to new sets of relationships and to members of additional groups."[2] Although at first glance they may appear to be contradictory, the terms "stability" and "adaptability" relate directly to that interplay and balance between tradition and change: between the South's varied yet uneven traditions of family, home, and religion, and the relatively recent presence of new waves of immigrants whose families, homes, and religions will almost certainly differ from its own. The development of these relationships leads to the creation of a Latino identity that is, in fact, a series of identities.[3] And while all of us may at some point juggle our different responsibilities through distinct behaviors appropriate for each moment and task, Latinos have entered into these exchanges, bringing the added factors of exile, displacement, and linguistic alienation, frequently compelling us to consider our customs, traditions, and surroundings from another's perspective.

There are a series of stereotypes surrounding the Latino population and presence in the United States: that they inhabit only a scattered number of cities and regions across the country, that the latest immigrants are principally rural, that their presence is relatively recent, that they cannot speak English well, that they are ignorant of U.S. culture and unwilling to assimilate, and that they are principally manual laborers, among other generalizations. The daily reality lived by Latinos in the United States belies these uninformed oversimplifications, as Latinos today are making their presence felt in nearly all aspects of the social, political, and economic fabric of the South and of the United States, with one of the most significant consequences being a very tangible remodeling of U.S. national identity through a curious yet effective balancing of varying degrees of assimilation into the host country and, along with their adopted communities, a shared sense of esteem and remembrance for the customs of home.

Due to the diverse nature of the Latino presence, misunderstandings, misconceptions, and miscommunications abound both within and outside Latino communities. According to the Miami-based journalist Jorge Ramos, for example, "the U.S. is afraid to look into the mirror and see a racially mixed country."[4] His critical assertion runs the danger of being as much a generalization of this country as those blanket statements looking to describe the homogeneous diversity of Hispanic immigrants. As varied as the population of this nation may be, what is expressed by Ramos's personification of the United States? More to the point: Who is, according to Ramos, "the U.S."? We may intuit that he implies the economic base, those who wield power, who define and protect the status quo. But the danger is that Ramos's point of reference, this inferred power base, is slowly becoming obsolete, as these individuals are being gradually viewed as a reactionary group, simply and primarily reacting in response to the fact that they are steadily becoming the "un-mainstream" as the margins gain demographic and economic power and bit by bit become the center, while the forces that have traditionally possessed the center ground are losing supremacy and are being shifted to the margins.

In an article published in 2004 in the journal *Foreign Policy*, the controversial professor Samuel P. Huntington declares that the "immense and continuing immigration from Latin America" to the United States constitutes "the single most immediate and most serious challenge to America's traditional identity."[5] His thesis centers on the fact that Latin American immigrants are not assimilating as easily or as completely as immigrants from other generations and nationalities. This, in essence, is forcing the economic and educational systems to accommodate these new populations and, in the process, explicitly exclude U.S. citizens who, for example, speak only English: "Because most of those whose first language is Spanish will also probably have some fluency in English, English speakers lacking fluency in Spanish are likely to be and feel at a disadvantage in the competition for jobs, promotions, and contracts."[6] In his opinion, this dawn of a multilingual United States and the continued influx of immigrants from Latin America does not herald new opportunities but rather warns of the accelerated fragmentation of national identity:

"Sustained numerical expansion promotes cultural consolidation and leads Mexican Americans not to minimize but to glory in the differences between their culture and the U.S. culture."[7] While there are certainly logistical concerns regarding the number of immigrants a community receives and the impact that these have on its infrastructure, Huntington's statement reflects his own ethnocentric fears, assuming that it is beneficial for a country to "minimize differences" and for an arriving population to assimilate into preestablished roles and societies. Unfortunately, his affirmation also assumes a standard of national homogeneity that, although its roots are firmly embedded in this nation's Puritanical past, remains unclear. As with Ramos's declarations, it is unclear what Huntington means by the apparently transparent phrase "U.S. culture." If a myriad of possibilities are present in this phrase—and it is plausible that they are—may that superficial distinction between "their culture" and "our culture" not be one of the most salient characteristics of contemporary "U.S. culture"? On the other hand, if his statement assumes the existence of a dominant, monolithic "U.S. culture" that is based solely on this nation's Anglo-Protestant past and present, then it is certainly time to disassemble those types of cultural constructions. In an interview that appeared in June 20, 2004, in the Spanish newspaper *El País*, Huntington's opinions acquire a tone that reflects a narrow perspective regarding a multiethnic United States and wistfully expresses yesteryear's apparently straightforward and rather one-dimensional vision of national identity. Speaking on the assimilation of Mexicans in the United States, he declares to the interviewer, "Assimilation is possible, but there are great difficulties that are also due to the attitude that Mexicans and Hispanics in general have toward teaching....There exists a real problem between Hispanics in regard to the topic of education and, for some reason, I think it is a part of their culture. They do not place much emphasis on teaching." Huntington's generalizations and oversimplifications reveal not only his personal opinions but also those of an unfortunately growing minority of United States citizens who feel threatened by the transformations that the country is undergoing.

Ideas similar to Huntington's may contribute more to the cultural and political climate surrounding a community's acceptance of Latinos than their assimilation or lack thereof. These attitudes often play a part in creating an atmosphere of distrust and misunderstanding in which the unfamiliar is placed almost permanently outside the reach and vision of unchanging communities that may be in need of an economic and cultural revival in order to thrive. By arriving throughout this country in

areas of nontraditional Spanish-speaking immigration, Latinos are entering into dialogue with their own past, present, and future, as well as
with the history of the United States. As Ilan Stavans has written, "By
accommodating ourselves to the American dream, by forcing the United
States to acknowledge us as part of its uterus, we are transforming ourselves inside El Dorado and, simultaneously, reevaluating the culture
and environment we left behind. Not since the abolition of slavery and
the waves of Jewish immigration from Eastern Europe has a group been
so capable of turning everybody upside-down."[8] Through this hybridity,
the new generation of Latino immigrants is "inventing identity in the
interstices,"[9] and setting the stage for a United States that will be a mirror
of the demographic changes undergone as a consequence of the arrival of
previous generations of immigrant populations, generations that are now
coming of age in communities across the country.

In a moment that will mark one possible political future for California,
Los Angeles recently elected its first Latino mayor in a state where one
out of three people is Hispanic.[10] On May 17, 2005, Antonio Villaraigosa
won the election against James Hahn, garnering 58.7 percent of the vote
by focusing primarily on public school reform and public transportation.
Although he had run and lost the 2001 mayoral election, his 2005 campaign centered on gaining support from non-Latino voters. Between
2001 and 2005, his vote from the white population increased to 50 percent,
up 9 percentage points; his vote from the black population jumped 28 percentage points, to 48 percent; "and his share of Asian voters increased by
9 percentage points, to 44 percent."[11] Currently, Villaraigosa has gathered
representatives from the Department of State and police chiefs from
Mexico, Honduras, El Salvador, Belize, and Canada in an effort to present
a unified front against the problem of gang violence.

While the election of Villaraigosa represents the increased number of
crossover voters between ethnic groups and the fact that it is becoming
decidedly more difficult to identify consistent voter behavior with a racial
or ethnic population, his victory also mirrored the growing number of
Latinos in California and other states across the nation. Entering the
United States in greater numbers, these more recent immigrants are also
altering the identity of the country through the linguistic, cultural, and
economic changes evident in communities across the nation. For the
writer Richard Rodriguez, the new Latin American immigrants embody
the characteristics of "Americanness" and gradually make obsolete anti-
quated notions of national identity: "I notice [Latino] immigrants are the
archetypal Americans at a time when we—U.S. citizens—have become

post-Americans, most concerned with subsidized medications."[12] Some
of the changes undergone by the country are affecting the very names that
children are being given. As Mireya Navarro noted in a *New York Times*
article on September 19, 1999, in 1998 José replaced Michael as the most
popular newborn boy's name in Texas and California. Is this simply the
expected consequence of the demographic transformations undergone
by states with growing Latino populations, or are there more profound
implications that suggest deeper changes in non-Latino cultures?
Could there be non-Latinos who are naming their children Miguel and
Rosalinda? Nomenclature—as a collection of topographical and linguistic
maps—may be read as propaganda: while our names represent our
spaces and ourselves, they are, more generally, cultural extensions of
our circumstances, of our context, of a time when a particular individual
rose above the rest and, therefore, became an instrument and an unwitting ambassador of their society. In much the same way, the Antonios,
Rosas, and Josés of this country are paving the way for a newer, different
understanding of Latino cultures, an understanding and acceptance that
begins with one's name. Miguel is not Michael, and María is not Mary:
it is María, with the accent on the "i" and the three terse vowels. If,
through a series of processes in which the individual determines that
"Michael" is as suitable as "Miguel," that the Anglicization of his
own name may bring an easier transition to a new environment, then it
is in the hands of that individual, not anyone else, to change that. If a
non-Latino is addressed as Juan instead of John, that individual has the
same right as the Latinos to correct their interlocutor and to remind their
listener that Miguel is not Michael: it is Miguel.

Changes in nomenclature and the detection of the Latino culture by
the popular media in the United States have also been reflected in the
opening of businesses targeted at Latinos and the adoption of specific
marketing strategies. In South Florida, for example, McDonald's has
included in its menu choices the Cuban sandwich, the Latin McOmelet,
and a pineapple-mango dipping sauce for McNuggets; M&Ms have come
out with a "dulce de leche" flavor; Puig F&PC USA launched "Spirit" by
Antonio Banderas; and Liz Claiborne has introduced "Mambo" cologne.[13]
The development of services and effects aimed at the Latino consumer
represents both the initiative of the transnational businesses and the
growth and economic success of the Spanish-speaking population,
as products are thrown their way for their consumption. This may in
fact represent the true, final integration of the Latino into the national
landscape: the Latino as consumer. Conversely, this also reflects the

consumption of Latino culture by non-Latinos, the creation and presentation of "Latinoness" (whatever that may be) as a desirable image worthy of mass consumption and worthy of being stereotyped and portrayed by advertisers. It is statistically true that many Latinos are manual laborers. They are also lawyers, monolingual landscapers, computer programmers, and bricklayers; but to Madison Avenue they represent the exotic and sensual, different in a way that welcomes cultural closeness and supplants and complements the Anglo-Saxon aesthetics of beauty and culture. Gradually, these same Latinos are defining distinctiveness and expressing their diverse voices through a series of social, economic, and political channels that, in some cases, have been taken for granted by the non-Latino population.

One of the ways in which the impact of these voices on the national landscape may be determined is by analyzing demographic statistics reflecting voter turnout. While overall voter turnout in the United States between 1994 and 1998 dropped 13 percent, Latino voting in nationwide midterm elections during this same period went up by 27 percent.[14] On its Web site, the Pew Hispanic Center reports that, demographically, in 2006 Hispanics represented 8.6 percent of eligible voters, with 39 percent of all Hispanics residing in the United States being qualified to vote. (Compared to 77 percent, 65 percent, and 51 percent of White, Black, and Asian voters, respectively.) States with the largest percentage of eligible Hispanic voters include New Mexico (37.6 percent), Texas (24.6 percent), California (22.5 percent), and Arizona (17.2 percent), with Southern states such as Georgia (2.3 percent), Louisiana (2.1 percent), and North Carolina (1.9 percent) being home to relatively small percentages of Hispanics eligible to vote among the population. The more recent midterm elections in November 2006 also present a complex image of Latino voters who are slowly beginning to vote outside traditional party lines and issues. In the 2006 elections for the U.S. House of Representatives, 69 percent of Latinos voted for Democrats and 30 percent for Republicans.[15]

The loss of votes by the Republican Party between the 2004 and 2006 elections is also represented and magnified by Latino voters, as "comparing exit polls from 2004 and 2006 suggests an 11-point swing in favor of the Democrats [58 percent to 69 percent]. Meanwhile, the swing among white voters was 6 percent [41 percent to 47 percent]. That suggests the movement away from the GOP was greater among Latinos than Whites."[16] Yet statistical generalization of the 2006 exit polls do not tell the whole story, as "Republican candidates in states with sizeable Latino electorates significantly outperformed their party's showing on the national level and received shares of the national vote comparable to Bush in 2004 [and his 44 percent share of the Latino vote]."[17] Generally speaking, Republican candidates in states with large Latino populations tend to receive a substantial amount of the Latino vote, as exemplified by Arnold Schwarzenegger's reelection to Governor of California (winning 39 percent of the Latino vote), Texas Senator Kay Bailey Hutchinson's reelection (44 percent of the Hispanic vote), and the victory of Nevada Governor Jim Gibbons (with 37 percent of the Latino vote).[18] "Republican incumbents prevailed in 8 of the 12 close [congressional] races in which Latinos could conceivably have played a decisive role."[19] In an interesting decision, "almost half of Latino voters (48 percent) in Arizona also backed the referendum that made English the state's official language," supporting "an issue that was heavily promoted by those in favor of a more restrictive immigration policy."[20] If the Latino voters in Arizona are practically split down the middle regarding an issue that should, at first glance, force the vast majority of the Spanish-speaking electorate to fall principally on one side or the other of the voting fence, then it is clear that, in the future, statistics extrapolated from national elections must take into consideration local context. In areas of the country such as the U.S. South, where politics and community have quite literally fought for their right to be intrinsically connected, the local voices of the new Latino immigrants will directly begin to shape the policies of their area in ways that will persistently defy categorization.

What do these changes mean for the dynamics of local communities, even in traditionally non-Latino areas? The long-term transformations that the nation and its distinct regions will undergo have yet to be fully evaluated due to the diverse nature of the immigrants' countries of origin, the historic presence that a specific national group has in a particular region, the linguistic and cultural imprint that the United States has left upon their homelands, and the lack of historical perspective. Regarding the South, the patterns of mutual assimilation evident in the relationships between communities and immigrant populations provide a window into this country's future, as nontraditional areas of extensive Latino immigration struggle to accept and, at the same time, transform a local infrastructure that will accommodate and be of assistance to the new inhabitants. We are not certain how this process will take place in each distinct town and city, but it will occur. As Richard Rodriguez has written, "I am not in favor of assimilation any more than I am in favor of the Pacific Ocean or clement weather. If I had a bumper sticker on the subject, it might read something like ASSIMILATION HAPPENS."[21] According to the *State of the South* 2007, "Latinos, spreading out beyond Texas, Florida, and California, have transformed large segments of the South from a biracial to a multi-ethnic culture."[22] Perhaps the future of Latino immigrants in this country—and the future of an interethnic United States—is more readily observed through the relationships forged in regions that are currently nontraditional centers of Latino immigration and settlement.

Regardless of the problems involving terminology and cultural topologies, it is clear that Latinos in the South belong to a divided cultural terrain and retain multiple identities. In doing so, they manage to inhabit a landscape of permanent partial assimilation as the South in all its varieties exerts its influence on Latinos and communities adjust to shifting cultures and demographics. Across the nation, the presence of Latinos has led to the belief that we are witnessing a new type of integration, one that manages to maintain those multiple identities. In a *New York Times* article from September 19, 1999, Mireya Navarro states that

> The phenomenon of assimilation alongside cultural affirmation is not unlike that experienced by other ethnic groups as they set roots in this country, some experts say. But the Hispanic population is likely to make its presence more deeply felt, these experts say, because Latinos make up the largest ethnic and linguistic group to arrive; they retain ties to their geographically close countries of origin, and the migration is continuing. All those factors reinforce Hispanic culture and the Spanish language while at the same time, assimilation dilutes them.

The sheer numbers of Latinos make this population a political, social, and economic force to be reckoned with. Latinos also inhabit a personal territory marked by decisiveness—the decision to uproot themselves in order to live and work in the United States, for example—divisiveness, and uncertainty, be it linguistic, economic, or cultural. In this arrangement lives the Latino, and within its porous walls the air of change exits and enters continuously, reminding us that adaptability and these shifting lives within a life are valuable assets in today's contemporary society.[23]

In this country today, the primary reason many Latin Americans emigrate to the United States and are willing to embark upon an existence in the margins of society is economic opportunity. According to Jorge Ramos, "As long as there are jobs in the north for workers in the south, there will continue to be undocumented immigration."[24] Whether as lawyers, gardeners, teachers, police officers, nurses, or construction or agricultural workers, Latin Americans have been present in the United States for centuries and are continuing to make an economic impact on their cities, regions, states, and host country. Nationally, the effect of immigration has been almost immediate. On its Web site, the Georgia Hispanic Chamber of Commerce reports that national Latino purchasing power of $798 billion dollars a year is expected to grow to $1.2 trillion by 2011, with, as Navarro reported, market researchers classifying 75 percent of Hispanic households across the country as middle or upper class, and Latino disposable income growing 160 percent between 1990 and 2004, to $580 billion.[25] With these statistics in mind, it would be fair to ask what constitutes a "Hispanic household." Does the term describe only Latinos who own their own homes, for example, or are those who rent also included? It is also wise to recall that many Latinos who reside undocumented in the United States undocumented may be unwilling to participate in surveys that request their household income. Undocumented workers may also make up a large part of the Latino workforce, a fact that has proven to be a thorn in the side of practically every presidential administration since Theodore Roosevelt. According to Jorge Ramos, "undocumented immigrants come for work, not social services. Moreover, the majority do not request government assistance. One, because they don't speak English. Two, because they are afraid of being deported. And three, because they don't even know how to get access to these services."[26]

In the U.S. South, the presence of the Hispanic labor force has been felt in practically every field of work, due not only to the arrival of immigrants from Mexico and countries in Central America but also to the national migration of Latinos to North Carolina, Tennessee, Georgia, and Arkansas from states such as California, Florida, and Texas, which historically have had a more visible Latino presence.[27] The economic impact that Latinos have had on a Southern communities is evident in a sampling of local news items across the region. In Tennessee, for example, "pork producers have formed a cooperative aimed at selling pig carcasses to Hispanic meat markets"; in South Carolina, Hispanic purchasing power "has sextupled over the past 12 years, to an estimated $22 billion [in 2003]"; and in Charleston, South Carolina, there is an AM Spanish-language radio station. *Vida Latina,* the city's first Spanish-language newspaper, was introduced by Randy Withers; and Los Puentes, a Hispanic market owned by Argentine immigrant Norma Jiménez, has opened three additional stores across the state in John's Island, Columbia, and Rock Hill.[28] In Louisiana, "many Latino migrants are reportedly now working in shipbuilding and fabrication yards in coastal areas of the state," attracted by companies that "had pre-existing connections to Texas" and that "[drew] on a Spanish-speaking labor pool" from that state.[29] The Latino labor pool in that area of Louisiana is, subsequently, growing and diversifying, as many of the "[i]mmigrant workers [who arrive] in Southern Louisiana are skilled craftsmen, not migrant farm workers, day laborers, or dishwashers."[30] Their arrival has also transformed the social dynamics of the region and has obliged certain immigrant populations who would otherwise not associate to be in close contact with each other. In Amelia, Louisiana, for example, a town with a population of roughly 2,400 people, "Most stores in this little town are owned by Vietnamese, and their customers are mainly Hispanic workers."[31] These small, Southern communities appear to be the places where the most recent distinct nationalities enter into communication and subtly alter the social fabric.

Besides demographic changes and the economic repercussions that these changes will have, there are additional factors to consider given the dynamics between Latin American immigrants and the Southern communities that they inhabit. Are relations between Latinos and African Americans actually and potentially more problematic than those between Latinos and white Anglos? At first glance, it would appear so, especially in rural areas of the South. Where African Americans have traditionally held the most demanding—and least-paying—jobs, they are now being displaced from these positions by the new wave of Latino immigrants who are willing to work harder and for less money than the African Americans who have traditionally inhabited the lowest rung on the South's economic ladder.

An employee at BC Rogers Poultry in Morton, Mississippi, places part of the blame on the local African American population: "I see an extremely poor black man. I see him accepting his poverty. They have not taken advantage of the circumstances."[32] Although we should take the speaker to task for what are blanket generalizations regarding African Americans, we would do well to remember the geographical context—Mississippi—and the entire series of historical determinants that have contributed to the formation of this opinion. The speaker is clearly observing the African American community from the outside, and although he personally suffered marginalization and persecution in a Latin American country under an authoritarian regime, he does not place himself any closer to the circumstances of the African American than the Anglo-Protestant culture in Morton. As in the speaker's case, the margins are relative and are constantly reminding us of what is both a part of us and persistently held at arm's length, of the changing social dynamics in this country, and of the social, political, and economic changes that are occurring across the South due to the growing Latino population.

3

The Immigration of Latinos
The Diaspora Within

The immigration of Latin Americans to the United States is and has been transforming areas of the country in ways that differ from the migratory customs of other more traditional European ethnic groups and that may, in fact, underscore local and national deficiencies. Robert D. Kaplan wrote in regard to international migration to this country, "As I had been told over and over again by businesspeople and other experts, it is far more cost-efficient to import the rest of the world's talent than to train citizens at home, especially as weak or nonexistent national education standards and insufficient tax revenues make a mockery of many local American schools."[1] A century ago, 90 percent of immigrants arrived from Europe; today, "out of every 100 immigrants, 45 come from Latin America, 26 from Asia, 23 from Europe, and the remaining 6 from other regions."[2] Startling as these figures may be, the stark reality for the vast majority of developing countries today is that a great many of their residents are leaving their homeland in order to begin a life in a developed nation. What does this entail? Displacement and diaspora in and of themselves are not unique to our times, but today's technological developments, relatively rapid access to international markets, and rippling political instabilities are certainly contributing to these dislocations. The United States offers Latin Americans the opportunity to flee from societies suffering the brunt of globalization and to begin their lives anew, to ground their futures in more stable economic ground than was available in their homeland.

Traditionally, Latinos in the United States have settled in one of a number of geographic areas that have included a sizeable population of immigrants that, at times, predated the establishment and expansion of the United States. The history and presence of Latinos in states such as California, Arizona, New Mexico, and Texas, for example, may be distinguished and differentiated in order to better understand individual motivations, demographic trends, and cultural factors that have influenced migration patterns. It is statistically undeniable that, historically, the majority of Latino immigrants have settled in these areas: 37 percent of Hispanics in the United States live in New York, Los Angeles, or Miami; and 87 percent of Hispanics are concentrated in Colorado, Arizona, New Mexico, Massachusetts, New Jersey, Illinois, Florida, California, New York, and Texas.[3] Of the new nontraditional Latino destinations in this country, 18 may be classified as "hypergrowth" due to the fact that between 1980 and 2000 "the Latino population [in these areas] grew by more than 300 percent."[4] Of these, four Southern cities make the list: Raleigh, North Carolina, Atlanta, Georgia, Greensboro, North Carolina, and Charlotte, North Carolina.[5]

When founded in 1996 by President Clinton, the President's Advisory Commission on Educational Excellence for Hispanic Americans comprised a total of 24 members: five from California, four from Texas and four from New York, two each from the District of Columbia, Florida, and Colorado, and one each from Illinois, Arizona, New Mexico, Massachusetts, and Puerto Rico. Statistically, these states represent the largest percentages of Latinos in this country, but Latinos in these states have only relatively recently begun to take advantage of their political and economic weight. At the national level, the National Hispanic Leadership Agenda (NHLA) has begun rating congressmen and women in an effort to "measure the responsiveness of the members of Congress on issues of concern to the Hispanic community."[6] The NHLA graded members of both the Senate and the House of Representatives according to the percentage of key ballots on which they voted in favor of a position endorsed by the organization. At the national level, for the 107th Congress the average for all senators was 51 percent; for members of the House it was approximately 47 percent.[7] Regionally, Southern senators and members of the House were less likely to be considered "pro-Hispanic" (i.e., more than 50 percent of positions on key votes agreed with the position endorsed by NHLA), as the averages for

Southern senators and members of the House[8] was approximately 36 percent for each (25 of 68 House members voted in accord with NHLA positions during the 107th Congress, as did 8 of the 22 senators). Interestingly enough, further analysis along Southern state lines indicates that there are a number of representatives and senators who are responding to the needs of the growing Latino population in their states: in Arkansas, three of four representatives (Marion Berry, Mike Ross, and Vic Snyder) and one senator (Blanche Lincoln) were at or above 67 percent. In North Carolina, five of the twelve representatives (Eva Clayton, Bob Etheridge, Mike McIntyre, David Price, and Melvin Watt) were at or above 56 percent (with Watt voting 94 percent of the time in accord with NHLA positions), and Senator John Edwards voted with NHLA positions 88 percent of the time. In Tennessee, four of the nine representatives (Bob Clement, Harold Ford, Bart Gordon, and John Tanner) scored at or above 56 percent, while in West Virginia, two of the three representatives (Allan Mollohan and Nick "Joe" Rahall II) and both senators scored at or above 69 percent.

Unfortunately, members of Congress from other Southern states that have received a recent influx of Latino immigration are not necessarily representing Hispanic interests accordingly. In Georgia, a state that has witnessed a significant increase in Latino immigration in the last ten years, only three of eleven members of the House (Sanford Bishop, John Lewis, and Cynthia McKinney) scored above 50 percent; in Alabama, only one of seven members (Earl Hilliard) and no Senators scored above 50 percent; and in Virginia, only three of eleven representatives (Rick Boucher, James Moran, and Bobby Scott) and no Senators scored above 50 percent. The numbers also fall along party lines, as Democratic senators and members of the House vote more frequently in accord with NHLA positions. Interestingly, there are exceptions, as Democratic members of the House like Robert Cramer (Alabama, 39 percent), Ken Lucas (Kentucky, 17 percent), and Gene Taylor (Mississippi, 33 percent), and the ubiquitous Democratic Senator from Georgia, Zell Miller (38 percent), all voted with NHLA positions in less than 50 percent of the key votes. Theoretically, as more Latinos in these states become United States citizens and register to vote, they will then be electing national representatives who reflect the state's demographic makeup and social transformations. Perhaps in the future, these states may suffer because of the short-sightedness of their elected officials in Washington. Today, however, Latinos have been generally grossly underrepresented in Congress, in state and city governments, and even in nonpolitical arenas such as the entertainment industry, where Latinos represent only 2 percent of the characters on prime-time television.[9]

While in the past more traditional areas such as California and Texas may have been attractive to Latino immigrants because of long-established community ties and the presence of a Spanish-speaking population, these states may also be anomalies regarding the future assimilation of Latinos, since higher salaries, lower costs of living, and a smaller and more effective cultural infrastructure may actually exist elsewhere. In the 1990s, for example, the economic recession in California "led to an exodus of Latinos to other states,"[10] Latinos who were principally Mexican in origin and who today "are more urban, they have more schooling and more resources than those who came before them, and if possible, they travel with the entire family."[11] While the Hispanic population across the country grew between 1990 and 2000 at a national average of 58 percent, states such as New York (30 percent Hispanic population growth), California (43 percent), and New Jersey (51 percent) actually witnessed the growth rate of the Hispanic population fall below the national average.[12] This statistic reflects the general sluggishness of population growth in those states for the majority ethnic and racial groups. Not unlike the U.S. South, other nontraditional areas of Latino immigration such as the Midwest are also witnessing the arrival of these more recent groups of laborers and allowing them the opportunity to fashion themselves in communities where the presence of the Latino population has not been as evident as Los Angeles, Houston, or New York, for example. As Marcos McPeek Villatoro has written, "In moving to the South, [Latinos] give up the ethnic connection of populations like those in Los Angeles or Dallas, where Latino-ness is intrinsic. Yet they also escape the street riots and organized gangs that have developed in the overpopulated barrios. The small population of immigrants here [in the South] lives relatively *tranquilo.*"[13] In a world in which national and transnational displacement is fast becoming the norm for those seeking greater economic opportunities and freedom from personal or social coercion, the presence of Latinos in areas of the South may be explained by geographic proximity and by the availability of material necessities and comforts. Frequently, the Latino arrives in search of simple stability, desiring a place safe from the "street riots and organized gangs" that may be present in cities like Houston, Los Angeles, New York, or Chicago, and that threaten a community's infrastructure from within.

What attraction does the Deep South hold that would lure immigrants away from traditional Latino areas of historical presence and settlement?

As Kochhar and others have noted, "Because the large growth in the Hispanic region is so recent, much of the impact of the new wave of immigration [in the South] is only beginning to make itself felt on the infrastructure of the host communities."[14] While there are common arguments—such as the nineties boom of the Southern economy and the agreeability of its climate—there are also regional differences and variations within the South that must be considered when evaluating the impact of any demographic trends. In Robeson County, North Carolina, for example, the "Latino population is younger and even more foreign-born than most new settlement counties, and far more male dominated"; while in Shelby County, Tennessee, "Only 54 percent of Latinos...were foreign-born, and the median age was 28. They were better educated; just 50 percent of foreign-born Latinos lacked a high school diploma."[15]

In an article by Stephen Gurr entitled "Hispanics in Athens: Out of the Shadows" that appeared November 21, 1999, in the *Athens Daily News/Athens Banner-Herald*, University of Georgia economic forecaster Jeff Humphreys declared that in Georgia, the pace at which Latinos have immigrated to the state caused the state's Hispanic buying power at the time—the disposable income after taxes—to expand twice as fast as the national rate. In January 1996, the Opryland Hotel in Nashville, Tennessee, held a job fair in Puerto Rico and by March of that same year had persuaded 250 Puerto Ricans to relocate and come to work in the city.[16] Sitting some 30 miles east of Jackson, Mississippi, Scott County and the town of Morton have seen their Latino population grow immensely in ten years. According to figures available on the U.S. Census Bureau Web site, the census reports that in 1990, Hispanics in Scott County numbered 141 (approximately 0.58 percent of total county population); ten years later, the Census registered 1,660 Hispanics—5.8 percent of the county—a jump of over 1,100 percent in a decade. (These statistics may not include immigrants who are wary of being counted or illegal immigrants.) In less than three years, North Carolina's Hispanic population quadrupled,[17] and in a national ranking of Roman Catholic Dioceses according to Hispanic population growth between 1990 and 1996, four of the top ten were located in the South (Charlotte, Atlanta, Raleigh, and Savannah).[18] Speaking of more recent generations of Latino immigrants to the South, a woman who arrived to Mississippi from Colombia in 1982 expressed a sense of adventure and freshness: "I don't want to go where everything is already made, where there are all kinds of Hispanic radio stations, all kinds of Hispanic newspapers, all kinds of activities, of festivals. I like the fact that we are pioneers. It has been difficult for us, but we are carving a path for the rest. Someone will reap the rewards of what I am doing. I have a social responsibility for those who are here and for those who are coming."[19]

As the President's Advisory Commission reported in 1996, the numbers of Latinos in the United States are increasing and will continue to increase well into the twenty-first century.[20] Consequently, shifts in national demographics will persist as the country expands its labor force and develops its efforts to include the Latino populations as active participants in their communities. In Richard Rodriguez's opinion, these most recent arrivals on the national landscape transform the nation and bring to the interior of their communities much-needed *outsider* realities: "The immigrant, in mythic terms, travels from the outermost rind of America to the very center of American mythology."[21] In this context, it is the South that will most likely witness the greatest political changes in its cities and towns. As Paul Simâo has indicated, "Hispanics in a number of states in the Deep South are for the first time seriously campaigning for seats on school boards, city councils and in-state legislatures."[22]

In the region, for example, "the arrival of Hispanics to work in poultry and fish-processing plants, in furniture factories and construction has changed the character of many small towns and the labor forces of those rural communities."[23] In Raleigh, North Carolina, St. Raphael Catholic Church holds at least three Spanish masses a week on Saturdays, Sundays, and Wednesdays, reflecting the growth of the Latino population in both the community and North Carolina, as "estimates now have the number of Hispanic Catholics equaling non-Hispanic Catholics in North Carolina."[24] As Eric Gonzalez noted in an *Athens Daily News/Athens Banner Herald* article dated November 28, 1999, the number of Hispanic children in pre-Kindergarten rose from 49 to 70 students from 1998 to 1999, a jump of over 40 percent in only one year; and, as Stephen Gurr reported in an *Athens Daily News/Athens Banner Herald* article November 21, 1999, over a period of four years, Hispanic patients in need of outpatient care at the Athens Regional Medical Center rose over 1,000 percent, from 79 in 1994 to a total of 833 in 1998. Overall, the City Data Web site indicates that, between 1980 and 1999, the Hispanic population of Athens, Georgia, grew by 263 percent, representing today 6.4 percent of the community's total population. As University of Georgia demographer Doug Bechtel noted in Gurr's article, "They used to roll through Georgia. That's not the case now. The Hispanics are staying in the state."

Latinos and Hispanics are not only staying in Southern states, they are taking advantage of the opportunities offered in these areas and, symbiotically, creating an awareness of their own needs among the population. As Hispanic Online reported on its Web site, of the top 25 national recruitment programs for Hispanics in the United States in May 2000, four of those corporations were located in the South: AT&T (Atlanta), Bank of America (Charlotte), BellSouth (Atlanta), and IBM (Raleigh). In 2001, there were a total of three (AFLAC, Bank of America, and Wal-Mart); and in 2002, AFLAC was the only remaining Southern-based company among the top 25 national recruitment programs for Hispanics. In 2005, 13 of the top 100 companies that offered the most opportunities for Hispanics were located in Texas alone, while twelve were located in all of the South: AFLAC, Bank of America, BellSouth, Cingular, Coca Cola, Delta Airlines, Freddie Mac, GlaxoSmithKline, Nextel, UPS, Wal-Mart, and Yum!Brands. Although part of the reason that there are not more Southern businesses on the list may be that Southern companies responsive to Latinos began to relocate outside the South or of the United States, another may be that, within a very short period of time, companies in the United States have vastly improved their efforts at recruiting Latinos and are more mindful of the benefits that multilingualism brings to their profit-making enterprises.

Latino demographics are changing nationally, but the growth of the Hispanic population in the South is rapidly outpacing other regions of the country. Drawn principally by job opportunities, the proportional Latino population in Southern counties has grown faster than the national rate. In a national ranking of the 30 counties with the greatest percentage increase in Hispanic population between 1990 and 1996, 14 were located in the South, with the top six spots held exclusively by Southern counties: 1) Gwinnett Co., GA (an increase of 118.8 percent in those six years), 2) Wake Co., NC (102.8 percent), 3) Cobb Co., GA (90.7 percent), 4) Loudoun Co., VA (90.4 percent), 5) Pulaski Co., AR (88.9 percent) and 6) Mecklenburg Co., NC (87.3 percent).[25] If we extend these figures to the 2000 census, between 1990 and 2000 the Hispanic population in Gwinnett County grew by 584 percent; Wake Co., 535 percent; Cobb Co., 354 percent; and Mecklenburg Co., 556 percent. During those ten years, the Hispanic population in a number of counties in the South grew by over 1000 percent: Gordon Co., GA (1138 percent), Murray Co., GA (1092 percent), DeSoto Co., MS (1195 percent), Alamance Co., NC (1019 percent), Cabarrus Co., NC (1039 percent), Randolph Co., NC (1470 percent), Union Co., NC (1166 percent), and Catawba Co., NC (1000 percent).[26] And the 2005 estimates available on the Census Web site place the percentage of Hispanics/Latinos even higher in some of these counties, with 16.2 percent, 7.5 percent, and 9.2 percent of Gwinnett, Wake, and Mecklenburg County residents respectively being Latinos. (Compared to the 2005 estimated national average of 14.5 percent.)

While the percentage of Latinos that live in these counties may be relatively small in comparison to the areas' overall population (in Randolph County, North Carolina, for example, a county with a total population of just over 67,000 people, the Hispanic population grew from 243 in 1990 to 3,815 in the year 2000), it is true that such increases of the local Hispanic population over a period of six or ten years necessitate a series of short- and long-term changes in the infrastructure of a community that may not initially be welcoming to the new residents. Public programs and services such as medical care, education, and public transportation will have to adapt to the changing needs of the population, much as the new population of Hispanic immigrants change and adapt to their host country.

As significant as these numbers were in the 1990s, it is also important to remember that they may actually underrepresent the number of Latinos in an area. Although I do not agree with the tone of Jorge Ramos's dismissive statement that "undocumented immigrants have more important things to do than answer the questions of the pollster from the Census Bureau,"[27] there may exist within a Latino community a certain apprehension about revealing or providing personal or professional information to an unknown census worker. If we are to judge the numbers as a somewhat accurate reflection of the growth of the Latino population in a certain community, we must recognize that it is practically inevitable that a symbiotic relationship will develop between the host community and the newly arrived Latinos.

In an area apparently unaccustomed to the presence of these 'outsider' immigrant populations, there exists a rich tradition of ethnicities predating and living alongside white Protestants who have, at times, found it difficult to assimilate the racial variety of their community. In her book *The Making of a Southerner* (1947), Katherine DuPre Lumpkin illustrates the typical racial attitudes towards those who were not white: In the South, "No one feared that a respectable white woman would ever intermarry with a black negro...but some...not respectable...will. While not over-nice white men, alas!, cohabit with negro women...whence in a generation or two persons of the color of skin of Spaniards or Italians would have no difficulty in forming alliances with genteel people...."[28] The fragment reflects the color scale upon which many White Southern Protestants have historically formed their judgments of individuals: at one extreme is the implicit "purity" of the white races; at the other is the darkness—the secretive, the unknowable, the forbidding, and the forbidden—of the "black negro"; and between them are the darker Europeans, the Mediterranean Spaniards, Portuguese, Greeks, and Italians. The Spaniards and Italians, she implies, would be sufficiently diluted "in a generation or two" so that they may forge "alliances with genteel people" (read "Whites"). Only in losing their 'ethnic' look—that is to say, in becoming whiter and, therefore, less threatening—would they truly find a place among the "good people" of the land.

Lumpkin's perspective both reflects and belies the centuries-long presence that ethnic populations have maintained in the South and the cultural, political, and economic exchanges that have taken place there for hundreds of years. In 1539, for example, the Spanish explorer Hernando de Soto was one of the first Europeans to travel through the area, meeting indigenous peoples along the way and stopping at communities that would later become Milledgeville, Greensboro, and Washington, Georgia, Edgefield, South Carolina, St. Clair, Alabama, and Macon, Mississippi, among others.[29] In 1670, the first European settlers of Charleston, South Carolina, became familiar with "Indians who spoke broken Spanish,"[30] raising the possibility that the first European language spoken on the North American continent was Spanish. In the 1730s, as the English began to establish their presence along the coast of Georgia, the border between these and the Spanish colonies witnessed the antagonism between European powers who fought "for the upper hand in the Indian trade."[31] In the eighteenth and nineteenth centuries —from 1763 to 1803—Louisiana was a Spanish colony under control of the Spanish Crown, and Mexico would have approximately one-third of its land confiscated by the United States government in 1848 after losing the Mexican-American War.

In essence, the South was one of the original multiethnic territories of the soon-to-be United States. As national borders began to form in the Americas during the end of the seventeenth and first part of the nineteenth centuries, the establishment of a national identity ran parallel with the development of a country's economy. The practical invisibility of these new borders and the first transformations during this time had little initial effect upon leaders, the majority of whom elaborated a nationalistic rhetoric void of substantial national strategies and were still greatly influenced by European governments that had no expertise in demographic transitions and transnational migrations. In the South, the unforeseen combination of American indigenous peoples, European immigrants, and African populations shaped an area that would have to come to terms with both the injustices and cruelty suffered by the many and the material wealth enjoyed by the few. Today, the arrival of Latin American immigrants to Southern states will continue to affect an area whose historical roots are being gradually remembered and brought to the surface.

The River's Edge
The Mexican Border and the Ohio River

The role of rivers as vehicles of economic development and locations of settlement is evident upon examining a map of the United States and studying the locations of cities such as San Antonio, St. Louis, Memphis, New Orleans, Pittsburgh, Cincinnati, or Louisville, for example. National urban areas such as Washington, D.C., were frequently founded along the shores of a waterway that provided both transportation and sustenance for a fledgling community, offering the chance to explore the surrounding territory without surrendering the opportunity to set down roots in an area. Across the globe, rivers also serve as national, transnational, and local borders that separate discrete lands and frequently function as buffers between distinct nation-states or cultures in conflict. Rivers, such as the San Juan (Costa Rica and Nicaragua), the Coco (Honduras and Nicaragua), the Usumacinta (Guatemala and Mexico), the Amur (Russia and China), the Senegal (Senegal and Mauritania), and the Congo (Zaire and Congo), are a few examples of waterways that divide or have divided countries and cultures. In the United States, the Ohio River in the nineteenth century represented the dividing line between Dixie and non-Dixie: between slaveholding states such as Kentucky, Mississippi, Alabama, Tennessee, Georgia, and South Carolina, and non-slaveholding states such as Ohio and Indiana to the north, marking the transition from slavery to freedom for the countless slaves who escaped their chains. Today, the Tijuana and Rio Grande rivers, which form part of the border between the United States and Mexico, are mere geographical barriers for the thousands of Latin American immigrants who cross illegally into the United States in search of a different type of freedom, one that liberates them from a troubled national economy and grants them opportunities unavailable in their home country.

Throughout much of the U.S.-Mexican border, there has arisen a transnational culture that thrives on the contact between both countries and gives birth to hybridized existences that live on and from both sides. The Southern Texas-Northeastern Mexican border, for example, "features a particularly high level of cross-border social, cultural, and economic interdependence."[1] On the Ohio River, the relations between neighbors on opposite shores of the river has long been proven to be symbiotic even to people on differing sides of the ideological spectrum, beneficial to those who choose to utilize the river more as a vehicle of communication and commerce rather than an impediment to these. By examining the historical, political, social, and economic parallels and differences between those fugitive slaves who crossed the Ohio River from the Deep South states in the nineteenth century and the Latin American immigrants that today journey overland from Mexico and enter undocumented into the United States in search of a more dignified life, we may be able to better understand the future that lies ahead for migrant populations who choose the U.S. South as their home.

BORDERS AND RIVERS

Although the ecological subsistence and continuation of rivers has merited a good amount of attention, little consideration has been given to the strategic importance of rivers as practically self-subsistent borders that depend solely and inherently on the dynamics between both shores. The critical emphasis has typically been on the individual territories separated by its waters and on the relations between these territories, quite literally leapfrogging the cultural identity of the river itself. Cities such as Buenos Aires, London, Bucharest, Paris, and Bombay, for example, have grown along the shores of principal waterways that both unite the inhabitants and separate the urban area into sections that are often as distinct as the neighborhoods found within them. Curiosity, customs, and business practices often motivate those from one side of a river to venture across the bridges and witness how life is lived on the other side of the city.

The crossing today of the Rio Grande section of the border between Mexico and the United States by undocumented Latin American migrants and of the Ohio River in the nineteenth century by escaped slaves seeking freedom has brought about a renewed curiosity about the determination and motivation of those who chose—and choose—to leave behind family, friends, and familiar country in search of a more dignified life. Open in 2004, the National Underground Railroad Freedom Center in Cincinnati, Ohio, introduces the visitor to the network of escape routes that existed in the nineteenth century for slaves seeking freedom across the Ohio River, and seeks to bring to light the work of those who, yesterday and today, have fought for the rights of the marginalized, contextualizing the fight against slavery within those historical circumstances. Exhibits include films, interactive displays, firsthand testimonials, documentation and *realia* of the cruelties of slavery, and an actual slave pen that was located in Kentucky and reconstructed in the Freedom Center. Such a desire to educate and learn more about the experience of marginalized populations has inspired a group of individuals in Mexico to organize trips that seek to emulate as closely as possible the nighttime experience of crossing the border between the United States and Mexico illegally. In "Run! Hide! The Illegal Border Crossing Experience," a February 4, 2007, *New York Times* article, Patrick O'Gilfoil Healy indicates that for 200 pesos— approximately $18—one can participate in a *caminata*—an organized walk—that "traverses desert, hills, brambles, and riverbeds in the Parque EcoAlberto, owned by the Hñahñu Indians" and includes simulated border police, gunfire, and narrow escapes that take place some 700 miles south of the border itself. According to organizers, their intention is "to offer tourists a taste of life as an illegal immigrant." As O'Gilfoil Healy indicates, "compared with actually crossing the border, the caminata is as watered down as an airport cocktail."

While the National Underground Railroad Freedom Center and the simulation of an illegal border crossing in the Parque EcoAlberto differ in their funding, intended public, scope, and magnitude, the principal objectives of both experiences coincide in that they seek to bring an individual as close as possible to the difficulties faced by those seeking an alternative life, free of social, political, and economic restrictions. This desire to replicate and emulate their struggles has as its primary objective for those who share in the experience to identify themselves in some way with those who have suffered in search of liberation from coercion and subjugation.

The Ohio River

As stages that have served as testimony to the struggles of escaped slaves and undocumented immigrants, the Ohio and Rio Grande rivers serve as ideal focal points for a comparative analysis of cross-historical border dynamics. The distinct knowledge shared by those who crossed these rivers under immensely dissimilar circumstances is differentiated by historical contexts, geographical determinisms, and political frameworks that place them squarely within their own categories of individuation; yet the possible parallels speak to the manner in which a domestic or transnational geographical border such as a river may be the touchstone that inspires individuals to seek a better life. In the United States today, contemporary border patrol organizations such as the Minutemen Civil Defense Corps, American Patrol, Border Rescue Arizona, Secure Borders U.S.A., 9/11 Families for a Secure America, and the Wake Up America Foundation have been founded by private citizens who seek to make the national border with Mexico more secure. Yet, their methods and principles of action may parallel those utilized by anti-abolitionists in the nineteenth century, whose determination to limit the condition of U.S. residency or citizenship were based principally on ethnic or racial features. It is from this comparative perspective that such borders begin to acquire a life of their own that often transcends any facile connection to environment and surroundings. Writing in 2006 of the border between Mexico and the United States, John A. Adams, Jr., remarked that, "In many regards the border is a microcosm of future U.S.-Mexico relations. Cross-border interaction brings numerous challenges and opportunities often overlooked in the broader scheme of binational priorities. With an annual economic growth rate of 8 percent over the past decade, if the border were a country it would rank ahead of Poland and just behind Thailand."[2] Often, the social, political, and economic health of the border zone forecasts the successful exchanges between bordering cities, states, or nations themselves, as the autonomy and virtual self-sufficiency of such boundaries are a window into an uncertain future. In the 1730s, for example, inhabitants of the border areas of coastal Georgia and St. Augustine, Florida, would witness the continuous conflicts between the English and Spanish forces that fought for command of the territories and trade with indigenous populations.[3] This situation would prolong itself for decades, foretelling the continuing decline in power of both the British and Spanish empires in this part of the Americas.

The Ohio River runs a 980 mile path, crossing a portion of the eastern United States from Pittsburgh to Cairo, Illinois, and connecting there with the grander Mississippi. As a mercantile waterway, in the early nine-teenth century the river facilitated urban development, trade, and trans-portation from Pittsburgh to cities such as Cincinnati and Louisville, which grew along its shores. Historically, the river has also served as one of the principal dividing lines between the customs of Northern and Southern states, a window into the conflict emerging from the friction between these distinct traditions: "The paradox that played out along the Ohio river presented a complex set of issues through which the United States would wade during the first century of its existence."[4] As Keith P. Griffler has written, "The waters of the Ohio River reflected an accurate though troubling image of the young American nation for nearly a century after its founding," serving as a symbol that "both divided and connected a nation."[5] The river was in an especially privileged position to witness the battle "between the forces of freedom and those of slavery," a fight that "would continue to plague the nation" for years to come.[6] Towns and cities along the river, particularly those such as Cincinnati and Ripley in Ohio, and Maysville in Kentucky that were located on the Ohio-Kentucky border, would emerge as busy shipping ports and develop into outposts that anticipated the arrival of the stereotypical Wild West. Founded in 1804, Ripley, Ohio, for example, was "A young, wild river town,...simply a hellhole. Shootouts and fistfights were as common on the streets of Ripley as muddy wagon wheels on rainy days."[7] The fact that it lay directly across from a slaveholding state and that its inhabitants interacted constantly with those living across the river only contributed to the reputation of this community.

When the Civil War erupted in 1861, the declared neutrality of the Commonwealth of Kentucky was consistently taken to task by both the Union and the Confederacy, both of whom sought to take advantage of its strategic location and natural resources. While Kentucky never seceded from the Union, the states that did essentially fought for a state's right to self-determination and noninterference in its affairs from Wash-ington (particularly in regard to the continuation of slavery). In effect, the Civil War would simply bring to a head the issue of slavery, a topic that had been smoldering on the national fires for a few decades. For many, Kentucky's refusal to take sides in the conflict was perceived as a practical ruse, since its representatives defended its condition as a slave state for many years. Although a number of Southern slaves had made their way to freedom by escaping to Mexico, for the vast majority it was only after following the more reliable northern route to freedom and passing through Kentucky entirely that slaves found themselves able to say that they were not bound to a master.[8] The dangers in Kentucky and Ohio for escaped slaves were, therefore, genuine, as slaveholders and those in their employment pursued this "escaped property" with a zeal that would belie the state's later neutral stance in the Civil War.

It is no coincidence that the Underground Railroad was born from the efforts of individuals who resided in northern towns and cities that bordered slaveholding states along the Ohio River. Ironically, the name of the Underground Railroad is reported to have originated when a slave-holder followed his slave across the river into Ohio, and, in his frustration at being unable to find him, declared that his slave had disappeared on an "underground road." Anecdotal as it may be, the Underground Road or Railroad only became recognized as such "when significant local and regional coordination of the efforts of the friends of the fugitives was achieved."[9] A "conductor" of the Underground Railroad, for example, frequently gave shelter to escaped slaves and would ensure that they arrived unharmed at the next safe house; a "shepherd" was an "escort for fugitives,"[10] not unlike some of the more humane Mexican *coyotes* that do not work for profit and lead undocumented immigrants safely across the border to the United States; and a "station" "might be a house, a barn, a church or any structure wherein freedom seekers could find sanctuary."[11] Cities as distant as Cincinnati—host to the pioneering abolitionist Lane Theological Seminary—and Baltimore—"a center of slave aid"—for example, attracted countless individuals whose principal purpose was to fight against the institution of slavery.[12]

In municipalities such as Louisville, Kentucky, Madison, Indiana, Cincinnati, Ohio, and Maysville, Kentucky, there were established a series of safe havens routed through individuals active along the Underground Railroad that fugitive slaves could use on their way further north. In Ohio, for example, one possible path would begin at Cincinnati and run through Xenia, Columbus, and Ashtabula, finishing on the lakeshore at Sandusky, Cleveland, or the Western Reserve (today Oberlin).[13] On the northern shore of the Ohio River, there were citizens in towns such as New Richmond, Moscow, Ripley, Aberdeen, and Portsmouth who actively aided the escaped slaves in their run to freedom. In Ripley, for example, the renowned Presbyterian Minister John Rankin (1793–1886) devoted most of his adult life to helping fugitives on their way to freedom, opening his home to slaves and "shepherds" who were on their way north. In effect, it was through Rankin's friendship with the Beecher family that Harriet Beecher Stowe "became acquainted with most of the real-life characters that formed the basis for *Uncle Tom's Cabin*,"[14] including the renowned Eliza, based in fact on the young woman who crossed a frozen Ohio river barefoot, with her two-year-old son in her arms.

Almost immediately after the inception of the Fugitive Slave Act in 1793 and before many of the territories north of the Ohio River had become states of the Union, the waterway became the legitimate line of change for many of the slaves who escaped their owners and looked for freedom in territories north of this border. Before crossing this inland division, slaves were classified as property and bound to their masters as such; after crossing the Ohio river, freedom was made more palpable due to the presence of free blacks who were their own masters and free black communities such as the Gist Settlement in south central Ohio, which represented an improvement in the face of Southern slavery.[15] The continued presence of discrimination and racism north of the Ohio River, however, would drastically temper their dreams, and "By the late 1820s, a definite note of discouragement set in among African Americans in the North."[16] Throughout the nineteenth century, the Ohio river would be an integral part of Southern identity, and the U.S. South would continue to be characterized by the philosophy of the slave owner and by the notion of an aristocracy permanently anchored to the land, while the North would be endearingly and idealistically portrayed as the homeland of meritocracy, of economic accomplishment, of the capability to advance one's position, and of justice and freedom in the face of life's cruel inequalities.

The Rio Grande and the U.S.-Mexican Border

If we project the North/South dissimilarities evident in the nineteenth-century United States to the whole of the American continent today, we find that many of the same images have been recast as contemporary stereotypes that look to easily categorize cultures south of the United States border with Mexico. As both a virtual and geographic location that distances the United States from other hemispherical neighbors, the border serves as a site of conflict that underscores the vast social, political, and economic differences present between continental neighbors, particularly with regard to economic indicators such as per capita income, gross domestic product, inflation, and unemployment. In both the United States and Mexico in the 1970s and 1980s, the growth of border populations taxed the ability "of education, health care, housing, and transportation to keep pace."[17] As Alma M. Garcia has stated, today, "Border cities find themselves without the social and economic resources to deal with the tremendous strain placed on them by such a dramatically increasing population."[18] Ironically, "While most economic barriers have been falling, barriers against the cross-border movement of labor have been rising in the form of more intensive policing."[19]

The vast political and economic inequalities that develop from these circumstances and can be found in both nations are reflected in the environment of the U.S.-Mexican border, as individuals compete for jobs in an endless cycle of scarcity that gives the illusion of affluence but offers few opportunities at real advancement for those on either side. As was reported in 2001, past Mexican President Vicente Fox (2000–2006) "stressed that workers leave Mexico out of an economic desperation that will only be alleviated by the implementation of economic measures that introduce sustained growth for the country [of Mexico]."[20] Gradually, however, an independent border zone is developing that is far removed from both Washington, D.C., and Mexico City and that is, ironically, practically unconnected to many of the laws and legislation approved by both national legislatures. In response to the growing migration, there has developed in the Tijuana area, for example, an underground economy that is outside the purview of both federal governments and is almost entirely dependent on undocumented migration. Manuela, a Mexican woman who lives in Tijuana, has profited from the exodus of her countrymen and women by setting up a "profitable café trade" every morning along the San Ysidro canyon: "She starts a fire in the blackened drum and puts an equally blackened grill on top of it. She uses this to roast chickens, to make quesadillas, to heat beans and tortillas, and to sear the beef for *carne asada*," making "about two hundred dollars a month" and tackling border life "as if it were a contest meant to challenge her intelligence."[21] Historically, while the majority of those who have crossed the border illegally have been Mexican citizens looking for work in the United States, recent changes show that Cubans, for example, who are avoiding the dangerous crossing to Florida, are taking advantage of the porous border between Mexico and the United States. In an article from the Spanish newspaper *El País* published on August 12, 2007, and titled "Los balseros cambian de ruta" ("The boat people change route"), Juan Jesús Aznárez reports that between October 1, 2006, and July 22, 2007, approximately 10,000 Cubans paid between $10,000 and $12,000 each, crossing the 140 mile stretch between western Cuba and the Yucatan peninsula in high-speed boats operated by immigration mafias. Upon their arrival in Mexico, the Cubans are taken by guides who facilitate their entry to the United States through California or Texas. If they happen to be detained by the U.S. Border Patrol, Aznárez reports, they declare themselves to be Cuban citizens and request political asylum. The attempts today at monitoring the migratory rerouting and the promising microeconomies of scale, and effectively patrolling the border between Mexico and the United States are, for many, unrealistic, as "boundary policing and militarization serve less their ostensible purposes than as a means for the two nation-states to impose surveillance and regulation over a regional society that has mushroomed, largely unsupervised, in recent decades."[22]

While the U.S.-Mexican border for many citizens of states in the U.S. South may be an erstwhile abstraction due to its geographical distance from places such as Murfreesboro, Tennessee, or Rock Hill, South Carolina, its tangible relevance to the region is singularly highlighted by the fact that "those born in Mexico make up 73 percent of foreign-born Latinos" in the states of Arkansas, Alabama, Georgia, North Carolina, South Carolina, and Tennessee.[23] Running over 1,900 miles long from Brownsville, Texas, to San Diego, California, the border between the United States and Mexico skirts a varied geographical terrain that includes the Rio Grande and Tijuana rivers. The states of Texas, New Mexico, Arizona, and California border Mexico on the northern side, while the six Mexican states of Baja California, Sonora, Chihuahua, Coahuila, Nuevo León, and Tamaulipas skirt the United States. On the U.S. side, the Rio Grande flows from southern Colorado and through New Mexico, forming the southern border of Texas with Mexico. On the Mexico side, the river is known as Río Bravo and touches the states of Tamaulipas, Nuevo León, Coahuila, and Chihuahua.

Obvious as it may appear, the border between the United States and Mexico has two sides, both of which legislate and arbitrate according to the moment's circumstances. Unfortunately, residents of the United States have rarely heard or read the opinions of their southern neighbor regarding border dynamics and Mexican relations with the northern colossus. In the nineteenth century, the distance between the capital of Mexico and the border with the United States was measured in light years and made difficult the construction of a Mexican identity, as "Patriotic ambiguity [in Mexico] at such a time reflected the frontier's distance from Mexico City and Mexico City's historic indifference to the frontier."[24] In 1852, "Tensions [between the United States and Mexico] escalated to the point...that both the Mexican state of Chihuahua and the new U.S. territory of New Mexico claimed jurisdiction over much of the same acreage."[25] In the early part of the twentieth century, U.S. expansion into the Americas was viewed as a threat by not only European powers, but also by Latin American nations. The Plan de San Diego in the 1910s, "an alleged secret plot calling for the overthrow of U.S. rule in the Southwest, the killing of most male Anglos over sixteen, and the creation of a Mexicano republic...seems to have been largely a reaction to deteriorating conditions along the border because of Mexican revolutionary activity and the frequent brutal conduct of the Texas Rangers."[26]

Since the war of 1848, when the United States dispossessed Mexico of approximately one-third of its territory and established the border as it remains today, the history of this transnational zone of conflict has been monopolized principally by efforts on the part of the United States to control the access of Mexican nationals into this country. From its beginnings, the border "provided a rugged refuge for outlaws of all sorts: escaped convicts, highwaymen, smugglers, felons, thugs, and simple ruffians."[27] From 1850 to 1900, the eastern part of the Rio Grande "provided egress for slaves fleeing from bondage and ready ingress for Mexican immigrants who came to pick the cotton."[28] Created in Boston in 1894 principally to campaign against the flow of European immigrants arriving daily on national soil, the Immigration Restriction League also had its impact on U.S.-Mexican border policy and on the construction of the border zone as a virtually autonomous region that merited special rules and legislation. As inhabitants of the border began to participate in the steady improvement of the area, the arrival of industrialization impacted the region in a number of ways and "[created] an environment for prejudice."[29]

The 1920s and 1930s were "times of heightened racial prejudices," which gave rise to the increased isolation of the United States from the rest of the world and witnessed a number of distinct changes in policy with regard to its border with Mexico and relations with its southern neighbor and other non-European nations.[30] The Immigration Act of 1924, for example, "effectively closed America to most of the world's peoples outside Europe. It reiterated the image projected in American's first naturalization act in 1790: To be an American began with being white."[31] The year 1924 also saw the formation of the Border Patrol, a force stationed principally along the U.S.-Mexican border that totaled approximately 450 officers and whose principal objective in those times was to seek out European and Asian immigrants.[32] The Mexican *pachucos* that began to arrive in the 1920s were also the victims of racism, prejudice, and bigotry, as they were frequently viewed as one of the principle causes of the deteriorating economy. At the time, as the situation in Mexico became more unstable in the wake of assorted attempts at post-revolutionary reforms and of the negative impact of the U.S. depression on their country, the United States began to see an increased influx of Mexican immigrants who looked for work across the border. In response to these changing conditions, the United States government later established the Bracero program, "a guest-worker arrangement in place between 1942 and 1964 [that] was created to provide a cheap source of labor for agribusiness."[33] Unfortunately, the long-term consequence of the Bracero Program was "to institutionalize mass labor migration from Mexico to the United States."[34]

More recent efforts to secure the border with Mexico have changed from focusing on strictly economic issues, broadening their perspective to add more security along the border and heavier policing of illegal immigration. The Immigration Reform and Control Act of 1986 "introduced employer sanctions, authorized an expansion of the Border Patrol, and offered a general legalization program."[35] The Illegal Immigration Reform and Immigration Responsibility Act of 1996 "authorized the hiring of 1,000 Border Patrol agents a year" and pronounced that there would be a "sharp increase in penalties against migrant smugglers."[36] The following year witnessed the launch of a number of different border operations that included, among others, Operation Safeguard, Operation Gatekeeper, Operation Hold-the-line, and Operation Rio Grande. In the wake of the September 11 terrorist attacks, "security concerns with Weapons of Mass Destruction (WMDs) and potential terrorists crossing into the United States changed the entire focus among law enforcement agencies,"[37] giving rise to an uneven distribution of resources among its international borders, as "more than 90 percent of immigration arrests" occur "at or near" the U.S.-Mexican border. In the opinion of John A. Adams, Jr., "The root of today's immigration policies and concerns dates from the mid-1960s, first due to the uneven economic conditions in Mexico and second, the gradual attraction to jobs on the border as a result of the Border Industrialization Program, which is better known as the maquiladora or twin plant manufacturing sector."[38] While the efforts of the United States federal government would seem to declare otherwise, transnational borders across the world are evaporating, and, as Luis Alberto Urrea affirmed, "no one knows what to do about it."[39]

MIGRATION: OHIO RIVER AND THE RIO GRANDE

The migration of human populations across national and transnational borders that have served as both obstacles and inspirations is nothing novel to the countless fields of study that consider the implications for the cultures of destination, for those Latin American communities that are witnessing their population diminish on a daily basis, and for the individuals making the choice to leave their homes, family, and friends behind in search of a better life. In the last approximately ten years, however, technology, incentives for emigrating, and the adaptation of human smuggling operations to more rigorous border controls have transformed the movement of populations, particularly those that look to move from developing nations in Africa and Latin America, for example, to developed countries in Europe and North America.

Migration as Resistance and Liberation

Historically, the movement and migration of peoples across international borders has frequently had its roots in a struggle against the inequities and uncertainties of human existence and the intransience of the search for a better life. The decision to quite literally pull up stakes and journey to a part of the world where one may have no immediate family or friends, where the customs represent singular ways of understanding life, and where the language may be as enigmatic as the clothing, may be qualified as an act of resistance that has, throughout history, subtly dismantled institutionalized structures of marginalization and oppression. In revolutionary Mexico, countless citizens left the northern part of the country in the early 1900s for the United States in search of a more stable national territory. In pre–World War II Europe, thousands of Jewish Germans and Poles began to flee Germany in active protest and concern over actions and legislation approved by a xenophobic National Socialist Party that had come into power in 1933. Beginning in the 1940s, Haitian citizens have immigrated to the Dominican Republic, on the other side of the island of Hispaniola, in search of better jobs and economic stability. Over the course of the 1940s, 1950s, and 1960s, thousands of Spanish workers and intellectuals left the country for Germany, France, Mexico, and the United States in order to find both economic opportunity and the chance to express their opinions freely without danger of reprisal. Beginning with the victory of the Cuban revolution in 1961, countless numbers of Cubans have sought political asylum on U.S. soil. In the 1960s, many citizens from newly independent African and Asian nations such as Algeria decided to emigrate to the corresponding European colonizer—in this case, France—transforming the ethnic, cultural, and economic dynamics of their host country. In the early 1990s, the world witnessed the decimation of Serbian, Croatian, Bosnian, and Kosovar populations over the course of the Balkan wars, coming to facilitate the emigration of these refugees to other European nations and the United States. And in the mid-1990s, citizens from Eastern European nations such as Bulgaria, Poland, and Rumania decided to take advantage of efforts on behalf of their governments and the European Union to subsequently include these countries in the group and relocated to Germany, France, Italy, or Spain. While many in the nations of origin either chose to remain behind of their own will or were unable to raise the money necessary for such a journey, those who crossed international borders did so in defiance of national conditions and laws that frequently created impediments to the movement, expression, and vocation of its citizens.

This resistance *vis-à-vis* migration to difficult economic circumstances, to a form of government or to an individual leader's rule and the authoritarian measures applied by his regime to keep the population in line, has as its intended consequence the ultimate liberation of an individual in the wake of social, political, and economic inequalities suffered back in his homeland. Within the context of these injustices, the contemporary connotations of the term *liberation* began to take form in the 1960s, when emerging movements of national liberation in Africa, Latin America, and Asia began to exert greater pressures on the *ancien régimes* of Europe and demand that the daily realities lived by citizens in nations such as Colombia, Vietnam, Algeria, Tunisia, and Korea correspond with the florid rhetoric of the superpowers of the period and with the intention to improve their quality of life. At this time, political figures, writers, artists, and theologians in both developed and developing nations began to work toward a systematic characterization of the origins of liberation, of its conditions, and of its ultimate consequences over the course of time. Writing on the topic in the mid-1980s, the Spanish theologian Ignacio Ellacuría, murdered in El Salvador in 1989 by paramilitaries, noted that liberation is "a process": "The liberation from unjust structures and the creation of new structures that give rise to dignity and freedom constitute, then, in the essential path to liberty, of liberty for individuals within their national context and liberty for people within their international context."[40] The interconnectedness between the domestic and global construction of just societies and the parallels between these and the continuation of dignity, freedom, and liberty, began, for Ellacuría, in very real changes made to the composition of societies across the globe.

Throughout history, the efforts of groups and populations whose suffering predated the political and social upheavals of the 1960s demonstrate that their cause is as relevant today as it was in their time. Inspired by the slave insurrection of Toussaint LOuverture in Haiti in 1804, Alphonse de Lamartine based "The Black Marsellaise" on the French national anthem of similar name, underscoring the plight of slaves in the Americas:

> Children of blacks, marginalized by the world,
> poor flesh made flock,
> what do you carry, terrible race,
> your own pain in your skin!
> Lift your head from the floor,
> dare to find everywhere
> women, children, a God:
> the name of Man is your conquest![41]

 Lamartine's lyrics, inciting blacks to find worth in their lives and to search for liberation, are a direct ironic complement to a French national anthem that describes all French citizens as sons and daughters of the country.

As children of slavery in the United States, the Exodusters, led by Benjamin "Pap" Singleton, were groups of African Americans who had left Southern states in the 1870s in search of better lives in Oklahoma, California, and other locations, emphasizing, through their name, their own particular quest for liberation and a promised land. Today, many Mexican and other Latin American immigrants arrive in the United States in search of opportunity and liberation from an undeserved fate, motivated by poverty and by the life they believe exists on this side of the Rio Grande, a life that serves as stimulus to sacrifice it all: "Night and day, the hungry watch us frolic in Disneyland. The lights are always on. They can see the glow reflected on the prism clouds of pollution. They want to come in and ride. Oh, and there's one more thing—if they don't get in the gates, their babies might very well die of starvation, disease, or misadventure. What choice would you make?"[42] Both the migration today of Latin Americans to the United States and the flight and rebellion of slaves in the Americas in the nineteenth century involve the direct resistance of marginalized populations to injustice through explicit action and movement that has, as its objective, the liberation and self-determination of the individual.

The Perceived and Established Lawlessness of Movement and Migration: Yesterday's Fugitive Slaves and Today's Latinos

The migration and flight of fugitive slaves from south to north in nineteenth-century United States and the immigration to the United

States of undocumented Latin American nationals represents a committed position in the face of national and international legislation. In the nineteenth century, for example, slaves were considered the property of their owners, who, from the inception of the 1793 Fugitive Slave Act,[43] had the support of the judicial system and the implicit approval of President George Washington, who signed it into law February 12 of that year, to hunt down and recover their "stolen" property.[44] Today, many immigrants throughout the world cross borders hidden in tractor trailers, under cover of night, or secreted in cargo holds in order to elude border posts, passport controls, and customs checkpoints, avoiding the very distinct possibility that they will be denied entry and turned back without proper documentation. By taking the risk to cross an international border undetected, today's immigrants entertain the possibility that their journey will meet with success upon establishing themselves in foreign territory.

Those who make the decision today to enter a country illegally are the modern day inheritors of nineteenth-century fugitive slaves who also went to extreme lengths in order to defy laws that restricted their movements and confined them to the status of mere chattel. The differences, however, between yesterday's escaped slave and today's transnational immigrant are varied and rather conspicuous in the face of dissimilar historical contexts. Slaves in nineteenth-century North America, for example, endured the brutality of plantation life and the indignity of being relegated to a status equivalent to a beast of burden, forsaken by the Constitution and unable to participate in a representative democracy. Their lot in life was to be born into the condition of *de jure* servitude and to suffer the truth that their misery was, on the whole, endorsed by the national representatives. Latin American immigrants who enter the United States unlawfully, however, enjoy a certain amount of representation and freedom that varies according to their country of origin, gender, ethnicity, and racial group. Mayans from Guatemala, for example, have traditionally suffered forms of marginalization distinct from those endured by mestizos in Mexico or El Salvador; recent dictatorships in Cuba, Argentina, Chile, and Guatemala have triggered the mass exodus of their citizens; and women, more than men, have typically been victims of the repression and cruelty of a regime, paramilitary force, or political leaders. Latin American nationals also have more access to technological advances in communication, such as cellular telephones, which provide an almost perpetual link to those left behind. Through the remission of monies to their families back home, these Latin American nationals are also creating their own representative process and circumventing established labor laws in their host country, subverting, at the same time, the existing paucity of jobs and economic opportunities in their national territories.

The case of fugitive slaves represents an exceptionally transparent example of migration as resistance and flight as liberation. Before deciding on escape as the only solution to their woes, countless slaves in North America and the Caribbean participated in active and allegedly lawless rebellion and resistance against slaveholders, who, ironically, "always seem to have been convinced that 'their' slaves were the happiest of earthly beings."[45] Examples of individual acts of shrewdly illicit resistance included "Doing nothing," "Arson," "Self-Mutilation," "Suicide," "Malingering, Bad Work, Lying, and Drunkenness," "pretending illness," and storytelling meant to subvert the slaveholder's world.[46] In the U.S. South, slaves also pretended ignorance, "worked carelessly, broke tools, damaged or set fire to property, and stole from their masters."[47]

Throughout history, slaves also united under a common banner and organized insurrections against slaveholders that were typically characterized by "a minimum of ten slaves involved; freedom as the apparent aim of the disaffected slaves; [and] contemporary references labeling the event as an uprising, plot, insurrection, or the equivalent of these terms."[48] In eighteenth-century South Carolina, for example, "The backbreaking nature [of rice cultivation] combined with the transgression of gender roles that had prevailed in Atlantic Africa gave male slaves a specific set of grievances against which to struggle."[49] The first documented slave insurrection "involving Negro slaves in English America occurred in Virginia, in 1663."[50] Later on, the 1730s would be known as "A decade of slave unrest throughout the New World plantation complex," and would include insurrections in the Bahamas (1734), Antigua (1735), St. John (1733), and Guadeloupe (1737).[51] Other rebellions in the English colonies and in the future United States would include the New York slave conspiracy (1712), the South Carolina Stono insurrection (1739), Samba's conspiracy in Louisiana (1763), Denmark Vesey's conspiracy in Charleston, South Carolina (1822), and Nat Turner's revolt in Virginia (1831), among many others. The historical contexts of those moments aid us in understanding the pronounced illegality of such actions: although slaves were the declared property of slaveholders who determined their rights (or absence thereof), were defined as such throughout the U.S. Constitution, and were subject to legislation that defined their position in no uncertain terms, the fundamental immorality of slavery and the ethical feebleness of the social, political, and economic pillars that helped support this "peculiar institution" gave slaves more than enough cause to actively rebel against the oppression they had endured for centuries.

Latin American immigrants who choose to enter the United States unlawfully via the southern border with Mexico are openly defying both national and international laws and legislation; yet, for many, this migration represents a fight against inequality and discrimination that equates economic justice with freedom of national and transnational movement. In their country of origin, Latin American nationals often find it challenging to support their families in a subsistence economy, and make the difficult choice to leave their homes, embark on a treacherous journey north, cross the United States border unlawfully, and begin the search for work that will enable them to both survive in the United States and aid their families back home financially. Upon arriving in the United States, their undocumented situation frequently permits employers, landlords, schools, and doctors to take advantage of them by overcharging for services or underpaying them for their work. In this case, their suffering parallels that experienced by fugitive slaves, who, in their deliberate "illegality," broke ties at home and, even upon reaching supposed freedom, continued to endure mistreatment and inequities.

Undocumented Latin American immigrants to the United States commonly experience attitudes and behavior that transcend legal guidelines and enter the realm of the harsh, cruel, and inhumane. Unfortunately, the United States has a dark, irrational tradition of treating the most recent immigrants and ethnic populations poorly. Writing in 1963, Thomas F. Gossett maintained that "Prejudice against ethnic minorities in this country has been immensely strong. Sometimes it has approached the point at which it seemed doubtful whether some ethnic groups were to be considered human at all, but there have always remained a nagging doubt that they *might* be."[52] This prejudice has frequently led to overt expressions of racism, as "Racism thus provides a rationalization for poor treatment of immigrants, both 'naturalizing' their socioeconomic inferiority and disarming them politically, oftentimes in the name of cultural supremacy or national security."[53]

Mexican nationals have recently suffered from this treatment, as their country shares a common border with the United States, and they have traditionally immigrated to this country in greater numbers than individuals from other Latin American countries. When the United States defeated Mexico in 1848 and appropriated approximately one-third of

Mexican territory, many Mexican nationals found themselves to be residents of a new nation without having moved their belongings, as the border crossed over them in the course of a single day. Immediately following the conflict, treatment of Mexican-American nationals "seldom satisfied the nation's highest legal standards,"[54] as many were expelled from new U.S. territory in Texas cities such as Austin, DeWitt, and San Antonio.[55] In Tucson, Arizona, the prevalent attitude reflected the fact that "Mexicans had lost the war, so they should suffer the indignities of peace."[56]

The entry of undocumented Latin American nationals into the United States may also make them easy targets for prejudice and racism. Writing on the experiences of many, Jerome R. Adams underscores the racial connections to their fate in the United States: "Immigrant families commonly cluster in neighborhoods and trailer parks, their breadwinners often unprotected by wage-and-hour regulations, their housing usually ignored by health and safety inspectors, and their well-being generally neglected. It would be difficult, if not impossible, to explain their condition in any way that did not acknowledge the widespread existence of prejudice."[57] Their sustained presence, however, will not force improvements of ethnic and racial relations in the United States: "As undocumented workers continue to seek opportunities, they will meet with increased hazards, opposition, and regrettably at times with loss of life."[58]

The breaking of laws by Latin American nationals does not occur, as in the case of nineteenth-century escaped slaves, the moment they decide to leave their homeland and walk or ride away from their families; the transgression of established regulations happens upon their undisclosed arrival in the United States and/or the unauthorized extension of their stay in this country. It is then that undocumented Latinos begin to suffer the consequences of their actions and to live life on the law's edge.

In this sense, both Hispanics and fugitive slaves are *outsiders* in that they sought and seek to make a place for themselves in societies by living outside the law: slaves by escaping the slaveholder's clutch and Hispanics by entering, working, and living as undocumented residents of the United States. The laws that were violated upon entering this country illegally have very little in common with the laws that defined African Americans in the nineteenth-century U.S. South as mere property to be used, mistreated, and exchanged, yet the very willingness of these two populations to break established legislation regarding their free movement in order to find a better life places them in anachronistic yet similar categories of human displacement.

There are other commonalities that connect the experience of fugitive slaves with those Latin American nationals who may be currently entering this country illegally, including their dissimilar yet mutual disenfranchisement from host cultures. Throughout history, attempts were made to transform prevalent attitudes and rewrite legislation, but failures have regrettably been more numerous than successes. In an effort to recognize the debt that the United States owes to its Mexican-American heritage, in 1975 "the Border Patrol began hiring Mexican-Americans. Instead of changing the agency's racist attitudes, [however,] it added the more brutal racism of the dark-skinned overseer, the one who proves himself to his white masters that he is loyal and who separates himself from his own people by brutalizing them."[59] The language utilized here by Earl Shorris draws a clear parallel between the situation today on the Mexican border and the plight of African American slaves in nineteenth-century North America, particularly with regard to authority and racial tensions. Sergio Ramírez, a Mexican-American border guard, declared in a 1990 interview, "They [undocumented immigrants] are not Americans," making it clear that "he has no feeling for them, no connection to them."[60]

The objectification of Mexican nationals that Shorris alludes to is symptomatic of the negative image perceived by non-immigrants and evokes the treatment of both contemporary undocumented Latin American immigrants who cross into the United States illegally and fugitive slaves in the nineteenth-century U.S. South. Through the animalization and corresponding dehumanization of these populations, authorities, cultural moguls, and the mass media have been able to find a scapegoat for the moment's woes, attempting to control an unmanageable situation by representing these individuals as brutish creatures meant to be contained in their respective pens.

In the national imaginary, African Americans in the nineteenth century were frequently portrayed as nothing more than animals that lived and reacted primarily according to instinct. Aside from the well-known caricatures and literary representations, blacks during this period were believed to have little free will and no curiosity about the world surrounding them, free to simply be mechanically content at having their time occupied by labor and some sleep. Writing in 1925, for example, Howard W. Odum and Gary B. Johnson indicated that "The migratory habits of the Negro are so well known that they need no explanation,"[61] using language that implicitly included the African American race within the domain of the fauna of the animal kingdom. In her short story "The Displaced Person," Flannery O'Connor utilizes her characters to comment on the racial dynamics between immigrants, African Americans, and whites in the 1950s U.S. South. Mrs. Shortley, a white worker who is being displaced by the arrival of an Eastern European immigrant family who will work for less pay, has an illustrative exchange with an elderly black man: "'The time is going to come,' she prophesied, 'when it won't be no more occasion to speak of a nigger.' The old man laughed politely. 'Yes indeed,' he said. 'Ha ha.'"[62] The comments of both individuals merit attention, as they reveal duplicitous positions on the part of the interlocutors: Mrs. Shortley's "prophesy," for example, may either be a racist wish that portends the end of the African American race in the United States or an idealistic desire to do away with this unnecessarily pejorative term, while the few words spoken by "the old man" either reflect his silent acquiescence in the face of a white authority figure or belie the resentment that lies seething inside of him.

The marginalization of immigrant populations in the United States began as early as the eighteenth and nineteenth centuries, when the oligarchy and middle classes, who were firmly entrenched in positions of authority, began to feel threatened by the new arrivals. In his 1895 poem "Unguarded Gates," the writer Thomas Bailey Aldrich railed against the masses of undesired immigrants arriving at the shores of the United States and drew apparent parallels between untamed animals and the arriving individuals that threatened the alleged purity of the country:

> Wide open and unguarded stand our gates,
> And through them presses a wild motley throng...
> These bringing with them unknown gods and rites,
> Those, tiger passions, have to stretch their claws.
> In street and alley what strange tongues are loud,
> Accents of menace alien to our air.[63]

During approximately the same time period, "Theodore Roosevelt's campaign against birth control was probably a reflection of the fears of certain old Americans that the native stock would be supplanted by the immigrants."[64] The new arrivals in the United States toward the end of the nineteenth century were from nations such as Ireland, Greece, and Italy, countries that generally did not enjoy the positive image bestowed upon those of British or German descent, for example, and that were seen as potential weights around the neck of the U.S. nation.

The current objectification of Latin American immigrants in the United States has also witnessed something of a renaissance in light of existing debates on the impact that undocumented immigration is having on this nation and in light of the increased spotlight placed on border dynamics: "For most of its existence the border has seen smuggling as a way of life, in recent decades automobiles into Mexico and drugs into the United States."[65] Of particular interest is the smuggling of Hispanics through the Mexican border and into U.S. territory, as these actions involve moving lawlessly and surreptitiously through populations that barely suspect their presence. Today's smugglers include *pateros* who "[lead] migrants across the Rio Grande," local or interior *coyotes*, "natives of towns and cities in the traditional migrant sending [Mexican] states of Guanajuato, Michoacán, Zacatecas, San Luis Potosí, and Jalisco," "friends and kin," and "border commercial smugglers."[66] As Josiah McC. Heyman noted, "Smugglers form organizations, some loose and band-like, others larger and more hierarchical, and rely on referrals and return business as well as recruitment of newly arriving migrants."[67] While the smuggling of human beings occurs in conjunction with the smuggling of foodstuffs, exotic animals, and commodities such as radios, refrigerators, or clothing, the language describing the specific phenomenon of human smuggling, however, has yet to develop a terminology of its own that distances the practice from other types of smuggling and re-humanizes those individuals who are being transported illegally or forcibly across borders, continents, and oceans.

One consequence of the perceived lawlessness of certain migrant populations is the development of racist attitudes and prejudices that are often fed by historical misconceptions. Both escaped slaves and today's undocumented immigrants skirt a number of laws that make them easy targets for those who wish to see in their lawlessness the very cause of the country's ills, stereotyping the journeys of these individuals and characterizing the vast diversity of their experiences as a monolithic totem of illicit adventures. Yet care must be exercised, as stereotypes represent the first step toward racist attitudes and come to reflect the insecurities of the majority. As Glenn T. Tsunokai has indicated, "Stereotypes and myths become more negative and persistent when the size of an out-group (e.g., an immigrant group) increases to a point where the dominant group believes their proprietary claim to certain areas of advantage or privilege are being threatened."[68] Subsequently, "Stereotypes and myths routinely serve as justification for more severe forms of prejudice and discrimination."[69] To this end, language participates in demarcating the rhetorical field of play, providing a semiotic authentication of negative depictions. In Spain, for example, there exist a series of set phrases that, although habitually used innocuously, racialize any exchange. Sayings such as "Trabajar como un negro" or "Trabajar como un chino" ("To work like a black man" or "To work like a Chinese man"), "Hablar en cristiano" ("To speak Christian," signifying speaking in Spanish), and "No seas judío" or "Qué judío eres" ("You're such a Jew," admonishing someone for being two-faced or excessively thrifty with their money), are used in a very general and denatured sense with anyone, yet their apparent innocence hides the racist undertone and damage that they are inflicting on these representative populations in the collective consciousness.

In the United States, the destructive portrayal of African Americans in the nineteenth century frequently served to further disenfranchise an already disenfranchised population, especially in regard to the issue of slavery and the potential participation of freed slaves at all levels of society. Writers in the 1860s drew attention to "the Negro's unfitness for civilization"[70] and wrote frequently on the negative impact that freed slaves would have on the country. In a representative 1866 article entitled *Free Negroism*, the anonymous author frequently beseeches the reader to consider the harmful effects of "free negroism" on those nations south of the Rio Grande and to view these as failed experiments to be avoided: "In order," he begins, "to see the really disastrous effects of free negroism, we must turn our attention to that vast tropical territory which has been cursed with this miserable delusion."[71] Due to this "delusion," "The entire continent of North and South-America, from the Rio Grande on the North to Brazil on the South, is to-day little more than a desert waste." The author further offers the opinion that "The improvements under the Spaniards are gone to decay and ruin, while the mongrel population do nothing except insult the name of 'God and Liberty' by indulging in pronunciamientos and revolution!"[72] While a society of liberated slaves is, in the writer's opinion, the cause of this anarchy, the language of his arguments represents an imperial mentality that, while reminding us of the alleged yet unstated "improvements [made] under the Spaniards" and advocating the beneficial effects of a civilizing enterprise, merely serves to promote his rather narrow and Eurocentric notion of *civilization*. Slaves in the nineteenth-century United States were frequently objectified and animalized by a Southern society that looked to extend its ideological supremacy over the land; yet their worst shortcoming was, as the piece looked to demonstrate, the fact that they were *uncivilizeable*: that they would remain as beasts, tied to their rudimentary cultures.

The rather frequent parallels made in the nineteenth century between populations in newly independent Latin American nations and African Americans in the United States offer attractive grounds for analyzing the first institutionalized attempts at justifying racist perspectives in the Americas. Published in 1866, the pamphlet *Abolition is National Death* compares the burgeoning situation in the United States to the situation brought about by those peoples "south of us" and expresses alarm at the potential consequences that would come from the freeing of slaves: "Like the mongrel populations south of us, [negroes] will work and fish, and hunt and live on in some miserable way, and while some few individuals may acquire wealth and distinction, the great mass will become poor and more miserable every year, until in the course of time they utterly perish from the earth."[73] While this notion may appear to us today as a racist generalization whose premise defies any attempt at systematic analysis, it casts its long shadow through the deterministic manner in which many contemporary residents of Europe and North America simply accept the condition of the world's poor and homeless, especially of those who choose to emigrate and risk their lives for a better paying job.

Undocumented immigrants who are currently entering the United States are frequent victims of prejudice and discrimination, initially evident in the language chosen to refer to this population. As James Loucky writes, "Today racist undertones may be seen when immigrants are referred to as 'aliens' or have imputed to them unsavory habits and maleficient motives."[74] These immigrants are also summarily lumped into one monolithic category that often extends individual inappropriate behavior or characteristics to the entire group and portrays it as a facile scapegoat for the country's ills, particularly if their arrival has unbalanced a community's infrastructure and sense of identity: "Situations that are atypical compared to mainstream culture are deemed alien and wrong. This makes it easy, in turn, to blame failure, anti-assimilation, dropout rates, and ethnic enclaves on immigrants or minorities themselves."[75]

As these sentiments continue to develop across the country, recent immigrants to the United States will not feel especially empowered or eager to step outside their "enclaves" and interact with what Loucky terms "the mainstream culture." The fact that they may remain within their neighborhoods and maintain an imposed and possibly chosen segregation amongst those who speak their language and live their own *outsider* culture represents a resistance to the homogenizing nature of their adopted community. Yet, as with fugitive slaves in the nineteenth century, their arrival in the Promised Land is only the first step toward liberation: these individuals must also establish their own homes, interact with the society that lives and breathes around them, and somehow coexist with existing legislation, whether it be the 1850 Fugitive Slave

Law or the Illegal Immigration Reform and Immigration Responsibility Act of 1996. Herein lay the challenge for African Americans who made it north of the Ohio river in the nineteenth century, and herein lies the challenge today for Latin American undocumented immigrants: to live life quietly, on the shoreline of the law.

PREPARATION AND MOTIVATION FOR MIGRATION. THE CROSSING

Understanding the preparation and motivation of fugitive slaves in the nineteenth-century U.S. South and of undocumented Latin American nationals looking to enter the United States today is crucial if we are to understand the journeys of these two populations and the consequences of their decisions once they arrive on the soil of the north. Their justifications for such a journey and the chosen means of transportation vary from the most practical to the most imaginative, meant to both carry them away from an unchosen life and toward a more singular, self-sustainable path.

Recognizing the motivation for leaving one's land and family is crucial to appreciating the presence of disenfranchised populations in territories of atypical migration. Born into a life of bondage, slaves chose to either remain on the plantation and acquiesce, remain and actively or passively rebel, or escape with the knowledge that they would either find a difficult freedom or be recaptured, returning to face an even worse fate. Whether they be fugitive slaves or undocumented immigrants, the rationale behind their decisions documents the life that they look to leave behind. Yet differences remain between the incentives for both populations. For escaped slaves, the decision was not made lightly nor easily, in spite of conditions that spoke to the contrary. As illustrated by the narrator in *Uncle Tom's Cabin*, the factors considered by the character of Eliza as she began her getaway were numerous: "Then there was the parting from every familiar object—the place where she had grown up, the trees under which she had played, the groves where she had walked many an evening in happier days, by the side of her young husband—everything, as it lay in the clear, frosty starlight, seemed to speak reproachfully to her, and ask her whither could she go from a home like that?"[76] In this passage, the effective romanticization of Eliza's home context evokes happier times that serve to implicitly juxtapose that which she is leaving behind—imagined security and tranquility—with what lays ahead for her: unknown hazards and perils. It would also appear that Nature herself is personified and contributes to this idealization of her past, as the "trees," "groves," and "starlight" seem to conspire and implore her not to leave.

What is Eliza's ultimate motivation? Freedom from the chains of slavery, which, to this end, justify sacrificing practically everything. The experience of Emeline Chapman, a fugitive slave who exchanged her life of slavery for one of freedom, is representative of the motivation behind her exploit: "In order to escape the responsibility attached to her original name, she adopted the name of Susan Bell. Thus for freedom she was willing to forego her name, her husband, and even her little children."[77] The weight of her name, her relationship with her husband, and the presence of her children were not enough to keep her from making the journey northward. Ohio, in particular, attracted many fugitive slaves, as "the presence of free African-American communities," "of anti-slavery whites," and of "reasonably direct routes from slave to free territory"[78] made a difficult decision somewhat more viable.

Latin American nationals who cross into the United States via the southern border with Mexico also struggle with the justification for embarking on such a treacherous journey northward. As Luis Alberto Urrea has written, "Imagine how bad things get to make you leave behind your family, your friends, your lovers; your home, as humble as it might be; your church, say."[79] Liberation from marginalization and the search for a better life requires taking chances that offer no guarantees and set compelling forces off against each other: "When tough but incomplete law enforcement faces off against the powerful motivations that drive migrants north (the need for family, the need for income), the result is extreme risk-taking."[80] As with fugitive slaves, conditions exist that endanger the lives of migrant travelers, yet the threats that lie along the way are not sufficient to hinder them in their journey.

For the vast majority of Latin American immigrants, the primary motivation for crossing the border illegally is economic: to earn more money than is possible in their homeland. According to Thomas J. Davis, "With legal immigration just about closed, illegal means remained the most practical entry for many. The stark contrast between poverty and plenty across what came to be called La Frontera from Mexico to the United States moved many."[81] The variety of jobs available to immigrants in the United States frequently surpasses the individual's experience and tests the patience of those who enter this country, yet the work does not stop:

"People wanted to work, and they didn't care what the work was like. They would do stoop labor, wrecking their backs and their knees picking strawberries or artichokes, and they would prune vineyards and orchards that had been sprayed with pesticides. They would swab floors, bathe infants, scrub pots and pans, and breathe in formaldehyde vapors in factories where particle board was made....They would agree to remove asbestos from heating ducts and to scrape lead-based paint from walls."[82]

The economic incentive to leave home and find work in the United States is also influenced by the ability to be able to wire U.S. dollars back to their families, as "The ability to send money home is one of the primary motivating factors to emigrate to the United States—legally or illegally."[83]

While the motivation for their journeys is distinctly different, the manner in which both nineteenth-century fugitive slaves in the United States and undocumented Latin American immigrants cross over into northern territory is similar. The well-known examples of slaves who hid in trunks, stowed away aboard steamships, holed up in the hull of a boat filled with turpentine, or simply made their way on foot across desolate and uninviting territory are paralleled by Mexicans who were hidden away in tractor-trailer trucks, Salvadorans who were led by a *coyote* through the desert in northern Mexico, or Guatemalans who simply begin walking north toward the border with Mexico. Along the Ohio River, many escaped slaves could count on the help of individuals along the Underground Railroad or on those who knew of the existence of people such as John Rankin, in Ripley, Ohio. In the case of the not-so-fictional Eliza in *Uncle Tom's Cabin,* her desperation as she flees across the frozen Ohio River is heightened by the sound of the barking hounds behind her, by the fact that she is carrying her infant son, and by her exhausted physical condition. As she arrives on the free soil of the Ohio side of the river, the narrator takes stock of her circumstances: "Her shoes are gone—her stockings cut from her feet—While blood marked every step; but she saw nothing, felt nothing, till dimly, as in a dream, she saw the Ohio side, and a man helping her up the bank."[84] Although the event is inspired by a slave woman who, in 1838, escaped across the frozen Ohio River, the passage from Harriet Beecher Stowe's novel admirably interweaves the difficulty of Eliza's crossing with the very patent possibility that, upon arriving on freedom's shore, her life will improve, using her adventure as an extreme albeit representative model that looked to bring to light the fugitive slave's experience and to shine a narrative light on what the narrator in *Uncle Tom's Cabin* calls "rich and joyous Ohio."[85]

In traveling overland from south to north, many Latin American immigrants also face physical dangers that, as in the case of fugitive slaves, also put their lives at risk. The efforts of Mexican-American *coyotes* and the "shepherds" that worked along the Underground Railroad are similar, as they both aid marginalized populations who wish to surreptitiously cross into the north. Writing about the *coyotes* who participate in these transnational ventures, John A. Adams, Jr., has emphasized the networks that exist on both sides of the border: "The smugglers, known as *coyotes* or *polleros*, maintain an extensive and well-organized operation targeting crossings at sparsely populated locations along a vast and harsh border."[86] The motivation behind their actions, however, differs vastly from those who led slaves from town to town along the Underground Railroad. The *coyote*, for example, is frequently ruthless in his dealings, suffers little to no punishment for his efforts, and works primarily for lucrative gain at the expense of a population who will pay practically anything to cross into the United States. In the nineteenth century, the "shepherds" and "conductors" rarely profited from their actions and were frequently persecuted by locals who opposed their activities and by bounty hunters looking to claim the reward offered for an escaped slave. While the *coyote's* job today is dangerous and involves eluding ground sensors, jumping over electrified fences, and shaking off border police, the lives of those who harbored and helped move fugitive slaves across lands both south and north of the Ohio River were in constant peril, as they were commonly publicly marked as abolitionists by individuals who were fighting to keep the wretched business of slavery alive.

Crossing the border as an undocumented immigrant—particularly as a Mexican or Central American national—remains a risky enterprise, as "illegal border crossings have always posed a serious threat to the safety of Mexican immigrants[,] with drowning accounting for large numbers of deaths."[87] The dangers, however, are not enough of an obstacle to keep Latin American immigrants from entering the United States illegally, and many of those crossing choose to hire a *coyote* who guides them across unknown terrain and may even make them aware of the difficulties that lie ahead. Bill Barich notes, "In the hierarchy of illegal immigration, *coyotes* occupy an odd niche between the vaguely heroic and the decidedly villainous, and this gives them a mythic stature on which they capitalize, outfitting themselves in fancy sweatshirts and high-top sneakers in the Air Jordan mode."[88] According to statistics, "Approximately 75 percent of these undocumented immigrants use a *coyote*...that charges anywhere from $250 to $1,500 per immigrant."[89] As they journey to the

United States, many Latin American nationals cannot afford to pay the fees required by *coyotes* and are taken advantage of by their guides and carriers, owing them a substantial amount of money. In the world of human trafficking today, "An important method for enacting debt bondage is for human smugglers to 'allow' individuals to contract for passage based on paying off the fee by work in their receiving country. Thus human trafficking is intimately connected to enslavement, and smuggling operations can produce cases of enslavement."[90]

In the cases of other immigrants who choose to cross the border through unguarded locations along the Rio Grande and do not have the money to pay the high fees charged by *coyotes*, the means may be somewhat more humble and the price a bit reduced, as individuals frequently simply "pay fifty cents to a man who brings them across in a rubber raft."[91] Notwithstanding the technique used to cross the border, the experience is daunting and reminds us of the very real hazards faced by fugitive slaves:

> You have walked, run, hidden in the backs of trucks, spent part of your precious money on bus fare. There is no AAA nor Travelers Aid Society available to you. Various features of your journey north might include police corruption; violence in the forms of beatings, rape, murder, torture, road accidents; theft; incarceration. Additionally, you might experience loneliness, fear, exhaustion, sorrow, cold, heat, diarrhea, thirst, hunger. There is no medical attention available to you.[92]

The details that Luis Alberto Urrea offers in this description of Mexican immigrants are, unfortunately, relevant to yesterday's fugitives and to the majority of today's global immigrant population who decide to cross illegally, continuing the diaspora of peoples throughout history as they seek a better life for themselves and their families.

THE CONSEQUENCES

The motivation for embarking upon journeys as hazardous as those faced by yesterday's fugitive slaves and today's undocumented Latin American immigrants was frequently rewarded by a successful escape to lands north of the Ohio and Rio Grande rivers, respectively. Regrettably, however, the ideals that compelled these peoples to uproot themselves and endure geographical and psychological displacement, physical pain, personal isolation, and economic uncertainty were at times toppled by the harsh reality awaiting them upon their arrival in the Promised Land.

Since slavery "was a system which lived on, by, and with fear,"[93] it would stand to reason that the horror ingrained in the slaves through the lifestyle and customs imposed by slaveholding societies in the U.S. South would leave its mark even in the lives of those who managed to escape the chains of slavery. As Peter J. Parish has written, "Most free blacks lived much more humble or even lives, sometimes suffering abject poverty, often performing menial tasks, and constantly harassed by authorities who were armed with more and more laws designed to crack down on this awkward minority group."[94] Undocumented immigrants who arrive in the United States today also find themselves persecuted by authorities and private individuals who call them simple criminals and subjectively choose how and when to employ them according to the moment's needs, causing them to suffer from the additional stress of living constantly on the margins of the law in the United States: "The stress of migration is coupled with the fact that undocumented immigrants are forced to live in fear and are vulnerable to criminals and unscrupulous employers because they have no legal recourse."[95]

For fugitive slaves in particular, their exit from the U.S. South and settlement in the North was often a disappointing experience, as the prejudice and racism they experienced as slaves and expected to diminish in locations where abolitionism flourished nominally continued over the course of their lives in much of the region. States such as Ohio (1804), Illinois (1819), Michigan (1827), Indiana (1831), and Iowa (1839), which entered the Union after 1804 and prohibited slavery, also banned blacks from residing within their territories.[96] The Fugitive Slave Law of 1850, in effect, made it illegal to give refuge to escaped slaves in non-slave states, obligating countless slaves to travel to Canada if they were to find true freedom. Years later, even the emancipation president Abraham Lincoln would express views that understood the plight of African American slaves in racially tinged tones. To them, he declared, "Your race are suffering, in my judgment, the greatest wrong inflicted on any people. But even when you cease to be slaves, you are yet far removed from being placed on an equality with the white race."[97]

Life on the northern shores of the Ohio River posed its own trials, as "Wherever slaves crossed, challenges abounded on the other side. Where to go. How to eat. Whom to trust."[98] As Anne Hagedorn has written, "Ohio may have been the land of the free, but it was also a land filled with hateful racial prejudice."[99] Many who arrived safely on northern shores kept moving along to other places in Ohio and beyond, ultimately finding safe haven through the help of ex-slaves and other individuals who dedicated themselves to the cause. As Griffler has noted, however, "For the thousands who remained [along the river], the territory immediately north of the Ohio was no Promised Land."[100] Fortunately there were also men such as David Walker, born of a free black mother and an enslaved father in North Carolina, and the author of *Appeal* (1829), a black nationalist and Pan-Africanist essay that looked to improve the plight of African Americans and promote racial equality in the United States.

Latin American undocumented nationals who have attempted to cross the border into the United States have frequently found themselves in an untenable position, particularly after trying unsuccessfully to enter through the area of the Tijuana River. As Luis Alberto Urrea has written, "If North America does not want them, Tijuana wants them even less. They become outcasts of an outcast region."[101] In this and other regions along the U.S.-Mexican border, immigrants who are turned back become the displaced amongst the displaced: they have been rejected from their destination and do not have the funds necessary to either attempt another crossing or return home, finding themselves in the position of living borderline existences that look only to step away, in one direction or another.

If Latin American nationals have the good fortune to survive the hazards inherent to border culture, elude border patrols, endure climate, fences, and topography and cross successfully—albeit illegally—into the United States, they may yet face the danger of unscrupulous *coyotes* who "will lead a migrant across, store him in a safe house, and then refuse to release him until his relatives in the United States cough up a ransom."[102] Fortunately, in the southwest there exist safe houses such as the Texas Key Shelters, which function within the law and serve as true sanctuaries for immigrants who have just arrived in this country. "In San Ysidro [CA], there are also safe houses, where, for a price, a migrant can hole up for a while. The safe houses look like the houses around them, but everybody on a given block can point them out."[103]

The ultimate degree of absorption of immigrants by the United States will more than likely be swift, as the national economy in the last ten to fifteen years has grown on the backs of these new immigrants. According to John A. Adams, Jr., "By the 1990s, 50 percent of the new jobs created were filled by newcomer immigrants—legal and illegal—to the United States."[104] Like fugitive slaves, Latin American immigrants who enter the United States illegally frequently find that, arduous as the physical journey northward might have been, the true exploit begins upon their arrival in their adopted places of residency. Unlike fugitive slaves, however, many of these Latin Americans arrive in nontraditional destinations such as Mississippi, Tennessee, and Georgia, where there are ample economic opportunities, and possibly a small but stable infrastructure to aid them in finding work, food, and shelter.

The parallels between the motivations, journeys, and consequences of the migration of fugitive slaves and undocumented Latin American nationals pale at the noticeable differences between the historical experiences of these two populations. Firstly, while the Ohio and Rio Grande rivers are respective examples of rather permeable borders, each waterway reflects the immense differences in domestic and international policy and legislation relevant to its effective administration. Although the globalization of local economies today is contributing to the localization of global economies across the world, the documentation and paperwork necessary for persons and material goods to travel from the United States to Mexico and vice versa parallels other international borders across the globe. Further restrictions on immigration and a closer watch on the personal items that a traveler brings into a country are now the norm across Europe, the Middle East, and Asia, particularly in light of the September 11 terrorist acts in the United States, the March 11, 2004, train bombings in Madrid, and the July 7, 2005, attacks in London.

Secondly, the historical circumstances and the present unmanaged economic and demographic growth of a locally globalized U.S.-Mexican border differ vastly from the frontier culture that developed along the localized Ohio River in the nineteenth century. According to John A. Adams, Jr., in the area today, "The primary impact and concern of border community leaders, given the historical shortfall of federal funding for border needs, is the growing list of unfunded federal government mandates to provide services and facilities for which there is little or no local funding."[105] While the conflict between federal and local authorities is a topic not new to the history of the United States, the manner in which the federal government has acted upon or ignored problems or threats evident along the border has reflected the international policies of respective presidential administrations and historical context more adequately. As Larry J. Estrada has written, "The [U.S.-Mexican] border represents one of the most dynamic boundaries in the world that is witness to high population growth, economic expansion, mobile labor forces, linguistic hybridization, high crime rates, and an artistic renaissance of the social and psycho-cultural character of each country."[106] The international impact of this border culture is extending beyond its geographical limitations, serving as both a model for countercultural evolution and a humanitarian example to avoid.

Lastly, the application and use of terminology such as "legal" and "illegal" to Latin American immigrants reflects the ideologies behind language that look to boorishly limit the impact of these individuals on communities across the United States and, in the process, attempt to fix the national identity in a very secure and static place. As we have attempted to demonstrate, the application of "illegal" should refer not to human beings themselves, but rather to human actions that transcend established laws and legislation. Slaves in the nineteenth-century United States, for example, were essentially disenfranchised noncitizens accepted into national society as property. Under the terms of the 1850 Fugitive Slave Law, they were simply considered lost property to be recovered if they willfully escaped their owners and sought refuge in other lands. The law did not apply to them as persons—only as chattel.

Both the plight of fugitive slaves and the situation of undocumented immigrants today share a number of commonalities, chief among them being the economic motive of exodus. The pursuit of escaped slaves in the nineteenth century was readily embarked upon by slaveholders who quite literally saw their income and investments dwindle away each time a runaway slave eluded their grasp. Their concern was not for the person who had escaped, but rather for the asset that had gone missing. Latin American immigrants who arrive successfully in the United States are frequently hired by building contractors, landscapers, hotels, and private citizens with the objective of maximizing their own profits. Since these immigrants entered the country illegally, they do not stand to benefit from minimum wage laws, insurance programs, or pension funds that are intended for citizens, residents, and those who entered the country "legally." Yet they, like fugitive slaves, financially contribute to a system that essentially looks to take advantage of their outsider status by setting them upon the razor's edge of survival and compelling them to either work under the imposed conditions or starve.

With the clarity of the choice looming before them, it is no wonder, then, that the escape from repression and the illegal entry into the United States by Latin American nationals is a form of liberation that seeks, above all, the capacity of an individual for self-determination. Liberated from slavery and economic stagnation, these individuals propel themselves forward toward unknown lands that, in theory, offer them the opportunity to start a new life. This liberation, however, does not come without risk, as their status as refugees would permanently identify them as those who had come from elsewhere. Today's immigrants are still "enslaveable," as they may be "recruited" as "1) child or domestic service, 2) farm workers kept in coerced labor camps under armed guard, 3) sweatshops, and 4) prostitution."[107]

As victims of prejudice and discrimination, both fugitive slaves and undocumented immigrants sought to carve their own quiet corner in some city or town where they would be free to realize their ideals and meet their obligations. In communities across the United States that are witnessing the unanticipated arrival of Latin American citizens, this may be difficult. As a city's infrastructure, for example, adjusts to this population growth, stereotypes frequently rise to the surface and serve as simplistic and inaccurate templates of what is deemed appropriate and lawful. According to Thomas J. Davis, "Dragnets for so-called illegals targeted people by physical profiles. Appearance, not behavior, served as the distinctive characteristic for law enforcement. Similarly, talk of 'Hispanics' and 'Latino' often obscured individuality and divergent backgrounds. Old-line racial views awkwardly clustered Spanish-speaking, Spanish-surnamed, Hispanic and Latino."[108] The generalizations surrounding a fugitive slave's capacity and condition in his adopted community may superficially remind us of what today's immigrants endure in the United States; yet efforts must be made to distinguish pre–Civil War slavery from today's contemporary forms of slavery: "[I]n new forms of slavery legal ownership is avoided, purchase costs and profits are very high, there is a surplus of potential slaves, relationships are short term, slaves are disposable, and ethnic differences are generally unimportant."[109] Currently we are witnessing the fragmentation and commodification of individual identities, to the point that there is little transparency on these fringes. As both Flannery O'Connor and Carlos Fuentes allude to in their works "The Displaced Person" and *The Glass Border*, respectively, there is always someone below who is willing to sacrifice in order to occupy the position that lies directly in his or her path. In this respect, the search for a more just existence was at the root and plight of fugitive slaves and is today at the heart of the difficulties endured by Latin American immigrants looking to enter the United States. Since the present does not offer many possibilities other than dehumanization and meager subsistence, these individuals place their hopes in the future.

For communities across the U.S. South today, it may be important to recall the lessons offered by the "peculiar institution" of slavery, as citizens from Mexico, Guatemala, El Salvador, Colombia, and the Dominican

Republic, among many others, rent or buy their homes alongside long-standing residents and look for work among the local businesses that will offer them an opportunity. As with fugitive slaves, their arrival signals the end of one part of the individuation process—the physical journey—yet heralds the beginning of another: the coexistence with others who may be unaccustomed to ethnically, linguistically, or culturally diverse populations and who may perceive them as a threat to their identity and "way of life." In nontraditional areas of Latino migration such as the U.S. South, Hispanics migrate and liberate themselves from disenfranchisement in their home country only to find that, upon arrival, they are still marginalized and chained to an identity that, not unlike "free" slaves, has been imposed from the outside, fabricated for the benefit of the dominant population. As Judith Warner has written, today's Latino laborers represent the new marginalized and are standing in for yesterday's oppressed African American population: "While previously those coerced into farm labor were primarily African-Americans, and sometimes homeless, alcoholics, or drug addicts, today it is often immigrant Latino farm workers who receive very low wages and endure poor working conditions and quality of life."[110]

The Ohio and Rio Grande rivers yesterday and today epitomize avenues of commerce and divisions between states and nations; yet they also remind us of the almost unstoppable phenomenon of domestic and transnational migration. As geographic touchstones, their waters both separate and unite the turbulent riverbeds that lie underneath, examples of the often inexhaustible capacity of natural borders to transcend the limitations imposed on them by human intentions. In this way, it is often as if, through their mere presence, these waterways cooperated with fugitive slaves and Latin American immigrants: by offering waters unblemished by the politics and legislation of the moment, the Ohio and Rio Grande rivers serve as impartial arbiters in the contest between those who flee and those who confine. Illegality, lawlessness, intention, or ultimate consequences appear not to matter to waters that continue their path, regardless of human legislation. If communities across the U.S. South could anticipate the arrival of nontraditional migrant populations and consequently dovetail with the emerging Latino presence, rivers as symbols of divisions and difficulties would be secondary to the social, political, and economic promise unleashed by multilingual and multiethnic cities and towns across the region.

Economics, the U.S. South, Latinos, and the Cultural Dollar

The origins and impetus of the colonial and imperial projects in the Americas have frequently been ascribed to religious factors or to an erstwhile nostalgia that compelled certain European powers to ignore the troubles of their national populations and look beyond their borders for their own particular identity. The migration of Mexican citizens and the appropriation of their territory, for example, has taken place in the shadow of public policies that rarely welcomed these workers to the United States. Yet these laborers have gone to extreme lengths to arrive in this country to work and suffer intense hardships simply to work a job, which, as Jerome R. Adams has noted, places them today in disproportionate peril: "Mexicans were 1 in every 24 workers in America, but they suffered one in every 14 workplace deaths."[1] While the economic mistreatment of undocumented Mexican and other Latino workers in the United States originates in a number of causes—which range from the laborers' own implicit dismissal of rights, rules, and regulations upon their undocumented arrival in this country to the systematic exploitation by unlicensed contractors—the economic transactions between residents of the Americas have historic and cultural origins that predate the first contacts between Europeans and non-Europeans on the American continent. These origins highlight the virtually indissoluble interconnection between the economic and the cultural arenas. Undocumented immigrants today "come here to make their best efforts, to work—to work *hard*—to better themselves, to enjoy a better world, to get educated, and to prosper. It's the American dream writ large. They're just writing it in Spanish."[2]

If we take Christopher Columbus's first voyage to the Americas in 1492 as a prequel to grander European endeavors intended to label the suitable (documented) and unsuitable (undocumented) citizen of the *polis* and as a sadly lasting example of colonial planning and motivation, the factor that emerges as the principal justification for which King Ferdinand and Queen Isabella agreed to finance his trip is the economic wealth that the Italian had guaranteed the Spanish Crown upon reaching his desired Asian destination and taking advantage of the spice trade. When the commander reached the first Caribbean islands and found that there were no spices, the grounds for his explorations were gradually modified and expanded to include the Christianization of the indigenous peoples that he encountered there, thereby attempting to make up for the paucity in economic riches and wealth that he dispatched to Spain.

Throughout the years, a compelling part of the U.S. South's history has been its economic upswings and downturns, violent changes that, initially, were brought about principally because of the South's social and economic dependence on a land which, in Howard Odum's opinion, the Southerner "has nonchalantly taken for granted."[3] Curiously, the rest of the nation has historically and, until very recently, perceived the economies of the Southern states to be as sluggish and leisurely as the stereotypes surrounding the region's population. These negative impressions of a substandard Southern economy may be viewed as relative commentary, since most observations and analyses were undergone or imposed from outside and frequently bordered on being cultural observations that were presented through an economic lens. The current reality is that, "In education as in the economy, the Southern story today is a mixture of heartening advances and disheartening disparities."[4]

In the eighteenth century, the South "did not feel itself to be a beleaguered or inferior region. The planter class bought the best goods from Europe and displayed far more obvious wealth than did the northern elites. Indeed, the per capita income of the region's white inhabitants was twice that of either New England or the middle colonies."[5] More specifically, between 1768 and 1772, "combined commodity exports from the Upper South (Chesapeake colonies) and the Lower South (the

Carolinas and Georgia) totaled almost nine million pounds sterling, which came to over 63 percent of the total value of commodity exports from the thirteen colonies during this period."[6]

The nineteenth century witnessed the growing Northern manipulation of economic standards, as the region defined and decided what was to be deemed "economic progress" and would frequently and erroneously deem the Southern economy to be sub par: "The Old South's economy [between 1860 and 1861] was backward by standards which equated progress with industrialization, urbanization, and diversification, but by other criteria it was quite dynamic. Between 1815 and 1860 it grew rapidly, but its growth was channeled into staple agriculture and related services rather than manufacturing."[7] By the second half of the nineteenth century, the Southern economy's dependence on cotton had worsened conditions throughout the area and created parallels between the region's economic state of affairs and the developing monocultural economies of Latin American countries (which, at the time, were suffering from the effects of a European and North American neocolonialism that looked to take advantage of goods such as coffee and minerals such as zinc and tin). At the time, slavery in and of itself turned into the moral pillar upon which the North would construct their arguments in favor of greater economic and personal freedoms for African Americans, who, in the North, suffered no less from de facto discrimination and racism. In sum, throughout the years, the backwardness of the South's economy has been due in part to a variety of factors, as the avarice and nearsightedness of Southern businessmen, the historical excesses of many Northern economic projects, and frequent northern desires to paint the region in a very specific negative light all collaborated to take advantage of a majority of the region's population.

The unanticipated dovetailing of the sluggishness of the Southern economy during the nineteenth century and the initiative demonstrated by a number of Northern businesses and businessmen at the time also represented and foreshadowed the very physical conflict that would erupt between a Southern agricultural culture that gradually saw its star waning on the horizon and the new industrial society coming to light in Europe and North America. Later on—and notwithstanding continuing negative impressions of the region's economics—from 1870 to 1950 the South "was generally in the vanguard of trade reform, supporting [the] Underwood-Simmons [Act in 1913][8] and, later, trade reciprocity, anticipating in many ways the world ushered in by Bretton Woods [Agreements in 1944]."[9]

As James C. Cobb has stated, the years after the Second World War began to witness the economic transformation of the region relative to other areas of the country: During this time, "Although the South remained a decidedly low-wage region, it emerged from [World War II] with an expanded industrial labor force and a markedly more affluent consumer pool, which became a crucial part of the region's postwar attraction for market-oriented industry."[10] Due in part, however, to "endemic poverty, one-party politics, and racial discrimination embedded in law, the South also lived in psychological and cultural isolation from the rest of America" during the twentieth century.[11] While the region still had a great deal of ground to make up regarding these and other issues, its economy began to grow and diversify its interests.

After 1945, the South proved to be in economic step with the rest of the nation, offering fertile soil to both factories and consumers and paving the way for what would be, in later years, the economic boom of the region. As Cobb has noted, "From an industrial development perspective, the South [today] may have become the nation's most globalized region."[12] Traditional Southern dependence on agricultural and heavy industry has today given way to a diverse collection of national and international businesses that have developed and/or relocated to the South and, in turn, have attracted more investment, diversified the area, and greatly contributed to an economic stability that looks to save the distance between the urban and the rural landscapes and promote the image of a diversified South. "Today there are not simply 'two Souths,' although a clear rural/metro divide persists. Today's South is a region of complex diversity, with fast-growth and slow-growth communities, with high-tech metro areas and backwater rural communities, and with coastal towns having emerged as vacation havens and older cities searching for a place in the economy."[13] In 1993, over half of the new jobs in the United States were created in the South; "At the end of the twentieth century, Dixie has twenty-one of the fifty largest ports [in the nation], and thirteen of the top twenty"; and during the period between 1993 and 1995, for example, the city of Atlanta added more jobs that any other city in the country.[14] In states such as North Carolina, Georgia, and Tennessee, "Economic growth in the new settlement areas created jobs for an additional 410,000 Hispanic workers and 1.9 million non-Hispanic workers in the 1990s."[15] According to *The State of the South 1998*, "Much of the capital invested from abroad, as well as new domestic capital investment, has gone into enterprises that are different from the South's traditional industries and that require a more skilled workforce."[16]

More recent installments of *The State of the South* have also recognized the pressure endured by many of the region's tax systems as one of the principal causes of the 2001–2002 economic crisis: "income tax collections plummeted as a result of both job losses and the drying up of capital gains; sales taxes took a hit from the drop in tourism; and corporate tax revenue dropped with the decline in profits."[17] Other sources and consequences of the recent crisis of the Southern economy include lost manufacturing jobs that "accounted for 21 percent of the nation's total," "globalization and technology [that] have become a tidal wave drowning white communities," and the "extended mass layoffs" in 2001 that resulted in the loss of over 375,000 jobs and plunged the region "into a trough of economic stagnation and widening income gaps."[18] The South today is still recovering from these changes and is, in effect, "the land of the working poor and the working near-poor," as "poverty remains a characteristic blot upon the face of the South."[19]

After the passing of a few years, it is evident that this "recent economic slowdown" has produced a variety of outcomes for the future of the Southern economy, as the crisis "has hastened the crumbling of the old small-farm and light-manufacturing economy, which anchored so many Southern towns and families. In addition, the plummeting of the telecommunications sector hit hard at some metropolitan areas that had, wisely, diversified."[20] The Southern economy has been gradually recovering from the 2001–2002 crisis and fashioning itself according to the requirements of an increasingly changing marketplace that includes multilingual populations and businesses. As Alfred Eckes notes, "The American South has become more diverse, more prosperous, and more like the larger American nation—vulnerable to the changing winds and fashions of the global marketplace."[21] A number of major corporations are still choosing to locate or relocate in the South, "bringing with them alternative ways of seeing and being in the world."[22] Some of these overseas corporations and their employees have expressed dissatisfaction at moving national jobs abroad. "With BMW moving into South Carolina for essentially the same [subsidy] reasons [granted to Mercedes Benz in Alabama], it is small wonder that some disgruntled German workers have taken to calling the South 'our Mexico.'"[23]

The globalization of the South has also had a negative impact on agricultural traditions, as "the same globalization and technological forces that have hammered manufacturing" have led to "a wrenching shift from family to corporate-style farming."[24] These economic consequences are intrinsically linked to a series of other factors that continue today to hold the region back from advancing, including "undereducated youth, chronic poverty, lingering health disparities, and civic frictions along the lines of class and ethnicity."[25] Between 1994 and 2000, for example, North Carolina "accounted for nearly 40 percent of textile job losses nationwide and lost more jobs in textiles and apparels combined than any other state."[26] Accordingly, "These similar influences have increasingly 'metropolitanized' the south and transformed it into a growing demographic power. By comparison, in 1980 there were only 10 metro areas of more than a million people; today, there are a total of 22, and only four states—Arkansas, Kentucky, Mississippi, and West Virginia—have more nonmetro than metro residents."[27] In today's South, almost 75 percent of the population lives in metro areas.[28] Unfortunately, "Southern states still treat big cities almost as aberrations and have yet to comprehend the full extent to which their economies depend on metro engines."[29]

Many places throughout both the rural and urban South are experiencing a renewed growth and vigor due to the influx of jobs for Latino immigrants. In areas such as Gainesville, Georgia, Silver City, North Carolina, and Jackson, Mississippi, for example, the poultry industry has brought employment and resources to communities that were in dire need of economic revitalization, providing work for members of the Latino population and attracting even newer waves of immigration to their communities. Yet this rebirth in economic activity and the role that Latinos are playing has proven challenging to the South, as "this formerly isolated region struggles with its unaccustomed role of serving as an employment magnet for immigrants speaking another language and arising from another culture."[30] In Silver City, North Carolina, alone, more than 50 percent of the kindergarten students and 40 percent of the student body in Silver City Elementary in 1999 were of Hispanic origin,[31] in a town of approximately 1,140 people. As Paul Cuadros has written, "If companies cannot move plants abroad to take advantage of cheap labor, they'll help bring the labor to them. A new South is rising indeed, but it is being built with Latino hands. It is the beginning of *el Nuevo Sur*."[32] By witnessing and suffering the burst of the 1990s economic bubble, the traditional populations of South are sharing in the difficulties of those more recent immigrants to the region who are struggling to succeed in the region and have common ground with others who live at the margins of society:

> For a period of time in the 1990s, the economy expanded so vigorously [in the South] that it raised the incomes of some of the poor, as well as the affluent. But many people who began the decade at risk ended the decade at risk. The at-risk included female-headed, single-parent families; men

who drop out of school without skills for anything but muscle work; aging factory workers whose plants have closed or downsized; and especially place-bound people with limited skills.[33]

On average, economic difficulties also appear to be affecting Latinos who live in the South more than those residing in other regions. In Arkansas, Alabama, Georgia, North Carolina, South Carolina, and Tennessee, for example, "65 percent of Latinos are renters compared with 52 percent of Latinos nationwide and 21 percent of whites and 44 percent of blacks."[34] The difficulty is that both individuals and regions appear to be caught in a cycle of poverty that has its roots in historical circumstances that somehow survive up to the present: for decades, low-income families have been concentrated in Central Appalachia, the Delta counties of Mississippi, Arkansas, and Louisiana, the Black Belt (Virginia, North Carolina, South Carolina, Georgia, Alabama, and Mississippi), and the Rio Grande Valley of Texas.[35] According to statistics that show that "The poverty rate among Latinos in the six Southern new settlement states [Arkansas, Alabama, Georgia, North Carolina, South Carolina, Tennessee] jumped from 19.7 percent to 25.5 percent between 1990 and 2000—a 30 percent increase compared with a 4 percent drop for Latinos nationwide,"[36] a number of Latino workers are fitting into the cycle of poverty that appears to be endemic in the South.

To this end, recent research suggests that in order to become financially more stable and continue to adapt to the arriving populations of Latino immigrants, the South must develop philanthropical resources from within and stop depending almost entirely on external funding for community ventures that may lie outside the purview of state or local agencies. "What the South needs is more foundations with statewide and regional reach because it needs more statewide and regional approaches to competitiveness and equity issues."[37] This more recent approach to regional success must concentrate on four fields of investment: "K-16 education; Economic development and Labor force preparation; Income enhancement and poverty reduction; and Public health and disease prevention."[38] By providing private financing that addresses the most pressing problems and is grounded in consistent and growing regional and local foundations and contributions, the South may be ahead of future population trends and gradually move toward providing a more dignified life for all of its inhabitants. As the 2007 MDC report declared, "For the better part of a century, philanthropy has served as a powerful force in the life of the South. Now the region has arrived at a moment in its history that calls for homegrown philanthropy to be a strategic tool for building the South of the future."[39]

In the countryside and in the cities, Southern advancement is directly related to demographic growth and to the general education level of a community. Generally, "Over the past 25 years, the South has outpaced the nation in population growth—40 percent growth for the South, 30 percent for the nation."[40] Yet this growth has not been evident in all areas of the region, where some places have actually lost population. This loss in a number of urban areas and the low education level attained by its residents have been a consistent negative factor in the development of these cities, as "the South's lowest-growing metros tend to have a lower percentage of the population with college degrees: New Orleans, 22.6 percent; Louisville, 22.2 percent; and Birmingham, 24.7 percent."[41] For these and other conditions to change, "the South requires leadership at two levels: at the grassroots to assure that all people have an effective voice locally and at the elective level so that governing bodies respond creatively to the complex issues arising from the consequences of the new economy."[42]

As Hurricane Katrina devastated the New Orleans-Mobile area in 2005 and left hundreds of thousands of people homeless and without work, it is no wonder that the disaster also left its impact on the approximately 300,000 Latin Americans who lived in the region, including the "up to 140,000 [estimated] Hondurans and their descendants [who] lived in and around New Orleans alone."[43] To aid in the post-Katrina recovery effort, a number of national organizations as well foreign agencies and businesses contributed resources that facilitated the economic recovery of the Hispanic residents. The airline company Aeromexico, for example, announced that "it would provide complimentary travel to Mexicans from Louisiana, Mississippi, Alabama, and Florida affected by Katrina."[44] And the Central American Bank for Economic Integration offered to provide assistance to Central Americans. Even the U.S. Federal Government "allowed special waivers of immigration law, which made it easier for employers to hire illegal immigrants,"[45] and directly contributed to the successful rebuilding of Gulf coast communities.

In the aftermath of Hurricane Katrina, there also arose a number of problems for Hispanic residents of the affected Gulf coast area during the immediate recovery period, chief among them being the discrimination against residents and workers. As María Elena Salinas reported, for example, "When it came time to provide shelter and housing, many Latino legal residents reported that they were turned away under the assumption that they were undocumented immigrants, while those who actually were undocumented were started on deportation proceedings."[46] In researching the impact of hurricane Katrina on the Latino population in a report entitled "In the Eye of the Storm: How the Government and Private Response to Hurricane Katrina Failed Latinos," Brenda Muñiz of the National Council of La Raza (NCLR) wrote that the Federal Emergency Management Agency (FEMA) "neglected to provide temporary emergency housing or shelter to Latinos it mistakenly presumed were undocumented."[47] The discrimination suffered by many Latinos during the recovery efforts was often justified by authorities in light of the tense situation, yet in a majority of reports it appears that both Blacks and Hispanics were the victims of prejudices expressed by private individuals and persons acting on behalf of federal, state, or local organizations.

Another troubling issue that became one of the principal stories in the aftermath of hurricane Katrina was the ineffectiveness of government agencies to deal efficiently with the massive problems faced by survivors and refugees of the storm. With respect to the Latino population, these unsuccessful efforts were frequently a simple and tragic extension of the region's inability to manage and assess the changes that increased numbers of Latinos were bringing to cities such as New Orleans and Mobile. As Muñiz wrote, "What transpired in the aftermath of Hurricane Katrina underscores in many ways the failure of public and private disaster relief institutions to respond adequately to rapid demographic changes."[48] As has also been studied in a number of analyses, a number of nongovernmental organizations such as the American Red Cross (ARC) frequently failed in their attempt to provide timely and adequate relief to the hundreds of thousands of people affected by hurricane Katrina. In the case of the ARC and their work with Latinos in the aftermath of Katrina, Muñiz clearly describes the principal problems with an organization whose staff was then 5 percent Black, 2 percent Asian, and 2 percent Hispanic:

> Due to its rigidity, both in structure and attitude, ARC failed to recognize some of the critical needs of the communities they were serving, which stemmed from both a lack of diversity within ARC's staff, board, and volunteer corps and a lack of knowledge and experience with diverse communities, resulting in several of the organization's mistakes during the response phase. These missteps included volunteers evicting hurricane victims on the presumption that they were workers and not actual survivors; preventing bilingual professionals from directly assisting

Spanish-dominant survivors; and requesting documentation proving legal status as a condition for receiving assistance.[49]

While the ARC aided thousands of individuals in the affected areas of the Gulf coast, the "rigidity" mentioned by Muñiz also prevented the organization from effectively being inclusive in the relief that they offered individuals and passively promoted the racialization of the recovery process.

As the reconstruction began in New Orleans, Mobile, and other Gulf communities that suffered the brunt of Hurricane Katrina, the manual laborers that were brought in to rebuild these areas were principally Hispanic. In New Orleans, for example, "almost half the reconstruction workforce" was Hispanic, with undocumented immigrants accounting for approximately half of the workers.[50] In the opinion of some, however, these manual laborers were basically unskilled workers, and their work demonstrated that "employing Latinos [was] one of the biggest reasons that the recovery effort has been such a failure. Inefficiencies due to the language barrier and shoddy workmanship due to unskilled labor [caused an] inordinate amount of delays and rework."[51] The actual reasons why many of the workers that were contracted for the rebuilding of the Gulf Coast were Latinos have their origins in the Federal Government: "The demand for these workers was generated by an emergency response hierarchy that has the federal government at the top. The Federal Emergency Management Agency handed out billions of dollars in contracts to many large and some medium-sized companies. These companies hired dozens of subcontractors. Some of the subcontractors have hired labor brokers in other states who are bringing in thousands of workers to the region."[52] While there are no studies or data supporting the allegations of "shoddy workmanship" of Spanish-speaking laborers who participated in the reconstruction following Hurricane Katrina, the economic reality was that Latino workers were contracted and brought into the Gulf area principally by U.S. companies who looked to take advantage of the reconstruction boom (not unlike what occurred in other areas of the nation that suffered from a catastrophic event such as a hurricane). In the end, it appeared that many of the Latino laborers could also count themselves among the discriminated victims of Katrina, as "Hundreds of workers hired for the cleanup of the affected areas complained that they had not been paid what was promised to them— [and] some weren't paid at all," and "Worker accounts of employer mistreatment, including both verbal and physical, along with threats to call U.S. Immigration and Customs Enforcement (ICE) and have workers deported if they complained, [were] also common."[53]

In writing her report for the NCLR, Muñiz also used the promise of and preparation for future catastrophes as a reference point and offered a list of recommendations to individuals and agencies that will be involved in the recovery efforts and will have to manage language barriers and other potential impediments to effective emergency management. If the ARC, for example, "is to improve its relationships with and better serve diverse communities," it should introduce a number of changes to its organization, including: "Create authority to minimize bureaucracy," "Diversify executive staff and Board of Directors," and "Foster key relationships with local and national organizations."[54] In light of the state and federal bureaucratic failures with regard to the appropriate distribution of aid and to responding to the needs of the Latino population, Muñiz also proposed that Congress and the Federal Government "Improve access to language assistance and materials for limited-English-proficient (LEP) victims of a disaster," "Extend legal status for immigrants who lose a family member or employer or their sponsor as a result of disaster," and "Improve immigrant access to benefits," among other suggestions.[55] As the Latino population in the United States continues to grow in the coming years, so too will their presence at all levels of society increase and subtly reflect both the shortcomings and advantages of a community. The United States has historically made it a habit to implement policies that ensure cities, counties, and states across the country are well prepared for any unforeseen catastrophic and potentially dangerous event, whether it is a fire in a grade school or a terrorist attack at a professional sports match. That local, state, and federal agencies as well as nongovernmental organizations seek community leaders and work toward including all the residents of a community in their preparation and recovery strategies from a disaster remains a challenge at practically all levels of government.

How are Latinos contributing to this need for community leadership in the U.S. South, specifically in light of Hurricane Katrina and the very real possibility of other natural or provoked catastrophic events? Are Latinos leading the push to find solutions and break the cycle of poverty in the region, or are they simply diversifying it and fitting into it? The answers may be complex, as they depend upon region (urban, rural, or metropolitan), social and economic class, and personal circumstances. What is clearer is the fact that Latinos are making a certifiable impact on their

community and on the South, whether it be by the pressure to produce a
State Driver's Education handbook and exam in Spanish, by the fact that
school districts are having to reexamine their policies and standards, or
by the creation of a Hispanic Chamber of Commerce in the area. Latinos
have subtly and stealthily placed the South in the unenviable position of
being a point of reference for Latinos in other parts of the United States
and abroad.

One example of the economic impression that Latinos are making on a
region is in the state of Georgia, where, as Doug Bachtel affirms, their
presence is felt throughout the state in practically every field. Interviewed
by Stephen Gurr for an article that appeared November 21, 1999, in the
Athens Daily News/Athens Banner-Herald, Bachtel declared that Latinos in
the state "live in south Georgia counties where row crop-harvesting jobs
abound; they live in north Georgia to work in the carpet mills; they are
drawn to the poultry industry in northeast Georgia; and they live in metropolitan areas to work jobs in landscaping, construction and restaurant
service." Similarly, in Louisiana "foreign workers are coming to the
employer, no matter how remote or nontraditional the destination may
seem."[56] The examples of Fruit County and Tobacco County, Georgia,
two areas south of Macon, illustrate how the reception that Latino immigrants have had in the state differs from the reception received by other
immigrant groups in the past and how their continued presence is now
dependent upon factors that differentiate the consequences of social integration from the impact of economic assimilation: "The hospitality
[toward the new immigrants in those two counties] probably stems from
economic self-interest rather than from the traditional values of the presumably gracious old South, and so the situation could change if economic
conditions worsen."[57] The growth rate figures for some of metro Atlanta's
counties help tell part of the story for Georgia. According to information
available on the Web site of the Georgia Hispanic Chamber of Commerce,
in Atlanta, nine of the city's top 25 minority-owned companies "are
owned by Hispanics"; and from 1990 to 2000, the Hispanic population in
Cherokee County grew by 517 percent; in Clayton County by 333 percent;
in Cobb County by 354 percent; in Dekalb County by 236 percent; in
Fulton County by 242 percent; and in Gwinnett County by 584 percent.[58]
As is to be expected, the Atlanta community has had to work to catch up
with the needs of this population, as the city's metropolitan services and
agencies were not prepared for such an influx.

Another part of the story is told by the fact that, as David McNaughton
noted in an *Atlanta Journal-Constitution* article published July 2, 2000, in

1999 a number of Atlanta-based companies employed Latinos at a rate well above the national average of 9.1 percent of Latinos that comprising the labor force, among them UPS (10.2 percent), Coca Cola (15 percent), and AFC Enterprises (20.6 percent). Although the growing presence of Latinos within these corporations reveals the impact that the individuals have had on their community, one of the concerns with these figures is that they reflect the total percentage of Latinos employed by the company without specifying whether there are a proportional number of them occupying management positions. Sadly, further research indicates that, as McNaughton reported, of the Atlanta-based companies, only BellSouth had a higher percentage of Hispanics who were members of management than total percentage of Hispanics employed (5 percent of management versus 4 percent of total employed). And only UPS came relatively close to their percentage of Hispanics employed (10.2 percent), with 7.3 percent of their management positions in the company being held by Hispanics. Unfortunately, none of these come close to the national average of 17 percent of Latinos employed across the country in a management, professional, or "related occupation."

Businesses in the Atlanta area that cater primarily to the Latino population have also vastly increased over the last five years. In an article written by Mark Bixler and published November 23, 1999, in the *Atlanta Journal-Constitution*, Samuel Zamarrón Jr.—owner and program manager for WAOS in Austell, WXEM in Buford, and WLBA in Gainesville, three Spanish language am-radio stations covering Atlanta and parts of other metro counties—stated that after he opened his first station in 1988, several companies declined to advertise with him. Now, his stations air ads for companies such as Sears, Budweiser, Western Union, American Airlines, and Wal-Mart. There currently exist in Georgia thirteen radio stations, and the first state daily newspaper in Spanish, *La Opinión de Georgia* In the Atlanta area alone there are or have been published up to a total of 21 periodicals or papers whose reading public is the Hispanic community in the city: *Comercio Newsletter, El Informador, El Norte de Atlanta, El Tiempo, El Volante, Estadio, Generación H, La Voz del Pueblo, México Lindo, Mundo Hispánico, Nuestro Semanario, Punto Hispánico, Textiles Panamericanos,* and *La Visión de Georgia.* Also, as the Georgia Hispanic Chamber of Commerce states on its Web site,there are "six radio shows and stations that are focused on serving the Hispanic population of Georgia." It would appear that the non-Latino as well as the Latino population in Atlanta and other cities across the South is investing directly in its own community, making information readily available, and setting down deep roots in areas where the economic presence of Hispanic immigrants is needed, noted, and valued.

Another area of Georgia that has undergone transformations due to the arrival of Latino populations has been Dalton, Georgia. Located in the northwest corner of the state—just across from Chattanooga, Tennessee—and originally named Cross Plains, Dalton's population of approximately 28,000 people has traditionally been linked to the textiles industry, specifically carpeting and floor covering, since, as the Golden Ink Web site states, "almost 90 percent of the functional carpet produced world-wide is made within a 25-mile radius of this north Georgia city." Today the city is also recognized as one of the centers of Latino populations in the South, as over 40 percent of the population is Hispanic. Due to the rapid growth of the tufted carpet industry, the residents of Dalton and Whitfield County were not numerous enough to "fit all of the industry's labor needs."[59] During the 1970s, the budding chicken-processing business in the northern part of the state began to attract Mexican workers, and many went to work specifically in Dalton's sizeable chicken-processing plant.[60]

In an effort to create new services and dovetail existing ones with the arriving immigrants, the Georgia Project was created in 1997 through a joint effort of business and community leaders in Dalton and Monterrey, Mexico. The four components of the plan included "placement of bilingual instructors from Monterrey in Dalton's schools; an intensive month-long summer institute for Dalton schoolteachers hosted by the Universidad de Monterrey; bilingual curriculum development; and the creation of an organization to promote leadership and involvement in Dalton's Hispanic community."[61] Over the course of the last ten years, "Dalton's carpet manufacturers have welcomed increasing numbers of immigrants" because of a difficult labor market and due to the fact that "Employers often perceive immigrants to be hardworking and loyal, willing to work for lower wages, and less likely to complain about working conditions than native-born workers."[62] The arrival of immigrant workers has impacted the community notably: two of the city's six elementary schools "reached more than 70 percent Hispanic enrollment by 1998";[63] the city established a task force that operated as an extension of the now-defunct INS, "staffed by local enforcement officers" and visited by immigration officials at least three times a week;[64] and the community now has two Spanish-language newspapers—*La Luz* and *El Informador de Dalton*—one Spanish-language radio station, and Spanish-language services at three churches. Although it is limited to a small, Southern city across the border from Tennessee, the cultural growth of

Dalton and how its residents have accommodated the new populations may portend the future of both small and large multiethnic communities across the United States. As James D. Engstrom has noted, "A multicultural Dalton may open up the possibility that multiple voices, and not just those of the carpet industry, can speak and that a more inclusive and democratic local political dialogue can emerge."[65]

The city of Nashville, Tennessee, has been transformed by the arrival of Latino immigrants and has had its share of civil unrest, especially during the late 1950s and 1960s as desegregation laws began to be implemented. Famously associated with country music and Vanderbilt University, its downtown avenues, restaurants, and stores are one part home to its past and present, another part sheer economic willpower. Boot-scootin' bars abound, and not an evening passes when somewhere someone is not trying to break into the city's music scene and become the next Nashville Miracle. But perhaps the next musical success story in this city will come not from a traditional or a cross-over country performer, but from a salsa or merengue band that manages to tap into the city's 100,000-plus Latino population and, ultimately, the national market. On the surface, Nashville is typical of some large Southern cities, as it has tried to remake itself by attracting companies such as BellSouth without completely losing its historical identity (something that Atlanta and Charlotte, for example, have not managed to do). But beneath the surface lies an intricate web of neighborhoods that—better than demographics and sheets of statistics—reflect how the presence of Latinos in the city has grown over the last ten years.

Traveling in 2000 to Nashville for the first time, I was struck by the naïve thought that the city is not one but many: its downtown is as different from the West End as the Belle Meade area is from Capitol Hill. Its shared history involving the Civil War, the presence of racial unrest in the late 1950s—including the bombing of the Hattie Cotton School in September of 1957—and the explosion of country music onto the national stage have created the illusion of a Nashville in tune with its past, present, and future. Now this apparent and unquestioned harmony is being taken to task by a Latino population that is gradually transforming the capital of Tennessee, which is witnessing the emergence of community centers such as Alianza Latina, Hispanic Catholic Community, Hispanic Family Resource Center, Hispanic Ministry, Spanish Outreach Services, Servicio Latino, and the Woodbine Community Organization, among others. Not unlike Atlanta, for example, where the Hispanic community has begun to establish businesses targeted at the Spanish speakers in the metropolitan area, there are two Spanish-language radio stations, two Spanish-language newspapers, a Hispanic Apostolate, and not one but three Hispanic Chambers of Commerce (the Nashville Area Hispanic Chamber of Commerce, the Tennessee Hispanic Chamber of Commerce, and Viva Nashville, all three located on Nolensville Pike, at 4050 and two at 4059, respectively). As I drove down Nolensville Pike—one of the neighborhoods in the city with a sizeable Latino population—I realized that, except for the orderly traffic, it could be Managua, Panama City, or Mexico City. There are blocks of store fronts with names and slogans in Spanish, advertising "La Ilusión" bridal shop, "Boriquén" music store, "Centro Botánico Azteca," "Joyería Diana," "Taquería La Hacienda," and "Discoteca México"—with, truth be told, the occasional pawn shop and White Castle thrown in for color.

The Hispanic Community center is located at 2608 Nolensville Pike, and it offers the Latin American immigrant a variety of services, including assistance with immigration paperwork, wiring money, faxes, photocopies, and—my favorite—"tikes de policía": parking or speeding fines. At the center I met Jesús, a young man who had moved away from San Diego and Los Angeles because of problems and conflicts within the Latino community there. Now in Nashville, he admitted he liked the peacefulness and the area's forests and lakes. Why not? The center was unintimidating: it sat off the main road, integrated into a neighborhood of apparently middle class homes. The entrance was spotless, and there were no people sitting idly by. Later, I realized that the Latino businesses and residences along Nolensville Pike balanced the extremes: it was not a Latino ghetto, nor had Latinos been completely acculturated. In this area of the city, the presence of the American entrepreneurial spirit coexisted alongside the varieties of Latin American culture and formed combinations not unseen in other parts of the country but unique to the urban South.

On the Vanderbilt University campus I met Norma Antillón and Pablo Garzón at the offices of International Programs and accompanied them on a visit to Murfreesboro Road and Patricia Drive, areas in Nashville where Latinos are concentrated. The sights they offered were unexpected after being led through the mansion-filled avenues, manicured lawns, and curved driveways of Belle Meade. The neighborhoods in the Murfreesboro Road area were primarily African American and Latino, sharing their streets with a low-end Mercedes Benz dealership, "Gun City USA," and "Ya Mamás Café" in the middle of it all (if the United States is not stereotypically represented by cars, guns, and home cooking, then we need to look at this country again). We drove through the Executive House Apartments, up on the hill, and we seemed to enter an exclusive albeit marginal community, as mostly male Latinos sat on porches and on the beds of pickup trucks, that eternal Southern symbol. Norma offered her opinion that apartment owners take advantage of Latinos, charging them $410 for a one bedroom apartment and $620 for a two bedroom apartment—but she told me that up to ten men live in some of the residences. (These figures take on additional importance when we realize that they are from over seven years ago.) Gangs are also a problem in the area, as groups of Latino youths have organized themselves according to their national background and announce themselves first and foremost as Mexicans, Salvadorans, or Hondurans. There were Latinos standing and talking at street corners, waiting to use the public telephones, and, as we left, I was struck by the sound of Norma locking her car door and Pablo, at the wheel, locking mine.

It appeared that the Hispanic community was omnipresent here, but upon returning to the Vanderbilt campus and the West End, there appeared to be almost no Latino presence there. Nor near the Union Station hotel. Nor downtown, waiting to see the Grand Old Opry or dancing bar side to the Dixie Chicks. Is Anglo society subtly ghettoizing other races and ethnic groups as they increase in number? Are other races and ethnicities choosing to live alongside instead of within Anglo society? And does economics supersede language and become the ultimate determining factor of the level or extent of their assimilation? Along Nolensville Pike, the businesses have sprung up in order to both satisfy and create the demand for their services. Along the way, they are changing both the makeup of the Nashville metropolitan area and the manner in which the Latino community is assimilating the forces of late capitalism and translating these to a language accessible to both populations. In trying to rent an Argentine movie, for example, the clerk requested that my wife or I present a Tennessee driver's license or "a *bill* del cable o de la electricidad" ("a cable or power bill"), presumably to prove local residence. A travel agency advertised "*tiques* a Colombia" ("[airline] tickets to Colombia"). Spanglish linguistic implications aside—for the moment— Latinos are creating the perfect commodity: an economic language that combines both English and Spanish and that straddles the economic division between those who have—monolingual speakers of English— and those who have not—monolingual speakers of Spanish.

On the outskirts of Nashville, Opryland is more than a hotel: it is an autonomous hub, an enormous self-enclosed community with various thematic interiors—cascades, riverboats, and tropical plants—a brook running through it, clothing stores and cafés, a world-within-a-world that, as the Opryland Web site announces, advertises how "Under majestic, climate-controlled glass atriums, you'll be surrounded by nine acres of lush indoor gardens, winding rivers and pathways, and sparkling waterfalls where you can unwind, explore, shop, dine, and be entertained to your heart's content." The tile floors shine to a reflective fault, the plants are green and very much alive, and the employees are bustling about, assisting the attendees of any number of conferences. Nearby rests the Opry Mills, which, according to its Web page, offers "a bargain shopper's paradise, with more than 200 manufacturer outlets, off-price retailers and unique specialty stores." Aside from the sheer size of the hotel and mall, one of the features that make Opryland unique is that in 1995 its human resources department decided to travel to Puerto Rico and recruit potential employees. When I read this, I remember asking myself "Why?" Why not recruit from the Nashville area?

As past employment manager for Opryland Hotel, Kathi Ferguson witnessed the arrival of dozens of Latino workers to the entertainment complex. In her thirties, with short, curly reddish-blond hair, Kathi answered my questions regarding the recruitment of Latinos and referred a few times to "Southern tradition" and "Spanish people." She struck me as someone who has become successful and is advancing steadily up her career ladder. When I asked her about the reasons behind the company's trip to Puerto Rico, she stated that in 1994 Opryland was approached the Human Resources Director at Amelia Island, who invited them to take part in the recruitment. Three months after the initial trip in January 1995, the Opryland people returned to Puerto Rico. By 1996, word of mouth had gotten around the island, and from 1995 to 1997 a total of four recruiting trips were made to the Commonwealth. For those who were laid off of jobs at the island, the Puerto Rican government bought their airplane ticket to Nashville as well as their shoes and coats.

During our conversation, the issue that emerged as the principal factor in Opryland's decision to recruit in Puerto Rico was that the hotel could not attract "good employees" in the Nashville area due to competition from other industries. Soon after they began arriving, paradoxically, Opryland began to receive negative press, as native and resident Tennesseans asked why they were bringing in a bunch of "Mexicans." What type of workers were (un)available in the area that would make the company travel to a United States Commonwealth to recruit and contract the residents? Was the trip in itself a subtle comment on the work ethic—or lack thereof—in Nashville, in Tennessee, in the United States today? Do Latinos work better because they work principally to send money home and/or to support a large household, or are these simple stereotypes that are defying statistical analyses of the phenomena? Unfortunately, there are stereotypes at work in the locals referring to the arriving Puerto Ricans as "Mexicans," in the reality that many principal assumptions function almost exclusively on generalizations and stereotypes, in the notion that Anglo Americans work principally to accumulate material gain and in the concept that Latinos work in order to support the cumbersome families that they have. While some of these notions may be true for specific individuals, the opposite may also certainly be the case: that there are Anglos who are struggling to raise a large family under today's circumstances, and that Latinos are also working to buy a better automobile, another television, DVD, CD player, iPod, or laptop computer.

The same local ignorance regarding the variety and diversity of the Latino community may also offer the advantage that, when compared to areas such as Los Angeles, Houston, New York, or Miami, in the U.S. South an immigrant is perhaps forced to better navigate the Anglo community due to the absence of a preexisting infrastructure of social and economic support for Latinos. At the Woodbine Community Organization Center in Nashville, Maggie Sapier, Roberto Melara, Terry Horgan, Monica Whitaker, and Pete Téllez spoke at length one afternoon about some of the advantages of living in the Nashville area. In Roberto's opinion, Nashville is "the perfect place. In Los Angeles you learn a lot, but life is faster-paced."

In other areas where Latinos are arriving at an unexpectedly rapid pace, one of the principal concerns is language, primarily the incentive for the immigrant population to learn and use English. In Terry's opinion, "there are two things going on: one is frequently talking about the melting pot, but we are expecting the foreigner to melt into our culture."[66] The incentives that a community provides for Latinos must somehow bridge the gap between their professional life (i.e., their economic motivation and incentive for being here) and their personal life. Throughout the conversation at the Woodbine Center, I had the sense that these individuals were genuinely committed to the advancement of the Latino community in Nashville, a community, according to Roberto, whose future depends on cohesion: "We try to make [Hispanics] see that the only way we will succeed is to be one race."[67] While the goals are logical, the reality is that creating a racial identity within the multicultural reality of Spanish-speaking immigrants will be very difficult, as what constituted "differences" back in their homeland will most likely contribute to their inclusion or exclusion from one group or another. Soccer, for example, may be a catalyst for social cohesion and collaboration, as one can participate in much the same way as back home, playing the position they preferred and training as often as they can; but the organization of the sport into leagues of individual teams may also lead to divisions within Latino communities, as teams are frequently based on regional Latin American alliances or on nationalities. As always, the inclusion within a specific group implies the often automatic exclusion from another, as choices are made and priorities established. It is ideal that Latinos strive to be "one race"—if such a thing exists—but perhaps what is most important is not that the end is achieved but that the consequences are sought.

After the interviews at the Woodbine Community Organization Center, Maggie, Robert, Terry, Monica, and Pete offered me the names of possible contacts in Nashville and Memphis and, as we said goodbye at 6.30 p.m., they stayed inside to continue working. Standing there, off of Nolensville Pike amongst modest ranch homes and in the light of a summer sun, I realized that the Center embodied the future of Latinos in Nashville and possibly within the South. Located within the Latino community, the members of the organization that I spoke with represented that link between the newly arrived immigrants and the long-term residents, between Nashville's needs and the Latino community's abilities, between the inflamed rhetoric of cultural separation and the economic reality of integration, consistently emphasizing the need to understand and to educate oneself, starting with the English language. The transition from a culturally homogeneous city to a multilayered web of communities has probably not been easy, but with the assistance of voices that emerge form the Asian, Anglo, and African American communities—among others—Latinos are unearthing their own voice in the Southern United States and contributing to the ongoing dialogue on the future of the area, engaging those outside their circle on a number of different issues. Nashville is growing, but my impression was that it is not so certain what to do with itself. It does not lay claim to the crystal cobwebs found in Charleston, South Carolina, nor does it have the blind economic drive of Atlanta, Georgia, either. In effect, this may ultimately be its best hope for the future: welcoming new populations by balancing the twin mountains of tradition and economic need.

Unlike Nashville, Jackson, Mississippi, seems a state capital forgotten by all except its inhabitants (and even they abandon downtown after 5 p.m.). While there appears to be a Latino presence in the area, it—like so many things in Jackson—surfaces only after an intense journey through and into the city. What primarily interested me in the area was located some 30 minutes east of the city: the BC Rodgers Poultry plant in Morton and surrounding Scott County, a business whose workforce consisted primarily of Latinos. These individuals have chosen to work in a section of the country where one can lose oneself easily among the rolling hills and summer heat, where opportunity seems to have hidden itself from even the most diligent, and the settled dust has given everything a look of immutability, of immovability. Arriving in the town, you sense that you have entered a small community that has developed too fast, even for a place such as Morton, where growth runs along the railroad line. Off the main road in town and right on the tracks are the offices of BC Rogers, where I met some of its employees, including Luis Cartagena, the Out of State Employment Supervisor. Chilean by birth, Luis came to Morton after being labeled an undesirable by the Pinochet government for his activities with cultural workshops in the capital. He studied history at the University of Chile but was unable to finish his thesis due to political problems in the country at the time.

When he arrived in 1990, the town "did not have more than 30 Hispanics, [and] today there are more than 3,000," in a community that numbers approximately 3,400 total inhabitants (of whom some 600 are Latinos employed by BC Rodgers, with 450 of them being documented residents). The community has indeed grown in little more than decade, and the statistics may not illustrate the entire impact of the growth. According to the 1990 census, there were a total of 141 Hispanics out of a population of 24,137 (a statistically insignificant 0.58 percent); for the 2000 census, "official" Hispanics already numbered 1,660—5.8 percent of the population—out of a total county-wide count of 28,423 inhabitants. The difference in the growth rate between the two populations is enormous. While the county grew approximately 17.8 percent between 1990 and 2000, the Latino population during that same period grew over 1000 percent. These changes affected the most basic workings of the town. On Wednesdays, for example, the Morton newspaper publishes a page written by Luis in Spanish, offering advice and information on topics such as immigration and legal resources. He states that he "tries to shape the mentality of what it means to be a foreigner," as he "wants to help people to get adjusted."[68]

When Spanish-speaking immigrants first began arriving in the town, "the Hispanic presence was resisted in an open way, and still some are resisting. In general, the population is accepting us more. It seems that we are accepted much more than blacks." For Luis, the "population" is the Establishment: the white, Anglo Protestants who have historically held the economic and political reins of the town. Interestingly, the assumptions behind Luis's use of the term "population" may reflect the polarized view of Southern society as being black and/or white. Implicitly, he may also include others in that term—Latinos, for example—that have lived there a shorter time than most and may be sensing the change that comes to a community, as they themselves are the vehicles of those transformations and have seen their world infinitely altered by their decision to emigrate to the United States and seek better jobs.

Visiting Morton, it is undoubtable that the community has been affected by the arrival of Latin American workers to the BC Rodgers plant. According to Luis, this influx meant a set of specific consequences for Morton and its neighbor Forrest, as "it has meant notable economic growth because we Hispanics are good at eating all foods and enjoying ourselves. When we arrived, this town never had a traffic jam; and now you go out between three and five o'clock [in the afternoon], and to cross to the other side [of town] there is a problem."[69] With Morton's growth have come the daily inconveniences of an economic boom, but the community is prepared to adjust, along with the new residents. Morton may not have the cultural diversity of Chicago or Los Angeles, or the economic infrastructure of Houston or Atlanta, but Morton does offer opportunities. Its manageable size, warm atmosphere, and job prospects, among other factors, may make arriving in the United States a less chaotic and disconcerting experience for Latino immigrants. Perhaps therein lies the subtle priorities of the new generation of immigrants to the South: they are looking for economic opportunity in a welcoming place, period. Morton, like other small towns across the South, is serving as an ideal petri dish for the observation and study of the impact of Latinos in a small community, where relatively little has changed since it was founded, when the state was essentially a territory of the United States.

Back in Jackson, I visited Elsa Baughman at her house on the outskirts of the city, where she introduced me to Esperanza Velázquez, who arrived in this country in 1982 from Colombia. According to both Esperanza and Elsa, Jackson—a state capital over 20 times the size of Morton that has no Spanish-language newspaper and no Spanish-language radio station—is witnessing different divisions, those between and within the Latino populations. Elsa underlines the economic divisions implicit within Latino society in the city: "The Hispanic who is 'up' does not want the riffraff to come. They will say 'I belong to this race.' That is in our blood."[70]

Beneath the sentiments expressed by the older generation of Latin American immigrants lies the principle of motivation: Why did they come to the United States? For many of them, the fact that the new wave of Latin American immigrants comes primarily in search of economic stability is difficult to understand, as they were members of an upper class and originally arrived in this country in the 1950s and 1960s in search of greater economic liberties, political freedom, and cultural opportunities. Now, the newer generations of immigrants are taking advantage of the economic opportunities that the region offers and finding themselves at home in the South. As a Hispanic woman in Jackson remarked, "We come with the idea of walking an extra mile. I have begun to feel like a Southerner. I feel as if I shared, in a certain way, the life of the South and part of its history. [Mississippi] is a state that has been beaten up by history. And the Latin American countries have been beaten up by the North. The history of the South is fascinating to me. It is fascinating how a state is so rich, so prosperous, how an event like the Civil War left them unable to raise themselves up; and it is still the slowest state in the country."[71] It is inevitable that parallels such as this one become self-evident after spending over 20 years in the area; and what brings the two together is a shared history of marginalization. At the time I did not ask, but the answer begs the question: Who is included by the pronoun 'we'? Is it all Latinos, the older or the newer generations? This purportedly implicit understanding of the word "we" has often carried with it baggage that includes as well as it excludes. While there may be a sense of a common, unified Latino presence and heritage, the diverse demographic and cultural daily reality lived by Hispanics in a community may in fact be dividing the individuals more than any common language could possibly unite them. The economic advancement of new immigrants in an area may be conditioned by the established presence of common regional and national groups.

In Jackson, Elsa's work with the Catholic Archdiocese has allowed her to observe firsthand the number of self-proclaimed Latin American Catholic immigrants that are arriving in the area and how those immigrants are almost immediately finding themselves more comfortable within a Protestant or Evangelical church that, as she said, gives them clothing and picks them up for church on Wednesdays and Sundays. Eventually, even this change of religious allegiances within the Latino community in Jackson implies a value judgment that places some "above" and some "below." According to Elsa, "The majority of the ones that change [religion] do not have much culture,"[72] a statement that underlines the differences between distinct generations of Latin American immigrants. Being "cultured" in the past was expected, as the most basic economic needs were met and those individuals belonging to the middle and upper classes possessed both spending money and leisure time and could dispose of each as they wished. Today, an immigrant's principle concern is meeting the most basic needs, at times providing for an entire family whose priorities generally center around economic survival, not around furthering their academic education or learning the English language.

Founded in 1971, the Casa de Amigos Migrant Center in Fairhope, Alabama, was located on the grounds of an old Southern plantation, on the shores of Mobile Bay and across the water from the city, offering schooling to migrant children in the area. At the time, finding it involved crossing the bay bridge from Mobile and then turning right onto Highway 98, down canopied tree-lined streets that seem to hide the harsh reality of lives spent harvesting potatoes. Before it closed in 2006, the Casa de Amigos took care of the children of migrant laborers who worked in the fields, picking them up in the morning and dropping them off once their parents had returned from work in the afternoon. Rosa Cabrales worked there for ten years, since 1996, and Ted Henken spent his summers volunteering at the center. As more immigrants arrived in the area, the Casa de Amigos attempted to accommodate this growth through a broadening of their services. Unfortunately, as Ted noted at the time, they still had to go out where immigrants worked, find the families, and register them with the Center, taking care of approximately 70 children on a daily basis. While the parents were working, the youngest ones were in large school rooms divided according to age. There was a church on the backyard of the property, overshadowed by a colossal magnolia tree with Spanish moss hanging off its branches. The main office of the Center was a newer A-frame construction, but the largest residence on the property was the old house, surrounded by a wrap-around porch that overlooked the magnolia tree and Mobile Bay.

In our conversations, Ted and Rosa emphasized the difficulties that the families had faced upon migrating to the area and finding work in agriculture, and both of them admitted that it was these same difficulties that stirred them to help the Latino population. In the area, the community reflected their positive attitude, as the support from the Anglo population has been consistent and dependable: the individuals and the community there have been donating their time and money to Latino causes. Due to the influx of immigrants into the area, workers from the

Department of Health informed Ted that the employees would begin taking Spanish classes and that a number of state agencies had begun to translate government documents into Spanish. Given the difficulties faced by Latinos, Ted and Rosa were also keenly aware of the tensions that exist between Latinos and other populations, specifically how the work of the center may paradoxically marginalize some Anglo or African American families, as the services that Casa de Amigos offered were primarily intended for Latin American immigrants. As Ted mentioned, "we do not go looking for black immigrant families."[73] The funds that they received from the United Way were meant for the schooling of the children and were earmarked to help the Latino community in the Fairhope area. As often happens, the Casa de Amigos did not have the resources to clothe, house, feed, or find work for all those in need in the county.

At the Casa de Amigos, I had the opportunity to accompany Ted to the house of one of the immigrant families, visiting María and her five children at their home in the country. Renting the trailer from one of the local potato farmers, María is an original pioneer of the area. Her home was a slapped-together dwelling made of plywood and pressed board and scented throughout with the fragrance of processed lumber. Directly to the west was another yellow trailer, a hay barn open to the elements and, further west, a rickety house. Behind Maria's house were clotheslines, toys strewn about, and an old refrigerator standing by a tree. There were also two satellite dishes in the yard, the larger one notched at eye level in the crook of a smallish tree. It was a humble home, but not necessarily a poor one. Their lawn was cut, they had four older cars, and there were some rose bushes planted around the tree that cradled the satellite dish. Clothes hung in the summer breeze: two pairs of black canvas tennis shoes, a red t-shirt, a pink towel with holes in it, and a pair of black, oversized jeans. There were cows to the east, where there were two more trailers and a small satellite dish under the shade of a large pecan tree.

The entrance to Maria's house was cluttered with the head and footboard of a small bed, two more refrigerators, a bag of potatoes, an upside-down plastic bucket, and two small filing cabinets. Inside, the walls were covered with plywood paneling. There was an entertainment center with a Santo television, two lamps, a couch and two chairs, and a ceiling fan with dusty edges. A wire ran up one of the walls and onto the ceiling, stapled into the pressed wood. It was evident that children lived here. Even absent they were part of the family, of the land, of the community, and the strewn toys were like colorful bookmarks left between the pages of home.

I am certain that I have just described a scene lived each day by thousands of Latino and non-Latino families across the United States, each of them working for the right to have three old refrigerators in their yards. So what, if anything, makes this one special? Why did María and her family choose to settle in the Fairhope, Alabama, area instead of El Paso, Nagadoches, or Denver? Some stereotypically believe that Southern culture may be more welcoming and more appreciative of Latino traditions.

Economic opportunities and culinary commonalities notwithstanding, there just might exist some clearly discernible parallels between the varieties of Southern culture and the diverse Latino populations, parallels that push a Southern community to adapt itself to the new Latin American immigrants and that may tell more about a genuinely multicultural once and future United States than Los Angeles, Chicago, or New York, diverse as these may be. Maria's case may certainly not be unique, but it certainly serves as an example of why and how Latin Americans are arriving in the South and carving out their own particular patch of land and home. For cities such as Nashville, Atlanta, and Mobile, the new wave of Spanish-speaking immigrants has meant a transformation of the most basic services and has represented the birth of a host of economic opportunities for both the Latino and non-Latino communities. In this manner, the cultural transformation of the U.S. South is being partially funded by those who are quite literally the most Southern of Southerners on the American continent and who are bringing with them new and distinct ways of being American.

6

Politics

Caudillos and Good Ole Boys

In the U.S. South and Latin America, the land has acted as a stage for the countless politicians who looked to curry favor with the local population in order to wield power in the area. The drawback was that these efforts often resulted in unambiguous examples of blackmail and bribery, of unethical political maneuvers that transformed the local politician into a national personality projected well beyond the small borders of his own personal fiefdom. In the U.S. South and Latin American, individuals such as Georgia Governor Herman Talmadge, Louisiana Governor Huey Long, Alabama Governor George Wallace, Dominican President Rafael Trujillo, Nicaraguan President Anastasio Somoza, and Paraguayan leader Alfredo Stroessner, among many others, have epitomized the Southern good ole-boy politician: a man who traditionally belonged to an exclusively male organization, micromanaged his political moves, looked to influence every level of local politics, paradoxically displayed both economic greed and a strong sense of moral "right" and "wrong"—without necessarily attending to the differences—and managed an administration whose tentacles reached deep into the community. Even today, when political and economic transparency are requisites to domestic stability and transnational commerce, there are countless examples in the U.S. South and Latin America of what Shang-Jin Wei has termed "crony capitalism," "the misallocation of financial resources to the friends and relatives of government officials."[1] In Honduras, for example, the new law on "access to public information" resists the current global trend toward transparency and asserts that "all information about humanitarian aid is secret."[2]

Corrupt politicians are certainly not exclusive to a particular nation or region of the world, but the U.S. South's good ole-boy history and network of political personalities establishes something of a sinister tradition and a murky pattern of societal evolution. Individuals such as Talmadge and Wallace were strict advocates of states' rights, going as far as, in Wallace's case, defying the National Guard in order to defend Alabama's supposedly sovereign right to legislate its own laws, regardless of national laws and regulations. Their manipulation of state funds, of electoral processes, and of individual civil liberties made them wealthy men and furthered an ideological agenda that centered on a strong sense of anti-federalism that would ultimately find a receptive ear in the rest of the country. Using George Wallace as the epitome of the Southern politician whose ideas would resonate outside the South, Peter Applebome has declared that "it was Wallace, preaching the gospel of pissed-off-ness decades before its time, who first attracted a national following based on the idea that neither national party was worth a damn."[3]

At the time, one of the more polemical voices heard throughout the region and the nation was that of George Wallace, a man whose apparently "Southern" characteristics foreshadowed an appeal that would ultimately extend far beyond the borders of Dixie. When he ran for president in 1968, "Wallace, whose white common-man campaign style, populist economics, and social reaction appealed to the whites of the countryside and the working class districts in the cities, won a plurality of the votes cast by blue-collar whites."[4] In the opinion of Augustus B. Cochran, Wallace's national popularity and the preeminence of Southern concerns on the national stage were the beginnings of what came to be the Reagan Revolution. According to Cochran, "Wallace discovered, and did much to foster, the antigovernment sentiment in Middle America that fueled the Reagan Revolution of the 1980s and proved to be Reagan's most lasting legacy for the 1990s and beyond."[5] Even Barry Goldwater's 1964 presidential campaign reflected theoretically Southern issues and "set the stage" for Ronald Reagan, as Goldwater lost the nomination but won five Deep South states—Georgia, South Carolina, Alabama, Mississippi, and Louisiana—and subtly announced the entrance of the Conservative Right.[6] In his 1970 campaign for president, Richard Nixon "denounced forced busing, criticized welfare as subverting the work ethic [and] railed against [racial] quotas," themes that, in Cochran's opinion, reflected "Nixon's attempt to send an encoded message, especially but not exclusively aimed at Southern whites, that the Republican party had now replaced the Democrats as the defender of White interests."[7] This apparent appropriation of national politics by a number of Southern politicians was simply the exploitation of seemingly regional Southern issues by national figures who realized the depth of discontent present in the South and how this discontent could be tapped into and addressed at the national level. Southern concerns became explicit national concerns in the 1970s, ultimately announcing and anticipating, as Cochran indicates, the Reagan Revolution and the gradual future turning of the tide in national politics.

The national resonance of Southern politicians has occurred principally among the more centrist and conservative spectrum of the population of the United States. But instead of forcing the rest of the nation to look deeply into its own prejudices, many contemporary extreme-right Southern politicians have served as lightning rods for a country that was looking for ideological scapegoats. According to Cochran, "The rise of the South's influence in national politics has contributed to, but not caused, the evolving structural deformities that weaken our contemporary democracy."[8]

Throughout the political history of the U.S. South there have emerged a number of personalities whose legacy embodies the characteristics of good ole boy politics and who may very well be compared with certain Latin American despots of the nineteenth and twentieth centuries. In our analysis of Southern politicians, we will offer evidence as to how those Southerners compare to certain Latin American autocrats and share characteristics that, while reflecting a very specific context, transcend those circumstances and share political perspectives, tactics, and attitudes with their hemispheric neighbors and possible contemporaries. Men such as George Wallace, Huey Long, Herman Talmadge, Theodore Bilbo, and Lester Maddox, for example, managed to balance the populism inherent and necessary in much of Southern politics with an oppressive heavy-handedness that often bordered on turning their respective administrations into little more than rubber stamp lobbies for the wishes of their *light* or soft dictatorship. As we examine these individuals, we will focus on themes—and their respective treatments—that are also discernible in the administrations of their Latin American counterparts: the level and practice of rhetoric and demagoguery, the presence and proliferation of corruption and racism, and the ultimate representation of the politician as dictator. Our intention is not to offer exhaustive studies of each political leader—those are available elsewhere—but rather to underscore the negative commonalities present between a representative sample of Southern and Latin American politicians. As Raymond Swing wrote in 1935 regarding the South, "Given a land in which the great majority are in want or in fear of it, in which democracy has not produced wise leadership or competent organs to conduct public affairs, in which 'big interests' have far more than their share of power, the easiest sacrifice that society seems ready to make, if only its prejudices can be stirred, is of its democratic freedom."[9] These same qualities may be carefully yet distinctly extended to some of the repressive regimes in Latin America, particularly those that existed in the twentieth century whose thick, totalitarian grasp managed to constrict their society through the justification that eradicating Communism, participating in the global economy, and instituting economic reforms largely dictated by developed countries and their respective transnational organizations would improve the quality of life for all those under their administration.

Throughout what may be considered modern history, authoritarian or totalitarian politicians in the U.S. South and Latin America have learned to promote a populist agenda, to appeal to popular sentiment, and—at least initially—to express a desire to help "the masses." If a burning and timely issue existed, the politician would learn to leap on it almost immediately, magnify the most sensationalist features, and create an immediate sense of urgency in the minds of the people on the street (for example, the bygone need in the U.S. South to ameliorate the "influence" of blacks in everyday life if they received the right to vote or the "damage" suffered by the "national identity" due to the increased number of immigrants arriving in the United States today). If such a burning issue was not present, the politician and his staff would frequently fabricate one through manipulation of statistics or playing upon a private fear that was visible in the public sphere. Such attempts were occasionally perceived by a willing public as honest intentions meant to genuinely improve their quality of life.

One of the first ground-breaking studies of U.S. Southern politics was *Southern Politics in State and Nation* (1949) by V.O. Key, a volume that, despite its anachronisms, remains pertinent today. In his work, Key divides his study of Southern politics according to a number of factors, including differences between states, behavior of the Southern electorate, restrictions on voting, and variations between "national" and "southern" politics. Due perhaps to the historical context, the work itself is rather racially tinged, as many of his arguments rest on his assertion that, in the South, race is everything. Writing in the late 1940s, Key declared, "In its grand outlines the politics of the South revolves around the position of the Negro."[10] While the moment's racial tension was certainly reflected in the political, economic, and cultural relationship between African Americans and Whites, there is a danger in generalizing the characteristics of these populations and viewing the U.S. South in polarized terms that tend to include only these two populations at the expense of other races and ethnicities that have been historically present in the region.

Using "the position of the Negro" as his theoretical point of reference, Key underscores the roots of the region's troubles: "The South's heritage from crises of its past, its problem of adjustment of racial relations of a scale unparalleled in any western nation, its poverty associated with an agrarian economy which in places is almost feudal in character, the long habituation of many of its people to non-participation in political life—all these and other social characteristics both influence the nature of the South's political system and place upon it an enormous burden."[11] Yet dating his writings to almost 60 years ago has not only left the importance of many of his ideas undiminished, it has also magnified their relation to the rest of the nation. The "crises of its past" and "adjustment of racial relations of a scale unparalleled in any western nation," among other statements, may be directly applied to a United States that has, as a nation, had a general tendency to overlook its past tribulations and focus on the future. Writing of the uniqueness of the U.S. South, Key also recognizes that the alleged one-party South was principally a region of factions paradoxically divided within one political organization that, in the South, turned into a no-man's land of political activity: "Consistent and unquestioning attachment, by overwhelming majority, to the Democratic party nationally has meant that the politics within Southern states…has had to be conducted without the benefit of political parties."[12] This one-party South that had until recently centered on the Democratic Party reminds us of the authoritarian, totalitarian, or oligarchic regimes that have abounded in Latin American history. As Key writes, "the Democratic party in most states of the South is merely a holding-company for a congeries of transient squabbling factions."[13]

In the larger analysis, there existed a number of Southern politicians who actually expressed concerns that were ultimately translated into real actions and policy changes meant to improve the quality of life for many individuals. For Key, these Southern politicians were characterized principally by a maverick attitude that endeared them to the people: "In the conduct of campaigns for the control of legislatures, for the control of governorships, and for representatives in the national Congress, the South must depend for political leadership, not on political parties, but on lone-wolf operators, on fortuitous groupings of individuals usually of a transient nature, on spectacular demagogues odd enough to command the attention of considerable numbers of voters."[14] Georgia's ubiquitous Tom Watson, for example, was a "spokesman for the laborer, sharecropper, tenant, miner, millhand, unemployed—both black and white" and "was decades ahead of his contemporaries in correctly identifying economics and not race as foremost on the southern agenda." Huey Long "reshaped the organism of an archaic state government, centralized it, made it easy to operate efficiently," "shifted the weight of taxation from the poor," and "devoted himself to the cause of education." George Wallace's administration was "progressive in economic matters, launching substantial programs for construction of Junior colleges and vocational schools and generally increasing state spending for education, roads, and other state services." And Governor Jeff Davis of Arkansas (1862–1913) employed a rhetoric that "was carefully orchestrated to articulate the masses' discontent, to personalize the causes of dissatisfaction by identifying the perpetrators of felt inequities, and to promise to thwart—if not punish—the privileged," giving the impression that he expressed a "genuine sympathy for the common man."[15] Understandably, their later actions would call into question the sincerity of their populist programs, as these men often ruled with an iron fist that tolerated no dissent from either within the political machine or from the working class, interested primarily in putting food on its table.

The unfortunate tradition of Latin American dictators and the corruption of their regimes were also upheld by an oligarchy interested in enriching itself at the expense of national resources and in propping up the leader that was most willing to protect their interests. At times, the relationship between oligarchy—military, economic, or political—and leader has been so symbiotic that it has been difficult to distinguish who supported whom first and whose power depends more on whom (the cases of the Somoza family in Nicaragua or Porfirio Díaz in Mexico, for example). The tradition of Latin American political corruption and dictators has been so cloying that a literary genre reflecting this world has been born: the novel of the dictator. These works have been written principally in the twentieth century and revolve around the particular unique figure of a leader whose strong arm is present in virtually every facet of national life. Novels such as *El señor presidente (Mr. President)* (1946) by the Guatemalan Miguel Ángel Asturias, *Recurso del método (Reasons of State)* (1974) by the Cuban Alejo

Carpentier, *El otoño del patriarca (Autumn of the Patriarch)* (1975) by the Colombian Nobel prize winner Gabriel García Márquez, *La novela de Perón (The Novel of Perón)* (1985) by the Argentinean Tomás Eloy Martínez, *In the Time of the Butterflies* (1994) by the Dominican-American Julia Álvarez, *Margarita está linda la mar (Margarita, the Sea is Beautiful)* (1998) by the Nicaraguan Sergio Ramírez, *La fiesta del chivo (The Feast of the Goat)* (2001) by the Peruvian Mario Vargas Llosa, and the futurist *La silla del águila (The Eagle's Chair)* (2003) by the Mexican Carlos Fuentes, among others, center around the figure of a dictator and his court. In many cases, the work is an explicit denunciation of the individual at the helm of the state—*La fiesta del chivo*, for example—while in other novels there is a candid condemnation of the entire system of totalitarian power and the web that the leader had woven over the entire country. The dictator in these works is the material around which the narrative revolves; he is the source that forms and informs the text and, as such, creates an autonomous existence both separate and within the borders of his country. Such was the life of dictators like Rafael Trujillo, Anastasio Somoza, or Juan Domingo Peron, individuals who considered themselves above the rule of law and free to impose upon their country their own particular interpretations of terms like "national security" and "freedom of expression."

For these reasons, the relationship between a national constitution and the authority of these corrupt dictatorial regimes has been inconsistent at best, as the letter of the law was conveniently disregarded according to the political or economic needs of the moment. In response to this blatant contempt for the rule of law, the distinct centers of power would frequently break off into entities uncontrolled by the federal government and, at times, in direct opposition to its policies. As Alain Rouquié has written, it is the distance between "the written constitution and the lived constitution," the difference between the intentions of a *legal* government and the free determination and lawful actions of a *legitimate* one.[16] At the same time, we must exercise caution in speaking, as Rouquié does, of the "frailty of the rule of law."[17] What concept of "law" are we projecting? If it is based upon the autonomous decisions taken and expressed in popular elections by the citizens of a country, upon how these decisions are incorporated into the fabric of their own particular social, political, and cultural identity, then there is a chance for success. However, if these laws are blindly based on Eurocentric or U.S.-centered notions of law and order—notions that have been unfalteringly and possibly mistakenly accepted as "universal"—then there is a danger that the legitimacy of such a project could falter and, in the end, fail miserably.

Throughout the course of Latin American history, the military and paramilitary have frequently emerged as the rewriters and reframers of an existing national constitution and have, therefore, enjoyed close relationships with both the oligarchy and the national leaders of the movement. In the case of Peru, for example, Alberto Fujimori's election victory in 1990 was viewed as a step toward the elimination of the terrorist group The Shining Path, as his election "provided the military with an opportunity to increase its political influence further, particularly in all matters relating to the conduct of the counter-insurgency struggle."[18] Chilean dictator Augusto Pinochet was a general in a military that, with the economic aid of the United States government and multinational corporations like ITT, violently overthrew the popularly elected president Salvador Allende from power in 1973. Others, from the Dominican Rafael Trujillo to the Argentinian generals presiding over military juntas during the 1970s and 1980s, have enjoyed and exploited the explosive relationship between a military that looks to shape the country in its image and a president who seeks to gain personally from his tenure.

Latin American dictators distinguish themselves in a number of ways from even the most extreme Southern politicians, as these dictatorships have commonly justified the use of mass disappearances, death squads, censorship, and corruption to a point that would have been intolerable in the United States. Still, there remains that commonality: the attraction held by groups that believe themselves to be above the law, such as paramilitary organizations or the Ku Klux Klan. If the U.S. South has that "tradition of vigilante action,"[19] then Latin American dictatorships and paramilitary groups reflect the extent to which vigilantism can manipulate and shape a nation's identity. There is no need to offer an exhaustive list, but it may serve to remember the Guatemalan death squads, the Acción Chilena Anticomunista in Chile, Somoza's National Guard in Nicaragua, and even Juan Manuel Rosas's *Mazorca* in nineteenth-century Argentina as examples of how both the letter and the spirit of a constitution are sidestepped or ignored simply to maintain "order" and for the sake of a very dubitable "national good." Compared to the relationship that a number of Southern politicians have enjoyed with the Ku Klux Klan or the Citizens' Councils of the 1940s and 1950s, the singularity of Latin American paramilitary organizations becomes something of a continental attribute, shared by even the best constitutional democracies.

Perhaps the first and most important piece of political artillery that a U.S. Southern or Latin American politician learned to handle was the spoken word, for it was during public appearances and debates that the candidate could most influence the voters and fashion himself as he truly wished to be identified. Although political oratory in the United States has been deftly utilized by politicians outside the Southern political tradition—for example, by Abraham Lincoln and Jesse Jackson—it has been in the South that the energy of the spoken word has reached its political zenith. In the region, oratory has at times reflected a degree of demagoguery or simply empty rhetoric as election time neared or as the need arose. Southern politics and such demagoguery have often had an intrinsically historic relationship, one that mirrors both the level of public discourse in the South and the extent to which politics in the region have been more a matter for the theater than for the electorate. According to I. A. Newby, the Southern rhetoric of men like Eugene Talmadge "derived from romance, not realism, for it reflected no understanding of social change or of the relationship between economics and politics, nor even the nature of political or economic power."[20] Due in part to the perceived and ambiguous "romantic" nature and visceral condition of such language, rhetoric in the South "early became a passion—and not only a passion but a primary standard of judgment, the *sine qua non* of leadership."[21] Both of these distinctions emphasize the principally emotional appeal of such rhetoric, expressed as it was to incite the senses and lead the audience down a very specific path.

If we stand back from the spectacle of rhetoric and its producer and byproduct the demagogue, it is evident that manipulative and incendiary speech has been one of the consistent characteristics in the sociopolitical development of humankind, beginning with the oratory of the classic Greeks and Romans, passing through the exclusivist language of the Spanish Inquisition in the sixteenth century, and up to the explosive ideological speeches of Hitler, Mussolini, Stalin, Idi Amin, Pol Pot, and other twentieth-century dictators. The "psychological strategy" is often the same, as the demagogue looks first to create "a popular crisis psychology," proceeds to "define the cause of the crisis as a single evil," and finishes by offering "a solution, a new faith, a new belief."[22] Many past U.S. Southern and Latin American politicians have implicitly or explicitly followed such a strategy, as they have looked to define a salient problem and offer themselves as the only solution available to the specific dilemma.

Although there are and always have been such demagogues in the United States, it is in the South that they have been most present, as so-called "'respectable' leaders [failed] to deal effectively with the problems of poor whites,"[23] and took no notice, for example, of the living conditions and circumstances of African Americans. These demagogues "not only never had any concrete program to offer the commons but never tried to do anything real for them once they were in office."[24] The Southern demagogue has frequently and historically been full of empty promises, ensuring only that their intentions—communicated in the most visceral, most sensationalistic, most alarmist manner—possessed no direct correlation to subsequent courses of action once they were elected into office.

Some specific examples of Southern demagogues and their respective misuses of the spoken and written word serve to illustrate how their proclaimed electoral platforms were simple ruses used to hitch their wagons to the plight of the voter (in today's politically cynical climate, one hopes that the electorate is more accustomed to the transparent attempts at political manipulation undertaken by candidates come election time; but in the traditionally rural South—and in a historical urban South still reeling from Reconstruction and from the ingress of new incomes—Southern demagogues were still taken for their word by a large number of readers and listeners). In his 1903 campaign for governor of the state of Mississippi, James Kimble Vardaman exploited years of "Yankee domination," underlined the Southern myth of the lost cause and the Agrarian myth, and held up "the poor but honest farmer or laborer as exemplifying the highest values of America."[25] The rhetoric of Mississippi governor Theodore Bilbo (1877–1947)—an admirer of Vardman—has been described as the "Bilbonic plague" and "reveals the recurrence of two predominant themes representing his basic objectives...preservation of states' rights against encroachment of the federal government [and] maintenance of white racial purity in the United States."[26] Georgia Governor Eugene Tallmadge's demagoguery led him to ban Howard Odum's classic volume *Southern Regions of the United States* (1936) from Georgia public schools, as the work criticized Southern sectionalism.[27] In his debates and pronouncements, for example, "Talmadge elevated the daily struggle of white Georgians to a kind of religious celebration of their lives of sacrifice."[28] The infamous George Wallace made national headlines during his fight against integration in Alabama schools and universities in the 1950s, as during the demonstrations in Birmingham and throughout the march from Selma to Montgomery he made efforts at "condemning the demonstrators and sometimes publicly linking their activities to communist subversion."[29] Arkansas governor Jeff Davis "liberally seasoned his speeches with the potent religious imagery loved by his backwoods fundamentalist audiences," utilizing aggressive terms such as "fighter," "tactics," "battle," and "warrior," and turning words like "red-neck," "hillbilly," "hayseed," and "yokel" into "terms of esteem, almost of endearment."[30]

The rhetorical maneuverings of these and other representative Southern politicians manifested both their demagoguery and their consistent use of language as virtually a means unto itself, an end that, if employed properly, could help dispense the candidate from any further action. The previous examples both serve to illustrate the diversity and consistency of Southern political rhetoric—particularly in the twentieth century—and aid us in identifying a few unadorned themes. Bilbo's concern for "white racial purity" and Wallace's battle against equal rights for African Americans, for example, reveal a racist sentiment that ran parallel to their fights for "states' rights"; and Jeff Davis's sensationalization of "the poor man's struggle" for economic stability, self-determination, and power runs common to Vardaman's mythification of the "honest farmer or laborer." Their rhetoric simplified complex issues, played sections of the public against each other—haves and have nots, blacks and whites, rural and urban—and took advantage of irrational future fears surrounding jobs, family/community livelihood, and personal safety and security. Though none of these characteristics may be exclusive to Southern demagogues, there proved to be a colorful preponderance of them in an area of the country whose population was especially vulnerable to their verbal onslaughts and selective paranoia.

Rhetoric was the first and perhaps the most important stone in the foundation of an authoritarian regime in another country. By defining the semantic field, by identifying the significant issues and limiting discourse to these matters, by seeking to move or inflame the populace, dictatorships in Latin America manipulated their citizenry in order to achieve a desired end. In the nineteenth century, the Argentinean leader and Federalist party member Juan Manuel Rosas sought to define his foes the Unitarian party in opposition to his ideals, demonizing their positions and, in the process, freeing himself from any possible criticism, as "he discovered the secret of using [the masses] to defeat his enemies and adversaries without compromising his own position."[31] Rosas's message regarding the importance of maintaining a vertical, hierarchical, and unquestionable social order translated simply into *his* type of social order, into *his* criteria for stability. *El hombre de orden*—"The man of order," as he was known—was not necessarily against *any* type of anarchy: he was simply in favor of "a certain type of social and political order," in opposition to other forms of order formulated by his political opposition.[32] The demagoguery of Rosas and the expression of his own particular concept of order transformed itself into violence, as dishonest criminal, popular, and institutional behavior was endorsed by the administration in order to better apply to the national stage the objectives of this "Man of Order." As Ricardo D. Salvatore has written, from 1820 to 1865 in Argentina "The construction of social order translated into the incarceration of black servants, the public execution of delinquents [not unlike lynching in the South], the 'dumping' of unfaithful or insubordinate wives, and an array of other forms of violence."[33] This violence was justified as being in line with the intentions expressed by the Rosas regime through its inflammatory rhetoric and its demonization of all things and people that did not fit into their image of "the national interest" (read, of course, within the context of "Buenos Aires," as Argentina was and remains to a large extent today a nation divided between Buenos Aires and the rest of the country, the only country in Latin America to celebrate two independence dates: 1810 and 1816, corresponding to the years when independence reached the region of Buenos Aires and the rest of the country).

The rhetoric of Rafael Trujillo's regime from 1930 to 1961 in the Dominican Republic also specified precisely what was in "the national interest" and attempted to distinguish the "patriots" from the "traitors," frequently using public forums, spectacles, and Trujillo family events as opportunities to further indoctrinate the populace. In 1955, for example, the capital city of Santo Domingo hosted the hazily named Free World's Fair of Peace and Confraternity and offered the world an example of surreal excesses, as Trujillo's daughter Angelita "was crowned Queen during the central Carnival parade. One-third of the nation's budget was spent on this gala affair....Queen Angelita's white silk satin gown was beyond fantasy proportions: it had a 75-foot train and was decorated with 150 feet of snow-white Russian ermine—the skins of 600 animals— as well as real pearls, rubies and diamonds."[34] This extravagance went not only toward displaying the riches of the Trujillo family but also toward exhibiting for the benefit of the citizens of his country all that he possessed, subtly reinforcing that which the people *did not possess* and, therefore, further distancing himself from the masses and mythifying even more the figure of the national leader. Not surprisingly, for the Fair, "the most effusive praises came from fellow strongmen Anastacio [*sic*] Somoza and Francisco Franco."[35]

The rhetoric of power enunciated during the Trujillo regime was also expressed more directly and traditionally in the form of articles in magazines or newspapers that denounced what had been deemed subversive behavior. In the newspaper *El Caribe*—the principle vehicle for the dissemination of Trujillo's ideology—there ran a column entitled "Foro Público"—"Public Forum"—an instrument for the condemnation of dissent and for the commendation of the national leader.[36] The column "had deep roots in Dominican popular culture" and, more than anything, "translated into print an oral genre—gossip and backbiting—that was especially characteristic of the mulatto lower middle classes in the Dominican Republic."[37] Classified by Derby as "a 'panoptical' regime in which no one escaped the purview of the state,"[38] Trujillo's dictatorship sought to establish itself in the life of every Dominican, whether through economic subjugation, the repression of human rights, or the formulation of a discourse that openly looked to polarize Dominican society. In this way, rhetoric became a faithful tool of coercion that constantly reminded Dominicans who was the supreme national authority in any and all matters.

The difference between action and intention evidenced by the rhetoric of a number of U.S. Southern and Latin American political figures has also been historically symptomatic of what may be an even greater evil: systemic corruption. As was the case with demagoguery, political dishonesty has never been the exclusive property of either region, but it has been unfortunately predominant in the behavior of many good ole boy politicians and the administrations of numerous soft dictatorships, from the smallest town in the foothills of the Tennessee Appalachians or the Peruvian Andes to cities such as Atlanta, Charlotte, Buenos Aires, and Bogotá. In cases of cronyism, bribery, voter list manipulation, or gerrymandering, corruption has taken on quite a variety of forms whose principal purpose is to sidestep or obfuscate established rules, laws, and norms so that a powerful minority may benefit. As a consequence, the status quo of the powerful is maintained and the alleged dangerous consequences of public participation and awareness are reduced to a minimum. In South Carolina in 1876, for example, 101 percent of the voting age population participated in the elections that year; and in the same state, in the 1924 national election there was a 6.4 percent voter turnout.[39] During the 1850s, the Argentine dictator Juan Manuel Rosas generated the only list of acceptable candidates for local and national positions and directed "its distribution through the justices of the peace."[40] In municipal elections in Tulúa, Colombia, in 1871, "one of the electoral tables was suddenly dragged away from the polling station by a man on horseback wielding a lasso."[41] While these somewhat anecdotal examples from the Palmetto State, Argentina, and Colombia may not compare in consequence to the purchase of political influence, a violent coup d'etat, the censorship of the press, the forced and violent disappearance of individuals, or the systematic incarceration of a marginalized people, they do allow us to begin to understand the roots of corruption and voter disenchantment with political figures in both the U.S. South and Latin America today. They also help us understand how, in cases such as Argentina, voters have lowered themselves to the standards set by their elected leaders.

One of the most controversial and corrupt figures in Southern politics was Louisiana governor Huey Long (1893–1935), assassinated only four months after declaring his candidacy for the Democratic presidential nomination and while he was serving as a United States Senator. Throughout his reign as governor of Louisiana (1928–1932), Long's reach over the workings of the state extended into virtually all areas of power and put him in standing with the authoritarian rule typified by many Latin American leaders throughout history. His "control of Louisiana," according to V.O. Key, "more neatly matched the power of a South American dictator than that of any other American state boss."[42] As Chairman of the state Ways and Means Committee, for example, bills were approved practically automatically, as Long exercised total control over the proceedings: "the chairman's only function [at the committee meetings] being to call for a vote, bring down his gavel, announce that the measure was approved."[43] Apparently, "the object of much of [this] legislation was patronage grabbing. One bill took from the city attorney the right to name more than three assistants. Hereafter this patronage goes to the Long machine through the Attorney General. Another bill transferred to the state the naming of all but five deputy sheriffs in any parish. Another required all police and firemen to hold a warrant issued by the state."[44] The bills essentially looked to make known Long's power in every position that could reflect it, from Lieutenant Governor to Sheriff's Assistant. The level of corruption discernible in his administration, therefore, was reflected principally by the political maneuverings that consolidated his authority, which protected his people and punished others. In one case, "He took powers to remove the elected mayor of Alexandria, the one town which had the temerity to shower him with eggs when he spoke there in the last campaign."[45] In his classic study, W.J. Cash analyzes Long's political ambitions and comes to the conclusion that he was one of the first Southern politicians to take calculated advantage of his demagoguery and connect it to his ability to manipulate the constituency: "He was, I believe, the first Southern politician to stand really apart from his people and coolly and accurately to measure the political potentialities afforded by the condition of the underdog."[46] Through a series of policies and dealings, Huey Long capitalized on the opportunities provided him by a political machine that could be controlled only by his yearning for even greater power.

The corrupt administrations of other Southern politicians also serve to illustrate the point that they have much in common with a good number of Latin American politicians. Ross Barnett of Mississippi, for example, tried three times to become governor, the third time in 1959. During this last campaign, "Barnett promised little...other than absolute devotion to the policies of white supremacy and, reputedly, an unusually large number of patronage positions for his supporters."[47] When he was successfully elected Governor of the state in 1960, his influence became readily visible in the first session of the Mississippi legislature to meet under his administration, as the assembly "distinguished itself primarily by lowering the income tax and raising legislative salaries; commending South Africa's racial policies, enacting a series of anti-sit-in and anti-civil-rights laws, and opening the state treasury to [the racist organizations known as] the Citizens' Councils."[48] When Alabama Governor George Wallace looked to seek reelection in 1966, "a group of anti-Wallace state senators filibustered to prevent passage of a state constitutional amendment that would allow the governor to be reelected." Wallace immediately "announced that his wife, Lurleen Burns Wallace, would seek the Democratic nomination."[49] She won 64 percent of the vote and became the first woman governor of Alabama. In another example of corrupt administrations, Mississippi Governor Theodore Bilbo dismissed in one day the heads of the University of Mississippi, the State College for Women, and the Mississippi Agricultural and Mechanical College, firing an additional 179 professors and teachers "for political reasons." Subsequently, "For president of the Agricultural and Mechanical College, he chose the director of public relations of the Mississippi Power and Light Company. [And] [f]or Chancellor of the State University he chose a real-estate salesman without a college degree."[50]

More than a few Latin American leaders have also been at the helm of dishonest regimes that sought to turn intention into action and overlook, ignore, or revoke established rules, laws, and norms that stood in the way of their advancement. As with Southern politics, there was, tragically, no paucity of political and economic machinations during the regimes of Latin American dictatorships. Leaders such as the

aforementioned Juan Manuel Rosas, Mexico's Porfirio Díaz, Venezuela's
Juan Vicente Gómez, Cuba's Fulgencio Batista, and Paraguay's Alfredo
Stroessner were in charge of administrations whose criminal practices
were meant principally to keep the oligarchy content and to preserve
the hierarchy of political power. Rosas, for example, had the political
talent to "manipulate symbols in the political theatre,"[51] declaring that
long sideburns in the shape of the letter "u" represented the opposition
party, the Unitarians. Ruling from 1876 to 1911, Porfirio Díaz amended
the Mexican constitution a number of times so that he could continue as
president.[52] Fulgencio Batista, president of Cuba from 1940 to 1944, lead
a successful coup in 1952 that kept him in power until 1959 and ultimately
manifested "the futility of the electoral system" in Cuba.[53] After the 1972
earthquake that left the city of Managua devastated, the Nicaraguan
Anastasio Somoza declared that "Nicaragua is my farm," and proceeded
to distribute to family and associates the aid received from the international community. During the presidency of the dictator Alfredo
Stroessner from 1954 to 1989, "Corruption and clientilism in their diverse
forms were tolerated and even encouraged [throughout Paraguay] as the
economic base and principal mechanism of support for the *stronato*."[54]
These few examples serve merely to illustrate the unfortunate extent to
which Latin American authoritarian leaders have used corruption both
to manipulate the populace and to further their own personal crusade
against the enemy of the moment, be it Communism, intellectualism, or
any other variation of those deemed unacceptable to a regime.

One of the archetypal examples of political corruption in Latin
America is the administration of the aforementioned Venezuelan Juan
Vicente Gómez, an example of what has been described as Sultanism.[55]
During his time, one of the principal commercial exports in the country
was cattle. Gómez gradually came to dominate every aspect of this
business, expanding his cattle empire immediately upon claiming the
presidency in 1908, becoming the largest landowner in the nation over
the course of his 27 years as president, and using funds primarily from
the public treasury rather than his personal monies.[56] If a rancher,
for example, wished to sell his livestock on his land, he was "required to
give Gómez or his local representative first option to buy."[57] Gómez also
established control over the butchering of cattle in the municipal slaugh-
terhouses of the major urban markets,[58] creating a virtual monopoly of
the industry and enriching himself from the work of his countrymen. In
daily life, the typical Venezuelan citizen's encounter with the corruption
of the Gómez regime "occurred through the hallmark of Gomecista

business networks."[59] As with the previous dictators, his reach extended far into the community, as he controlled election results and distributed economic favors according to political and familial ties.

In more recent years, charges of corruption continue to be leveled against Latin American leaders, their immediate circles, and their administrations. Carlos Salinas de Gortari, President of Mexico between 1988 and 1994, "disappeared from the country in the midst of grave accusations of corruption, such as laundering money, inexplicable growth of personal fortunes, and among others electoral fraud." Ecuador's Vice-President from 1992 to 1996, Alberto Dahik Garzón, was accused of corruption and, like Salinas, ended up fleeing to another country. The ubiquitous Alberto Fujimori also escaped Peru in 2000 in the midst of massive demonstrations against the rampant corruption of his administration. On its Web site, the Revista Interforum indicates that Juan Carlos Wasmosy, President of Paraguay from 1993 to 1998, was sentenced in April 2002 to four years in prison for illegal economic transactions. Other leaders such as Nicaraguan President Arnoldo Alemán (1997–2002), Panamanian President Mireya Moscoso (elected in 1999), and Guatemalan President Alfonso Portillo (elected in 1999) have also overseen administrations accused of numerous violations of voter law and/or systematic corruption.

Another recent example has occurred in Peru, where the wife of President Alejandro Toledo, Elaine Karp, was forbidden by a federal judge in 2004 from leaving the country and ordered to remain and respond to a number of charges regarding influence peddling and enriching herself from illegal funds. According to an article written by Ramy Wurgraft and published July 30, 2004, in the Spanish newspaper *El País*, Toledo had not yet assumed the presidency in July of 2001 when his wife named herself Director of CONAPA, the National Commission of Indigenous, Amazonian, and Afro Peruvian Peoples. Immediately thereafter, she fired the Treasurer of the organization, Julián Acevedo, and raised their annual budget from $12 million a year to $28 million a year. Intriguingly, the visits that the First Lady made to the mountain regions and the Amazon and the low salaries earned by the CONAPA personnel did not match the average $2 million a month spent by the organization between September 2001 and January 2003.

A few months before the 2001 elections, Karp founded the organization "Pacha para el Campo"—"Pacha for the Countryside"—a nongovernmental organization (NGO) dedicated to promoting indigenous cultures and the well-being of their peoples. Persuaded by her arguments and by her plans for 23 different projects, the World Bank awarded her approximately $45 million dollars for the undertakings. Of the 23 initiatives, there was truly only one that was ultimately implemented by Karp and her NGO: a campaign intended to convince the indigenous communities not to watch television, listen to popular music, or drink Inca Kola (an imitation of Coca Cola), as these were all "intrusive elements from Western culture." As Wurgraft indicated, the project "only made her look like the outsider that she was to these communities, as they would watch her exit the presidential helicopter with a chic copy of the indigenous attire that her village hosts would be wearing that day." The mythification of this first lady had begun much earlier, as stories began to appear in the newspapers heralding her tireless work for the poor of Perú, twenty-four hours a day. In August 2002, this myth came apart as it was discovered that Karp was earning $10,000 a month as a consultant to the Weise Sudameris Bank, the same business that aided both Alberto Fujimori and his right-hand man, Vladimiro Montesinos, in removing from the country the millions that they had both made from drug trafficking.

The organized corruption of these and other Latin American and U.S. Southern political figures reminds us of other political leaders, specifically of many in Latin America who practiced practically the same types of dishonest policies in order to sink their talons into nearly every facet of society. Juan Domingo Peron of Argentina advanced an anti-intellectual crusade in the 1950s under his slogan "Shoes not books" and had his wife María Estela Martínez de Peron succeed him as President upon his death in 1974. Thousands of Chilean intellectuals fled the country after the 1973 military coup organized by General Augusto Pinochet aimed at deposing elected president Salvador Allende. And Marta Sahagún, the wife of Mexican president Vicente Fox (2000–2006), rescinded her decision and announced that she would *not* seek the presidency of México in 2006 (unlike the wife of Argentine ex-President Néstor Kirchner, Cristina E. Fernández, who was recently elected president of Argentina). Corruption in the Americas is both endemic and pandemic, as politicians across the face of the continent have demonstrated over the years that, on occasion, the darkest of common denominators are those that impel an individual to seek illegitimate avenues to power.

Historically, racism has been at the center of the discourse enunciated by a great many authoritarian leaders throughout history. Hitler's genocidal campaign against the Jewish culture, Mao Zedong's purges of Tibetan thought and identity, the 1990s ethnic battles between the Hutus and the Tutsis in Africa, the Balkan conflicts of the 1980s and 1990s endorsed by individuals such as Slobodan Milosevic, and the "scorched earth" campaigns of Guatemalan president Efraín Ríos Montt against Mayan villages that were allegedly aiding guerrilla movements, are but a few distressing examples of the connections between totalitarian/authoritarian regimes and racist discourse. One of the objectives of political corruption in the Americas has been to preserve the racial divisions present in a country and maintain the hegemony that a specific ethnic group has enjoyed. Historically, the diversity among distinct races and cultures already existed in populations living on the continent when English boats and Spanish explorers were making their way toward the land. Both the English and the Spanish would encounter markedly different ethnicities, and each of these colonial powers would, in turn, subjugate the peoples and marginalize them from any position of political or economic power in their nascent societies. The relative ease of the subjugation would continuously support the colonialist notions that these were peoples who were clamoring for the civilization of the White race.[60] In this sense, racism is an intrinsic part of the colonial enterprise and the extension of an empire; but it is not unique to these. Racism in Latin America was made manifest during the occupation of the continent by the Spanish and Portuguese and became particularly evident in the eighteenth century—when the declarations regarding African inferiority reached their climax[61]—and the nineteenth century, on the heels of independence from the European powers. At this time, the leaders of the new nations embodied what may be viewed as contradictory discourses: on one hand, many of the Latin American founding fathers such as Simón Bolívar sought to distinguish themselves from the "Mother Land" and from its supposed backwardness when compared to other European powers such as France, Germany, or England. On the other hand, these same founding fathers kept in place many of the colonial institutions that had been established by Spain, particularly in places where the indigenous cultures had been enslaved and oppressed by a Spanish crown that was gradually weakening. Circa 1870, the industrial development of colonial nations altered their undertakings and turned them into imperialist projects that used racist theories to advance their causes. During this time, "racial theories were conveniently arriving to justify the political ambitions and international strategies, to maintain economic ambitions across the seas, and to provide new impetus for the missionaries charged with civilizing the pagans, Christianizing them."[62] A number of peoples across the globe in places such as Australia, North America, Vietnam, Laos, South Africa, Indonesia, and Puerto Rico would come to be systematically eliminated via racial discrimination and the construction of structural prejudices.

In the U.S. South, racism proved to be both a consequence of and a pillar of support for slavery, as West Africans were forcibly brought to the United States over the course of the eighteenth and nineteenth centuries and made to participate in an economic project that was neither fair nor just. Over time, some would come to view the laws impressed upon the South during and after Reconstruction as a factor that exacerbated the racism expressed by many inhabitants of the region, as whites —the perceived losers of the Civil War—continued to brutally, and irrationally, fight for states' rights and against any regulation imposed by the federal government. As W.J. Cash observes—albeit somewhat datedly—Reconstruction "established what I have called the savage ideal as it had not been established in any Western people since the decay of medieval feudalism, and almost as truly as it is established today in Fascist Italy, in Nazi Germany, in Soviet Russia—and so paralyzed Southern culture at the root."[63] Eurocentrisms aside, Cash notes the possible origins of contemporary Southern racism: a racism that resulted from a visceral reaction to "Northern" victory and subsequent dominion, a racism that was uncomplicated in the worst possible way, a racism that would ultimately cause some aspects of Southern culture to stagnate indefinitely. In these respects, many Southern politicians built for themselves a comfortable political platform that attempted to reclaim the alleged historical importance of "whiteness": the illusory ideal of a homogeneous white family, white culture, and white race. Deep down, these efforts harkened back to the times of slavery—when human beings materially possessed other human beings—and belied the allegedly altruistic efforts and claims of Southern politicians to unite Dixie under the banner of a more modern and therefore progressive neoconfederacy.

While not unique to the nation, the U.S. South's sadly profuse tradition of racist politicians began in earnest in the eighteenth century, continued through the nineteenth century—during the zenith of the plantation era—and exists well into that bridge-time that encompasses both the twentieth and twenty-first centuries, when the civil rights battle is carried on in the blink of history. More contemporary politicians like Lester Maddox, Ross Barnett, William Rainach, and David Duke have fit all too well into a tradition that marginalizes the African American population and exclaims the supremacy of "the white race," expressing their misguided nostalgia for other times and other laws. In 1988, for example, David Duke presented himself as a Republican candidate "in a special election to fill the seat of the 81st legislative District" in Louisiana,[64] and almost immediately became nationally notorious due to his extremist ideas regarding racial issues.

His formation, however, had begun long before that date. In 1964, at the age of 14, he heard of and began attending meetings of the White Citizens' Council and participated at the local level in Barry Goldwater's national campaign for president.[65] After working his way through the Republican party ranks, he found himself elected to the Louisiana Legislature, where he advocated an apartheid system for the state and promoted legislation that was, in effect, "considered racially motivated:...1) abolishing affirmative action programs; 2) increasing penalties for possession and sale of drugs in public housing projects; 3) cutting off welfare benefits to convicted drug offenders; 4) providing financial incentives for public assistance recipients to use contraceptives."[66] As his ideas began to polarize opinion in the state legislature, Duke began to gain notoriety on a national level, attracting not only dissenters with policies of the federal government but also individuals who agreed with his initiatives. As Dennis Hevesy noted in a November 5, 1991, *New York Times* article, his national appeal was evident when he ran for governor of the state in 1991, as 47 percent of Duke's campaign contributions that year came from outside Louisiana.

As Jack Wardlaw noted in a March 15, 1992, article in the *New Orleans Times Picayune,* in the 1992 presidential election year, the Republican Pat Buchanan began to co-opt and therefore legitimize Duke's message of racial separation, inequity, and urgency. Duke's intentions that year had been to run for president and tilt the Republican platform even further right by presenting an active racial agenda that looked to promote "white" interests and cut benefits that, in his opinion, nonwhites were receiving simply because of the color of their skin. However, as Evel Elliott and Gregory S. Thielemann note, his ideas would not find a receptive northern audience in the early primary contests of that year of 1992, as "there was not the potent combination of economic discontent and racial anxieties present in the South."[67] Interestingly, Buchanan's message was essentially the same, except from a different messenger, and he proceeded to appropriate "the symbols of Duke's infamy and [wrap] them in his greater legitimacy."[68] Perhaps David Duke's regional political persona could not transcend the borders of the South and, in particular, Louisiana; but in many ways his ideas reflected those attitudes already present in other parts of the nation, something proved by the votes and the popular attention garnered by Buchanan. Ultimately, that Super

Tuesday in 1992 proved to be decisive in the downfall of Duke's national campaign, as he won no more than 3.1 percent of the votes in states outside the South.[69] As T. Wayne Parent writes, the consequences to his national campaign were clear. In the past, "Candidates have won elections by addressing legitimate problems in distinctly racist terms. Such candidates should recognize the long-term social costs of such short-term thinking."[70]

There are numerous examples of U.S. Southern politicians who have gained local, regional, or even national prominence and contempt due to their racist views and the manner in which they expressed them. Mississippi governor Ross Barnett had, like Wallace, also "stood in the schoolhouse door at the State University and had achieved a deserved reputation for segregationist fanaticism."[71] The infamous Georgia governor Lester Maddox was active in a number of white supremacy organizations, including the White Citizens' Councils and GUTS, Georgians Unwilling to Surrender. Anecdotes abound surrounding his Pickrick restaurant, from his showing a pistol in order to prevent blacks from dining in his restaurant to rejecting the desegregation of his establishment as mandated by the 1964 Civil Rights Bill by temporarily changing his business "into a curiosity shop specializing in the sale of items like axe handles, labeled 'Pickrick drumsticks.'"[72] In his 1957 and 1961 campaigns for mayor of the city of Atlanta, "Maddox fervently championed the virtues of segregation, free enterprise, and Protestant fundamentalism, and often associated social and ideological change with communism."[73] Another political figure, William E. Rainach, a state senator from the late 1950s little known outside his home state of Louisiana, "became chairman of the Joint Legislative Committee to Maintain Segregation, which plotted segregationist strategy, concocted and drafted all manner of anti-integration legislation, carried out white supremacy propaganda campaigns, investigated integrationists and communists, and encouraged purges of blacks from the voter registration rolls."[74] In this context, we cannot but mention the likes of Theodore Bilbo, author of *Take your Choice: Separation or Mongrelization* (1947), who in a number of speeches emphasized the necessity of "purifying" the white race in order to stabilize society. On June 6, 1938, in a four-hour address to the Mississippi Senate that predated the rhetorical excesses of Fidel Castro, Bilbo proclaimed his support for the racial beliefs maintained by the Germans of the time: "the Germans appreciate the importance of race values. They understand that racial improvement is the greatest asset any country can have."[75] In another speech that year,

Bilbo again spoke at length about "the racial problem," comparing it to the situations of other countries, and drew attention to the "dangers" inherent in miscegenation. Quoted at length, the speech provides ample evidence not only of Bilbo's racism but of his prejudices toward nonwhite cultures:

> The amalgamation of the white with the colored races has destroyed the civilization of the Caucasian race not only in Egypt and India but in Abyssinia, Nigeria, Uganda, Mashonaland, Babylonia, Phoenicia, Persia, Cambodia, Ceylon, Java, New Zealand, Polynesia, Northern China, Korea, Portugal, Spain, Italy, Greece, the Balkans, Mexico, Yucatan, Peru, and Haiti; and today the same cause of amalgamation between the white and colored races is threatening the destruction of the civilizations in practically all of the Latin Americas and many of the white colonial possessions in Africa.[76]

His comments explicitly champion the dominance of "the Caucasian race" over practically all others in regions where said "Caucasians" have been a historical minority or cultural trespassers, connected to the conquered area only through colonialism and subjugation.

Bilbo's racist views reflected his own particular vision for the future of the U.S. South, but unfortunately, they somewhat mirrored the views of those Southerners who saw their homeland deconstructed, reconstructed, and thrust back into the country right before their eyes. Reconstruction was certainly no excuse for their attitudes, but the vehement racism of some Southern politicians emphatically implies an entrenched resentment of Federal ("Northern") interventions in matters pertaining to the individual states. For them, that a human being should or should not be considered property was not a legislative matter for politicians: it was a moral issue that rested with the individual and, therefore, could not be legislated from Washington. For these Southern politicians, "racism" was a nonexistent, unidentifiable term: it was how life was lived, how society was organized. It was an attitude so transparent that it needed no novel term to define or describe it, as the action existed long before the term came into being. The linguistic transparency of their convictions may be comparable to a belief in God: as soon as we announce "God exists," we begin to doubt the existence of God, as his presence should be so evident to a believer, so transparent, that it should not need declarations of existence. In this sense, Nietzsche's announcement that "God is dead" did more to sustain and possibly strengthen a belief in God than would be evident at first glance; for it is frequently through an attempted *refutation* of the other that a *verification* of being and otherness occurs.

For many Southern politicians—particularly those reared between Reconstruction and the 1950s—racism as a term, as a verbalized suspicion, did not exist as such, as it was the patent tribal attitude of the day. There was no need to enunciate such an evident word. Because of those and other reasons, institutionally supported racism in the South began to break down during the Civil Rights battles of the 1950s and 1960s, as an appropriate language for confronting and eradicating locally sponsored bigotry and intolerance began to be applied from outside the centers of conflict and by those who had suffered and continue to suffer the brutal consequences of racist ideologies.

A number of Latin American leaders that we have mentioned were also overtly racist or promoted a racist agenda, effectively dividing their country between the lighter-skinned (those descended from Europeans, the economically privileged, and the oligarchy) and the darker-skinned indigenous or African descendants. Considering the ethnic and racial diversity of Latin America and the economic difficulties of practically all its nations, other ethnicities became comfortable targets for those in power who looked to find a scapegoat for national troubles. In Caribbean countries such as the Dominican Republic or Haiti, for example, those frequently found at fault for many of the country's problems have traditionally been the direct descendants of African slaves (a topic treated by the Cuban author Gertrudis Gómez de Avellaneda in her 1847 novel *Sab*, a work published about five years before *Uncle Tom's Cabin*). In Mexico, the institutional powers have frequently blamed the indigenous populations in Southern regions like Chiapas for their own troubles. In Nicaragua, the hierarchy of the Sandinista revolution marginalized the Miskito and Rumi peoples that live along the Caribbean coast (many of whom, in the 1980s, would join the Contras in the fight against the Sandinista government). And in Guatemala, Panama, Bolivia, Honduras, Peru, and Ecuador, among others, indigenous groups have represented a part of the population that, statistically, ranged from a substantial to outright majority. Historically, however, these populations have had very little say or control in national affairs. With the advent of global movements of liberation in the 1950s and 1960s in Africa and Asia and the emergence of groups like the Ejército Zapatista de Liberación Nacional (National Zapatista Army of Liberation) in Mexico during the latter part of the twentieth century, indigenous communities in Bolivia, Ecuador, and other countries are gradually recovering lost political and geographical territory and fighting against the institutional racism that pervades many aspects of Latin American societies. The recent election in Bolivia of

President Evo Morales and his active campaigning on a pro-indigenous platform demonstrates the consistent relevance of indigenous affairs to the present and the future of many Latin American nations.

There are a number of Latin American leaders who have repeatedly repressed indigenous peoples or have worked to enact legislation that would disallow or eliminate the presence of any ethnic voice in public policy. Once again, the figure of the Argentinean Juan Manual Rosas stands above the others, as during his regime he fought actively and principally against the Pampa and Ranquel peoples in the interior parts of the country, bringing down upon them such government violence that the genocide begun by the European powers in the sixteenth and seventeenth centuries appeared to continue through the nineteenth century.[77] Other examples are useful. Over the course of his 35 years as president, the Mexican Porfirio Díaz opened his country up to foreign investment and directed a number of campaigns against ethnic populations (he himself was reported to have been so self-conscious of his indigenous heritage that every morning he allegedly sprinkled rice powder on his face in an effort to "whiten" himself, not unlike the eighteenth-century European monarchs). Known as "Guatemala's Pinochet," President Efraín Ríos Montt waged an active and violent campaign in the 1980s against the indigenous populations, accusing them of aiding subversive terrorists who were looking to destabilize his governments. In Peru, Bolivia, and Guatemala—nations with significant indigenous populations—national governments and their respective administrations have done very little for the distinct ethnicities and offer only token shows of support, such as appointing members to nominal positions within their government, marginalizing the ethnicities from a national political scene that centers exclusively on the capital city, or emphasizing the importance of integrating themselves within a larger nation-state that will, assuredly, paternalistically look after their interests. After centuries of struggle, indigenous groups like the Quechua and Aymara in Peru and Bolivia are waging their own organized battle for their rights, disrupting commercial traffic that passes through their lands, protesting government policies, and coordinating general strikes against administrations or institutions that do not make attempts at addressing their concerns or including their voices in the decision-making process. Even in the fields of advertising and public relations, indigenous groups have been protesting against both the stereotypical depiction of indigenous cultures and against their absence in advertisements that reinforce clichés and that seem to portray the national populace as a uniform set of light-skinned individuals. Racism in Latin America has been blatantly evident in the deeds and actions of authoritarian, xenophobic leaders who looked to fashion a static, monocultural nation whose image would reflect many of their own biases and prejudices and little of the demographic reality of the cities and countryside. If indigenous groups in Latin America are, in fact, reclaiming their identity from within the borders of national political boundaries, it is not because the institutional powers have allowed it, but rather because ethnicities and indigenous groups have begun to organize alliances that have a direct effect on national policy.

Both Latin American dictators and Southern politicians in the tradition of a "lighter" dictatorship have, not surprisingly, had supporters within the national oligarchy and among the masses, as these leaders learned to appeal to specific economic interests and popular sentiment. The jury may still be out on populist politicians, as they have at times pushed a country forward through a period of growth and construction—roads, schools, hospitals—reforms—increasing the minimum wage, improving the statewide health care system—or pet projects—the founding of a university or the building of an airport. The Argentine president Juan Domingo Peron is a case in point. As Tomás Eloy Martínez indicated in an editorial that appeared in the Spanish newspaper *El País* on August 1, 2004, between 1944 and 1952 Peron's power was paradoxical, oscillating between authoritarianism and social transformation. While he "stimulated hundreds of laws that returned dignity to the workers and to the most ignored sectors of society, [he also] demanded from the community absolute submission to the orders of his party, overwhelming the country with unceasing propaganda and censuring almost every voice of the opposition." Alberto Fujimori of Peru "was able to build on public sympathy through his government's successes in dealing with hyperinflation and guerrilla violence";[78] the Nicaraguan Anastasio Somoza became involved in a 1936 general strike on behalf of "taxi drivers, construction workers, railroad employees, artisans and domestic servants";[79] and the Pinochet government used economists from the University of Chicago and stabilized the Chilean economy in the 1970s and 1980s, making the country into an economic player on the international scene. In many cases, what was at stake was not solely the economic future of a nation, but rather how that future was to be molded and what was to be sacrificed in the process. In the case of Pinochet, for example, his government justified its repressive measures against any type of domestic dissent by denouncing intellectuals, students, or workers who were anti-Pinochet as "subversive," anti-patriotic, and contrary to the national interests of a regime that allegedly looked only after the stability and prosperity of its citizens.

Due to the variety of many of the dictatorships throughout the course of Latin American history, we may further categorize the distinct types of totalitarian or authoritarian governments on the continent. H. E. Chehabi and Juan L. Linz, for example, include Rafael Trujillo, Fulgencio Batista, and Anastasio Somoza as examples of what they term *sultanistic* regimes. Writing on the government of Juan Vicente Gómez (1857–1935) in Venezuela, Doug Yarrington defines "sultanism" and specifies its characteristics: "extreme cases of patrimonial authority characterized by the concentration of discretionary authority in the hands of a ruler who advances state and personal power through a mixture of rewards and repression."[80] In his research on the authoritarianism of the administrations of Alberto Fujimori, John Crabtree indicates that some governments in Latin America may also be considered *hybrid regimes*—"regimes that adhered to the basic norms of democracy but which embodied strongly authoritarian features"—specifying further that "such regimes are personalist, involve a concentration of power and bypass representative institutions to create a direct, top-down relationship between government and the mass of the population," and offering as a paradigm Fujimori's rule.[81] Over the course of Latin American history, certain governments have not attempted to disguise their efforts at "stabilizing" and "pacifying" their country—as was the case with the Argentinean military in the 1970s and 1980s or the Guatemalan Ríos Montt, for example—and, consequently, their disregard for the voice of the majority population or the results of popular elections. For most Latin American dictatorships, the commonality has been the power of a single generally misguided vision for their nation: the projection of a unique moral mission upon the people of the country. Within this mission, all variations were possible and "stability and progress"—as defined by those in power—would be within the reach of those who toed the line and acted according to the intentions of the government.

At first glance, it would seem an exaggeration to compare the discourse, administrative corruption, and racist remarks and behavior of a number of Southern politicians to the racist ravings of Pol Pot, Benito Mussolini, Augusto Pinochet, or Saddam Hussein. Upon reflection, however, there are more parallels than one is willing to acknowledge. A number of past U.S. Southern politicians may be classified as dictatorial, as supreme leaders of a regime in which "those governed do not have the possibility to separate the officials from power through regular or institutionalized procedures."[82] It is in this respect that they may be compared to a type of soft or *light* dictator—particularly those in Latin America in the twentieth century—as, notwithstanding the democratic processes put into place in order to ensure the accountability of elected leaders, these politicians managed to circumvent the electorate in a blatant attempt to manipulate election results, distribute wealth disproportionately and in an unlawful manner, actively discriminate against one or more ethnic or racial sectors of the population, and/or squelch dissent within the ranks of their constituency and of their political machine. In this sense, there has thankfully come a time in the regimes of these leaders when their heavy-handed rule has been denounced. (As was the case in 1936 when an editorial in the *Atlanta Constitution* "warned of the 'nazi' methods of [Eugene] 'Talmadgism.'"[83]) When this has occurred, there have been institutions and processes in place that have frequently allowed for the reparation of the damage; but until this has happened, Southern soft dictators have often held too tight a rein over the land.

Perhaps the two Southern politicians whose personalities and administrations best characterize that variety of soft or *light* dictatorship are Huey Long and Theodore Bilbo. In many ways, their administrations, political machinations, and personalities suggest the attributes of a despot. Their administrations were to a large extent dictatorships that exercised supreme authority over their land. The case of Huey Long is possibly the most apparent within the framework of our study. As I.A. Newby wrote, Huey P. Long "became the nearest thing to a dictator that any American state ever had."[84] In his somewhat dated albeit essential work *Forerunners of Fascism* (1935), Raymond Swing writes extensively about Long's totalitarian tendencies and contextualizes them within a specific historical moment in which Adolf Hitler's plans regarding the marginalization and intended elimination of the Jewish people were slowly gaining momentum both in Germany and abroad. In his work, Swing first establishes resentment as a theme common among many dictators and proceeds to compare Long and Hitler to other authoritarian leaders: "Resentment lies in the hearts of many because of the hardships they bore as children, the dreary hours of work they endured, the advantages they saw given to others but were not fated to enjoy. Hitler tapped that resentment in building up his great German host. Huey Long has tapped it in Louisiana and he is confident that he can tap it in forty-seven other states."[85] Swing then offers a list of justifications for his classification of Long as a dictator: Long is waiting "to Hitlerize America"; "He rules, and opponents had better stay out of his way. He punishes all who thwart him with grim, relentless, efficient vengeance"; and, in a final comment on the political organization that remained long after his death, Swing declares, "The machine Huey left as his legacy is a fitting memorial to the hillbilly firebrand who might have become the first American Fuehrer."[86] Like many totalitarians and authoritarians through history, Long possessed the ability to cultivate popular support among the masses of voters and herd them along necessary paths. Yet his populist style was a means and not an end unto itself, as throughout his political career Long amassed an incredible amount of both political and material wealth that he would, according to his whims, redistribute in a deceitful show of compassion and connection to the "common people."

The actions and administration of Theodore Bilbo may also be interpreted through an authoritarian lens. The Mississippi politician frequently invoked the sanctity and purity of his power, exalting the need for a heavy hand in matters of the state. When he was last governor of Mississippi from 1928 to 1932, "he ran the state in a ruthless manner and declared that what Mississippi needed was a Mussolini."[87] He also admired "the race theories of Adolf Hitler" and advanced the idea that 12 million "Negro-Americans" should have been deported to Liberia in the 1920s and 1930s.[88] As was mentioned in the case of Long, it is not surprising that, at a time when Charles Lindberg was decorated by Hitler, individuals would express an appreciation for the revitalization of Italy and Germany after World War I. What is astonishing is that, at the time, the "race theories" of Hitler and the strong hand of Mussolini's regime would attract admiration from Southern politicians whose ideas and lives had flourished in circumstances vastly different from those of Italy and Germany in the 1930s. Perhaps part of the reactions expressed by Southern politicians like Long and Bilbo may be understood—but never justified—by recalling the immigration that, in those years and in the previous decades, had arrived in the United States from Europe. These Southerners saw firsthand how the new generations were quietly but firmly transforming "their" country and with it the religious, cultural, and political inheritances of the Anglo founders of the United States. Today, there are many politicians both inside and outside Dixie who are resorting to the same nativist xenophobic discourse, expressing the need for a strong hand in all things immigrant, from the idea that "American jobs are for Americans" to declaring support for a wall along the United States border with Mexico and opposition to any and all bilingual education or worker visa programs. As past Southern politicians came to learn, the issue is not *if* a community will change, but rather *how well* it will adapt to the shifting circumstances generated by the population. The soft dictatorships of Long and Bilbo may have disappeared, but a land in transition and transformation is always susceptible to the discourse of those who are most threatened by the unmistakable process of change taking place in their world.

The dictatorial qualities of a few Southern politicians are perhaps the clearest parallel between these and a number of Latin American leaders who have taken full social, political, and economic advantage of their positions. Historically, the democratic tradition in Latin American countries is lacking in individuals that have upheld a national constitution or observed the will of the electorate. In this sense, the South has been dramatically different from a number of Latin American countries, as democratic processes were put in place in order to curb the corruption of its elected leaders (whether these processes were followed depends upon the historical moment and the strength of these democratic institutions in the South). The colonial legacy inherited by the newly independent nations of Latin America at the beginning of the nineteenth century has contributed to determining the political path that each country would subsequently follow. As has been indicated, the manner in which the majority of Latin American nations became independent in the nineteenth century was distinctly different from other colonial movements of liberation, especially those that would come later, in the twentieth century. When nations such as Egypt, India, Morocco, Algeria, or Vietnam freed themselves from the colonial control of France, England, or Germany, for example, the newly independent nation typically underwent a radical reconstruction of its social, political, and economic infrastructure in an attempt to recover from the gaze and grasp of the colonial overseer and to subvert and modify any hint of colonial authority. Latin American leaders of countries that claimed their independence between 1800 and 1820 were primarily from the upper classes of their societies and, therefore, generally wished to maintain the internal social order that the Spanish empire had established (with one difference, of course: the political and cultural absence of Spain). Latin American history throughout the course of the nineteenth and twentieth centuries, then, has represented a power play between the different ideological branches of the ruling classes (with the occasional popular revolution thrown in). The Argentinean Federales and Unitarios, the Mexican PRI party, and the polarization of post-revolutionary politics in Nicaragua and El Salvador, for example, bear the marks of a colonial empire in which society was divided between two ranks: the colonizer and the colonized.

While racism, corruption, and rhetoric are not the sole characteristics of a dictatorship, they are three of its principal engines. When run "effectively" in conjunction with institutionalized repression, violence, and censorship, the ideological apparatus ultimately penetrates into every facet of society and reminds each citizen of their "patriotic duty," of the need to promote "civic pride" and unambiguously support the national leader. Historically, Latin America has had its share of dictatorial regimes whose leaders sought to benefit economically from their tenure, to mold a nation in their image, and to articulate a very specific mission for the nation and her citizens. While the governments have not been identical —compare, for example, the most obvious differences between Diaz's regime in Mexico and Somoza's in Nicaragua to Castro's in Cuba—there are commonalities that allow us to better understand these governments within the context of Interamerican politics, specifically Southern politicians in the United States. The dictatorship in Argentina of the infamous Rosas, for example, forms part of a tradition apparently rooted in a set of national—Argentinean—and continental—American—circumstances, as he created paramilitary groups like the *Mazorca* in order to sow terrorist intimidation and physically throw his political adversaries out of the city of Buenos Aires.[89] In the 1950s, 60s, 70s, and 80s, his future compatriot Juan Domingo Peron and generals such as Leopoldo Fortunato Galtieri and Jorge Rafael Videla attempted to control the nation through repression, formulating a technique known as "disappearing" someone: kidnapping, murdering, erasing that person and leaving no physical trace—no body, no traces, no marks—through which they would be remembered. By transforming the adjective "disappeared" into the transitive verb "to disappear," the cruel progression of events turned the word into an active process. Individuals were simply "disappeared" without explanation, without anyone knowing their fate or being able to locate their remains. Ironically, the Falklands war of 1982 that the military government hastily concocted in order to circle their international allies and distract fellow Argentineans from the national crises also led to their downfall, as the neutrality and even antipathy of traditional friends like the United States and the loss of the war to England allowed the nation—and the world—to view the farce that the junta had devised.

Over the course of the twentieth century, Latin American dictatorships have survived in spite of international opposition and thanks, in part, to the support of several U.S. presidents and their administrations. From the Mexican-American War of 1848 to the invasion of Panama in 1989, a number of U.S. administrations have sought to either benefit from the relationship they enjoyed with a despot—Somoza in Nicaragua, Duvalier in Haiti, Pinochet in Chile—or to export the U.S. national ideology by overthrowing or attempting to overthrow a leftist government that had been democratically elected—in the case of Salvador Allende in Chile or the Guatemalan Jacobo Arbenz—or that had rebelled against an ignominious dictatorship—in the case of the Sandinistas in Nicaragua, for example.

The dictatorship in Chile of General Augusto Pinochet from 1973 to 1989–1990 proved particularly oppressive and even offered the international community a brutal petri dish in which one could consider the level and extent of repressive state measures. Upon Pinochet's exit from power, the Chilean nation began to gradually come to terms with the injustices committed by his government. Released in 1991, the Rettig Report details the human rights abuses committed in Chile between 1973 and 1989 and describes the three stages of repression that the Pinochet regime exercised during this time: "1) Sept.-Dec. 1973: massive detentions throughout the country, prisoners interned in concentration camps, political prisoners and peasants involved in the process of agrarian reform executed, and a 'social cleaning' of young people in urban squatter settlements took place; 2) 1974–1977: the regime developed a systemic policy of repression in order to exterminate those whom it deemed a political threat; and 3) 1977–1989: a familiar pattern of violence."[90] The regime of the Dominican Republic's Rafael Trujillo and his own personal power "was based as much on the consumption of women through sexual conquest as it was on the domination of enemies of state. His charisma was founded as much on the concrete numbers of women he acquired (and their class status) as it was on violence and the near mythological fear he inspired by eliminating men."[91] The "softer" dictatorship of Peru's Alberto Fujimori was also characterized by the authoritarian reshuffling of government powers that looked to consolidate his own control of Peruvian citizens and institutions. In 1992, for example, he closed down the national congress and struck down his own government in what was called a self-coup and termed a manifestation of his "electoral authoritarianism," "[capitalizing] on the disarray of Peru's main parties and [seeking] to exclude them from the arena of decision-making," "[making] it clear that he was at the centre of all decision-making."[92]

The desired omnipotence—and ultimate downfall—of Latin American dictators and U.S. Southern politicians suggests specifically that the land may indeed breed a unique variety of leaders. As always, though, political reality is not that simple. Latin American and U.S. Southern politics have traditionally presented an image that combines historical legacy, geographic determinism, and callously ambitious individuals who looked to take advantage of the fortunes inherent in the natural resources of their respective regions and to prolong the poverty of their citizens. Thankfully, there have been notable exceptions to this despotic tradition. In the U.S. South, Hoke Smith, Governor of Georgia from 1907 to 1909 and in 1911, and U.S. Senator from 1911 to 1921, was considered a progressive "for the times," as "he greatly strengthened the Railroad Commission's power to regulate railroads, increased public school funding, [and] established the juvenile court system."[93] Alben Barkley, U.S. Senator from Kentucky, was one of the few Southern politicians to defend Franklin Delano Roosevelt's New Deal in 1938. Serving as Governor of Tennessee from 1953 to 1959, and again from 1963 to 1967, Frank G. Clement "promoted the first free textbook program for all public school grades," and was "the first Southern governor to veto a segregation bill."[94] Winthrop Rockefeller, Governor of Arkansas from 1967 to 1971, worked toward the integration of Arkansas schools, organizing state draft boards that possessed the best integration of any state in the United States. One of his last acts before leaving office was to commute the sentences of every person on the state's Death Row and to urge other governors to do the same. Between 1954 and 1969, "non-segregationists won nearly one-quarter (23 percent) of the governor's races,"[95] quietly serving as a counterbalance to that portion of the U.S. Southern population that vehemently defended segregation.

In Latin America, Vicente Fox's electoral victory in Mexico in 2000, the granting of the Nobel Peace prize in 1987 to Costa Rican president Oscar Arias, the 1990 national election loss by the Sandinista party in Nicaragua and the democratic transition to being an opposition party, and the 2002 election of Colombian president Álvaro Uribe, for example, also serve as positive examples of transparently democratic political processes in Latin America. Regrettably, the commonalities shared by a number of U.S. Southern and Latin American politicians throughout the nineteenth and twentieth centuries have been primarily negative in nature. The manipulation and abuse of the electorate through rhetoric and demagoguery, the political and economic corruption evident in their administrations, the blatant and veiled varieties of racism, and the repressive measures of a number of U.S. Southern and Latin American politicians place these individuals in similar categories that blend dissimilar personalities. The electoral manipulations, press censorship and control, and attempted eradication of dissenting opinions expressed at all levels of society distance the actions of Latin American political figures somewhat from their U.S. Southern counterparts, but not necessarily their intentions. Like U.S. Southern politicians who sought to control and maneuver the free exchange and expression of ideas and accumulate political and economic capital, Latin American dictators represent only the extreme of that which might have been in the Southeastern United States, had it not been for the differences in colonial history, aristocratic ambitions, and the intense insistence of democratic institutions that, while they may have faded from view for periods of time in the southern United States, never entirely disappeared.

Literature as Mirror

For Latino communities in the U.S. South, the struggle for a political, social, and economic voice has found common ground with the fight of other ethnicities, in particular African American and indigenous populations. In the past, this voice was unambiguously appropriated by others and took on a number of different forms, from gerrymandering political districts to denying bank loans to individuals based on the color of their skin. Subtly—albeit soundly—cultural representations such as music, literature, or paintings also contributed to the gleaning of the distinct types of power through the illustration of archetypes that look to construct stereotypically exaggerated images of those "different" from the mainstream (i.e., White Anglo-Saxon Protestant), partly to create an irrational fear of those "others." Fortunately, there also existed cultural statements to the contrary: songs, literature, or paintings that sought to subvert the constructed image of the "differents" and, therefore, advocate a more inclusive attitude toward individuals who did not share in the community's power base. As Marie-Chantal Barre has noted, "Culture is a feature of resistance."[1]

Many literary constructions emanating from the U.S. South and Latin America have included an element of subversion that has aided people in coping with the preventable cruelty of daily life and has originated in exactly that marginalization of the African American, the indigenous, the female, the poor, or the homosexual, among others, from both within and outside that referent. One of the reasons slave stories developed in the U.S. South, for example, was "[to help] provide hope for the future and [to serve] as a survival kit for the present."[2] As societies change, so do their margins and points of reference, bringing about a literature that is constantly in flux and that shares a number of stylistic and thematic elements that originate in a people, a social structure, and a geography and serve as their own *raison d'etre*. As he traveled through the U.S. South in 1961, Gabriel García Márquez, the future Nobel prize-winning author from Colombia, noted his impressions of the region and the interconnections he perceived between Latin America, the Deep South, and Southern literature: "I found evidence—on those hot, dusty roads, with the same vegetation, trees, and great houses—of the similarity between our two worlds. One mustn't forget that Faulkner is in a way a Latin American writer."[3] Did the road and the land of Faulkner inspire García Márquez? The critic Deborah N. Cohn seems to think so. In her studies, she has devoted a considerable amount of effort to establishing the base of a literary interamericanness and to studying the parallels between Latin American literature and Southern literature. Both of these traditions, notwithstanding the "sheer number of differences that separate the South and Spanish America,"[4] were also born from historical circumstances shaped to placate, pacify, "civilize," or strictly colonize the respective regions.

The designation of a U.S. Southern or Latin American literature is in itself problematic and may be directly linked to readers, writers, and themes. Does the writing of a novel by an Argentine author, for example, allow the work to be included under the rubric of "Latin American literature"? Within the expanding canon of all that is literature, most would argue that yes, the novel is certainly considered Latin American literature. If the work is written *from* Latin America, the reader may experience a greater awareness of authenticity and authority, a growing sense— perhaps unjustified—of believability and accountability. Moreover, if the Argentine novel is written by an Argentine who resides in the country, the authority of the work—the power that it communicates—may be more easily accepted by a reading public critical of outsider voices. This postmodern centering and focusing of the narrative voice may be repeated ad nauseam. In order to, say, write a novel about a 50-year-old upper-class Mexican male suffering from a mid-life crisis due to his unrestrained consumer tendencies, then, in order to speak and write with authority, the author must supposedly be a 50-year-old Mexican male from the upper class who is suffering or has suffered from this same crisis. This posturing and critical need to attach a biographical referent to every published work seems to have met a decisive end some time ago with the advent of science fiction novels, western paperbacks, and romance stories (the "popular culture" of Culture), but there still remains the question of authority. Who is speaking? And is anyone listening?

The mark left by U.S. Southern and Latin American literatures is shared equally by the writer and reading public (at times non-sequentially). Works may be written in a certain style, from within a specific historical context, exercising discernible thematic and stylistic patterns, but a work may also distance itself from its context, bridge two or more worlds, or inhabit all at the same point in time. Such is the case, for example, with the novel *Rayuela* (*Hopscotch*) (1963) by the Argentine Julio Cortázar. While the text itself is an insurrection against all things literary and a recalibration of the relationship between reader and author, the action *per se* of the novel is more uncomplicated and takes place—representatively—in Paris and Buenos Aires. Both cities, then, may lay claim to *Rayuela*, but *for what* may be distinctly different reasons: Buenos Aires is where the action of the novel ends—if this novel truly ends at all—where the events culminate and consequently drop off; it is also the city where the author began to write. Paris, on the other hand, is where the action begins—if this novel has a beginning at all—where the protagonists learn to ruminate and wander the streets of the French capital in search of meaning, human warmth, and experiences. It was also the home of Cortázar, as it was there that he spent the last 30-plus years of his life in residence, using it as a base from which to write and travel.

Rayuela—and, by extension, Cortázar himself—belongs to Buenos Aires and Paris, to both Argentina and France, to those individuals in Latin America, Europe, and beyond who see themselves reflected in the lives of characters such as La Maga, Héctor, Treviranus, and others who are in a constant state of flux and who appear to be tirelessly searching for their place under the sun. Very little is assumed in the novel except that nothing is assumed. In this manner, Cortázar gave voice to a generation that already felt prematurely displaced by its predecessors, that looked to separate itself from its past via ideas and actions, radical escapes from the shadows of their fathers and mothers. To this end, Latin American writers like Julio Cortázar, Octavio Paz, and Gabriel García Márquez, and Southern writers like William Faulkner, Tennessee Williams, and Flannery O'Connor, have been crucial in the creation of an identity that, without forsaking its regional roots and idiosyncrasies, extended beyond itself and into the uncertain realm of the non-particular, to the extent that non-Southern or non-Latin American writers began to appropriate Southern or Latin American themes and incorporate them into their own *zeitgeist*. As W.J. Cash wrote in 1941, for example, U.S. Southern literature in the nineteenth century came to be a commodity that was marketed and whose styling would be emulated in the North: "In Northern literature and even more in the Northern theater romantic Southern themes grew constantly in popularity, until in the 1890s they were near to dominating all others."[5] This imitation gradually came to veil the authority supposedly inherent to a text, as it occurred that those unfamiliar with Latin America or the South began to inhabit their cultural territories and write about each (something that is not necessarily a topic new to the written word).

Today the issue of authority has taken center stage in the debate regarding verisimilitude and representation in literature and the arts. In their study "The Northern Origins of Southern Mythology," Patrick Gerster and Nicholas Cords offer notable examples of what are today known as emblematic examples of Southern literature or music but, in actuality, were originally written or composed by non-Southerners. The New Englander Harriet Beecher Stowe wrote *Uncle Tom's Cabin* (1852) with "extremely limited first-hand experience [of the South]," constructing "inflated images" that "contributed to their share of myth to the nation's understanding of slave conditions in the Old South." The abolitionist work *Cotton is King* (1855) by the Ohioan David Cristy represented an effort "to obscure the realities of the South's diversified economy and create the impression that Dixie was an empire of plantations and slaveholders." And Stephen Foster composed the songs "Susanna" (1847) and "Old Folks at Home" (1851) "prior to a one-month excursion into the South in 1852."[6] While the South's social institutions at the time demanded attention, it would seem that much of this attention—at least initially—came unfortunately from outside, originating in a desire to shape the region from a distinctly non-Southern perspective and to call attention to the injustices of slavery, further distancing the North from Southern society. Gerster and Cords maintain that, in reality, the truth was very different. In times of social turbulence and economic uncertainty, they say, the South served as "an enviable brand of social stability, when crisis, flux, and anxiety were the order of the day on northern fronts."[7] In fact, the works of Northern writers such as Henry James, Herman Melville, and Henry Adams condemned the perceived "Yankee civilization" of the 1870s and 1880s in an effort to "compare the progress and optimism of the early South with the stagnation and despair of America's 'age of excess.'"[8] This, in essence, was one of the principal justifications in the

United States of the representation and manipulation of Southern themes by non-Southern authors: to revel in the longing for a time past in which life was apparently simpler (at least for those who were white and belonged to the upper classes).

A representation and manipulation of identity from the outside is also evident in the literature and culture of Latin America, as popular figures such as Frida Kahlo and Eva Peron, indigenous peoples of Guatemala and Peru, and revolutionary movements in México, Nicaragua, and Bolivia, for example, have been lionized from outside their homeland, reworked according to the usurper's needs and nostalgias, and returned to their country in the shape of a cultural commodity, converted into the recognizable and familiar forces of a kinder market subversion that emanates security, comfort, and warmth. This appropriation and these constructed parallel paths of history are part of what connect the U.S. South and Latin America. The South, as Deborah N. Cohn observes, has come to be like Latin America due to historical and economic circumstances: "the impact of industrialization on the agrarian South in the first half of this [twentieth] century aggravated or produced conditions resembling those increasingly characteristic of Spanish American nations: poverty, malnourishment, illiteracy, and low standards of living."[9] These traits— "poverty," "malnourishment," and "illiteracy"—have come to represent part of the historical legacy left by both Latin America and the U.S. South.

In the case of Latin America, that legacy was first recorded by the chronicles of Spanish explorers in the fifteenth and sixteenth centuries, as these men accounted for their actions in the New World on behalf of the Spanish Crown. The letters and accounts of chroniclers such as Bernal Díaz del Castillo, Cabeza de Vaca, Bartolomé de las Casas, and Guamán Poma de Ayala have today come to represent the first written expressions of literature from within an ethnically heterogeneous Latin America: communications by those outside that sought to categorize, understand, and explain the New World to others. It is no surprise, then, that these descriptions were tainted by interests—personal or otherwise—that shaped the message of the text and placed the reader at an immediate disadvantage due to the fact that the writer was often writing years after the narrated events and thousands of miles away from his subject.

Contrary to the English colonization of North America, Spanish colonization of the Americas looked to extend the empire's power beyond its peninsular geography and to impose itself upon the conquered, using the tools provided by the State and the Church in order to reap material and spiritual riches for the Crown. The writers who recorded the travels and transactions of the Spanish king's representatives turned the New World into a land rich in possibility, abundant in dangers, and far from the stagnant familiarity of Spain.

The same romantic, astonished tone that chroniclers of Latin America gave their letters and manuscripts would later find its mirror image in the field research of Alexander von Humboldt and the writings and ideals of Jean Jacques Rousseau regarding the "noble savage" on the American continent, persisting well into the nineteenth century. Curiously, the writings on and from the Deep South of the Cuban patriot José Martí, champion of Cuban self-determination and independence from Spain, also contain romantic nuances that set the region apart from the rest of the United States. When he visited Charleston, South Carolina, immediately following the 1886 earthquake, Martí presented images of the homes and the perceived romantic spirit that inhabits them and distinguishes them from the North. He wrote that the city "abounds in beautiful residences, not built shoulder to shoulder like these immodest and slavish houses in the North, but with that noble detachment which contributes so much to the poetry and decorum of life," referring to the city in general as "a place of scanty science and abundant imagination."[10] In his descriptions, his choice of language belies an attitude established before his actual visit to the city, and what he does not write is as important as what he writes: the "immodest...slavish houses in the North" are contrapuntal constructions to the generous and elegant homes—and, by association, culture—of the South, the "scanty science" of the city underlining its life, its vitality, its lust for subjectivity, and its aversion to objectivity. History, it seems, has once again intervened between a writer and his subject, filtering impressions through the looking glass of the moment and leaving little room for those marginalized from the social, economic, and political centers of society.

If historical memory is in fact the inspiration for much of Latin American poetry and narrative, it is truly no different for the U.S. South. While we may evoke the first novels, the first short stories, poems, or essays to be considered definitively Southern, we must today recover and give priority to accounts that have emerged from the margins: slave narratives, indigenous traditions, letters sent by sons, wives, and fathers during the Civil War, truncated attempts at communication. These and other literary expressions have been formed and informed by history, and what I. A. Newby wrote regarding Southern writers may be true for Latin American ones: "History is a heavy weight, an obstruction to overcome, an obstacle to justice and truth and liberation."[11] This "heavy

weight" lies more squarely on the shoulders of the historically marginalized, those who have been isolated from positions of power because of
their economic status, the color of their skin or their gender, voices that,
over time, have manifested the diversity of literary manifestations. Examples include writers such as the Cuban-born Gertrudis Gómez de Avellaneda and her novel *Sab* (1841)—an abolitionist work that argues for a
woman's right to self-determination—and the book *Aves sin nido* (*Birds
Without a Nest*) (1889) by the Peruvian Clorinda Matto de Turner, a narrative fiction that places itself squarely within the boundaries of a feminist
movement and champions women's right to self-determination. In the
U.S. South, there has also been an abundance of narrative voices that have
spoken out against the traditional role imposed by men and in favor
of a more contemporary role for women. A few examples include Kate
Chopin, who in 1899 wrote *The Awakening*, a novel centering on the
frustrations of a married woman who attempts to communicate her disil-
lusionment to her husband and, ultimately finding no satisfaction in her
relationship with either her husband or her lover, chooses to end her
own life; Belle Kearney, who in works such as *A Slaveholder's Daughter*
(1900) wrote against "the influence of the southern lady ideal" without
being able to escape it; and the novel *The Comings of Cousin Ann* (1923)
by Emma Speed Sampson, which "contrasts the typical Southern belle"
and "the new Southern woman."[12] Further examples include other writers such as Evelyn Scott (*Escapade* [1923]), Frances Newman (*Dead Lovers
are Faithful Lovers* [1928]), Zora Neale Hurston (*Their Eyes Were Watching
God* [1937]), and Harriet Arrow (*The Dollmaker* [1954]),[13] all of whom
questioned the myths surrounding the U.S. Southern woman. In Latin
America, women such as Sor Juana Inés de la Cruz, Rosario Castellanos
(*El eterno femenino*), Elena Poniatowska (*Tinísima*), Gioconda Belli (*De la
costilla de Eva*), Isabel Allende (*La casa de los espíritus*), and Nélida Piñón,
among many others, offer written accounts of the struggles and ideals of
women throughout the course of Latin American history. In U.S. Southern
and Latin American literature, these and other writers exemplify the
multiple concerns of the marginalized voices of women, speaking to the
particular context of each and to the possibility of joining this distinctiveness with a collective consciousness of themes that transcends both
geographical borders and the spatial limitations of time.

For many writers in the U.S. South and Latin America, part of
their charge has been to recover history from the hands of others and to
rediscover their own memories. As Cohn has noted, "For both Southern
and Spanish American authors, memory, the point at which notions of

time and individual perspective intersect, came to be a particularly powerful correlative to explorations of historical consciousness."[14] Memory, as Cohn alludes, is that place where the particular and the collective assemble, bound together through time, corroborating one's evidence with the other's presence. In this way, that which has been neglected may, once again, be brought to the light of history, and the vanquished and the lost may again offer their voices to time.

Due to the defeat suffered at the hands of Union forces over the course of the Civil War, the South proved to be the only region in the continental United States with a clear and distinct memory of loss. When the conflict concluded in 1865, it was deemed lost by the Confederate States of America, a "nation" forced to capitulate, to extend to the Union Army the full benefits of victory and to bear the brunt of defeat. As Newby has indicated, "Southerners learned many things from the war, none of them more important than the meaning of defeat, of knowing it is possible to strive and sacrifice and do one's best and still lose."[15] Militarily, the United States has, since the end of the Civil War, known defeat—or at least the absence of a victory—but it has always tasted it on foreign soils: the Cuban Bay of Pigs invasion in 1962 and the Vietnam War, for example. Even the most recent problematic victory against oppression in Iraq and its leader Saddam Hussein, has not meant loss of national soil, the burning of homes on its own land, the death of citizens on its own territory. The losses—defeats, even—have occurred far from home and have run the danger of turning each successive campaign into an abstract struggle distant from the lives of the vast majority of residents in the United States. As a region familiar with loss and defeat, the South may be in a privileged position to better understand the disappointments and failures of armed conflict. Perhaps this is why the region has been witness to the emergence of its fair share of written and oral testimonials, of texts that seek to both disclose and come to terms with the suffered incongruities of life. From the *Narrative of the Life of Frederick Douglass, An American Slave* (1845) to *All God's Dangers* (1974), the memories of Theodore Rosengarten, a poor elderly black man in Alabama, many U.S. Southern writers have sought to incorporate their own voices into a web of expression. Canonically, this same web of expression had kept these voices at a literary distance, shelving them as winsome "essays" or "memoirs" and condemning them to the same fate from which they were born: the potential commercial anonymity of autobiography. In the second half of the twentieth century, the restorative power of the autobiographical narrative was rediscovered, and both fiction and nonfiction have sought to incorporate the styling of

Southern testimonials. William Styron's Pulitzer prize-winning *The Confessions of Nat Turner* (1967), for example, is the imagined narrative of the 1831 Southampton slave insurrection. And Allan Gurganus's bestseller *Oldest Living Confederate Widow Tells All* (1989) gives voice to 99 year-old Lucy Mardsen—the widow of the last surviving Confederate soldier—and recounts from memory her life story, evoking the most minute details of her existence in order to come to terms with her particular moment in time and with the world around her.

The writing of memoirs and testimonials in the U.S. South has also been an attempt to reassert one's potentially misplaced identity and to recover a historical space within the composition of a nation whose paths to political, social, and economic power were occupied by a minority that had frequently assumed this mantle as their birthright and, paradoxically, undermined any possible subversive voices. The written and spoken word has frequently illustrated the fight against the powers of these cultural omnivores. According to Cohn, "As literature has frequently served as a space for redressing the failure of official channels to address social and political issues, writers have often sought to restore untold tales to the record, rewrite their history, and participate in the construction of a collective id."[16] Interestingly, the three verbs "restore," "rewrite," and "participate" have proven to be contentious, as writers have offered themselves as surrogate parents, as voices for the voiceless, and may be charged with contaminating the original message of the text. Rigoberta Menchú's work *My Story and the Story of all Poor Guatemalans* (1982) offers the representative story of one Maya-Quiché woman's struggle against repression, yet proved to be, some years after its publication, a sensitive point of debate for many academics who were forced to choose sides when David Stoll published *Rigoberta Menchú and the Story of All Poor Guatemalans* (1999). In his work, Stoll criticizes Menchú for either fabricating or exaggerating a number of essential details in her work, from the importance (or lack thereof) of her formal education to the number of people that the Guatemalan military forces murdered in her village. Critics on one side of the debate applauded the analysis of Menchú's selective memory, echoing Stoll and claiming that Menchú's accounts "are distorted and slanted, when they are not embellishments," that "Menchú altered the facts throughout to suit her purposes," and that her work "is specifically adapted to suit the purposes of the guerrilla insurgency with which she had become associated."[17] Other academics defended the representativeness of her testimony, overlooking seemingly insignificant inconsistencies and declaring that "her book is important because tens of thousands of people were killed or brutalized by Guatemalan soldiers during the country's 36-year war," and stressing that "it is important to remember that Menchú's book is a narrative, not a piece of legal testimony."[18] The compromise between both perspectives—one that offers a testimonial account of the suffering of a people, another that takes the work to task for its factual errors—appears to be nonexistent, as the two are positioned on either flank of the ideological debate and are therefore unwilling to give any discursive advantage to the other side.

The doubt regarding the truthfulness, authenticity, and authority of this and other nonfiction works will nonetheless remain, as the reader consistently seeks the difference between an author's pen and a witness's own voice—if they are indeed two separate and distinct subjects—and looks to detect any hint of discursive manipulation. For this reason, perhaps, U.S. Southern literature has distinguished itself vehemently from the rest of the nation. While today's Southern writers may have explicitly little in common with the Faulkners of the past, there is still a historical debt running through much of their contemporary works, an intonation that redeems itself in the face of history and that looks to scrap with the adversary. It should be no coincidence, then, that Reconstruction and Northern presence and intervention in Southern affairs immediately following the Civil War gave rise to a Southern literature that "represented basically the patriotic response of the men of talent to the absorbing need of the South to defend itself, to shore up its pride at home, and to justify itself in the eyes of the world."[19] As has been previously mentioned, the presence of an enemy has made it much easier for a people to define themselves within a given historical moment.

In Latin American literature, the relatively recent eruption of the testimonial genre upon the literary scene has represented a thematic and stylistic revolution, one that has taken as its inspiration the plight of the marginalized. Beginning with the establishment of the prestigious Casa de las Américas prize for testimonial narrative in 1970, the testimonial as literature has informed practically all Latin American literary genres, from Ernesto Cardenal's poetry to the essays and communiqués of sub-commander Marcos, leader of the Ejército Zapatista de Liberación Nacional (Zapatista Army of National Liberation) in Chiapas, Mexico. Authors such as Menchú, Omar Cabezas, and Domitila Barrios have enunciated personal events that represent the experiences of thousands of other individuals in Guatemala, Nicaragua, and Bolivia, respectively, infusing each narrative with a weight that transcends the merely personal and placing the narrator squarely within the borders of history (or, better yet, expanding the limits of history so that its borders include the experiences of the narrative/narrated voice). As with U.S. Southern writing that takes historical memory as its starting point, Latin American testimonial literature represents the reassertion of a misplaced identity, the recovery of specific blanks existing over the course of a nation's history. As Cohn has noted, "Southerners and Spanish Americans alike self-consciously reclaim their histories by telling their own stories; they simultaneously challenge the versions presented as truth by a dominant voice and call into question the voice's authority."[20]

The research carried out by Cohn in 1999 and 2004 has looked to compare and contrast Southern and Latin American literary expressions, extending the seminal work of Earl Fitz in the field of Inter-American Studies, where the languages, literature, music, paintings, and political history, among others, are studied from a comparative perspective and treat the American continent as a whole, searching for both the commonalities and the distinctions between the cultures of the Americas. This relatively recent interest in uniting the continent and transcending national borders, from Canada to Argentina and Chile, has its current origins in the work of Professor Herbert E. Bolton, particularly his book *History of the Americas* (1918). Lewis Hanke's 1964 volume, *Do the Americas Have a Common History?*, also made a significant impact upon the field of Inter-American Studies by studying discrete themes in the national cultures of American countries.[21] The growing interest in the field also reflects the growing transparency of cultural interactions between American societies and the increased globalization of the continent: "[T]he Americas are taking note of each other as never before, and the Inter-American paradigm (understood as involving both Francophone and Anglophone Canada, the United States, Spanish America, Brazil, and the Caribbean) offers an excellent, though by no means foolproof, method of ensuring that this difficult process of [continental] rediscovery and reconsideration proceeds with fairness and accuracy."[22] As Fitz has noted, Inter-American Studies draws on interdisciplinary strategies that permit us to situate ourselves in the position of the other: "Crossing borders and boundaries in ways that increasingly integrate even such historically separate disciplines as the humanities, social sciences, law, engineering, and medicine, Inter-American Studies allows us to displace our traditional and very restrictive understanding of the term 'American' with a nomenclature and methodology that include all the cultures and nations of the New World."[23] For the field of Inter-American Studies to remain relevant in the future, there are a number of issues that underscore its most salient characteristics today and that must be addressed, including cohesion between the distinct academic programs, underscoring the importance of the Inter-American dissertation, supporting the revision of existing courses and the creation of new ones "that have representation from all five of our New World literatures,"[24] and, most importantly, requiring that students and faculty in the field of Inter-American Studies be linguistically competent in "at least three of our New World languages."[25] At the moment, the field of Inter-American Studies "represents an alternative way of studying things 'American,'"[26] and shows extreme potential to academically and systematically bring together the American continent.

Yet the field of Inter-American literary studies is only now uncovering the richness of analytical and comparative possibilities and finally stepping beyond the simple and repetitive examinations of the influences of the work of William Faulkner in the novels of Gabriel García Márquez. In Cohn's volume *History and Memory in the Two Souths*, many of the works cited in the "Criticism, History, and Theory" section of the bibliography center on the presence and evolution of magical realism in the literary production of both of these authors. In the co-edited work *Look Away! The U.S. South in New World Studies*, Cohn and Jon Smith assemble a group of essays that focus on the historical, political, demographic, cultural, and economic parallels existent between the Deep South and Latin American, Asian, African, or minority populations within the United States. The cultural strength and resonance of the studies in both volumes certainly lends itself to a wealth of interpretative possibilities; but there are also a variety of other hermeneutical options that Cohn and others intimate and explore only superficially.

One of the suggested characteristics of an inter-American or trans-American literature is the possible commonality between the works of the Southern Renaissance writers (1920s–1950s) and Latin American Boom literature (approximately 1950 to 1970). Many of the texts written and published in those contexts and during those times reflect reactions to a distinct period in history in which the distance between the author and the reader was bridged by themes manifesting the cultural anxieties of the moment: In the South, for example, "the works of the Southern Renaissance reflect an intense preoccupation with the South's history and the sense of a disjunction between the region's traditionalism and the questionable value(s) of modern industrial society."[27] And Latin American writers such as Mario Vargas Llosa and Gabriel García Márquez, who began writing in the 1950s and 60s and were termed the

Latin American Boom Generation, sought to incorporate the historical moment into their texts in order to transgress the conventional linear narrative style, in the process implicitly questioning the relationship between author (producer) and reader (consumer). According to Cohn, "As in the fiction of the Southern Renaissance, Boom fiction reexamines the past, assesses local (and international) forces competing for economic and political control, as well as their impact on social dynamics, and speculates on the region's future."[28] It is important to note that the technical and thematic disruptions to the Latin American and Spanish literary landscapes set in motion by Boom literature were accompanied by an editorial push sponsored by some of the largest publishing houses in Latin America, including Editorial Sudamericana in Buenos Aires and Siglo XXI in Mexico City. The question has been posed a number of times: Did the readers create the authors (and therefore the publishers), or did the publishing houses, by providing relatively inexpensive access to innovative novels, poems, essays, and short stories, create a market for the works? The relationship seems to have been symbiotic, as Boom writers arrived on the Latin American scene during the global political upheavals of the 1950s and 60s, at a time when the reading public was hungry for and exceptionally amenable to texts that challenged preestablished perceptions of literary purpose, structure, and construction. Once a writer had earned a reader's trust, the public began to search for their works and to expect more than merely a solipsist author ensconced in a purely linguistic theater.

One term that has frequently been used to describe the works of this period—particularly those of Gabriel García Márquez—has been magical realism. First coined in 1924 by the German artist and art critic Franz Roh, magical realism was "a way of representing and responding to reality and pictorially depicting the enigmas of reality."[29] In literature, the expression has been applied to works in which the fantastic (a floating woman, a group of butterflies carrying someone heavenward, a column of ants abducting a baby) catches the attention of the reader but does not seem out of place as dictated by the narrative structure of the text. A quintessential work of magical realism is *One Hundred Years of Solitude* (1967), by Gabriel García Márquez. Throughout its pages, the novel tells the story of the Buendía family and how destiny appears to have dictated their entire future (including even the names of the family members, as many of the principal male characters are named either José Arcadio or Aureliano and possess the characteristics of their namesake). A series of episodes and events illustrates how magical realism was perhaps the most appropriate and stylistic channel for the novel. When José Arcadio II is murdered in his own house, for example, the trail of blood trickles away from his body, down the streets of the town, over walls and under closed doors, until it crosses the village and reaches his mother's feet, who had earlier thrown her son out of the house. There is also the death of Remedios the Beautiful, who was so stunning that she simply one day floated away; or the implicit death of the last member of the Buendía family, carried away as a baby by a colony of ants. These examples, taken from one of the most representative works in Latin American literature, illustrate the extent to which literature has reflected the fantastic or the marvelous qualities of life in Latin America. As the Cuban writer Alejo Carpentier developed his ideas of life in Latin America as being what he termed "lo real maravilloso"—the marvelously real, the incredible fact that, given the socioeconomic circumstances for the majority of the population, life in Latin America is undoubtedly still lived and enjoyed—and used this as a vehicle in his writings, so too has magical realism been a part of the subtext of much of the literature, music, and painting produced in Latin America after the 1940s.

In U.S. Southern literature, there has existed a certain type of magical realism, a tendency toward a contemporary gothic, a union of the fantastic, the tragic, and the realist within a narrative, that which Cash broadly described as the Southerner's "naïve capacity for unreality."[30] A work such as *Look Homeward, Angel* (1929) by the North Carolinian Thomas Wolfe, for example, uses a first-person narrative to tell the story of Eugene, a boy growing up in Altamont, North Carolina (a veiled portrait of Asheville, Wolfe's home town). Throughout this semi-autobiographical novel, Wolfe uses a lyric stream of consciousness that illustrates Eugene's sensitivity to his family and his surroundings and generates dreamlike images that occasionally blur the division between the real and the imagined. When his brother Ben dies of pneumonia toward the final pages of the novel, for example, Eugene dreams and meets his deceased brother—speaking with him, listening to his advice—and imagines that a statue moves: "With a strong rustle of marble and a cold sigh of weariness, the angel nearest Eugene moved her stone foot and lifted her arm to a higher balance. The slender lily stipe shook stiffly in her elegant cold fingers."[31] In other moments of the novel, Eugene reflects on his existence and at times fashions for himself a type of alternate life, fueled by his relationships with those around him, by his reflections on solitude, and by his imagination. Cash has somewhat tenderly written regarding this perceptive stream of consciousness so evident in the Southern disposition: "It is a mood, in sum, in which directed thinking is all but impossible, a mood in which the mind yields almost perforce to drift and in which the imagination holds unchecked sway, a mood in which nothing any more seems improbably save the puny inadequateness of fact, nothing incredible save the bareness of truth."[32]

A variation on magical realism may also be found in the writings of Tennessee Williams. Known primarily for his theatre, Williams wrote a number of short stories such as "One Arm," "Hard Candy," and "The Field of Blue Children" that often appreciated that "inadequateness of fact" and created a world of the imagined and the surreal (his first short story was "The Vengeance of Nitrocis," published in 1928 in *Weird Tales*). Although both the short stories of Williams and Wolfe's *Look Homeward, Angel* are products of distinct contexts, different from *One Hundred Years of Solitude* or *The House of the Spirits* (1982) by Isabel Allende, the works of these and other Southern authors use the fantastic as a fulcrum from which reality may be raised and examined, as a stage upon which action fits into unexpected patterns and reflects the purposes of a writer intent possibly on transforming our understanding of a logical narrative event.

Another commonality between Southern literature and Latin American literature is the presence of voices descended from the African continent. In the South, writers such as Frederick Douglass, W.E.B. Du Bois, Zora Neale Hurston, Richard Wright, Alice Walker, and Joyce Carol Oates create and replicate the variety of themes that have been evoked in literature throughout the years, mirroring historical periods and individual sets of circumstances, ethical and aesthetic concerns and priorities. In the U.S. South, African American writers have fought to have their voice heard above the racial noise produced by publishers and reading public, a double-edged cacophony that, historically, looked to either pigeonhole them within the confines of "Colored" literature or disenfranchise them altogether. In Latin American literature, the presence of the African voice also evokes the themes of injustice and slavery, of Spanish galleons transporting people to the Americas from the West African coasts. Particularly over the course of the twentieth century, the voice of Blacks and the spirit of "Négritude" has gained strength and public (read "commercial") visibility—especially in Central America and the Caribbean—asserting itself alongside a growing awareness of identity. Writers such as the Cuban Nicolás Guillén have echoed the concerns of the question posed by Langston Hughes: "What happens to a dream deferred?" In his writings, Guillén responded by composing poems that combined a consciousness of the Afrohispanic voice in Cuba with concerns over the fate of the poor and marginalized in an industrialized world, crafting poems as cultural statements that looked to erode stereotypes and deconstruct race-based prejudices and immigrant mythologies.

The myriad of possible commonalities mentioned here are only a few of the possible points of departure for the comparative analysis of U.S. Southern and Latin American literatures and cultures, particularly with respect to the creation of a Latino literary identity within the geographical context of the Deep South. Works delving into the historical memory of a people, written by women, or posing the issue of discursive authority are connecting cultures across the Americas and rewriting the literary canon through a reexamination of continental, national, and regional identity. The field of Inter-American Studies must balance, however, the significance of local context with a larger, transnational framework that frequently provides the operational background for understanding smaller communities across the continent and emphasizes the importance of literary works as not only the *expressions* of distinctiveness but the *locations* of cultural identity. Only in this way will the interactions between the literary varieties of U.S. Southern and Latin American cultures be understood within proper theoretical and practical perspectives that look to understand the migrational dynamics occurring across the American continent.

FLANNERY O'CONNOR AND "THE DISPLACED PERSON": IMMIGRATION NOW, IMMIGRATION TOMORROW, IMMIGRATION FOREVER

In U.S. Southern literature, an example of the deconstruction and demythification of regional and transnational identities is the short story "The Displaced Person," by Flannery O'Connor. As a narrative, the story introduces the reader to themes such as immigration and the creation of community within the context of the South and the cultural framework that it offers. Moreover, it is about how one perceives the other and how such a perception can be altered by life's immediate circumstances and by the shifting terrain of ethnocentrism and an irrational fear of those different from us. First published in 1954 in the *Sewanee Review,* it should be seen as no coincidence that the story appears in the midst of the McCarthyist furor and of the period's right-wing impetus to create and maintain the traditional image of the homogeneous nuclear family in the United States. Although the action centers principally around a farm in the South, its themes cross both geographic and temporal divides, offering lessons for other areas of the country and for other times.

The title of the story lends itself to a variety of interpretative possibilities: the displaced persons may be the Guizacs, a family that has emigrated from Poland to find work in the rural South, on land owned by Mrs. McIntyre's. The displaced persons may also be the members of the Shortley family, who also work with Mrs. McIntyre's but are forced to leave and find their fortune elsewhere when they are fired because she can no longer afford to pay them their "normal" wages. The displaced are also the African Americans who work on the farm, as they are marginalized and descended from those taken by force from their homes. The attitudes depicted in the story reflect the fragmentation of historical identity and how one's discrete distinctiveness may be inseparable from those we considered to be outside of our community (a realization that carries with it the seeds of an irrational fear of the other). In the story, the personalization and representation of just such a phobia is the character of Mrs. Shortley, a woman whose prejudices rise to the surface when she learns that she and her family will lose their jobs because the Guizac family has arrived and is prepared to work for much lower wages. Her attitudes are evident in her reactions to the Poles. When she hears, for example, about how the family had escaped from a German concentration camp, Mrs. Shortley associates those evils with the family and thinks: "If they had come from where that kind of thing was done to them, who was to say they were not the kind that would do it to others?"[33] Mrs. Shortley is concerned that her country and the lifestyle she enjoys will be unavoidably altered by the arrival of immigrants. She projects her nation as a virgin territory, ripe for being overridden and conquered by hordes of uncivilized barbarians yearning to establish themselves, to turn the nation on its head, to rule from coast to coast and from the country to the city, the rural and the urban governed alike by the dictates of the new populations.

While in the twenty-first century the primary targets of those irrational nativist fears are immigrants arriving in the United States from developing countries in Asia, Africa, and Latin America, in the 1950s the scapegoats were Europeans, primarily those who came from countries whose social, political, and economic traditions were not historically related to the German or English cultures in the United States. In the short story, Mrs. Shortley boorishly views all of Europe as a dangerous unknown, a continent whose enigmas and maladies are personified by Mr. Guizac: "Every time Mr. Guizac smiled, Europe stretched out in Mrs. Shortley's imagination, mysterious and evil, the devil's experiment station."[34] For her, the Pole represents the sum of her fears and the expression of differences that look to destroy her world, embodied by a European lack of progress that constitutes an immediate threat to the stability of the United States: "In Europe they probably got some different way to make liquor but I reckon they know all the ways. They're full of crooked ways. They never have advanced or reformed. They got the same religion as a thousand years ago. It could only be the devil responsible for that. Always fighting amongst each other. Disputing. And then get us into it."[35] From her vantage point, the United States has always had to save Europe from itself and fight their battles for them, on a foreign territory that has little to offer her—save cheap labor. Even this, however, is not balanced by centuries of religious stagnation and, in her opinion, the proliferation of cheats and scoundrels.

The landscape upon which a conflict occurs corresponds to both a geographical territory and a cultural realm that may not respect geopolitical borders and may be transported easily as legitimate personal baggage. The terrain of languiage is just such a landscape, one of the moveable fields upon which otherness is defined. As a distrustful monolingual, Mrs. Shortley resents any individual who does not communicate in her own *lingua franca*, English. When the town priest attempts to convince the land owner Mrs. McIntyre to take in another immigrant family, for example, Mrs. Shortley's own fears multiply as she imagines the tensions and conflicts that will result from such an "invasion." She creates a collection of linguistic victims comparable to the Holocaust:

> It suddenly came to Mrs. Shortley that [the priest] was trying to persuade [Mrs. McIntyre] to bring another Polish family onto the place. With two of them here, there would be almost nothing spoken but Polish! The Negroes would be gone and there would be the two families against Mr. Shortley and herself! She began to imagine a war of words, to see the Polish words and the English words coming at each other, stalking forward, not sentences, just words, gabble gabble gabble, flung out high and shrill and stalking forward and then grappling with each other. She saw the Polish words, dirty and all-knowing and unreformed, flinging mud on the clean English words until everything was equally dirty. She saw them all piled up in a room, all the dead dirty words, theirs and hers too, piled up like the naked bodies in the newsreel.[36]

Her imagination perceives the fight as a violent battle for power where the foot soldiers will be the words and each language will be unmistakably representative of each culture: the Polish words, "dirty and all-knowing and unreformed," versus "the clean English words." For her way of life to survive, the English language must remain inaccessible to other cultures and hold on to its privileged communicative position, not giving ground to other languages. As she declares later on in the story, "That's where we make our mistake, letting all them people onto English. There's be a heap less trouble if everybody only knew his own language."[37] Being monolingual is compartmentalization, especially if the language spoken is the language of the dominant culture being apparently and gradually displaced. In this sense, a monolingual culture breeds and supports its own idea of power through the support of one-language laws and institutions. Monolingual cultures hitch their own linguistic domination of the other to the horses of irrational fear that individuals may have of a multilingual society, which may itself be as exclusive of them as they are of those who speak other languages.

In the story, Mrs. Shortley's fears stem primarily from her lack of interaction with individuals different from herself, an ignorance grounded chiefly in the acceptance of facile stereotypes and in the refusal to encounter other persons as individuals instead of as assorted compilations of characteristics. She fights to distinguish herself from the Guizacs, but events force her to share emotional space with the Polish family as she and her family are fired and, therefore, displaced from their environment. Her children ask her, "Where we goin', ma? Where we goin'? While their mother, her huge body rolled back still against the seat and her eyes like blue-painted glass, seemed to contemplate for the first time the tremendous frontiers of her true country."[38] If we follow the characterization that the narrator offers, the adjectives "tremendous" and "true" emphasize Mrs. Shortley's plight: regardless of citizenship, the country's size is no longer a portent of possibility but rather an inevitable weight to carry in one's search for a place. This, in turn, is one of the truths of her country: that individuals risk losing themselves in it, no matter where they are from. For many immigrants to the United States, this country inspires a degree of fear combined with the promise of a better life. For Mrs. Shortley, the United States also inspires a degree of fear, but a fear absent of potential and economic promise. She has been displaced and, as labor, replaced by the arrival of another family, one that is not from that place but that has come looking for theirs.

Mrs. McIntyre, the owner of the farm, pursues apparently selfish motives, as she helps the Guizacs out of her own economic self-interest and not out of some altruistic impulse. In considering the Polish family,

Mrs. McIntyre mythifies and distorts their image until something emerges akin to an admission of cultural guilt: "Mr. Guizac probably had everything given to him all the way across Europe and over here. He had probably not had to struggle enough. She had given him a job. She didn't know if he was grateful or not. She didn't know anything about him except that he did the work. The truth was that he was not very real to her yet."[39] She envisions how easy his life must have been in Europe, congratulates herself for giving him work, and allows that she does not know Mr. Guizac as an individual, only as a set of larger traits. Her tacit admission underlies the fact that she, herself, through contact with the Guizacs and through recognizing that they had not yet acquired individual characteristics, has been witness to the displacement of her own identity. She is beginning to step outside herself, outside her preconceived notions regarding the foreign. Implicit in her admission is that, like Mrs. Shortley, Mrs. McIntyre also believes in a truth, in a concept that is in direct contradiction to her own personal experience. For Mrs. Shortley, her country emerges as something unknown and indefinite; for Mrs. McIntyre, however, a fellow human being from a foreign land begins to acquire depth.

Throughout the story there are additional themes and subthemes that resonate with current national attitudes toward immigration and both extend and subvert common stereotypes. Ethnocentrism, cultural self-centeredness, and stereotypical ways of thinking with regard to the influx of immigrant labor are present throughout the narrative, especially when the three narrated cultures—the Southern Anglo-Saxon, the Polish, and the African American—come into direct contact with each other and reveal the unanticipated commonalities between them, particularly between the Polish and the African American characters in the story. Is there a narrative common ground? Both ethnicities are presented in opposition to the dominant Anglo culture of Mrs. Shortley and Mrs. McIntyre. Is there a *cultural* common ground? Due to imperialism and war, both the African American and the Polish cultures have suffered from displacement. In the story, both are also presented as victims with a common fate.

It is no surprise that the black workers in the story express both empathy and understanding toward the plight of the Guizac family—empathy and understanding that the Polish family awkwardly returns when Mr. Guizac decides to "give" a black worker one of his Polish cousins, "promising him that she will marry him when she is older."[40] Aside from the clear parallel that this "arrangement" has with ideas regarding the individual as property and with the relationship between Mr. Guizac and Mrs. McIntyre, it is also troubling that someone would agree to such an understanding. When she learns of the verbal contract, Mrs. McIntyre's only concerns center around the racial elements of the exchange and she chastises the Pole for his apparent naïveté: "Mr. Guizac...that nigger cannot have a white wife from Europe. You can't talk to a nigger that way. You'll excite him and besides it can't be done. Maybe it can be done in Poland but it can't be done here and you'll have to stop."[41] Her language represents the black man as an animal, dominated by sheer emotions and passions that defy logic. And while Mr. Guizac may not be African American, Mrs. McIntyre makes it clear throughout her sermon that he does not belong in her own racial category, either. Her declaration that "It can't be done here and you'll have to stop" carries the cultural weight of time and place: our customs are different here, and you may not continue—but again, because of the perceived characteristics and opinions of the African American race, not out of an ethical or humanitarian concern regarding the selling of another human being. In the end, Mr. Guizac's response to Mrs. McIntyre brings him even closer to the black workers—"[My cousin,] She no care black. She in camp three year"[42]—and emphasizes the importance of socialization and cultural experience. For his cousin, being married to a black man is unimportant, as she was a prisoner in a German concentration camp for three years.

By the end of the story, the three ethnic lines of divergence—the white, the black, and the Polish—come together in time as Mr. Shortley returns and asks for his job back, explaining that Mrs. Shortley had died and they had nowhere else to go. Mrs. McIntyre acquiesces, and shortly thereafter the incident occurs that brings the story to a dramatic close: as Mr. Guizac is lying on the ground, repairing a small tractor, a larger tractor runs over him, breaking his back and killing him. Mr. Shortley, Mrs. McIntyre, and a black worker who had witnessed the episode and could have prevented the tragedy, apparently and silently cement their alliance against this displaced person, as they had seen it coming but had done nothing to warn the man about the impending danger: "[Mrs. McIntyre] had felt her eyes and Mr. Shortley's eyes and the Negro's eyes come together in one look that froze them in collusion forever."[43] What common interest "froze them in collusion forever"? Why actively or passively seek the failure of the Guizac family on the McIntyre farm? Apparently, because the success of these immigrants would have meant failure for those who refused to accept the equal status of migrational populations and the changing realities of their community and of the world around them.

A contemporary reading of the story sheds light on the difficulties that Latino immigrants face in the United States and emphasizes the same themes: prejudice, racism, rejection, and ultimate spiritual poverty for a community that cannot accept its own growth and transformation. As Cohn suggests, both Latinos and the South share these same troubles: "The marginalization of the South and Spanish America has been internal as well as external. On the one hand, both regions have fought the political, economic, and cultural expansionism of a northern neighbor, whether the northern U.S. or the nation in its entirety. On the other, they reduplicate their own subordination in the dispossession by race, ethnicity, gender, and class that has created 'fourth world' populations within their perimeters."[44] As an expression of popular culture, literature has and will continue to act as mirror in which a people may follow the evolution of their own soul and perhaps even anticipate the eventual future that awaits them upon the turn of the calendar page.

CARLOS FUENTES AND *THE CRYSTAL FRONTIER*: MOVEMENT AND PASSAGE

As with the short story by Flannery O'Connor, Carlos Fuentes's work *The Crystal Frontier* (1995)—"A novel in nine stories"—also delves into the world of immigration, contextualizing the narrative within the contemporary framework of the Mexico-United States border and articulating itself from a position that observes the daily reality of the border culture in both countries. This work, above all, speaks to the future of the United States, as other areas of the nation that are not necessarily international border zones continue to receive Latin American immigrants and, in the process, become themselves a type of periphery where the unexpected combination and interrelation of two or more cultures produces a third that is found, simultaneously, at the borders of the community and at the center of the power struggle between the new immigrants and the long-standing inhabitants of the area.

As the subtitle of the work indicates, the novel is composed of nine independent yet interconnected stories in which a number of characters shift from one chapter to another. Individually, each narrative stands apart as a specific moment in time in the lives of individuals whose existence revolves around the Mexico-United States border culture; collectively, their accounts form a tapestry of experience that highlights the diversity of understanding and the power of the border to form, control, and determine the assorted relationships. As was the case with O'Connor's short story "The Displaced Person," Fuentes's novel portrays the impact of immigration upon a society, highlights the transitory nature of those whose lives depend on the border, and turns the geographical space of the frontier into a cultural space that may actually migrate and move with the immigrant. As the title indicates, the principle focus of the novel is itself the border: its residents, its impression, its genuinely illusory nature. The theme of the border is touched on in each of the nine stories, as many of the characters attempt to balance cultural responsibility with economic need and to come to terms with an environment that combines the hypocrisy, the injustice, the racism, and the commanding economic potential of both countries. These factors, then, contribute to its undefinability as, in the process of aiding or hindering an individual's efforts at making use of the opportunities available, the border, in effect, dissipates and becomes slowly part of that individual. That a political border exists between the two countries is undeniable; that the Rio Grande forms part of that border between the two countries is also difficult to contradict. However, the border's permeability and ultimate futility is also indisputable, as these same political and geographical divisions are unable to stop the flow of Mexican immigrants from entering the United States.

In the novel, Fuentes's characters and narrative voice describe the border as a place of transit that, more than anything, serves as stage and witness to the thousands of daily maneuvers and machinations: "Properties, customs offices, real estate deals, wealth and power provided by control over an illusory, crystal border, a porous frontier through which each year pass millions of people, ideas, products—in short, everything (sotto voce: contraband, drugs, counterfeit money, et cetera)."[45] More than creating an iron-clad border, the policies of Mexico and the United States have breathed life into an area that has become its own master, as it allows or forbids movements according to economic necessity and reality, not political mandates dictated by a federal capital so potentially alienated from its margins.

Throughout the stories, a number of characters come to represent the distinct and subtle connotations of the term "border." In one chapter, "The Line of Oblivion," Leonardo Barroso's unnamed brother reflects upon his destiny from the perspective of his wheelchair. For him, the border is everywhere: in front of him, beneath him, above him, playing a decisive role in the fate of his family and of those who live from and for it:

Sunrise. The run rises with silhouettes I watch from my chair. Posts and cables. Barbed-wire fences. Pavements. Dung heaps. Tin roofs. Cardboard houses perched on the hillsides. Television antennas scratching the ravines. Garbagemen. Infinite numbers of garbagemen. Plantations of garbage. Dogs. Don't let them come near me. And the sound of feet. Swift. Crossing the border. Abandoning the earth. Seeking the world. Earth and world, always. We have no other home. And I sit here immobile, abandoned at the line of oblivion. Which country do I belong to? Which memory? Which blood?[46]

The physical characteristics of the border and its unbreakable cycle of poverty do not mask its territorial consciousness and the constant emergence of those whose lives disprove the simplistic and naïve definitions of that land between lands. Heard above the din of physical necessity is the cry of its inhabitants, those who search for a home and implicitly acknowledge that their place is no-place, their country is no-country, their blood a historic amalgamation of crossings and tinctures that no government has been able to circumscribe. While borders are an attempt to separate, they also contribute to the perpetual unity and flux of the world: the greater the political, cultural, or economic distances between bordering nations, the more necessary that the "movement" between them continue and flourish (not in order to homogenize both countries or to create two parallel indistinct nations, but rather to encourage relationships based on respect, understanding, and a shared awareness of future).

Appearing in only a few pages toward the end of the work, the character of José Francisco represents the synthesis of cultures and the promise that this offers for the future. As José Francisco rides his Harley-Davidson along the border, the narrator recognizes his uniqueness as being born of fusion: "He bore something that couldn't happen on either side of the frontier but can happen on both sides. Those were hard things to understand on both sides."[47] We sometimes look for a clear division of space, something that will soothe us in the search for our place among so many and for our time amongst so much. Identity has rarely been as unambiguous as when it has reflected interstices and conjunctions, and this may disorient those who consider themselves to be of unadulterated lineage or nationality; but the product of two distinct integers is frequently more unique than one of those integers, as it incorporates the history of *two* digits and not just one. In the work, José Francisco is this product— and he realizes this—using his writing to collect these border stories and disseminate them throughout the world into which he has been thrust:

and when he began to write, at the age of nineteen, he was asked, and asked himself, in which language, in English or in Spanish? and first he said in something new, the Chicano language, and it was then he realized what he was, neither Mexican nor gringo but Chicano, the language revealed it to him, he began to write in Spanish the parts that came out of his Mexican soul, in English the parts that imposed themselves on him in a Yankee rhythm, first he mixed, then he began separating, some stories in English, others in Spanish, depending on the story, the characters, but always everything united, story, characters.[48]

The result of José Francisco's realization of his own border identity is not only the production of texts that move easily between two languages—and therefore two worlds. It is also the creation of a singular individuality—a border consciousness—which not only takes from two cultures but, more importantly, *is* two cultures. As he himself expresses later, "I'm not a Mexican. I'm not a gringo. I'm Chicano. I'm not a gringo in the USA and a Mexican in Mexico. I'm Chicano everywhere. I don't have to assimilate into anything. I have my own history."[49] The narrations emanating from borders and the formation of border cultures is what European and North American histories have largely ignored over the course of centuries. Although these frontier areas have inhabited the physical margins of the nation-state, they have represented that which has been geographically and culturally furthest from the political center of the country. Through his denial of a single history tied exclusively to one nationality, José Francisco creates for himself an identity that acknowledges the contributions of both the United States and Mexican cultures and that endows him with a sense of pride. His declaration that "I have my own history" acknowledges his own uniqueness and the uniqueness of his heritage, a heritage born of the permanent duality inherent in border zones.

It is evident that, in the novel, the border is the philosophical touchstone that attempts to reveal the enormous complexity of border life and relations. Fuentes's description of life at the U.S.-Mexican border is a revelation of that which exists in the shadows, in the forgotten corners of our national cultures: bilingual poverty, political corruption, fraud, marginalization, and racism. As in O'Connor's short story, Fuentes uses his characters to unmask many of the biases and prejudices surrounding the immigration of foreign nationals to the United States.

One of the principal opinions evident in many of the novel's characters concerns the hypocrisy of some citizens of the United States regarding individuals who may be different from themselves—such as Mexican citizens—and their arrival in this country. In the work, the Tarleton Wingate family, for example, serves as host to Juan Zamora while he is in Ithaca, New York, studying medicine at Cornell University in the 1980s. The family is a conservative one, belonging to the upper middle class and making no secret of the fact that "They watch television every night and applaud the decisions of the new president, his movie-star smile, his desire to put a halt to excessive government control."[50] The Wingates are the new conservatives of a country that, in the 1980s, declared its allegiance to Ronald Reagan and to the conservative vision that he offered in which all citizens would prosper if the wealthy prospered first. In the novel, the ideological side of these particular Reaganites emerges gradually, as they cautiously express their point of view "that the expression *free world* is synonymous with *free enterprise*." Jim Rowlands, Juan's lover, does not agree with the Wingate's ideology and, speaking to Juan, criticizes his host family's double standards: "They're a bunch of cynics. They want free enterprise in everything, except when it comes to weapons and rescuing thieving financiers."[51]

When Juan decides to return to Mexico because he discovers that Jim is engaged to be married to a woman from his hometown, the Wingate family "felt relieved" at his departure, as, in their opinion, Juan had been associating with someone as undesirable as Jim Rowlands. In the process, the narrator asks of the family, "Had they allowed themselves to succumb to irrational prejudice? They certainly had. But prejudices could not be removed overnight; they were very old, they had more reality—they did—than a political party or a bank account."[52] In this case, the prejudice and the hypocrisy of the Wingate family extends to other United States citizens who may not act or think exactly like them; but their attitudes are justified, as, allegedly, the prejudices would still exist tomorrow, and trying to eliminate them was an exercise in futility. What's more, these prejudices may actually be comforting, as they represent a degree of self-validity and can safeguard them from those on the *outside* who do not share their values and their approach to life.

An integral part of the hypocrisy of the United States as represented in the novel is the economic double standard practiced by both the government and transnational corporations, which is imposed upon U.S. -Mexican relations (specifically upon the Mexican immigrants arriving in the United States looking for employment). In "The Line of Oblivion," for example, a second voice answers the concerns of the Mexican wheelchair-ridden protagonist of the chapter and underlines the rigid nature of the economic relations between the two countries: "Those you call your brothers will keep coming. When their arms are wanted, they'll cross the line and no one will bother them. Everyone will look the other way. But when they're no longer needed, they'll be rejected. They'll be beaten up. They'll be killed in the streets in broad daylight. They'll be kicked out. The world won't change."[53]

In another chapter, the Mexican businessman Leonardo "Len" Barroso reflects U.S. attitudes on labor and comments on the transitory and frequently hypocritical attitudes and behaviors of North American companies that choose to do business in Mexico: "If we [in Mexico] enforce work-safety rules, they move on. If we're strict about applying the Federal Labor Law, they move on. If there's a boom in the defense industry, they move on. You talk to me about job rotations? That's the law of labor."[54] As with the Mrs. McIntyre in O'Connor's short story, the principle motivation behind U.S. immigration and corporate law is an economic self-interest that benefits both businesses in the United States and large landowners in Mexico. The hypocrisy is not only forbidding entry into the United States nor controlling immigration consistent with national laws, but rather applying such laws sporadically—according to the moment's economic circumstances—without affecting a change in policy that will accommodate fiscal fluctuations. Mrs. McIntyre, as we noted previously, cared little for the plight of her immigrant laborers, for, if she hires the Polish Guizac family and intends to fire the Shortleys, it is out of the need to maximize profits and the desire to pay her workers less. Mr. Guizac is, as she admits, a means to an end—"The truth was that he was not very real to her yet"[55]—who represents a minimization of costs. Equally, in Fuentes's novel, many of the immigrant workers are simply pawns—manipulated by individuals who interpret immigration laws according to the whims of the market—and rarely do these persons become tangible men and women in the eyes of U.S. business interests.

Fuentes's novel manages to skillfully represent the impulses that frequently exemplify the injustices suffered by the Mexican immigrants in their efforts to work in the United States, from outright discrimination to subtle political or economic marginalization. In the work, the opinion of plant managers in the United States regarding Mexicans who came to the United States seeking jobs, for example, is that "the advantage of the Mexican worker was that he did not become a citizen and did not organize unions or go on strike, the way European immigrants did."[56] In another section, the *coyote* Gonzalo Romero helps 54 Mexican workers cross illegally into the United States and hands them over to the "contractors" on the U.S. side. These contractors, however, declare that they did not need such a large number of workers, and begin to lower the wage offered in an attempt to whittle down their ranks: "From their truck, the contractors first said that there were too many, that they couldn't contract for fifty-four wetbacks, although they'd take anyone who would work for a dollar an hour even though they'd said they'd pay two dollars an hour. All fifty-four raised their hands, and then the contractors said, Still too many—let's see how many will come with us for fifty cents an hour."[57] In these cases, the injustices suffered by the Mexican immigrants may be understood given the laws of supply and demand and the paucity of opportunities in Mexico; but it does not justify their dehumanization. The Mexican worker may not necessarily "become a US citizen nor organize unions and strikes," but, like the Guizac family, they are deserving of humane working conditions and the right to organize if these conditions do not exist. Likewise, the fact that they will work for one dollar an hour does not give an employer the right to lower this wage even further, as the contractor is already considering himself above the law by illegally hiring workers—international or otherwise—and paying them less than the federally mandated minimum wage. As a variation on the theme of unfairness, economic injustice is frequently the first step toward political or social discrimination, marginalization, or even violence (in all its ugly permutations). If in his work Fuentes draws attention to the economic injustices suffered by Mexican immigrants who arrive in the United States seeking employment, it is, perhaps, to present a mirror before the face of the country: this treatment of the other is who you are, and you are much better than that.

Throughout the work there are additional examples of injustices suffered by Mexicans who chose to work and reside in the United States. The situation of the aforementioned medical student Juan Zamora is a case in point, as he tells the story of Mexican immigrants who, after the passing of Proposition 187 in California in 1994 and the subsequent loss of education and health care services for illegal immigrants, feared going to the hospital, as they were scared that the authorities would turn them in to the police. In light of the times, Mexican parents also stopped taking their children to school, as "a child of Mexican origin is easily identified."[58] They asked Juan, "What are we doing to do?...We pay more, much, much more in taxes than what they give us in education and services. What are we going to do? Why are they accusing us? What are they accusing us of? We're working. We're here because they need us. The gringos need us. If they didn't, we wouldn't come."[59] The anonymous voice of these parents represents the multitudes of Mexican immigrants who suffer a systematically inhumane treatment that begins at the legislative level and trickles down to the individuals. It is not "fair" that there are Mexican immigrants who pay their share of taxes yet do not receive their share of benefits; it is not "fair" that their children's skin color may dictate the quality of their education; and it is not "fair" that the immigration dilemma is dropped neatly into the laps of Mexicans and the Mexican government, as if, similar to the United States campaign against the production and refinement of cocaine in Colombia, the problem stemmed simply from the supply and not the demand.

Originating in economics, these injustices touch all facets of immigrant life, from the personal to the political, and from the momentous to the mundane. In the novel, the character of the Chicano writer José Francisco draws attention to the presence of these prejudices in the educational system where he resides—on the U.S. side of the border—demanding, through pressure and publicity, "that students—blacks, Mexicans, whites —be seated in the classroom by alphabetical order and not by racial group."[60] In the text, he is the first character to truly assume his bicultural condition, grow from it, and gradually rebel against an administrative authority that categorizes someone according to the color of their skin. Many more like him are needed, though, in order to prevent the inequalities and the violence against Mexican immigrants who, like the 23 workers killed by skinheads in the novel, are simply giving the United States the manual labor it needs to continue to harvest the crops, prepare the hospital rooms, construct the buildings, and much, much more.

In much the same way as O'Connor's short story, certain characters in the novel are representative of the hostility and the blind racism encountered by Mexican immigrants upon their arrival in the United States. Amy Dunbar, for example, is a wealthy, rude spinster living alone in the Chicago suburbs, whose abusive treatment of her domestic help always forces them to leave the house. Upon the departure of her latest employee, one day her nephew Archibald hires Josefina, a Mexican woman whose husband is in jail wrongly accused of murder and who agrees to work for Ms. Dunbar in order to help defray the legal costs that are accruing in her husband's case. Even before Josefina's arrival, Ms. Dunbar bares her prejudices as she reacts to her nephew's hiring of a Mexican, declaring—twice—that Mexicans "are supposed to be lazy!"[61] When Josefina begins to work in the house, she too suffers the opinions and abuse of Ms. Dunbar. In the afternoons, for example, her employer sits and watches television, "commenting on everything she saw with sarcasm, insults, and disdain for blacks, Jews, Italians, Mexicans. She delivered it all out loud, whether anyone heard or not."[62] Gradually,

Ms. Dunbar constructs a relationship with Josefina based on an apprehension that, as is slowly evident, manifests more her dread of those different from her rather than Josefina's fear of Ms. Dunbar.

In actuality, Josefina never expresses a fear of her employer, addressing her respectfully and honestly, never in a subservient manner, accepting the abuse that Ms. Dunbar bestows. When the older woman attempts to manipulate her and to force her to lose her temper, Josefina simply reacts with deference, replying, "Because you're a good person" or "As you say, ma'am."[63] Gradually, "Miss Amy" becomes more aware of the difficult situation that Josefina and her husband are in—as he is incarcerated—and slowly opens herself up to her employee until, by the end of the chapter, she allows Josefina to dress her for bed, to arrange her pillows, until finally, as Josefina is about to leave one night, Miss Amy brought "her maid's hands to her lips, [and] kissed them."[64] Although much more outward affection may not pass between them, they have become, by the end of the chapter—and as the title foreshadows—"Las Amigas."

Although written over 40 years after the publication of "The Displaced Person," Fuentes's "novel in nine stories"—like O'Connor's text—observes the situation of immigrants in the United States, offering the perspective of the other in a series of narratives that center on the Mexican-U.S. border. Read in a vacuum, the work presents a glimpse into the relations between the two countries, the risks for those Mexicans who cross into the United States, and the benefits gained by both nations. Compared with "The Displaced Person," Fuentes's work enters into dialogue with the creation of an immigrant identity in the United States and with the construction of self by those traditionally marginalized from the centers of social, political, and economic power. In this respect, both Fuentes and O'Connor reproduce and assemble a specific moment in time on the national landscape of the United States, each of them subtly emphasizing, through literature, the impact that immigrants have upon regions such as the U.S. South and the potential interconnectedness of the immigrant experience.

8

What Lies Beneath
Music and Land in the U.S. South and Latin America

As an expression of human emotion, experience, and historical context, music has commonly arisen from the relationship between an individual and the land, and is at the heart of both Southern and Latino cultures. Beginning with more traditional types of lyrics and instruments and ending with today's multifaceted expressions of intercategorical explosions and cross-over successes, music continues to be that transborder language that needs no language. As country and folk music in the United States celebrate the importance of land and homeland in one's life, so too do Mexican *rancheras* and Colombian *cumbias* rejoice in the relationship between a community and the geography it inhabits. Recent Mexican *corridos*—traditional songs of life and love—have incorporated circumstances that have affected Mexican immigrants living in the United States. As Randal C. Archibald noted in a *New York Times* article on July 6, 2007, The Mexican artist José F. García has composed a number of *corridos* that absorb the headlines from recent events, writing songs about September 11 ("Tragedia en Nueva York") and, in the song "Beautiful Memories," about "the loss of his family's ranch in Michoacán to development after he left 15 years ago and his inability to ever return." In the song "Latinos Unidos," García writes of the efforts to stop Mexican immigration and of the determination to seek a new and better life in the United States: "Now they are putting up barriers in front of us so we don't return, but that is not going to block us from crossing into the United States, we leap them like deer, we go under them like moles."

The lyric of the land unites us, and it is no coincidence, for example, that the song "Décimas" by the Colombian Carlos Vives proclaims the similarities between New Orleans and Barranquilla, Colombia, that Scott Joplin's 1899 composition "Maple Leaf Rag" is "a work with a very Cuban feel," that the banjo's origins are inherently African, that in 1931 the Southern Music Company "set up an office in Havana and began to sign publishing deals with Cuban composers," or that "historical factors [have] combined to make [New Orleans] the strongest center of African musical practice in the United States."[1] In the U.S. South, the distinct roots of the varieties of regional music can be found in cities like Nashville, New Orleans, and Birmingham, in the lives of the Appalachian communities, and in the songs passed down by African American slaves and white impoverished field workers.

In one of the first works to classify and analyze "Black" music existent in the United States from an outsider's perspective, Howard Odum and Gary Johnson's 1925 work *The Negro and His Songs* systematically approached these songs as a corpus redolent of themes such as spirituality and manual labor, and applied research methods and opinions that, today, seem a bit dated in their romanticization of the songs of the African American race in the United States. For example, Odum and Johnson remarked that in music composed by "Blacks" one finds "an improvised arrangement of words which makes the dominant feeling that of mingling successfully words and cadences."[2] During the singing of a spiritual, for example, "Their senses are all turned toward the perception of one attitude, and besides a wonderful tranquility of feeling, they also feel and see visions," during which they may observe or sense the presence of Jesus.[3] Today we may read their words and notice the paternalistic tone, generalizations, and racially tinged overtones of the period, as Odum and Johnson often objectified African Americans instead of recognizing their voices as the expressed subjection of a collective identity expressed through music. As Frederick Douglass wrote in his autobiography regarding the songs intoned by slaves, "I have sometimes thought that the mere hearing of those songs would do more to impress some minds with the horrible character of slavery, than the reading of whole volumes of philosophy on the subject would do."[4] Odum and Johnson's attitudes are represented as 'science' and portrayed as quasi-scientific, objective, empirical research, and may revealingly reflect the times; yet the study provides ample and fascinating documentation of songs, artists, and popular themes that were present in African American music for decades. In essence, the study may be one of the first ethnographic volumes dedicated to cultural studies in the twentieth century. For us—while observations regarding "the Negro's musical nature" and how "the Negro was and is passionately fond of dancing" blur the line between anthropology and stereotypical generalization—the volume is a worthy effort that attempts to understand the impact, influence, and importance of African American music in the United States and the possible thematic parallels that these songs have with more traditional compositions found in Latin America.[5]

Later musicians such as Elvis Presley, the Beatles, Bob Dylan, and the Rolling Stones incorporated many African American rhythms into their music and subsequently gave contemporary lyrics in English to the more traditional blues of the Mississippi valley and country tunes of Tennessee and Alabama. They transformed the songs into rock and roll and its later incarnations as punk music, disco, rap, and more contemporary hip-hop. At its birth in the early twentieth century, the blues transgressed all convention by offering another way of life that not only rebelled against society but defied the rules established by a primarily white Anglo patriarchy, reveling in the independence and spirit created by the transgression of such norms. The blues subverted White society's ideologies by offering "an alternative lifestyle in which rambling, hedonism, aggressive sexuality, and a general disregard for authority were the norm."[6] Gradually forging a relationship that created avenues into virtually all aspects of society, the blues and gospel music are evidence of the link between the physical and the spiritual worlds and of the sensualization of religion, as churches became arenas where passionate, forceful, even rowdy voices were not only allowed but encouraged (something distinctly different from most Anglo Protestant services that are non-charismatic or non-evangelical). Music—specifically the blues—became the point at which individuals came face to face with the conjoining of their physical presence and their spiritual being, witnessing the melding of each into a community that thrived on this weekly catharsis and reflecting that which W.J. Cash vaguely characterized as the South's "unusual proneness to sentimentality."[7]

In the Latino cultures, voices and songs imploring forgiveness, searching for a lost love, or lamenting one's fortune can be found in practically every society's form of music, from the Argentine tango and the Mexican ranchera to the Cuban habañera. In Spain, the "cante jondo" ("deep song") popular in flamenco music has its origins in the Gypsy culture, a population that, in Spain, has been historically known for its nomadic nontraditional lifestyle and has also suffered consistent marginalization and disenfranchisement not unlike the African American population of the United States. If the songs of the blues, for example, originate in a lament, the "cante jondo" uses as its point of departure a "duende" (literally "ghost"), a presence that takes possession of the singer and allows him to reach down into his soul, exposing and giving voice to the generations of suffering that lie within. The singers are frequently better known by their nicknames, as their given names do not appear to reflect the depth of commitment to their gypsy culture and to their art form. Camarón de la Isla ("The Shrimp from the Island"), La Niña de los Peines ("The Girl of the Combs"), La Niña Pastori ("The Pastori Girl"), and Tomatito ("Little Tomato"), among many others, represent a musical tradition that has evolved into other possibilities and musical arrangements. Today, while flamenco purists denigrate the transformation of flamenco music, the fact is that "cante jondo" is at the roots of the flamenco rock played by Ketama, the flamenco chill of Chambao, and other contemporary variations of conventional flamenco music, such as the guitarrist Paco de Lucía's chart-topping collaboration in 1996 with the Canadian Bryan Adams on his song "Have You Ever Really Loved A Woman."

Frequently, the musical expression of African American and Gypsy cultures and identities involves an otherworldly inspiration that manifests itself via the singer. During his stay in New York in 1929, the Spanish writer Federico García Lorca came to know the Harlem neighborhood and to appreciate the parallels between the music that he encountered there and the flamenco songs of his native Granada, Spain. In a letter home dated July 14 of that year, García Lorca describes a party he had attended in Harlem and the music he heard there: "What marvellous songs! Only our Andalusian *cante jondo* could be compared to them."[8] His fascination with the African American culture in New York City came to a head in his book *Poet in New York*, a collection of poems that express García Lorca's empathy for those who suffer and that relate his angst at encountering the underprivileged amidst the wealth of the city, searching to understand the role that African Americans play in the workings of the metropolis. In the poem "The King of Harlem," García Lorca writes of "the place where the blacks wept" and "the murmuring blacks," concluding, "*Ay*, Harlem, threatened by a mob of headless suits! / I hear your murmur." As Ian Gibson notes, "The poem suggests that Lorca had perceived a connection, not only between Black music and *cante jondo*, but between the predicament of the Blacks, condemned to third-class citizenship in a situation of virtual apartheid—they were not even allowed into the Cotton Club, despite the fact that its best performers were Black—and the Gypsies of Andalusia, harassed by an intolerant society."[9] Other parallels between *cante jondo* and the blues are evident if we reflect on the manner in which many of the musicians were inspired to sing or perform. The famous blues guitarist Robert Johnson, for example, supposedly played the guitar so well because he had sold his soul to the devil. That same emphasis on a connection to some other-worldly force exists for many performers of *cante jondo,* as they begin their songs by inaudibly allowing their voice to rise up from within themselves, and then to exit deeply and gradually, as if channeling a possessing spirit. Many of the flamenco singers and dancers also quite literally transform their faces into expressions of agony and emotional pain that mirror the themes expressed in their music. While these and other characteristics are present in other types of musical expressions found throughout the world, what is unique to both the blues and *cante jondo* is how each has evolved from a historical context of displacement and marginalization. Both the Gypsy and African American cultures have suffered the inequities of racism and ignorance, and both cultures have used music as a vehicle through which to articulate their suffering.

The origins of the blues in the U.S. South may be found in the inequities and sufferings provoked by slavery, as African Americans were cruelly objectified, treated as mere property, and forced to live and work on a land that, in their master's eyes, would never belong to them. The paramount position that land has occupied in the U.S. Southern cultures originated partly and simply in the fact that the region has been historically agricultural in nature and that rural communities have depended on it almost entirely for their subsistence. Southern rural communities forged a relationship with the environment in which the land became practically a part of the family, a living being compelling the Southerner to, as Alice Walker has written, "loving the earth so much that one longs to taste it and sometimes does."[10]

A curious state of affairs has contributed to the privileged position that land has held in Southern society in the United States through the years: the necessity of bracing and supporting the plantation myth, in which the Southern land was owned by genteel families who had only the best interest of their workers—read "slaves"—at heart. In effect, the plantation myth was created by Southern landowners in order to defend the land,[11] endorsed by the North as a way "to hide their own mistreatment of the black man behind the façade of an 'anti-slavery myth,'"[12] and to justify the concentration of land in a few hands, as the plantation system "had blocked [poor whites] off from escape or any considerable economic and social advances as a body."[13] In this version of the U.S. South, the land is often the equivalent of ancestors, descendants, and household, as it offers both sustenance and shelter, omnipresent even during challenging times. In his book *A Turn In The South*(1989), the Nobel prize-winning author V.S. Naipaul writes of the land around Greensboro, North Carolina, as being "flat, like the pampas of Argentina or the llanos of Venezuela," of how the "oak trees of South Carolina had the same shape and spread of the saman trees of Central America," and, upon visiting a Mississippi plantation, of the sensation that, "In the estate house, at lunch, one might have been in Argentina, on an *estancia*."[14] Land in the South was and continues to be a source of social stability,[15] and the Southerner became, in the words of Cash, "a direct product of the soil."[16]

The notion of an aristocracy—of the distinctly and stereotypically un-American notion that some individuals are simply born into better families and, therefore, bred for success—exists today in the United States in places such as Boston and New York, where surnames and family lineage may still play a role in determining one's social position and economic situation. Nowhere is the historic presence of an aristocratic landed gentry more evident, however, than in Southern cities such as Savannah, Charleston, New Orleans, or Nashville, communities where some families have spent centuries prospering from the land—frequently at the expense of others—and benefiting from lax, ignored, or nonexistent labor laws and pollution standards. Notwithstanding negative reactions against a number of Southern goods, products such as cotton and tobacco have paradoxically helped Southern gentry remain connected to the land and have allowed them to expand their empire and to seek alternative sources of income such as chicken or cattle, subletting their land to large companies such as ConAgra. Due to these and other factors—such as the ideal location of their ports—Southern farmers looked to conceal racial inequities and were frequently the first in the United States to take advantage of geographical circumstances and establish commercial ties with Europe and other parts of the world. The Southern shoreline runs from Louisiana to Chesapeake Bay and has historically offered more opportunity for trade and industrial growth than the interior of the country.

As early as 1874, Southern farmers began to come together and form organizations that would protect their interests. The Southern Alliance of

Farmers, for example, merged with the Louisiana Farmers' Union in 1876 to form the National Farmers' Alliance. As I. A. Newby states regarding this new organization, "Because so many of their initiatives—voluntary acreage restriction, controlled marketing arrangements for important crops, for example—depended upon government action, Alliance leaders decided to take the organization into politics. The decision was momentous, for it transformed the Alliance, the farmer movement, and Southern politics."[17] If we were to follow the course of Latin American history in nations such as Mexico, Argentina, Guatemala, or Colombia, we would agree with James Petras and conclude, "In most national contexts, the states, both federal and provincial, have been enemies of peasant movements."[18] We would also conclude that political developments in a number of Latin American countries have often occurred as a result of peasant, farmer, or agrarian frustrations with a central government that was unresponsive to their needs. In Mexico, "the state has severely repressed peasant movements in Chiapas, Guerrero, Oaxaca, and throughout southern-central Mexico"; in Colombia, "thousands of peasant leaders have been assassinated by paramilitary groups associated with the Armed Forces"; and in Venezuela, "over 110 peasant leaders, many of them land reform beneficiaries, have been murdered between 2001 and 2004 by landlord 'private armies' with the complicity of local officials."[19]

The recent elections in various Latin American nations of heads of state open to negotiating a more equitable distribution of land give witness to the fact that peasant indigenous movements on the continent have "the power to topple governments,"[20] and underline the significance that agrarian political movements still have today, particularly in nations with a notable indigenous population. As Marie-Chantal Barre has written regarding the relationship between the indigenous and the land, "The land is the privileged medium for the development of community ties with others, as freedom does not mean to be alone nor to follow one's way in solitude, but rather to live in intimate relationship with others and with nature, as constitutive elements."[21] According to Petras, "Over the past twenty years, the peasantry [in Latin America] has re-emerged, playing a central role in changing regimes, determining national agendas, leading struggles against international trade agreements (ALCA, or Free Trade of the Americas), as well as establishing regional and local bases of power. In many countries, coalitions of landless farm workers, small family farmers and peasants have been central to national struggles against neo-liberal regimes and free-trade policies."[22] Mexico's recent struggles between the federal government and the Zapatista Army of National Liberation (EZLN), for example, typify the local agrarian roots of many land disputes throughout Latin America, as many of the EZLN's active members "are drawn from the forests, mountains and small towns of the region [of Chiapas], both from the indigenous and linguistically diverse population, and from immigrants from Central and Northern Mexico."[23] In southern Guatemala there has also emerged a peasant movement called the Movimiento Campesino Pro-Justicia Nueva Linda (Pro-Justice Peasant Movement Nueva Linda), which has mobilized against the interests of cattle farmers, ranchers, and large landowners who pay their hired hands approximately four to five dollars a day,[24] a fraction of what other workers earn. In Bolivia, the recent election of president Evo Morales is due in large part to the Movimiento Sin Tierra (Landless Movement), a coalition that includes such organizations as Federación de Mujeres Campesinas de Bolivia Bartolina Sisa (Bartolina Sisa Federation of Bolivian Peasant Women). As J. Marirrodriga reported in an article published in the Spanish newspaper El País on June 25, 2007, in Argentina, some 1,300 miles southwest of the capital of Buenos Aires, in the provinces of Río Negro, Chubut, and Neuquén, the October 11 Movement represents the interests of the Argentina Mapuche Indians who, in the last few years, have begun to occupy territories that currently belong to large multinational companies such as Benetton, alleging that these lands were once owned by their ancestors. In other countries such as Honduras, Colombia, and Peru, there have also emerged a number of organizations such as Movimiento Madre Tierra (Mother Earth Movement), defending the interests of peasants and agricultural laborers and advocating, as the EZLN did in Mexico, "the return of cultivable lands to the indigenous and poor campesinos so that they can have the material basis for organizing their lives and cultures."[25] For many of the indigenous and non-indigenous cultures in Latin America, the fortunes and the troubles of their nation-state and the contemporary identity of their country have a direct relationship with the land, particularly with the cultural role that it plays in all societies and the necessity of reaching some type of sustainable development that balances a respect for pre-Columbian traditions with continued economic growth.

While the U.S. South remains strongly agricultural today, this economic base began to undergo a transformation as early as World War II, due principally to "the outmigration of blacks and the move [in the region] to industrialize."[26] Gradually, the industrialization of the South has, it appears, not led to a separation from the land but rather to a multinationalization of the land, as companies have looked to acquire products such as corn or chicken, sell them more in the international markets than at home, and paradoxically promote "job growth [that] has been accompanied by widening income disparities."[27] This de-agriculturization of the South was brought about by many factors, including "absentee landlordism," the "[loss] of its foreign market to cotton," and the Depression.[28] Today, many landowners have become something of a twenty-first century serf, as they answer principally to the company and to the business interests that purchase their goods. The positive side is that it is an assured cash inflow, as the corn or chickens will have a place in a relatively constant marketplace, regardless of fluctuations. The negative consequences are that the Southern farmer is being homogenized and colonized by interests that, while assuring his survival, also guarantee that the land and that which it produces will, through possible exploitation and structural manipulation, slip gradually from his arms and into the hands of enterprises that focus exclusively on their profit margin.

Many of the U.S. South's private landowners today now hire Latin American migrant workers to plant and harvest their crops, clean the chicken houses, and basically tend to the land. Besides the most obvious benefit—inexpensive labor—of this practice, Latin American workers are reportedly more willing than United States-born laborers to work hard under the most difficult of circumstances; and while there are other immigrant populations whose success in the United States depended largely upon their farming skills—Germans and Northern Europeans in the Midwest or Asians on the West coast—Latin Americans are contributing to the economic health of areas in the South that were already agriculturally successful in the variety and consistency of their harvests and that shared a number of commonalities with the immigrant population.

In his article written only ten days after the Charleston, South Carolina, earthquake in 1886, even the Cuban writer José Martí seemed to identify more with the land than with the structures built by human hands, describing the damage suffered by the flora of the city more extensively and passionately than the destruction to Charleston's buildings or streets: "Within a radius of twenty miles inland the ground was everywhere parched and cracked," and "even the withered jasmines on the branches and the stooping, faded roses seemed to take their share of the damage."[29] This familiarity with and empathy for the land and with the rhythm of life that surrounds agricultural customs in different countries has aided many Latin American workers in gently assimilating into their respective Southern communities. And while this assimilation has come on the heels of economic disadvantages, linguistic difficulties, and contemporary labor lords, knowledge of the land and a willingness to work the soil have aided in bringing together the Southern and the Latin American cultures. If between 1940 and 1945 alone "more than 20 percent of the South's farm population abandoned the land,"[30] the demographic loss that this statistic represents is being recuperated due to the influx of Latin American immigrants who have breathed new life into Southern communities, who are bringing with them land-centered customs and traditions, and who are gradually helping to turn rural Southern towns into microcosms of resourceful transnational communities through, among other reasons, encountered parallels found in the music and in the land of the Americas.

Religion
An Equal Praise

The omnipresence of countless varieties of religious worship is self-evident in the cultures of the U.S. South and Latin America, from each nation's unique celebration of Christianity's Holy Week to the growing strength of evangelical movements in countries such as the United States, Mexico, Nicaragua, Colombia, and Peru. As early as 1699, the Spanish language was believed to have been a useful vehicle for potential conversion to the Protestant faith, as it was that year that Cotton Mather published in Salem, Massachusetts, a catechism in Spanish entitled *La fe del cristiano* (*The Faith of the Christian*).[1] More currently, the historical similarities between Latin American and U.S. Southern political expressions of faith and the preeminent position that religion occupied and continues to occupy in U.S. Southern society may be perceived in statistics available on the USA Today Web site, which reflect the percentage of residents who consider themselves to be active members of the Baptist Church: Georgia (37 percent), Alabama (37 percent), North Carolina (38 percent), Tennessee (39 percent), South Carolina (43 percent) and Mississippi (55 percent), states that were and continue to be strongly and eminently Baptist. In Latin America, authoritarian leaders such as the Somoza family of Nicaragua, Pinochet in Chile, and Stroessner in Paraguay all believed—not unlike Francisco Franco in Spain—in a strong nation firmly rooted in a Roman Catholic faith and identity. Other post-dictatorial Latin

American political figures such as Vicente Fox and Álvaro Uribe are either practicing Catholics or were brought up in the Catholic faith. While Roman Catholics and U.S. Southern Baptists vary in their rituals and traditions, both faiths have played significant roles in the lives of regional and national leaders on the American continent. For many U.S. Southerners, for example, worship and church attendance are of primary inspiration and significance. What Howard Odum wrote in 1936 regarding the U.S. South is still true today: "Like politics, religion is closely interwoven in the fabric of Southern culture. In its church membership, in its Protestant representation, in its church colleges, in the position which the church holds in the community, and in its general influence upon social policy, the Southeast outranks the other regions of the nation."[2]

In a time that witnesses a nationally strong conservative Christian coalition of businesses and individuals that effectively influence changes in policies and legislation across the United States, the U.S. South may in fact have announced this trend. Today, a vast majority of U.S. Southern Baptists attend church on Sundays and Wednesdays, using these days to connect with their community and, as Odum discerned, benefit from the church as a common meeting ground, a sort of democratic think tank in which common religious beliefs help solidify old acquaintances and form new ones. In the traditional U.S. South, the community centers around the church, Sunday afternoon picnics, unfailing tithing, construction and growth, children's day care, and, of course, worship. Members of a community have a vested interest in maintaining a noticeable church presence, as lawyers, car mechanics, teachers, plumbers, bankers, and nurses all attend a church—and possibly the same church—often in order to remain visible in the community and to demonstrate that they, too, lead an active religious and spiritual life.

For many Latin American immigrants to the U.S. South, the presence and expression of a strong religious faith remains one of the salient characteristics of the recently arrived populations. Although Roman Catholicism as an expression of personal beliefs has traditionally centered on the iconography of Jesus Christ, his mother Mary, and the saints, Latin American immigrants to the U.S. South are arriving in a strange land and finding that a shared religion builds bridges. As evidenced by the creation of a number of organizations intended to foster and improve the Catholic Church's relationship with the Spanish-speaking community in the United States, over the course of the second half of the twentieth century there has developed a national awareness of Spanish-speaking Catholics, as evidenced by the creation in 1945 of the Office for the Spanish Speaking under the sponsorship of the National Catholic Welfare Council and supervised by the previous Bishop Robert E. Lucey, Archbishop of San Antonio; by the 1969 formation by the National Conference of Catholic Bishops of the Division for the Spanish Speaking under the Department of Social Development; by the naming in 1970 of Archbishop Patrick Flores, the first U.S. Hispanic Bishop; and by the First National Hispanic Encuentro in 1972, which called for "greater participation of the Spanish speaking in leadership and decision-making roles at all levels within the Catholic Church [in the United States] and for the establishment of structures for ministry to be implemented."[3]

In the United States, the Catholic Church currently divides the nation into 13 geographical regions numbering I to XIII. On its Web site, the U.S. Conference of Catholic Bishops indicates that, from 1990 to 2000, the Hispanic Catholic population across the country increased approximately 58 percent, from 22,354,059 to 35,305,818. Over that same period of time, Region IV (FL, GA, SC, NC, VA, WV, DE, MD, DC) saw a 99 percent increase of the Catholic Hispanic population, from 2,132,751 to 4,243,946; and the population of Catholic Hispanics in Region V (KY, MS, AL, LA, TN) increased 116 percent. In Region IV in 1999, 21.8 percent of priests were Hispanic, compared with 6.3 percent of priests and 13 percent of seminarians on the national level in 2003. Are they preparing for something that the rest of the nation ignores? Does the Catholic Church represent more than a common faith for the new immigrants from Latin America? As Beatriz Morales has written, for the immigrants "the Catholic Church provides stability by continuing to reinforce the norms and values that people have transplanted from their homelands."[4]

On its Web site, the U.S. Conference of Catholic Bishops states that, nationally, there are 1,230 Catholics per U.S. priest; but there are 9,925 Hispanic Catholics per Hispanic priest. Further—and still on a national level—statistics reflecting the growth of the Latino community and the influx of Hispanics who identify themselves as Catholic tell a compelling story: Hispanics account for 71 percent of Catholic population growth since 1960; 39 percent of U.S. Catholics are Hispanic; 20.6 percent of U.S. parishes have a majority Hispanic presence; and there are approximately 4,000 parishes in the United States with Hispanic ministries, with 20.6 percent of these parishes boasting a majority Hispanic presence. While the growth of Catholic churches across the U.S. South is outpacing the growth of other dioceses in the United States and is beneficial for Catholic churches in the region, Catholic communities are preparing for the challenges that lie ahead. The Southeast Pastoral Institute (SEPI) is an educational and service organization that aids the Catholic Bishops of the southeastern states. Founded in 1979 in response to the necessity of organizing a program that centered around Hispanic education, SEPI began to formulate objectives that would ultimately comply with the Third National Hispanic Encuentro in 1985. SEPI lists many of its objectives on its Web site, including, among others: "The correct analysis of reality is an essential element of pastoral action," "The analysis of reality and pastoral planning have to be carried out periodically," and "Pastoral action must adapt itself constantly to changing reality." A number of these principles would, in fact, integrate the most basic ideas of Liberation Theology, developed by Latin American theologians and philosophers in the 1960s in order to address the relationship of the Roman Catholic Church to the marginalized and oppressed throughout the world.

Over the course of U.S. Southern history, the interconnectedness of church and society has been almost sensibly transparent: community leaders, bank presidents, renowned athletes, teachers, doctors, and lawyers have been expected to be God-fearing, Bible-reading people, to attend church regularly, and to be known within Christian circles. As is the case with many other matters, the South is the reflection and the exaggeration of the United States: it is the ideology, the philosophy, the ontology of that "American Way of Life" raised to the *nth* degree. If the founding fathers of the country declaimed "In God We Trust," Southerners—particularly White Protestant Southerners in the tradition of Southern Baptists— would seem to sometimes cry *"Only* In God We Trust." In the U.S. South, daily life frequently exists as an extension of the church community, supposedly bringing to being through daily chores and activities those values pronounced at the pulpit and read from the Good Book. The relationship, however, between action and intention, and between the public and private spheres, has often been blurred, as historically in the South, "religious orthodoxy was a prop for secular orthodoxy, especially in matters involving morals and sin."[5] In the nineteenth century, for example, the presence of religion in "public life" bred a conformity and intolerance that tended to homogenize and firmly establish the social hierarchy of the community, bringing stagnation to an otherwise vibrant city or town.[6] Even before the Civil War, many churches "had endorsed slavery and puritanical moral codes, and made themselves integral parts of the social system."[7] After the Civil War, in the 1880s, a number of churches in the South strengthened their dominion, "not only allying themselves with a particular political and economic establishment but making themselves a part of its apparatus of social control."[8] Those who visited Southern states during this period in history were struck by the incongruousness of the situation and the little sense that it all made. As the Cuban writer José Martí wrote in 1886 upon visiting Charleston, South Carolina, only days after the city had suffered an earthquake, "Country folk fill the churches and listen in dread to the words of ire the stupid pastors visit upon their heads."[9]

Churches in the U.S. South have also had a very positive impact upon their communities, as they have helped to clothe and feed those in need, build homes for the poor, and fund new schools. Habitat for Humanity, ex-president Jimmy Carter's organization, for example, declares on its Web site that it is "a non-profit, ecumenical Christian housing ministry" that openly relates its work to a higher ethical purpose. In its mission statement, the organization declares, "The work of Habitat is driven by the desire to give tangible expression to the love of God through the work of eliminating poverty housing. Habitat's mission and methods are predominantly derived from a few key theological concepts: the necessity of putting faith into action, the 'economics of Jesus,' and the 'theology of the hammer.'" The positive impact that Habitat has had on communities across the country is tangible, particularly in areas where low-income residents have little or no opportunity to buy a house of their own. In their work, Habitat manages to integrate the economic reality of owning a house with a spiritual dimension that puts into practice the lessons gleaned from reading the Bible.

In Latin America, the hierarchy of the Catholic Church has historically merited both positive and negative appraisals. In the past, many individual churches have aided the needy, yet the upper echelons of the clergy have been accused of ignoring the physical and material well-being of their parishioners while disseminating a message that promised the flock their reward in Heaven if only they would suffer in quiet dignity the inequities of this earthly life. Historically, Catholic opinions of Protestantism have often reflected a resistance to dialogue and, ultimately, to understanding. After World War II, these attitudes critical of Protestantism and other divergent systems of belief began to undergo a systematic transformation within the Catholic church in Europe, as many French and German priests experienced a crisis of personal faith due to their having witnessed the incarceration and murder of hundreds of thousands of Catholics and non-Catholics alike in ghettoes, prisons, and concentration camps. When these attitudes crossed the Atlantic in the late 1940s and early 1950s, they found fertile ideological ground in the poverty and destitution of Latin America and in the growing wave of Marxist consciousness and its subsequent political or revolutionary expressions.

In response to mounting unrest and discord within the Catholic Church, in 1962 Pope John XXIII inaugurated the Second Vatican Ecumenical Council in Rome. Lasting until 1965, one of the focal points of the meetings was to turn the Catholic church both literally and figuratively toward the people (declaring, for example, that the celebrating priest may face the parishioners during the mass—changing the previous custom of facing the altar—and that the mass may be celebrated in a language other than Latin). These changes reoriented the Catholic Church toward the impoverished citizens who make up the vast majority of Latin America's population and recognized both their presence in the physical church and the authority of a culture separate and distinct from Rome's.

Brought together in Medellín, Colombia, in 1968 to implement the changes advocated by the Second Vatican Council, the Roman Catholic Cardinals who lived in Latin America began to elaborate a theology whose point of departure would be the poorest and most marginalized individuals. Because of the poverty experienced by an immense majority of Central and South America's population, the "preferential option for the poor" as it became known represented one of the pillars of the new Theology of Liberation espoused by priests, bishops, archbishops, and cardinals such as Gustavo Gutiérrez, the brothers Leonardo and Clodovis Boff, Pedro Casaldáliga, and Ernesto Cardenal. Granting the differences between each national set of circumstances, clergy and intellectuals who expressed positions that supported the basic principles of liberation theology were often accused of being Marxists in disguise, as they frequently employed a Marxist framework to contextualize their ideas. The charges were frequently found to be groundless, as these theologians merely used the Marxist concepts of property, consumption, and class as eyeglasses through which they could better see and understand the daily reality lived by the vast majority of Latin Americans and to work toward changing it. In order to communicate more effectively with their parishioners, priests began to dialogue with the faithful, to relinquish some of their authority so that the people could actively participate in the liturgy. The celebration of mass became a series of interpretative exchanges, as the priest would explicitly include the parishioners in the ritual, asking those present, for example, what they understood to be the messages of the day's readings and embarking upon a practical and hands-on application of the Gospel. In this way, the abstract names, locations, and events mentioned in the Bible were made relative to the people and their day-to-day circumstances, particularly to the material poverty shared by many.

Particularly relevant to many who shared in the ideas espoused by liberation theology was the book of Exodus, used by many priests as an example of a people's struggle and fight to reach a very physical and tangible Promised Land here on earth that actually had little to do with the intangible paradise promised in the hereafter. If we examine the book of Exodus, there are passages that are relevant to the liberation of a people and to the founding of a promised land directly on earth. When God speaks at the burning bush, for example, the land that He promises Moses and His people is a concrete land here on earth: "Then the Lord said to him, 'I have seen the deep sorrows of my people in Egypt, and have heard their pleas for freedom from their harsh taskmaster. I have come to deliver them from the Egyptians and to take them out of Egypt and into a good land, a large land, a land 'flowing with milk and honey'" (3: 7-8). Later, the voice of the Lord underscores the physical reality of liberation: "I promise to rescue [my people] from the dangers and humiliation they are undergoing, and to take them to a land now occupied by the Canaanites, Hittites, Amorites, Perizzites, and Jebusites" (3: 17). This very tangible presence of a biblical promised land has been perceived by others who, throughout history, wished to lead a people out of oppression and to a better life and place here on earth. With regard to slavery, for example, "the most constantly reiterated theme was deliverance and the coming of the promised land, in which the spiritual and temporal were inextricably mixed."[10] As Phillip Berryman has written, "Exodus is not simply an event but a pattern of deliverance that provides a key for interpreting the Scriptures and for interpreting present experience."[11]

While liberation theology as a philosophically and ethically constructed model for daily life in Latin America is not necessarily new—its origins may be traced as far back as the writings of Fray Bartolomé de las Casas and Guamán Poma de Ayala in the sixteenth and seventeenth centuries—it is not until the twentieth century that we witness the confluence of theologians and philosophers who sought to create a Latin American theology that would reflect the life of the majority of the continent's population and that was unique within the Asian, African, and Euro-American traditions. At different moments during the twentieth century, the Peruvian writer José Carlos Mariátegui, the Mexican essayist Leopoldo Zea, the Brazilian pedagogue Paulo Freire, and the Peruvian priest Gustavo Gutiérrez, among others, looked to advance a Latin American philosophy and theology rooted in the daily existence of a majority of Latin American individuals. As was to be expected, the hierarchy of the Roman Catholic Church took issue with the worldly emphasis of "liberation theology" because, in its opinion, it was *too* rooted in the material concerns of daily life and, therefore, too overtly political. As Cardinal Ratzinger—later Pope Benedict XVI—wrote in the 1985 document entitled "Instruction Regarding Certain Aspects of Liberation Theology," and available on the Vatican's Web site, "Liberation is first and foremost liberation from the radical slavery of sin." In a series of interviews with the Italian journalist Vittorio Messori that occurred at approximately the same time, Cardinal Ratzinger underscored that a Catholic priest's exaggerated emphasis on historical context and analysis often distances him from the Church's path and exacerbates an already difficult situation: "In recent years theology has energetically dedicated itself to make faith and signs of the times accord with each other in order to find new ways for the transmission of Christianity. Many, however, have finally come to the realization that these efforts have often contributed more to the aggravation than to the resolution of the crisis."[12] Above all, Ratzinger claimed, liberation theology "constitutes a fundamental threat to the faith of the Church."[13]

As evidenced by Cardinal Ratzinger's comments in 1984 and 1985, the Catholic Church's initial reaction was to silence all dissent—including imposing a year of "obsequious silence" on the Brazilian priest Leonardo Boff in 1985—discrediting the new theology and chastising any clerics who might appear to espouse the ideals of liberation theology (one of the best-known incidents also occurred in 1985 when, upon landing in the capital of Managua, Nicaragua, Pope John Paul II descended the airplane's steps, passed through the receiving line, and openly chastised Nicaraguan priest Ernesto Cardenal for his participation in the country's political affairs). Toward the end of the twentieth century, the Catholic Church hierarchy had realized that the social philosophy espoused by liberation theologians was particularly relevant to a vast majority of the developing world and gradually co-opted many of the tenets expressed by the theology.

In post–World War II Europe, a progressive Catholic theology had grown from the terrors sown by the conflict, but it was never a liberation theology in the sense that Latin American theologians—particularly those who participated in the Latin American Bishop's Conference in Medellín, Colombia, in 1968—elaborated and defined through their conceptual framework. As it came to be characterized by German theologians such as Johannes Baptist Metz and Jürgen Moltmann, Political Theology centered upon the elaboration of a progressively religious discourse emanating from within the European heart of the Catholic Church. The concerns were similar to liberation theologians' distress regarding the poor in Latin America, but its focus was distinctly different: in Europe, present as they were in the continent's daily life, the economically poor simply did not represent a majority of its inhabitants and could, therefore, be rhetorically swept under a carpet that lay at the feet of many European Catholics. Subsequently, liberation theologies began developing within the Jewish, feminist, and gay communities, and in locations such as Asia, India, and Africa.

In the United States, there had been strains of progressive Catholicism that dated back to the nineteenth century, but liberation theology never truly took root in the mainstream of North American Catholicism simply because it was not perceived as a broad necessity. There were—and continue to be—poor Catholics in the United States, but there were also a great many of them who belonged to the middle and upper classes. When writing in 1845 about organized religion in the United States, for example, Frederick Douglass declared, "Indeed, I can see no reason, but the most deceitful one, for calling the religion of this land Christianity: I look upon it as the climax of all misnomers, the boldest of all frauds, the grossest of all libels."[14] In response to the growing number of impoverished parishioners, churches in the late nineteenth and early twentieth centuries from a number of denominations began to construct what may today be considered a "liberational" message that was based on providing the most basic of material necessities here on earth and ensuring that everyone in a particular parish or community had clothes, food, and a home. After slaves were liberated in the nineteenth century, for example, "Black churches provided some of the organization, and black preachers much of the leadership, which saw the freed slaves through the troubled years following emancipation."[15] In the U.S. South especially, poor Catholic and Protestant churches began to spread a gospel that recognized their marginal status within the borders of the United States and shared certain characteristics with the principles established by Latin American liberation theologians.

As was the case with Latin America, economic circumstances existing over the course of U.S. history also dictated the context from which this gospel would surface and how churches chose to respond. In 1929, for example, the Great Depression "dramatized the unresponsiveness of churches to economic and social problems and thus [underscored] their irrelevance in times of social crisis."[16]

Fortunately, this "unresponsiveness" of churches and their unique "irrelevance" changed in the 1950s and 1960s—particularly in the South, when the civil rights movement in effect "grew out of black churches in the South and the religious groups committed to furthering social justice issues."[17] Considering the dramatically dissimilar national circumstances, how do we account for the similarities between the emergence of liberation theology in Latin America in the 1960s and the growing role that Southern Protestant churches played in the struggle for civil rights during approximately the same period? Both the African American culture in the United States and the Latin American poor have been historically denied a central voice in their representation and respective social and political infrastructures, and have been forced to take advantage of their positions at the margins of society to search for and express their particular voices. The Southern Baptist churches in the South, for example, began to teach that the fight for one's rights within the context of an experienced daily reality was a noble enterprise that should be supported. Reflecting a similar attitude that translated abstract theory into explicit action, many Latin American priests who were in accord with the principles of liberation theology began to sell church property in order to feed, clothe, and house their flocks. Both African American Baptist churches in the South and Latin American parishes that were led by priests who defended the ideals of liberation theology formulated programs that looked to respond to the economic and spiritual injustices of daily life with tangible actions meant to alleviate, resolve, or repudiate said prejudices and inequalities. As many clergy in Latin America in the 1960s and 1970s began to create a "popular" Catholic church that reacted to the physical and spiritual needs of the people, so too were a number of African American churches in the South in the 1950s and 1960s involved in the struggles of their members, providing pulpits for individuals who, like Martin Luther King, Jr. or Vernon Johns, looked to articulate the concerns, hopes, and fears of the voiceless in the Southern United States. Today, the Catholic Church in the U.S. South has integrated the Civil Rights struggle and the philosophical bases of liberation theology for Hispanic Ministry, including the growing proselytism of Hispanic Catholics, the fact that the demand for services in Spanish is outpacing the Church's response, the need to hire, as the U.S. Conference of Catholic Bishops states on its Web site, "Hispanic Ministers who are familiar with the collective history of Hispanic ministry," and to avoid employing a "multicultural" model that "often dilutes the identity and vision of Hispanic Ministry and those of other ethnic ministries," recognizing above all "the ethnic and linguistic variety of Latin American immigrants to the United States."

The transplantation and manifestation of Hispanic norms and values may coincide at a very basic level with Southern norms and values that have frequently announced ideological changes in the national climate. According to Peter Applebome, these Southern ideological touchstones have become currents that have helped form national trends and attitudes across the country:

> Think of a place that's bitterly antigovernment and fiercely individualistic, where race is a constant subtext to daily life, and God and guns run through public discourse like an electric current. Think of a place where influential scholars market theories of white supremacy, where the word 'liberal' is a negative epithet, where hang-em-high law-and-order justice centered on the death penalty and throw-away-the-key sentencing are politically all but unstoppable. Think of a place obsessed with states' rights, as if it were the 1850s all over again and the Civil War had never been fought. Such characteristics have always described the South. Somehow, they now describe the nation.[18]

For Latin American workers who immigrate to the region, the United States is represented by a South whose Protestant religious traditions may ironically serve to better acclimate and comfort new residents who are practicing Catholics, to remove some of the uncertainty and hostility that one may sense upon residing in another country. In Southern communities in the United States, the constancy of worship and the presence of this worship in many areas of daily life help to remind the newcomer that there are spiritual necessities that run parallel to the material needs of the immediate present and that, while these difficulties shall perhaps one day pass, it is also important to connect with our respective community, to perceive those different from us, and to be aware of how we ourselves may be different from others.

Tensions

As the percentage of Hispanics in U.S. Southern communities unaccustomed to transnational immigration continues to increase in the years to come, it is also a distinct inevitability that tensions will rise between and within these populations. There may be attempts at cooperation, at dialogue, at presenting a united front in the face of a number of community issues, but both external and internal forces will unhinge these fronts and underline the tenuous balance that exists within the diverse elements of each group.

LANGUAGE

Possibly the most critical point of tension is language, as many U.S. Southern communities today are monolingual and not traditionally accustomed to the presence of a multilingual immigrant population. As Jorge Ramos writes, "Language is framed and developed at home, at work, between friends, in front of the *tivi*, and listening to *la radio, man.*"[1] While these may not be the *only* places where this occurs, these may now be difficult moments for institutions like schools or hospitals that have never considered catering to a non–English-speaking population. These very same difficulties and tensions are also the first signs that a community is preparing to take its initial steps toward an inclusively multilingual future. One significant example of this tension occurred when, as reported in the *Atlanta Journal-Constitution* on August 23, 2000, six Mexican bricklayers were arrested in Smyrna, Georgia, for violating the city's ban on construction after six o'clock pm. At the work site, an officer saw them working and requested that they stop, but, since they did not understand English, they continued. Smyrna Mayor Max Bacon stated, incredulous and oblivious, that "they just blatantly refused to quit. That amazed me more than anything else." A few days later, a city judge dismissed the charges and threw out the ordinance prohibiting construction after six, saying it was too vague. Mayor Bacon was content with how everything worked out, "but he still believes the bricklayers deserved their trip to jail."

The language barrier at the center of the conflict between the law enforcement personnel and immigrant laborers is unfortunately not a new phenomenon to communities that have been recently receiving disproportionate numbers of nontraditional Hispanic immigrants. As these populations and the respective residential towns and cities continue to grow, however, the pressure will be on both Hispanics and non-Hispanics to confront the consequences of knowing only one language. As reported in the *Atlanta Journal-Constitution* article, in Mayor Bacon's opinion, the issue is primarily economic, as "city taxpayers shouldn't have to pay to teach police Spanish so they can communicate with the city's growing Hispanic community." But the matter also has significant political ramifications and reminds us of the traditional Southern position that defends and advances states' rights in the face of national concerns. Some hold that Washington is ultimately responsible for the flow of immigrants and must, therefore, pay for the language training of police officers. If we approach each of these points separately, Mayor Bacon's position regarding federally funding the teaching of police to speak and write in Spanish and to understand the language seems the most untenable: as the community of Smyrna will be the primary beneficiary of a multilingual police force, should it not fund the Spanish classes for the officers? If nothing else, the police officers will be able to better communicate with an ever-diversifying Smyrna population.

Regarding the role that the federal government plays in "the flow of nationals coming into the country," Bacon should be familiar with the statistics regarding the benefits to a community of both documented and undocumented immigration from Latin America. While typecasting Washington as the epicenter of the nation's woes has never gone out of vogue, it is also Washington that provides much of the funding for the Smyrna Police Department. Ultimately, separating the political from the economic is as elusive as the idea of unconnected Anglo and Latino populations: there may be neighborhoods, schools, or offices where one race or ethnicity predominates, but in the end, a mutually inclusive coexistence is an inevitability that these communities will soon witness—if they have not done so already. For Smyrna, a police force that speaks both English and Spanish will reduce miscommunications, facilitate dialogue, and ultimately help do away with stereotypes surrounding Anglos, African Americans, Latinos, and potentially other populations.

The implementation of Spanish in classrooms, hospitals, courtrooms, and banks, for example, will depend partly on the motivation of the English-speaking community, but Latin American immigrants who arrive in the United States must also find it valuable and sensible to be as fluent as possible in English. And though learning the language of one's adopted country appears to make good sense, it is also terribly easy for an immigrant to associate himself exclusively with the Spanish-speaking community and depend almost entirely on multilinguals to conduct any matters which may require the use of English. This is one reason the Latino population in the South has been ghettoized: the continued linguistic isolation imposed on immigrants through a dearth of efforts on the part of both the Anglo community and the non–English-speaking individual. Paradoxically, a consequence of the ghettoization of the Hispanic population has been the emergence and usage of Spanglish—that hybrid that combines the vocabulary, grammar, and syntax of both English and Spanish—as individuals and communities who, in their home country, were exclusively monolingual have found themselves immersed in the necessary trappings of the English language: street signs, newspapers, telemarketers, billboards, overheard conversations, songs, and so on. Due to the fact that many Latino immigrants choose to function exclusively in Spanish, the border between the two languages becomes increasingly pocked as English filters inevitably into Spanish—and vice versa—bringing into being that hybrid of all hybrids, Spanglish.

The influence of one language upon another is not a topic new to sociolinguistic or anthropological studies. Consider, specifically, border areas: in the Pyrenees mountains between France and Spain, the French, Spanish, Catalán, and Basque languages have historical interconnections dating back centuries; the agglomeration and combination in the Swiss Alps of French, German, and Italian have created a multifaceted set of cultures; and, in many regions of Africa, colonialism has left its legacy in the remains of European languages—English, German, French, Spanish, or Italian—that have combined with other tongues. The controversy today regarding the use of Spanglish is not novel, but the passions it is producing are, especially to the United States, a country accustomed to having its immigrant populations rapidly assimilate themselves to the country and to its communities. The use of Spanglish and the increased presence of Latin Americans, Africans, Caribbeans, and Asians in the United States may indeed signal a revolution, as Sonia Torres indicates: "We would do well to ask if a revolution is not already occurring through the subversion of the [English] language and of the customs of Anglo-Americans."[2]

There are two sides to this debate: one claims that Spanglish is an unacceptable bastardization of the Spanish language, a violent twisting that promotes misspellings and incorrect grammatical usage; another perspective is that Spanglish is the future of the Spanish language, especially in the United States. As Torres has written regarding the specific situation of *Nuyoricans* in New York, for example, "The use of *Spanglish* and the changing of the linguistic code serves as an instrument of resistance and of representation of the *Nuyorican* as someone who, being 'American,' represents the vast inequalities between Americans."[3]

In supporting the acceptance and widespread use of Spanglish, the Mexican-American journalist Jorge Ramos believes that this blend of English and Spanish "is the bicultural as well as the bilingual code of what it means to be Hispanic in America," that "Whoever refuses to use Anglicisms, Spanglish, or cyber-Spanish will have a difficult time communicating efficiently on the internet," that "In the future there will be no pure Spanish for Hispanics," that "I have heard lawyers and doctors speak Spanglish with their servants and cleaning people," that "it is easier to refer to a word [in Spanglish] than a long and incomprehensible explanation," and that Spanglish "should be a language that reflects reality (not the whim of academics)."[4] Ramos's reference to an "Academy" directly addresses the colonial past of Latin America and its inhabitants: in the eighteenth century, Spain established an Academy of Language in order to standardize its usage—as did France. This project became a double-edged sword due to the fact that, at the same time that it dictated what was acceptable within the limits of the language, it implicitly defined that which was unacceptable and outside the cultural canon. Proponents of Spanglish today rest their arguments on an ideological imposition that has its roots in eighteenth-century Eurocentrism (more specifically, Francocentrism). In Ramos's opinion, "We must forget about the academics and the *tichers* of the Royal Academy of the Spanish language."[5] Ironically, *Spanglists* such as Ramos are gradually becoming more like the academics they criticize, as they are imposing not only the acceptance of Spanglish rules but the exclusive use of Spanglish at many levels of discourse.

Ramos's observations regarding the use of Spanglish need to be addressed, as they may cause misunderstandings both within and outside the bilingual community. When he writes that "Spanish should be a language that reflects reality,"[6] for example, we should question the ambiguous use of the term "reality." What "reality" would be reflected in the Spanglish mirror? Perhaps a cook, a bricklayer, or a waitress, but not necessarily a doctor, nurse, or practicing lawyer who works within the limits of an accepted linguistic code that has, in effect, permitted him to contribute to the community distinctly and differently from others who choose to use Spanglish in their occupations. Ramos's previous advice that "we must forget about the academics and the *tichers* of the Royal Academy of the Spanish language" ignores the symbiotic dynamics extant between an individual and a language: people—such as academics—make the language, but language also makes a people. As we construct discourse, we also participate within an established linguistic stratum. Language, then, has the power to elevate a people or sink them into a realm of complacency and egocentrism that looks only to satisfy their most immediate communicative needs. Ramos and others believe that this opinion is elitist, that it equates the concept of a "correct" Spanish with a "better" class of person; but the fact remains that, while community leaders may be fluent in Spanglish and all its current variations, they are also able to adapt themselves to situations where Spanglish would be more an impediment than an aid to communication and to the betterment of society.

Ramos's observation that "Whoever refuses to use Anglicisms, Spanglish, or cyber-Spanish will have a difficult time communicating efficiently on the internet," also merits consideration. We should question the univocal importance of emphasizing the exclusive role of the Internet as a vehicle of expression and "communication." Without denying the need to commune "effectively" online, we must also acknowledge that there exist other types of formal and informal discourse or speech in which the use of Spanglish may actually hinder the message and that require us to deftly manage either Spanish or English: business letters, résumés, and essays on job or school applications, for example. These and other forms of communication not only assume a working knowledge of a language, but also base part of a decision on how well that language is brought into play. Effective communication on the Internet is a laudable goal, but it can only be *part* of a program that endows both children and adults with high levels of literacy. To paraphrase Oscar Wilde, instead of lowering the language, let us raise the level of discourse.

Therein lays the crux: what or whom is the reference point? Whom are we talking to and about? When Ramos accepts the all-encompassing potentiality of Spanglish, is he condemning Spanglish-speaking immigrants to the level of the lowest common (popular) denominator? It may certainly be true for some that, in Spanglish, "it is easier to refer to a word [in Spanglish] than a long and incomprehensible explanation." Again, the observation begs the question: "a long and incomprehensible explanation" for whom? Can we not work toward raising the English and Spanish linguistic proficiencies of Latin American immigrants instead of accepting these as they are and, therefore, pigeon-holing them within a very closed—and ultimately isolated—linguistic community? If Ramos's intentions regarding the use of Spanglish in the United States are perceived correctly, we respect and understand his opinions, as he seems to be searching to create a linguistic space for the thousands of Latin American immigrants who arrive in this country every year; but I believe this space can be created by making available to them the resources needed to elevate themselves, not by demonizing those who insist on the accurate use of a language.

In his work *The Other Face of America*, Ramos writes, "In the future there will be no pure Spanish for Hispanics."[7] However, has there ever been a "pure Spanish"? There may have been attempts at codifying, establishing the norms and patterns of the language, even imposing a Peninsular type of Spanish syntax and lexicon (particularly in the eighteenth and nineteenth centuries), but there have always been more exceptions to the rules than rules themselves. Within Spain, for example, the distinct regions have consistently fought for their particular variety of Spanish (not to mention the distinct Catalan, Basque, and Galician languages spoken in the country). Among Latin American countries, the differences between particular styles of the Spanish language have fragmented and resonated from coast to coast, coming to the point where the same word means something distinctly different elsewhere. Somehow, the Spanish-speaking nations still manage to communicate effectively amongst themselves, regardless of regional and transnational variations. Caution should be exercised in suggesting the structural acceptance of Spanglish and imposing its usage within certain contexts, as this imposition may be, in effect, as discriminatory as efforts to completely exclude it from our daily lives.

As a citizen of both Spain and the United States, I am constantly in awe of the magnificent variations that exist within both of my languages, and I am beginning to understand how colonialism and economics have played a part in the perception, imposition, and unending elaboration of both languages. However, many years have passed since the English spoken in the United States was a "pure" British English and the Spanish spoken in Latin America was a "pure" Peninsular Spanish. In effect, both languages ceased to be unadulterated—if they ever were—as soon as individuals left their homelands and set sail in search of other lands and other words with which to describe that which they had already begun to imagine and. Spanglish may be, in effect, a variation on those themes of travel, search, and destination; but it need not be the only vehicle that carries cultures forward into communion with themselves and with other peoples and destinations.

If the situation regarding the use and knowledge of English by Latin American immigrant populations is to improve, we must do away with any legislation that declares any language the "official" language and work to integrate both the Spanish and the English languages into an increasingly diversified community that will cooperate with other multilingual populations. Different generations of Latinos and non-Latinos may learn a second language at different levels—some may even feel illiterate as the journey begins—but through the process of learning and employing this new language, a community may well discover its hidden applications for the future.

LATINOS AND AFRICAN AMERICANS

In many Southern communities the linguistic miscommunications occurring between heritage Spanish speakers and Anglo-American monolinguals exist alongside racial tensions, especially between African Americans and Latinos. The racial and ethnic diversity present in many of these areas is creating a polarization of opinions and behaviors that reflects national attitudes: some prefer to isolate themselves from contact with other ethnic groups, while others work toward the complete integration of a population within the established Anglo community. In many areas that have witnessed the arrival of immigrants from Latin America or other parts of the United States, tensions have frequently arisen between Latinos and African Americans due to a number of factors that include jobs, political control of a community, immigration policies, and the racial distribution and behavior of the police force, among others.

Writing on the Web site Black Agenda Report, Glen Ford declares that, "It must be said that African Americans have been conditioned to be much more 'Anglo' in their perceptions of Latino political assertiveness than most of us are willing to admit." Speaking at a business forum on October 6, 2005, on the economic tensions arising in the wake of hurricane Katrina, for example, New Orleans mayor Ray Nagin referred to the substantial numbers of Latino workers that were working on the reconstruction of the city and asked rhetorically, "How do I ensure that New Orleans is not overrun by Mexican workers?"[8] As Raymond A. Mohl noted in more general terms, "Employers' seeming preference for Hispanic workers, often praised as being more compliant and having a strong work ethic, has rankled black communities across the South."[9] Curiously, these tensions are also a sign that the South belongs to the American continent in a much broader sense. As Jon Smith and Deborah Cohn have indicated, "If we define 'America' hemispherically, for example, the experience of defeat, occupation, and reconstruction— particularly if this historical trauma is broadened to include the African American experience of defeat under slavery—is something the [U.S.] South shares with every other part of America."[10]

In his book *The Presumed Alliance. The Unspoken Conflict Between Latinos and Blacks and What It Means for America*, Nicolás Vaca traces the antipathy that often characterizes the relationships between many Latino and African American communities in the United States, studying the impact of institutional restructurings such as the 1986 Immigration Reform and Control Act on the dynamics between both populations. He also studies events such as the 1965 riots in Watts, Los Angeles, pointing out that when whites began to leave Compton, Blacks "view[ed] Latinos as challenges to the gains they fought so hard to achieve and [held] them at arm's length."[11] In regard to the systematic discrimination of Latinos by African Americans, Vaca also analyzes issues such as education resources, public sector jobs, and representation of African Americans and Latinos on school boards and City Councils (where no Latino had held elected office in 20 years).[12] For Vaca, the roots of much of the national tensions between these two groups lie in the Immigration Reform and Control Act of 1986, which, among other stipulations, "imposed federal, civil, and criminal penalties on employees who knowingly hired, recruited, or referred aliens who are not authorized to work by the Immigration and Naturalization Service."[13] Many employees who feared breaking this law began to openly discriminate against Latinos, and the NAACP soon announced its support of the Act. Two

Latino organizations, the Mexican-American Legal Defense Fund and the National Council of La Raza, sought the help of the African American community in repealing the Act, but the leadership conference on civil rights wavered, stating that they needed to study the issue more.[14]

Today, tensions between African American and Latino populations are evident wherever economic conditions are creating competition for work, particularly over positions involving manual labor. For many, these tensions originate in a resentment of the numbers of Latinos arriving in this country and purportedly taking jobs that have been the traditional—but not exclusive—domain of African Americans. Recent research, however, has shown that this resentment has no basis in daily reality, as "Employment trends for black workers specifically also show no signs of job displacement from the rapid influx of Hispanic workers."[15] The Federation for American Immigration Reform—a peripheral organization that looks to curb Latin American immigration to the United States—illustrates this anxiety by offering as an example Greenwood, South Carolina, where, as the organization states on its Web site, "There were some early tensions with the city's minority black population over what was seen as job competition." Another example of rising tensions occurred in May 1991, when riots ensued in the Mount Pleasant neighborhood of Washington, D.C., after an African American police officer shot a Latino immigrant, Daniel Enrique Gómez.[16] The journalist Jorge Ramos has also written on these tensions, observing in 2002, "Although we [Latinos] outnumber African-Americans, there are thirty-nine African-American members of Congress [as opposed to 19 Hispanic members]."[17] Miami, the city of Ramos's residence, has also been witness to conflicts between police officers and the African American community, sparked in part by the 1989 shooting of a Black motorcyclist by a Latino officer.[18] In a city known for its ethnic diversity and linguistic porousness, "African-Americans [have] confronted something they had not seen before in other parts of the United States—a power structure that felt no apparent guilt or empathy for their plight, or any desire to extend special privileges to them as a disenfranchised group."[19] Nelson Mandela's 1990 visit to Miami Beach also revealed tensions between the communities, as the South African statesman had publicly thanked Fidel Castro for his years of supporting the African National Congress.[20] The bilingual, mostly conservative Latino middle class in Miami excluded the African American population from their circles and, through the power of their vote, "rendered the Black vote almost meaningless."[21] In the opinion of many, Latinos in Miami were succeeding in the 1980s at the expense of Blacks through the establishment of "economic beachheads in the traditionally Black areas of Miami" after the arrival of the Marielitos in 1980.[22] The diversity of the Miami population is unique given the sheer numbers of Latinos and the economic and political power that these individuals wield. As exceptional as the conflicts may be, however, they may also herald a new dimension of racial tensions in the United States.

For the majority of the history of the United States, racial tensions in the United States have been defined strictly as a binary relationship between "opposing" groups: Blacks and Whites, Whites and Latinos, Blacks and Latinos, Asians and Whites, etc. The sheer and unexpected presence of Latinos in some areas of the country has turned this polarity into a multicolored blueprint, as three or more ethnic groups are substantially represented in an area and struggle to further their own sets of priorities. This situation has instigated the racialization of community relationships through the stereotyping of Spanish-speaking immigrants. According to James Loucky, these stereotypes "deny immigrants the right to be judged and treated as individuals."[23] Similarly, the stress between African Americans and Latinos in the U.S. South reflects a new and potentially encouraging dynamic in the history of identity consciousness in the United States, as a growing number of small and large communities make efforts to be both inclusive of new populations and protective of existing ones. These struggles in the region may reveal more about the future of the United States than any close analysis of Latino migration to and from Los Angeles, New York, or Chicago, for example, as these large urban areas have historically entrenched traditions of diversity that have required them to gradually and systematically make efforts at including the whole of its population and to adopt what may be perceived as sink-or-swim attitudes toward more recent waves of immigrant populations.

Problems and solutions to the rising tensions between Latinos and African Americans have already been identified and proposed. Across the South, the anxiety expressed by members of both populations is often masked by the historic tension that has marked relations between Anglos and African Americans and that has tended to paint the region with a very broad white or black brush. Statistics show that "At the end of the '90s, only 8 percent of the rural South's African American adults aged 25-64—and only 5 percent of Hispanics—had a four-year college degree. For nonmetro whites, the figure was 17 percent....More than half of the rural South's Hispanic adults ages 25 to 64 had not completed high school, along with 28 percent of African Americans and 18 percent of whites."[24] Consequently, "To sustain and build the South's economy in the future, the region cannot squander the assets embodied in the young people who currently live in rural shadows. The competitiveness of the region requires us to educate all our people—and to meet the special challenge of raising the educational attainment of African Americans and Latinos."[25] As Latinos have immigrated to urban and rural Southern communities, resentment has grown among all ethnic groups. According to Nicolás Vaca, "the Latino arrival brings a new complexion to the Black-White South."[26] The impressions of the relationships between Latinos and African Americans tend to oscillate between generally positive opinions that believe in a future of possible cooperation between both groups and a strong desire that Latinos and the issues salient to their community not be identified with those of the African Americans.

While a blind drive toward integration may not be the answer to these tensions, the (self)segregation of these populations may only contribute to the miscommunications and misunderstandings. As MDC, Inc., indicated in its *State of the South 2004* report, "School systems that increasingly isolate white students from blacks and Latinos—and isolate children of the poor from children of the more affluent—will fail to prepare young people adequately for participation in an equitable society and a competitive economy."[27] In a city such as Memphis, Tennessee, coexistence between Latinos and African Americans is practically obligatory, as the two communities share the same urban space, living in both the middle-class suburbs of rising affluence and in marginalized neighborhoods marked by crime and poverty. Have Latinos and African Americans alienated themselves from wealthier areas of the city, or have they been marginalized by subtle urban techniques such as the creation or manipulation of a school district or tax base? Although in Memphis Latinos may live in neighborhoods that have been traditionally African American, this does not guarantee social, political, or economic interaction between the two groups. (As a Nashville lawyer remarked to me in rather racist terms, "Hispanics do not like to live where there are many blacks."[28]) If, for both populations, there is a shared history of marginalization and struggle, why is cooperation between Latinos and African Americans so difficult?

Some Latinos fear that African Americans may think of them as usurpers: bottom-dwelling social climbers, economic opportunists, political lackeys of the Anglos. Elsa Baughman in Jackson, Mississippi, believes that African Americans may resent the Latino population because "the one above does not want to associate with the one below."[29] In this vertical and hierarchical representation of human existence, who is above and who is below may be a matter of perception. In Elsa's opinion, are the

African Americans "above," witnessing the arrival of an economically disadvantaged population that may commandeer jobs held by African Americans? Or are the Latinos "above" the African Americans due to a seemingly intrinsic set of advantages (or, more importantly, the absence of the same disadvantages historically suffered by the African American population in the United States)? If the first possibility is true, then Elsa is reaffirming the daily reality of many Latin American immigrants in the South who arrive to this country looking for economic security (and, at times, finding it by offering themselves for positions of manual labor at wages earned below those made by others and below the federally mandated minimum wage). Multiple opinions of Latino and African American perceptions serve as a double filter and contaminate relations from the beginning, as they appear to set individuals in direct competition with one another and force the creation of apparently incompatible economic goals: the perception is that African Americans in the South occupy the lowest rung on the socioeconomic ladder; the perception is that Latinos look to occupy that rung and displace African American workers; and the perception is that non-Latino landowners and managers will be the primary beneficiaries of their labor competition. As a Latino resident of Mississippi stated, "I see an extremely poor black man. I see him very resigned to his poverty. They have not taken advantage of the circumstances."[30] Will the new generation of Latin American immigrants in the South "take advantage of the circumstances," because, as is the case elsewhere, perceptions appear to be creating a great portion of daily reality in Southern states? If these perceptions indeed become realities, then many Southern communities must learn to transform these opinions and look to be inclusive of the variety of races and ethnicities found if the community is to attract newcomers to the area and to remain competitive in an ever-globalizing South.

For all the tensions between Latinos and African Americans, there are many reasons to hope that there will be continued dialogue and interaction that will lead to the pursuit of shared economic, political, and social priorities. As the *State of the South 2007* noted, "Blacks and Latinos have traditions of benevolence, and as their economic wherewithal expands, they will be in a position to develop institutions for organized living."[31] In North Carolina, for example, the Black Workers for Justice and the Latino Workers Association "created an African American/Latino Alliance to find common ground among blacks and Hispanics. In Durham, the Piedmont Peace Project, the North Carolina Black-Latino Reconciliation Project, and the Operation TRUCE Campaign engaged in similar work."[32] Even today, the personal experiences of some Latinos give witness to the strength of opportunities that transcend any racial or ethnic divisions. The understanding shared with an individual marginalized by society transcends, in many cases, any differences there may have been between Hispanic and African American women working under the same roof. Both Latinos and African Americans will struggle with cultural differences if they are to introduce themselves into the workforce and into schools, hospitals, and city halls, on equal terms with the non-Latino and non–African American populations. For the future, this struggle represents a possible common starting point for dialogue between Latinos and African Americans in Southern communities. The positive impact of any population upon a community and the increasing interaction between them is noted first and foremost within the entering group, be it Latino, African American, or Korean; but when this positive impact is noted by other groups and affects them within the community, then the creation of a society potentially inclusive of all individuals will have begun (perceptions notwithstanding).

For this to occur, the acceptance of differences between cultures is crucial. An employee at the National Civil Rights Museum in Memphis perceived positive consequences in the influx of Latinos into the city, as "They bring in a spice of life, new cultures, new ways of dress. Once a community becomes diverse, then you don't have to be afraid anymore." The fear mentioned by the speaker is at the heart of many conversations about ethnic and racial diversity and its impact on a community. Where does this potential fear of the Other originate? In the simple unknown and in ignorance? Is it a fear of losing one's job, of cultural displacement, or an existential fear that forces one to look deep into the mirror of individual identity? It is there—and beyond. It is the fear of past, present, and future rolled up and identified with a very specific race or ethnic group that threatens to destabilize a community, with another individual whose aptitudes are perceived as threats and are all too readily blamed for one's limitations and difficulties. And it is the possible fear of connecting with others, as similarities with those apparently radically different from us may reveal more than the tastes and distastes we share with those whom history and circumstances have taught to live under the same economic, social, or political roof as us or that belong to our own inscribed community. As Vaca affirms, "For each analysis that finds that Latinos and Blacks have a 'natural' basis for mutual support because of a common history of suffering and oppression, there are others that find great antipathy between the two groups."[33]

A possible first step in recognizing this fear is an awareness of others and of their circumstances. As the employee of the National Civil Rights Museum in Memphis revealingly and sympathetically declared of Latinos in that city, "I'm pretty sure it's hard on them, too." While this phrase may be somewhat subjective, its explicit attention to and recognition of the geographical, emotional, and psychological displacement suffered by Latin American immigrants grants these same Latinos a sense of identity, an otherness, an understanding that confers dignity upon a marginalized population. In advocating a more positive perspective, Glen Ford affirms on the Black Agenda Report Web site that, "For the sake of our common interests, Black progressives are obligated to do everything possible to cleanse the African American dialogue of parochialism, insults against other ethnicities, useless nostalgia that keeps us fixed in a past time and—most importantly—the nativism inherited from our historical oppressors." Despite the fact that "in the real world the ostensible moral and philosophical base for coalition politics have largely fallen apart because of competing self-interests,"[34] it is in both acknowledging these "competing self-interests" and finding social, political, and economic common ground that many of the tensions between Latino and African American communities may begin to be addressed. What is required is a perception and a recognition of the Other that manages to bring together the circumstances of the moment and a vision of better future days, and not just a list of shared economic goals that describe human existence in numerical approximations that reduce individuals to a set of glyphs not unlike those on an Egyptian cartouche.

The Future

Economic concerns will play an important part in determining the future of a Latino family, but these must be balanced with a sense of history and of progress, of goals shared between the individual and the immediate community. As Paul Simão has written, "Poor access to quality health care, difficulties obtaining government services and towering high school dropout rates are the problems most often cited as barriers to Hispanic prosperity in Southern states."[1] It is no wonder that the South's possible future difficulties and those faced by the emerging Latino population in the area are connected. For the region, "Now, more than in the past, undereducated youth, chronic poverty, lingering health disparities, and civic frictions along the lines of class and ethnicity complicate the South's ability to keep pace in a local race."[2] While history is not doomed to repeat itself, it does appear in the U.S. South that, in many respects, it is continuing some of the most inelegant traditions of its past.

In this sense, knowledge of past and present circumstances transforms the Latino in the U.S. South today into an active part of the public sphere. In the past, for example, landlords in the region pursued wealth in labor more than in land, gauging their affluence according in part by the number of slaves they owned and later, after emancipation, by the workers that were "hired." In the twentieth century, wealth as capital was the land that an individual owned, particularly the acreage one possessed and what cash crop was planted and harvested. Currently, the influx of migrant farm workers into the South and other areas has made for a redefinition of what constitutes "wealth," including both the land that an individual owns and the number of migrant workers that are needed over the course of a season. This de-personalization of the value of labor risks portraying every migrant worker in a very general light that both ignores individual differences within the migrant worker population and objectifies the thousands of human beings who work in Southern fields and farms.

Another salient issue for the majority of farm worker populations is the presence of children as laborers. As Steven Greenhouse noted in a *New York Times* article on August 6, 2000, "Child farm workers are divided into three groups: unaccompanied migrants, children of migrant farm workers, and about 40,000 minors who are the children of farm owners and who start milking cows and harvesting at an early age to learn how to operate the farms that they may someday inherit." Among the children who may be considered migrant workers, there exist work conditions that, as Greenhouse notes, would be considered illegal in any part of the country: "Child farm workers are often paid less than the $5.15 minimum wage, sometimes receiving $2.50 an hour. Growers often do not provide them with toilets and drinking water, and some child pickers say growers occasionally order them to resume picking even when the twenty-four hours required by law have not passed after pesticides are sprayed." Besides the physical consequences, how will this affect the children psychologically? What impressions will this leave on a nation whose agricultural production is dependent upon a generation of illegally paid migrant workers? Perhaps this is allowed to happen because the children are a foreign population—frequently undocumented or undocumentable —or because migrant workers are a virtually uncountable group that moves with the harvest calendar. Regardless, if these families remain in the United States—and statistics show that they will—these marginalized, unschooled children will grow up to be adults who participate in the social, political, and economic life of Southern communities. These will be significant contributions, but one cannot help but wonder how much more their families, their communities, and their host nation would be enriched if the motivation existed to establish roots in a community and for landowners to hire a rotating labor force that they would share in contractual agreement with the workers and with other businesses and agricultural property holders in the United States. The benefit for the landowner would be the hiring of an experienced labor force, while the migrant workers would have the possibility, if they wished, of completing the same harvest cycle every year in the same place, supported by a contractual agreement. The abuses of migrant workers would in all likelihood persist, but there would be even more legal recourse and stabilization of their labor conditions so that they may be relatively assured of their continuance and of their economic support.

In the U.S. South, the virtually uninterrupted presence of Latinos is a contemporary reality that is transforming both local Southern communities and the Spanish-speaking populations that inhabit them. Local school systems are also being challenged, as administrators and teachers across the region face the unanticipated arrival and exponential growth of a population whose first language is not English. As Kochhar and others have noted, "The Hispanic school-age population (ages 5 through 17) in the new settlement areas of the South grew by 322 percent between 1990 and 2000. Over the same period, the corresponding white population grew by just 10 percent and the black population by 18 percent."[3] In Arkansas, Alabama, Georgia, North Carolina, South Carolina, and Tennessee, "Latinos accounted for 43 percent of the people added to the population of these states in the pre-school age range."[4] School systems are being required to adapt to changing circumstances, offering classes in Spanish or courses in English as a Second Language for the new immigrants. At first glance, these circumstances would appear to be anomalous: Are the majority of Latinos not concentrated in ten states, none of which are in the Deep South (Florida notwithstanding)? Do a number of Southern states not rank at or near the bottom of national categories such as household per capita income, level of education attained, and health care coverage? Are 37 percent of Hispanics not living in the three very non–Deep South cities of Los Angeles, New York, and Miami?[5] Does the U.S. South not have an awkward history of race relations that involves the objectification and mistreatment of human beings different from the mainstream and dominant racial group? The arrival of nontraditional immigrants to the U.S. South poses a number of questions and obligates the traditional populations to adjust to the changes in their community. The extent of communication between both groups and the skill that their respective leaders show in adapting to and foreseeing these variations will determine the continued success and longevity of these communities. As Jared Diamond has written, "Leaders who don't just react passively, who have the courage to anticipate crises or to act early, and who make strong insightful decisions of top-down management really can make a huge difference to their societies. So can similarly courageous, active citizens practicing bottom-up management."[6]

As paradoxical as it may seem, the uncertainties may help the South attract more Latinos by offering a wealth of economic opportunities, a sense of identity distinct from other parts of the country, and a land that is historically conscious of its past. According to Peter Applebome, "The South's past may offer up more wrong turns than right ones, but its experience...is as good a distillation of the nation's search for its soul as we are likely to find."[7] There are Latinos in the South, and they are making a discernible impression in rural areas such as South Georgia, central Mississippi, and the coastal Carolinas, and on the cities and metropolitan areas of Charleston, Nashville, Memphis, Mobile, Charlotte, Jackson, Savannah, and Atlanta. Through a type of cultural symbiosis that permits an exchange of cultural attributes that does not efface or erase communal features and characteristics, the South is also present in Latinos. Even though both Southerners and Latinos may be described and illustrated through a variety of statistics and research, at times the diversity inherent to any group also makes empirical categorizations problematic as the discrete populations have been marginalized by larger, national communities that have frequently looked to stigmatize them, to represent them through a series of distinct, trouble-free stereotypes, and to ultimately blur the fact that there exists a group of Southern Latinos that consistently defies characterization. What W.J. Cash wrote to describe the South circa 1940 may certainly apply to the United States today:

> Violence, intolerance, aversion and suspicion toward new ideas, an incapacity for analysis, an inclination to act from feeling rather than from thought, an exaggerated individualism and a too narrow concept of social responsibility, attachment to fictious and false values, above all too great attachment to racial values and a tendency to justify cruelty and injustice in the name of those values, sentimentality, and a lack of realism—these have been its characteristic vices in the past. And, despite changes for the better, they remain its characteristic vices today.[8]

How prophetic is this statement? Does this set of characteristics currently reflect the nation at large? As Gregory Stephens has written, "A multicentered model of intergroup relations in the South would undertake what I see as a fundamental challenge of inclusive democracy: building institutions and social spaces in which commonality and social difference can exist."[9] The "commonalities" between the immense variety of Latino cultures and Southern populations, the mutual interests, and the shared geographic stage upon which these lives unfold, will not only draw the communities closer together; they will speak to the future of the United States as a vibrant, polychromatic land and to the willingness of its citizens, residents, and leaders to continue to welcome the diverse races, religions, and ethnicities that form its national communities.

Notes

INTRODUCTION

1. Adams, Jerome R. *Greasers and Gringos. The Historical Roots of Anglo-Hispanic Prejudice*, 189.

2. O'Connor, "The Displaced Person," 203.

3. Heyck, "Introduction: Latinos, Past and Present," 1.

4. Fraga, Luis, Herman Gallegos, Gerald P. López, Mary Louise Pratt, Renato Rosaldo, José Saldivar, Ramon Saldivar, and Guadalupe Valdés. "Still Looking for America. Beyond the Latino National Political Survey," 244.

5. Key, *Southern Politics in State and Nation*, 4.

6. Kochhar, Rakesh, Robert Suso, and Sonya Tagoya. "The New Latino South: The Context and Consequences of Rapid Growth," i.

7. While we recognize the linguistic and political distinctions inherent to each term, throughout the work we will be using the terms "Hispanic" and "Latino" interchangeably.

8. Oboler, "Hispanics? That's What They Call Us," 4; Oquendo, "Re-imagining the Latino/a Race," 62; Gimenez, "Latino Politics—Class Struggles: Reflections on the Future of Latino Politics," 168.

9. Mendieta, "The Making of New Peoples. Hispanizing Race," 47.

10. In discussion with author, May 2000. The majority of the interviews were conducted in Spanish. The translations are therefore my own.

11. Ibid., May 2000.

12. See note 6 above, 27.

13. Yale-Loehr and Chiappari, "Immigration: Cities and States Rush in Where Congress Fears to Tread," http://millermayer.com/new/nylj_locallaw.html.

14. Chen, "Legal Fight over Harsh Illegal Immigration Law Moves Forward," http://newstandardnews.net/content/index.cfm/items/3628.

15. Yale-Loehr and Chiappari, "Immigration: Cities and States Rush in Where Congress Fears to Tread."

CHAPTER 1

1. Hoffman, Paul E., "Lucas Vásquez de Ayllóńs Discovery and Colony," 36.

2. Ibid., 42–43.

3. Fernandez-Shaw, *The Hispanic Presence in North America*, 287.

4. Middleton, *Colonial America. A History, 1565–1776*, 392.

5. Posada, *Alonso de Posada Report, 1686*, 49.

6. Middleton, *Colonial America. A History, 1565–1776*, 416–17.

7. Fernandez-Shaw, *The Hispanic Presence in North America*, 145.

8. Ortuño Martínez, "España-Estados Unidos. Fronteras imposibles," 45.

9. Fernandez-Shaw, *The Hispanic Presence in North America*, 156.

10. Ibid., 133–35.

11. Ibid., 135.

12. Ibid., 73.

13. Ibid., 74.

14. Ibid., 74.

15. Beers, *French and Spanish Records of Louisiana*, 40.

16. Ortuño Martínez, "España-Estados Unidos. Fronteras imposibles," 46.

17. Ibid., 47.

18. Ibid., 47.

19. Fernandez-Shaw, *The Hispanic Presence in North America*, 148.

20. Davis, Thomas J. *Race Relations in America*, 71–72.

21. Adams, Jerome R. *Greasers and Gringos. The Historical Roots of Anglo-Hispanic Prejudice*, 135.

22. Stavans, *The Hispanic Condition*, 23.

23. The information regarding the direct or indirect participation of Hispanics in the Civil War may be found on the Hispanic Heritage Page of the Sons of Confederate Veterans: www.scv.org/education/edpapers/hisphst.htm.

24. Davis, David Brion. "The Comparative Approach to American History: Slavery," 61.

25. Tannenbaum, Frank. "Slavery, the Negro, and Racial Prejudice," 5.

26. Poloni-Simard, "La América española: una colonización de antiguo régimen," 217.

27. Klein, Herbert S., *Slavery in the Americas*, 59.

28. Elkins, "Slavery in Capitalist and Non-capitalist cultures," 19.

29. Parish, *Slavery. History and Historians*, 11.

30. Jordan, "Modern Tensions and the Origins of American Slavery," 115.

31. Ibid., 117.

32. Rose, *A Documentary History of Slavery in North America*, 20.

33. Jordan, "Modern Tensions and the Origins of American Slavery," 117.

34. Klein, Herbert S., *Slavery in the Americas*, 2.

35. Davis, David Brion. "The Comparative Approach to American History: Slavery," 62.

36. Parish, *Slavery. History and Historians*, 99.

37. Berlin, "Time, Space, and the Evolution of Afro-American Society on British Mainland North America," 135.

38. Rose, *A Documentary History of Slavery in North America*, 70–74.

39. Ibid., 67.

40. Parish, *Slavery. History and Historians*, 19–20.

41. Aptheker, *American Negro Slave Revolts*, 163; Ibid., 132.

42. Davis, David Brion. "The Comparative Approach to American History: Slavery," 67.

43. Parish, *Slavery. History and Historians*, 21; Berlin, "Time, Space, and the Evolution of Afro-American Society on British Mainland North America," 130.

44. Parish, *Slavery. History and Historians*, 21.

45. Rose, *A Documentary History of Slavery in North America*, 176.

46. Ibid., 182.

47. N'diaye, "Los esclavos del sur de los Estados Unidos," 150–51.

48. Parish, *Slavery, History and Historians*, 26.

49. Ibid., 26.

50. Ibid., 27.

51. Ibid., 4.

52. Parish, *Slavery, History and Historians*, 50.

53. Ibid., 44.

54. Ibid., 59.

55. Ibid., 55.

56. See note 27 above, 6.

57. Ibid., 27.

58. Bernand, "Imperialismos ibéricos," 208–10.

59. Klein, Herbert S., *Slavery in the Americas*, 38, 85.

60. Elkins, "Slavery in Capitalist and Non-capitalist cultures," 23.

61. Ibid., 22.

62. Davis, David Brion, "A Comparison of British America and Latin America," 72.

63. Davis, David Brion. "The Comparative Approach to American History: Slavery," 66.

64. Parish, *Slavery, History and Historians*, 115.

65. Ibid., 115.

66. Poloni-Simard, "La América española: una colonización de antiguo régimen," 246.

67. Bernand, "Imperialismos ibéricos," 177; in the opinion of Marie-Chantal Barre, "Indigenism is the ideology of the non-Indians, while Indianism is the ideology of the Indians[.] " (19).

68. Poloni-Simard, "La América española: una colonización de antiguo régimen," 222.

69. Barre, *Ideologías indigenistas y movimientos indios*, 7.

70. Ibid., 19.

71. Goodwin, *Global Studies. Latin America*, 7, 10, 36, 49, 99, 89.

72. Pearson, Edward A. "A Countryside Full of Flames," 568.

73. Martin, Ken. "Neutrality and the Alliance with the Confederate States of America," http://cherokeehistory.com/confed.html.

74. The Creek handed over some 23 million acres of land to the U.S. government, and in 1830 the Cherokee signed over approximately 10.5 million acres of land to the federal government in the Treaty of Dancing Creek.

75. MDC, Inc., *The State of the South 2002,* 6.

76. Smith, W. Thomas Jr., "An Influx of Hispanics Causing Growing Pains for the South," www.latinolink.com/news/us/0309sur.php3.

77. Barthes, *Mythologies,* 110.

78. Ibid., 120.

79. Ibid., 143.

80. Channing, "Slavery and Confederate Nationalism," 223.

81. Newby, *The South. A History,* 92.

82. Daniels, *A Southerner Discovers the South,* 8.

83. Wyatt Brown, Bertram. *The Shaping of Southern Culture: Honor, Grace, and War.*

84. Page, *The Rebuilding of Old Commonwealths,* 125.

85. Gray, "Negotiating Differences: Southern Culture(s) Now," 226.

86. Lumpkin, *The Making of a Southerner,* 101.

87. Fry, *Dixie Looks Abroad. The South and U.S. Foreign Relations, 1789–1973,* 106.

88. Newby, *The South. A History,* 250.

89. Ibid., 288.

90. Cash, *The Mind of the South,* 4.

91. Ibid., 163.

92. Ibid., 178.

93. Ibid., 292.

94. Ibid., 430, 431.

95. Himes, "Introduction: Background of Recent Changes in the South," 1.

96. Douglass, "Reconstruction," 764. Emphasis added.

97. Douglass, "An Appeal to Congress for Impartial Suffrage," 117.

98. Cash, *The Mind of the South,* 108.

99. Cohn, *History and Memory in the Two Souths,* 185.

100. Newby, *The South. A History,* 259–60.

101. Ibid., 298.

102. Ibid., 261.

103. Ibid., 261.

104. Ibid., 275.

105. Ibid., 275.

106. Ibid., 276.

107. Cash, *The Mind of the South,* 109.

108. Ibid., 114.

109. Ibid., 139.

110. Newby, *The South. A History,* 235.

111. Cohn, *History and Memory in the Two Souths,* 6.

112. Newby, *The South. A History,* 298–99.

113. Ibid., 299.

114. Ibid., 299.

115. Ibid., 299.

116. Ibid., 300.

117. Mencken, "The Sahara of the Bozart," 158, 159, 160.

118. Ibid., 160.

119. Ibid., 158.

120. Ibid., 159.

121. Ibid., 163.

122. Daniel, *Standing at the Crossroads: Southern Life in the Twentieth Century*, 3.

123. Newby, *The South. A History*, 238.

124. Naipaul. *A Turn in the South*, 306.

125. Gerster and Cords, "The Northern Origins of Southern Mythology," 573.

126. Ibid., 574.

127. Ibid., 572.

128. Ibid., 567.

129. Ibid., 570.

130. Ibid., 570.

131. See note 90 above, 242.

132. See note 81 above, 289.

133. Grantham, "Henry Grady," http://www.anl.org/articles/16/16-00647.html.

134. Grady, *The New South*, 17–18.

135. Newby, *The South. A History*, 290.

136. Cash, *The Mind of the South*, 188.

137. Quoted in Cobb, *Redefining Southern Culture*, 150.

138. Smith and Cohn, "Introduction: Uncanny Hybridities," 3.

139. Newby, *The South. A History*, 99.

140. Cochran, *Democrcacy Heading South. National Politics in the Shadow of Dixie*, 174.

141. Applebome, *Dixie Rising: How the South is shaping America*, 344.

142. Smith and Cohn, "Introduction: Uncanny Hybridities," 9.

143. Gerster and Cords, "The Northern Origins of Southern Mythology," 576.

144. Jefferson, *The Papers of Thomas Jefferson, vol. 8*, 468.

145. Odum, *Southern Regions of the United States*, 25.

146. Newby, *The South. A History*, 443.

147. Roberts, "Living Southern in *Southern Living*," 90.

148. Cited in Dalrymple, "Dixie's Dead, Long Live the South," 3.

149. Newby, *The South. A History*, 256.

150. Kanellos, *Thirty million strong: reclaiming the Hispanic image in American culture*, 70.

151. Dalrymple, "Dixie's Dead, Long Live the South," 2.

152. Tindall, *Natives and newcomers: ethnic Southerners and Southern ethnics*, 16.

153. Fry, *Dixie Looks Abroad. The South and U.S. Foreign Relations, 1789–1973*, 77.

154. Gerster and Cords, "The Northern Origins of Southern Mythology," 581–82.

155. Cochran, *Democrcacy Heading South. National Politics in the Shadow of Dixie*, 23.

156. Ibid., 23.

157. Ibid., 87.

158. Ibid., 205, 226.

159. Ibid., 24.

160. Gray, "Negotiating Differences: Southern Culture(s) Now," 221.

161. MDC, Inc., *The State of the South 1998*, 3.

162. Cobb, *Redefining Southern Culture*, 3.

163. Cash, *The Mind of the South*, 188.

164. Cobb, *Redefining Southern Culture*, 4.

165. Cobb, "Beyond the 'Y'all Wal;': The American South Goes Global," 5.

166. Cochran, *Democrcacy Heading South. National Politics in the Shadow of Dixie*, 51.

167. Tindall, *Natives and Newcomers: Ethnic Southerners and Southern Ethnics*, 19.

168. MDC, Inc., *The State of the South 2002*, 6.

169. Channing, "Slavery and Confederate Nationalism," 224.

170. MDC, Inc., *The State of the South 2002*, 4.

171. Cobb, *Redefining Southern Culture*, 185.

172. Hill, "Contemporary Issues in Anthropological Studies of the American South," 22.

173. Cochran, *Democrcacy Heading South. National Politics in the Shadow of Dixie*, 91.

174. Cash, *The Mind of the South*, 345.

175. Bullock and Rozell, "Southern Politics at Century's End," 5.

176. Cohn, *History and Memory in the Two Souths*, 189.

177. Applebome, *Dixie Rising: How the South is shaping America*, 61.

178. Ibid., 88.

179. Ibid., 131.

180. Cash, *The Mind of the South*, 51.

181. Ibid., 56, 87, 320.

182. Odum and Johnson, *The Negro and His Songs*, 19; Ibid., 31.

183. Martí, *Marti on the USA*, 102.

184. Griffin, "Why Was the South a Problem to America?" 23.

185. Applebome, *Dixie Rising: How the South is shaping America*, 139.

186. Pozzetta, "Migration to the Urban South: An Unfinished Agenda," 202.

187. Ibid., 202.

188. Gray, "Negotiating Differences: Southern Culture(s) Now," 226.

CHAPTER 2

1. Trueba, *Latinos unidos: from cultural diversity to the politics of solidarity*, 47.

2. Ibid., 156–57.

3. Ibid., 155.

4. Ramos, *The Other Face of America*, xxxiii.

5. Huntington, "The Hispanic Challenge," 32.

6. Ibid., 40.

7. Ibid., 44.

8. Stavans, *The Hispanic Condition*, 19.

9. Leland and Chambers, "Generation Ñ. Latino America," 53.

10. Ramos, *The Other Face of America*, 46.

11. Álvarez and Nagler, "Antonio Villaraigosa's Victory in Los Angeles: Any Democratic Lessons for Winning Latino Votes?" http://www.emerging democraticmajorityweblog.com/donkeyrising/archives/001247.php.

12. Rodríguez, Richard, "'Blaxicans and Other Reinvented Americans," B11.

13. Ramos, *The Other Face of America*, xxv–xxvi.

14. Chambers, Figueroa, Wingert, and Weingarten, "Latino America," 51.

15. Pew Hispanic Center, "Latinos and the 2006 Mid-term Election," 1. http://Pewhispanic.org/files/factsheets/26.pdf.

16. Ibid., 2

17. Ibid., 3.

18. Ibid., 3.

19. Ibid., 4.

20. Ibid., 4.

21. Rodríguez, Richard, "'Blaxicans and Other Reinvented Americans," B11.

22. MDC Inc., *The State of the South 2007*, 9.

23. Trueba, *Latinos unidos: from cultural diversity to the politics of solidarity*, 22.

24. Ramos, *The Other Face of America*, 8.

25. Porter, "The Surging Hispanic Economy," 1. http://www.wsjclassroom edition.com/archive.

26. Ramos, *The Other Face of America*, 21.

27. MDC, Inc., *The State of the South 1998*, 10.

28. Porter, "The Surging Hispanic Economy," 1–3.

29. Donato, Bankston, and Robison, "Immigration and the Organization of the Onshore Oil Industry: Southern Louisiana in the late 1990s," 105, 108.

30. Ibid., 112.

31. Ibid., 111.

32. In discussion with author, May 2000.

CHAPTER 3

1. Kaplan, *An Empire Wilderness. Travels into the heart of America*, 95.

2. Ramos, *The Other Face of America*, 110.

3. Chambers, Figueroa, Wingert, and Weingarten, "Latino America," 51.

4. Vaca, *The Presumed Alliance. The Unspoken Conflict Between Latinos and Blacks and What It Means for America*, 23.

5. Ibid., 23.

6. National Hispanic Leadership Agenda. *Congressional Scorecard 107th Congress. First and Second Sessions*, ii. http://www.nclr.org/policy/score card2003/NHLA_Scorecard.pdf.

7. These statistics and those following were taken from the National Hispanic Leadership Agenda's *Congressional Scorecard 107th Congress. 1st and 2nd Session*. Available online at: www.nclr.org/policy/scorecard2003/NHLA_ Scorecard.pdf.

8. For our intentions, "Southern" Senators and members of the House included those representing the states of Alabama, Arkansas, Georgia, Kentucky, Louisiana, Mississippi, North Carolina, South Carolina, Tennessee, Virginia, and West Virginia.

9. Cortes, "Latinos woefully underrepresented in US media, panelists say." http://www.freedomforum.org/templates/document.asp?documentID=15096.

10. Ramos, *The Other Face of America*, 161.

11. Ibid., 6.

12. Kochhar, Suso, and Tagoya. "The New Latino South: The Context and Consequences of Rapid Growth," 6. http://pewhispanic.org/files/reports/50.pdf.

13. McPeek Villatoro, "Latino Southerners: A New Form of Mestizaje," 107.

14. Kochhar, Suso, and Tagoya. "The New Latino South: The Context and Consequences of Rapid Growth,", ii.

15. Ibid., 17.

16. MDC, Inc., *The State of the South 1998*, 8.

17. Thompson, "Putting Down Roots," 13.

18. Washington National Conference of Catholic Bishops, *Hispanic Ministry at the Turn of the New Millenium*(conducted by Rev. Raúl Gómez and Dr. Manuel Vásquez). http://usccb.org/hispanicaffairs/studygomez.shtml.

19. In discussion with author, June 2000.

20. President's Advisory Commission on Educational Excellence for Hispanic Americans, *Our Nation on the Fault Line: Hispanic American Education*, 27–44.

21. Rodríguez, Richard, "Blaxicans and Other Reinvented Americans," B10.

22. Simâo, "Hispanics Flex New Muscle in Southern U.S," 1. http://www.puertorico-herald.org/issues/2002/vol6n27.

23. MDC, Inc., *The State of the South 1998*, 10.

24. Thompson, "Putting Down Roots," 13.

25. MDC, Inc., *The State of the South 1998*, 10.

26. Kochhar, Suso, and Tagoya. "The New Latino South: The Context and Consequences of Rapid Growth," 26.

27. Ramos, *The Other Face of America*, 154.

28. Lumpkin, *The Making of a Southerner*, 61.

29. Hudson, "The Hernando de Soto Expedition," 76–77.

30. Tindall, *Natives and newcomers: ethnic Southerners and Southern ethnics*, 11.

31. Pearson, "A Countryside Full of Flames," 579.

CHAPTER 4

1. Spener, David. "Smuggling Migrants through South Texas: Challenges Posed by Operation Rio Grande," 130.

2. Adams, John A., Jr., *Bordering the Future. The Impact of Mexico on the United States*, 45.

3. Pearson, "A Countryside Full of Flames," 579.

4. Griffler, *Front Line of Freedom*, 2.

5. Ibid., 1.

6. Ibid., 2.

7. Hagedorn, *Beyond the River. The Untold Story of the Heroes of the Underground Railroad*, 43.

8. Sadly, state and national politics during the nineteenth century would frequently play with a slave's right to freedom. In 1839, "The Ohio Fugitive Slave Law" declared a maximum penalty of 60 days jail time and a $500 fine for anyone attempting to interfere in the arrest or detention of a runaway slave by a representative of the law (Hagedorn 182). In an attempt to strike a compromise over California's entry into the Union as a free state, the national Fugitive Slave Law proposed by Henry Clay in 1850 was novel in its detail, as "it struck down the right of habeas corpus, it demanded that every person in sight be responsible for the successful return of the slave to his or her alleged owner, it raised all fines and terms of imprisonment for violation of such procedures, it allowed any citizen to be appointed by a circuit court as commissioner, and it provided financial incentives for the commissioner to retrieve the slaveholder's property" (Hagedorn 241).

9. Hudson, J. Blaine. *Encyclopedia of the Underground Railroad*, 6.

10. Ibid., 8.

11. Ibid., 7.

12. Hagedorn, *Beyond the River. The Untold Story of the Heroes of the Underground Railroad*, 68; Hudson, J. Blaine. *Encyclopedia of the Underground Railroad*, 3.

13. Hudson, J. Blaine. *Encyclopedia of the Underground Railroad*, 4.

14. Ibid., 174.

15. Ironically, the Gist Settlement was an incentive of the American Colonization Society, whose "message was that white and black people could not, and should not, cohabit in the same nation" (Griffler 21).

16. Griffler, *Front Line of Freedom*, 26.

17. Adams, John A., Jr., *Bordering the Future. The Impact of Mexico on the United States*, 48.

18. Garcia, Alma M. *The Mexican Americans*, 169.

19. Andreas, Peter. "The Transformation of Migrant Smuggling across the U.S.-Mexican Border," 107.

20. Garcia, Alma M. *The Mexican Americans*, 176.

21. Barich, "La Frontera," 54–55.

22. McC. Heyman, "Border Control," 43.

23. Kochhar, Rakesh, Robert Suso, and Sonya Tagoya. "The New Latino South: The Context and Consequences of Rapid Growth," 13.

24. Adams, Jerome R. *Greasers and Gringos. The Historical Roots of Anglo-Hispanic Prejudice*, 139.

25. Ibid., 145.

26. Meier and Gutiérrez. *The Mexican American Experience. An Encyclopedia*, 313.

27. Ibid., 38.

28. Ibid., 345.

29. Adams, Jerome R. *Greasers and Gringos. The Historical Roots of Anglo-Hispanic Prejudice*, 162.

30. Garcia, Alma M. *The Mexican Americans*, 28.

31. Davis, Thomas J. *Race Relations in America*, 13.

32. Andreas, Peter. "The Transformation of Migrant Smuggling across the U.S.-Mexican Border," 109.

33. Ibid., 109.

34. Ibid., 109.

35. Ibid., 112.

36. Ibid., 114.

37. Adams, John A., Jr., *Bordering the Future. The Impact of Mexico on the United States*, 46.

38. Ibid., 45.

39. Urrea, *By the Lake of Sleeping Children. The Secret Life of the Mexican Border*, 14.

40. Ellacuría, "Liberación," 698, 699.

41. Ferro, "Sobre la trata y la esclavitud," 141.

42. Urrea, *By the Lake of Sleeping Children. The Secret Life of the Mexican Border*, 10–11.

43. Declaring that "slave owners and their agents" "had the legal right to ´ seize or arrest´ their slaves in free states, without a warrant and without the presence of a civil official" (Hagedorn 17), the Act passed both Houses of Congress with little debate.

44. Hagedorn, *Beyond the River. The Untold Story of the Heroes of the Underground Railroad*, 17.

45. Harris, "The Myth of the Friendly Master," 44.

46. Rose, *A Documentary History of Slavery in North America*, 256, 267, 283, 284, 257; Aptheker, Herbert. *American Negro Slave Revolts*, 140–44.

47. Parish, *Slavery. History and Historians*, 73.

48. Aptheker, *American Negro Slave Revolts*, 162.

49. Pearson, "A Countryside Full of Flames," 579.

50. Aptheker, *American Negro Slave Revolts*, 164.

51. Pearson, "A Countryside Full of Flames," 579.

52. Gossett, *Race. The History of an Idea in America*, 431.

53. Loucky, "Racism," 272.

54. Davis, Thomas J. *Race Relations in America*, 9.

55. Adams, Jerome R. *Greasers and Gringos. The Historical Roots of Anglo-Hispanic Prejudice*, 146.

56. Ibid., 156.

57. Ibid., 175.

58. Estrada, "U.S.-Mexico Border," 343.

59. Shorris, "Borderline Cases," 82.

60. Ibid., 79.

61. Odum and Johnson, *The Negro and His Songs*, 161.

62. O'Connor, "The Displaced Person," 206.

63. Available on the Web: http://oxroads.virginia.edu.

64. Gossett, *Race. The History of an Idea in America*, 305.

65. Meier and Gutiérrez. *The Mexican American Experience. An Encyclopedia*, 51.

66. Spener, David. "Smuggling Migrants through South Texas: Challenges Posed by Operation Rio Grande,", 134, 136, 136, 137.

67. McC. Heyman, "Border Control," 42.

68. Tsunokai, "Stereotypes," 318.

69. Ibid., 317.

70. Smith, John David, *Anti-Black Thought. 1863–1925. "The Negro Problem,"* 123.

71. Ibid., 38–39.

72. Ibid., 39, 40.

73. Ibid., 20–21.

74. Loucky, "Racism," 270.

75. Ibid., 270.

76. Beecher Stowe, *Uncle Tom's Cabin*, 57.

77. Still, *The Underground Rail Road*, 157.

78. Hudson, J. Blaine. *Encyclopedia of the Underground Railroad*, 4.

79. Urrea, *Across the Wire. Life and Hard Times on the Mexican Border*, 12.

80. McC. Heyman, "Border Control," 43.

81. Davis, Thomas J. *Race Relations in America*, 248.

82. Barich, "La Frontera," 64.

83. Adams, John A., Jr., *Bordering the Future. The Impact of Mexico on the United States*, 52.

84. Beecher Stowe, *Uncle Tom's Cabin*, 68.

85. Ibid., 467.

86. Adams, John A., Jr., *Bordering the Future. The Impact of Mexico on the United States*, 56.

87. Garcia, Alma M. *The Mexican Americans*, 171.

88. Barich, "La Frontera," 56–57.

89. Wilson and Armstrong, "Unauthorized immigration," 335.

90. Warner, "Enslavement," 94.

91. Shorris, "Borderline Cases."

92. Urrea, *Across the Wire. Life and Hard Times on the Mexican Border*, 12.

93. Parish, *Slavery. History and Historians*, 22.

94. Ibid., 109.

95. Wilson and Armstrong, "Unauthorized immigration," 335.

96. Davis, Thomas J. *Race Relations in America*, 6.

97. Ibid., 95.

98. Hagedorn, *Beyond the River. The Untold Story of the Heroes of the Underground Railroad*, 41.

99. Ibid., 41.

100. Griffler, *Front Line of Freedom*, 6.

101. Urrea, *Across the Wire. Life and Hard Times on the Mexican Border*, 19.

102. Barich, "La Frontera," 57.

103. Ibid., 53.

104. Adams, John A., Jr., *Bordering the Future. The Impact of Mexico on the United States*, 54.

105. Ibid., 46.

106. Estrada, "U.S.-Mexico Border," 341.

107. Warner, "Enslavement," 94.

108. Davis, Thomas J. *Race Relations in America*, 19.

109. Warner, "Enslavement," 93.

110. Ibid., 95.

CHAPTER 5

1. Adams, Jerome R. *Greasers and Gringos. The Historical Roots of Anglo-Hispanic Prejudice*, 191–92.

2. Urrea, *By the Lake of Sleeping Children. The Secret Life of the Mexican Border*, 18.

3. Odum, *Southern Regions of the United States*, 29.

4. MDC, Inc. *The State of the South 2007*, 19.

5. Middleton, *Colonial America. A History, 1565–1776*, 203.

6. Coclanis, "Globalization before Globalization: The South and the World to 1950," 23.

7. Newby, *The South. A History*, 128.

8. "The first successful downward revision of the tariff since the Civil War, the Underwood-Simmons Tariff Act enacted an across-the-board reduction in tariffs, making manufacturers more efficient and providing consumers with competitive pricing. To compensate for lost revenue, a rider to the act created a small, graduated income tax" (Public Broadcasting System)

9. Newby, *The South. A History*, 29.

10. Cobb, *Redefining Southern Culture*, 32.

11. MDC, Inc. *The State of the South 2007*, 9.

12. Cobb, "Beyond the'Y'all Wall': The American South Goes Global."

13. MDC, Inc. *The State of the South 2002*, 4.

14. Eckes, "The South and Economic Globalization, 1950 to the Future," 46; Applebome, *Dixie Rising: How the South is shaping America*, 9.

15. Kochhar, Suso, and Tagoya. "The New Latino South: The Context and Consequences of Rapid Growth," iii. http://pewhispanic.org/files/reports/50.pdf.

16. MDC, Inc. *The State of the South 1998*, 24.

17. MDC, Inc. *The State of the South 2002*, 6.

18. MDC, Inc. *The State of the South 2007*, 15; MDC, Inc. *The State of the South 2002*, 10;MDC, Inc. *The State of the South 2007*, 7.

19. MDC, Inc. *The State of the South 2007*, 16.

20. MDC, Inc. *The State of the South 2002*, 22.

21. Eckes, "The South and Economic Globalization, 1950 to the Future," 62.

22. Hill, "Contemporary Issues in Anthropological Studies of the American South," 20.

23. Cobb, "Beyond the 'Yall Wall: The American South Goes Global," 2.

24. MDC, Inc. *The State of the South 2002*, 11.

25. MDC, Inc. *The State of the South 2007*, 7.

26. Cobb, "Beyond the 'Yall Wall: The American South Goes Global," 3.

27. MDC, Inc. *The State of the South 2002*, 16.

28. Ibid., 16.

29. Ibid., 27.

30. MDC, Inc. *The State of the South 2007*, 10.

31. Cuadros, "Hispanics Targeted for Hate in the New South," 3.

32. Ibid., 2.

33. MDC, Inc. *The State of the South 2007*, 7.

34. Kochhar, Suso, and Tagoya. "The New Latino South: The Context and Consequences of Rapid Growth," iv.

35. MDC, Inc. *The State of the South 2002*, 8.

36. Kochhar, Suso, and Tagoya. "The New Latino South: The Context and Consequences of Rapid Growth," iv.

37. MDC, Inc. *The State of the South 2007*, 29.

38. Ibid., 36.

39. Ibid., 7.

40. Ibid., 13.

41. MDC, Inc. *The State of the South 2002*, 18.

42. MDC, Inc. *The State of the South 2007*, 27.

43. Muñiz, "In the Eye of the Storm: How the Government and Private Response to Hurricane Katrina Failed Latinos," 2.

44. Cevallos, "Latin American Immigrants Harmed by Katrina."

45. Belsie and Axtman, "Post-Katrina, New Orleans coming back more Hispanic."

46. Salinas, "Latinos paid dearly after Katrina."

47. Muñiz, "In the Eye of the Storm: How the Government and Private Response to Hurricane Katrina Failed Latinos," 4.

48. Ibid., 2.

49. Ibid., 9.

50. Belsie and Axtman, "Post-Katrina, New Orleans coming back more Hispanic."

51. "Hispanics Getting GC Jobs that Americans Want." http://www.katcons.com/2006/03/.

52. Radelat, "An Avalanche of Aid. Hispanic workers flood the Gulf Coast."
53. Salinas, "Latinos paid dearly after Katrina"; Muñiz, "In the Eye of the Storm: How the Government and Private Response to Hurricane Katrina Failed Latinos," 13.
54. Muñiz, "In the Eye of the Storm: How the Government and Private Response to Hurricane Katrina Failed Latinos," 19–20.
55. Ibid., 16–17.
56. Donato, Bankston, and Robison, "Immigration and the Organization of the Onshore Oil Industry: Southern Louisiana in the late 1990s," 112.
57. Studstill, Nieto-Studstill. "Hospitality and Hostility: Latin Immigrants in Southern Georgia," 80.
58. Kochhar, Suso, and Tagoya. "The New Latino South: The Context and Consequences of Rapid Growth," 26.
59. Engstrom, "Industry and Immigration to Dalton, GA," 46.
60. Ibid., 48.
61. Wexler, "A Possible Dream."
62. Engstrom, "Industry and Immigration to Dalton, GA," 44, 49.
63. Ibid., 48.
64. Ibid., 52–53.
65. Ibid., 54.
66. In discussion with author, May 2000.
67. In discussion with author, May 2000.
68. In discussion with author, June 2000.
69. In discussion with author, June 2000.
70. In discussion with author, June 2000.
71. In discussion with author, June 2000.
72. In discussion with author, June 2000.
73. In discussion with author, June 2000.

CHAPTER 6

1. Wei, Shang-Jin. "Local Corruption and global Capital Flows," 304.
2. Mejía, "A Murky Transparency Law."
3. Applebome, *Dixie Rising: How the South is shaping America*, 95.
4. Bartley, and Graham, *Southern Politics and the Second Reconstruction*, 127.
5. Cochran, *Democrcacy Heading South. National Politics in the Shadow of Dixie*, 104.
6. Ibid., 92–93.
7. Ibid., 94, 94.
8. Ibid., 168.
9. Swing, *Forerunners of American Fascism*, 106.
10. Key, *Southern Politics in State and Nation*, 5.
11. Ibid., 4.
12. Ibid., 11.
13. Ibid., 16.

14. Ibid., 16.

15. Graylee, "Tom Watson Disciple of 'Jeffersonian Democracý," 93, 86; Swing, *Forerunners of American Fascism*, 75, 76; Bartley, and Graham, *Southern Politics and the Second Reconstruction*, 118; Shelby, "Jeff Davis of Arkansas," 26, 18.

16. Rouquié, "Dictadores, militares y legitimidad en America Latina," 12, 13.

17. Ibid., 12.

18. Crabtree, "The Collapse of *Fujimorismo*: Authoritarianism and Its Limits," 291.

19. Cash, W.J. *The Mind of the South*, 45.

20. Newby, *The South. A History*, 394.

21. Cash, W.J. *The Mind of the South*, 53.

22. Fishman, "The Rise of Hitler as Beer Hall Orator," 250–52.

23. Newby, *The South. A History*, 395.

24. Cash, W.J. *The Mind of the South*, 257.

25. Strickland, "James Kimble Vardaman. Manipulation Through Myths in Mississippi," 79.

26. Newby, *The South. A History*, 392; Hendrix, "Theodore G. Bilbo. Evangelist of Racial Purity," 161.

27. Newby, *The South. A History*, 454.

28. Logue, "The Coercive Campaign Prophecy of Gene Talmadge, 1926–46," 214.

29. Bartley, and Graham, *Southern Politics and the Second Reconstruction*, 117.

30. Shelby, "Jeff Davis of Arkansas," 30, 33, 43.

31. Ansaldi, "La forja de un dictador: El caso de Juan Manuel de Rosas," 87.

32. Ibid., 89.

33. Salvatore, "Repertoires of Coercion and Market Culture in Nineteenth-Century Buenos Aires Province," 410.

34. Derby, "The Dictator's Seduction: Gender and State Spectacle During the Trujillo Regime," 1112.

35. Ibid., 1124.

36. Derby, "In the Shadow of the State: The Politics of Denunciation and Panegyric during the Trujillo Regime in the Dominican Republic, 1940–1958," 299.

37. Ibid., 299.

38. Ibid., 301.

39. Bartley, and Graham, *Southern Politics and the Second Reconstruction*, 5, 10.

40. Posada-Carbó, "Electoral Juggling: A Comparative History of the Corruption of Suffrage in Latin America, 1830–1930," 631.

41. Ibid., 611.

42. Key, *Southern Politics in State and Nation*, 156.

43. Swing, *Forerunners of American Fascism*, 68.

44. Ibid., 68.

45. Swing, *Forerunners of American Fascism*, 71.

46. Cash, W.J. *The Mind of the South*, 291.

47. Bartley, and Graham, *Southern Politics and the Second Reconstruction*, 74.

48. Ibid., 74.

49. Ibid., 118.

50. Swing, *Forerunners of American Fascism*, 114–15.

51. Ansaldi, "La forja de un dictador: El caso de Juan Manuel de Rosas," 74.

52. Skidmore, *Modern Latin America*, 224.

53. Ibid., 267.

54. Lambert, "A decade of electoral democracy: continuity, change and crisis in Paraguay," 381.

55. Yarrington, "Cattle, Corruption, Venezuelan State Formation During the Regime of Juan Vicente Gomez, 1908–35," 11.

56. Ibid., 13, 14, 16.

57. Ibid., 15.

58. Ibid., 17.

59. Ibid., 13.

60. Coquery-Vidovitch, "El postulado de la superioridad blanca y de la inferioridad negra," 804.

61. Ibid., 780.

62. Ibid., 803.

63. Cash, W.J. *The Mind of the South*, 137.

64. Kuzenski, "David Duke and the Nonpartisan Primary," 4.

65. Ibid., 5.

66. Boeckelman, Arp, and Tenadot. "Messenger or Message? David Duke in the Louisiana Legislature," 24, 25.

67. Elliott, and Thielemann. "The White Knight Faces to Black: David Duke in the 1992 Presidential Campaign," 149.

68. Ibid., 151, 154.

69. King, Rose, and Crozat. "The Downfall of David Duke? Duke, Republicans, and the Structure of Elections in Louisiana," 127.

70. Parent, "Race and Republican Resurgence in the South: Success in Black and White?" 126.

71. Bartley, and Graham, *Southern Politics and the Second Reconstruction*, 119.

72. Ibid., 113.

73. Ibid., 113.

74. Ibid., 58.

75. Cited in Michie and Rhylick, *Dixie Demagogues*, 105.

76. Cited in Hendrix "Theodore G. Bilbo. Evangelist of Racial Purity," 164.

77. Salvatore, "Repertoires of Coercion and Market Culture in Nineteenth-Century Buenos Aires Province," 422.

78. Crabtree, "The Collapse of *Fujimorismo*: Authoritarianism and Its Limits," 295.

79. Gould, "'For an Organized Nicaragua': Somoza and the Labor Movement," 357.

80. Yarrington, "Cattle, Corruption, Venezuelan State Formation During the Regime of Juan Vicente Gomez, 1908–35," 11.

81. Crabtree, "The Collapse of *Fujimorismo*: Authoritarianism and Its Limits," 288.

82. Rouquié, "Dictadores, militares y legitimidad en America Latina," 20.

83. Logue, "The Coercive Campaign Prophecy of Gene Talmadge, 1926–46," 228.

84. Newby, *The South. A History,* 395.

85. Swing, *Forerunners of American Fascism,* 88–89.

86. Ibid., 107, 74, 109.

87. Michie and Rhylick, *Dixie Demagogues,* 89.

88. Ibid., 89–90.

89. Ansaldi, "La forja de un dictador: El caso de Juan Manuel de Rosas," 81.

90. Valdivia Ortiz de Zarate, "Terrorism and Political Violence during the Pinochet Years: Chile, 1973–1989," 187–88.

91. Derby, "The Dictator's Seduction: Gender and State Spectacle During the Trujillo Regime," 1113.

92. Skidmore, *Modern Latin America,* 214; Derby, "In the Shadow of the State: The Politics of Denunciation and Panegyric during the Trujillo Regime in the Dominican Republic, 1940–1958," 297, 293.

93. Maysilles, "Hoke Smith." http://www.georgiaencyclopedia.org/nge/Article.jsp?id=h-2121.

94. Griggs, "Frank G. Clement." http://tennesseeencylopedia.net/imagegallery.php?EntryID=C107.

95. Black, "Southern Governors and Political Change: Campaign Stances on Racial Segregation and Economic Development," 711.

CHAPTER 7

1. Barre, *Ideologías indigenistas y movimientos indios,* 221.

2. Parish, *Slavery. History and Historians,* 90.

3. Guibert, *Seven Voices. Seven Latin American Writers Talk to Rita Guibert,* 327.

4. Cohn, *History and Memory in the Two Souths,* 4.

5. Cash, *The Mind of the South,* 128.

6. Gerster and Cords, "The Northern Origins of Southern Mythology," 569.

7. Ibid., 573.

8. Ibid., 577.

9. Cohn, *History and Memory in the Two Souths,* 6.

10. Martí, *Marti on the USA,* 95, 96.

11. Newby, *The South. A History,* 459.

12. Manning, "Southern Women Writers and the Beginning of the Renaissance," 245, 249.

13. Goodwyn Jones, "Women Writers and the Myths of Southern Womanhood," 275–89.

14. Cohn, *History and Memory in the Two Souths,* 26–27.

15. Newby, *The South. A History,* 238.

16. Cohn, *History and Memory in the Two Souths,* 190.

17. Tredoux, "Review of *Rigoberta Menchú and the Story of All Poor Guatemalans,* by David Stoll."

18. Wilson, Robin, "Anthropologist Challenges Veracity of Multicultural Icon."

19. Cash, *The Mind of the South*, 146.

20. Cohn, *History and Memory in the Two Souths*, 41.

21. Fitz, "In Quest of 'Nuestras Américas' or Inter-American Studies and the Dislocation of the Traditional 'American' Paradigm or (with apologies to José Martí and Stanley Kubrick) How I Learned to Stop Worrying and Love Academic Change."

22. Fitz, "Inter-American Studies as an Emerging Field: The Future of a Discipline," 13.

23. Fitz, "In Quest of 'Nuestras Américas' or Inter-American Studies and the Dislocation of the Traditional 'American' Paradigm or (with apologies to José Martí and Stanley Kubrick) How I Learned to Stop Worrying and Love Academic Change."

24. Fitz, "Inter-American Studies as an Emerging Field: The Future of a Discipline," 20.

25. Ibid., 14.

26. Fitz, "In Quest of 'Nuestras Américas' or Inter-American Studies and the Dislocation of the Traditional 'American' Paradigm or (with apologies to José Martí and Stanley Kubrick) How I Learned to Stop Worrying and Love Academic Change."

27. Cohn, *History and Memory in the Two Souths*, 18.

28. Ibid., 21–22.

29. Moore, "Magical Realism."

30. Cash, *The Mind of the South*, 60.

31. Wolfe, *Look Homeward, Angel*, 515.

32. Cash, *The Mind of the South*, 48.

33. O'Connor, "The Displaced Person," 196.

34. Ibid., 205.

35. Ibid., 207.

36. Ibid., 209.

37. Ibid., 233.

38. Ibid., 214.

39. Ibid., 219.

40. Ibid., 220.

41. Ibid., 222.

42. Ibid., 223.

43. Ibid., 234.

44. Cohn, *History and Memory in the Two Souths*, 193.

45. Fuentes, *The Crystal Frontier*, 25.

46. Ibid., 109.

47. Ibid., 250.

48. Ibid., 252.

49. Ibid., 252.

50. Ibid., 34.

51. Ibid., 44.
52. Ibid., 48.
53. Ibid., 98.
54. Ibid., 128.
55. O'Connor, "The Displaced Person," 219.
56. Fuentes, *The Crystal Frontier,* 220.
57. Ibid, 257.
58. Ibid., 245.
59. Ibid., 245.
60. Ibid., 250.
61. Ibid., 147.
62. Ibid., 15.
63. Ibid., 155.
64. Ibid., 165.

CHAPTER 8

1. Sublette, *Cuba and Its Music,* 325, 165, 397, 167.
2. Odum and Johnson, *The Negro and His Songs,* 11–12.
3. Ibid., 28, 38–45.
4. Douglass, *Narrative of the Life of Frederick Douglass. An American Slave,* 31.
5. Odum and Johnson, *The Negro and His Songs,* 31, 34.
6. Cobb, *Redefining Southern Culture,* 98.
7. Cash, W.J. *The Mind of the South,* 85.
8. Gibson, *Federico García Lorca. A Life,* 255.
9. Ibid., 256.
10. Walker, *In Search of our Mother's Gardens: Womanist Prose,* 144–45.
11. Cash, W.J. *The Mind of the South,* 70.
12. Gerster and Cords, "The Northern Origins of Southern Mythology," 575.
13. Cash, W.J. *The Mind of the South,* 23.
14. Naipaul. *A Turn in the South,* 4, 80, 172.
15. Dalrymple, "Dixie's Dead, Long Live the South," 4.
16. Cash, W.J. *The Mind of the South,* 31.
17. Newby, *The South. A History,* 334.
18. Petras, "The Centrality of Peasant Movements in Latin America: Achievements and Objections."
19. Ibid.
20. Klein, Naomi. "The Threat of Hope in Latin America."
21. Barre, *Ideologías indigenistas y movimientos indios,* 165.
22. Petras, "The Centrality of Peasant Movements in Latin America: Achievements and Objections."
23. Cleaner, "Introduction."
24. Ibid.
25. Ibid.
26. Cobb, *Redefining Southern Culture,* 31.

27. MDC, Inc., *The State of the South 2007*, 16.
28. Cash, W.J. *The Mind of the South*, 405, 408, 415.
29. Martí, *Marti on the USA*, 100.
30. Cobb, *Redefining Southern Culture*, 27.

CHAPTER 9

1. Ortuño Martínez, "España-Estados Unidos. Fronteras imposibles," 44.
2. Odum, *Southern Regions of the United States*, 141.
3. United States Conference of Catholic Bishops, "Demographics."
4. Morales, "Latino Religion, Ritual and Culture," 194.
5. Newby, *The South. A History*, 411.
6. Ibid., 98.
7. Ibid., 324.
8. Ibid., 324.
9. Martí, *Marti on the USA*, 101.
10. Parish, *Slavery. History and Historians*, 82.
11. Berryman, *Liberation Theology*, 50.
12. Ratzinger, with Messori. *The Ratzinger Report. An Exclusive Interview on the State of the Church*, 71.
13. Ibid., 175.
14. Douglass, *Narrative of the Life of Frederick Douglass. An American Slave*, 120.
15. Parish, *Slavery. History and Historians*, 162.
16. Newby, *The South. A History*, 414.
17. Bullock and Rozell, "Southern Politics at Century's End," 14.
18. Applebome, *Dixie Rising: How the South is shaping America*, 8.

CHAPTER 10

1. Ramos, *The Other Face of America*, 202.
2. Torres, Sonia. *Nosotros in USA*, 23.
3. Ibid., 87.
4. Ramos, *The Other Face of America*, xvi, 205, 209, 211, 207, 203.
5. Ibid., 203.
6. Ibid., 203.
7. Ibid., 209.
8. Muñiz, "In the Eye of the Storm: How the Government and Private Response to Hurricane Katrina Failed Latinos." 14.
9. Mohl, "Globalization, Latinization and the *Nuevo* New South," 80.
10. Smith and Cohn, "Introduction: Uncanny Hybridities," 2.
11. Vaca, *The Presumed Alliance. The Unspoken Conflict Between Latinos and Blacks and What It Means for America*, 128.
12. Ibid., 128–29.
13. Ibid., 4–5.
14. Ibid., 4–5.

15. Kochhar, Suso, and Tagoya, "The New Latino South: The Context and Consequences of Rapid Growth," 27.

16. Vaca, *The Presumed Alliance. The Unspoken Conflict Between Latinos and Blacks and What It Means for America*, 6–8.

17. Ramos, *The Other Face of America*, xxxiii–xxxiv.

18. Vaca, *The Presumed Alliance. The Unspoken Conflict Between Latinos and Blacks and What It Means for America*, 108 ff.

19. Ibid., 110.

20. Ibid., 115–28.

21. Ibid., 111.

22. Ibid., 115.

23. Loucky, "Racism," 319.

24. MDC, Inc. *The State of the South 2002*, 12.

25. Ibid., 12.

26. Vaca, *The Presumed Alliance. The Unspoken Conflict Between Latinos and Blacks and What It Means for America*, 24.

27. MDC, Inc. *The State of the South 2004*, 43.

28. In discussion with author, May 2000.

29. In discussion with author, June 2000.

30. In discussion with author, June 2000.

31. MDC, Inc., *The State of the South 2007*, 43.

32. Mohl, "Globalization, Latinization and the *Nuevo* New South," 81.

33. Vaca, *The Presumed Alliance. The Unspoken Conflict Between Latinos and Blacks and What It Means for America*, 186.

34. Ibid., 188.

CHAPTER II

1. Simâo, "Hispanics Flex New Muscle in Southern U.S.," 2.

2. MDC, Inc., *The State of the South 2007*, 25.

3. Kochhar, Suso, and Tagoya, "The New Latino South: The Context and Consequences of Rapid Growth," iv.

4. Ibid., 38.

5. Chambers, Figueroa, Wingert, and Weingarten, "Latino America," 51.

6. Diamond, *Collapse. How Societies Choose to Fail or Succeed*, 306.

7. Applebome, *Dixie Rising: How the South is shaping America*, 344.

8. Cash, *The Mind of the South*, 439–40.

9. Stephens, "Monolingualism and Racialism as Curable Diseases: *Nuestra América* in the Transnational South," 214.

Bibliography

Note: In the text, translations into English from works whose titles are in languages other than English are my own.

Adams, Jerome R. *Greasers and Gringos. The Historical Roots of Anglo-Hispanic Prejudice.*Jefferson, NC: McFarland and Company, 2006.

Adams, John A., Jr. *Bordering the Future. The Impact of Mexico on the United States.* Westport, CT: Praeger, 2006.

Álvarez, Julia. *Something to Declare.* Chapel Hill, NC: Algonquin Books, 1998.

Álvarez, Michael and Jonathan Nagler. "Antonio Villaraigosa's Victory in Los Angeles: Any Democratic Lessons for Winning Latino Votes?" Accessed April 5. http://www.emergingdemocraticmajorityweblog.com/donkey rising/archives/001247.php.

Andreas, Peter. "The Transformation of Migrant Smuggling across the U.S.-Mexican Border." In *Global Human Smuggling. Comparative Perspectives,* edited by David Kyle and Rey Koslowski. Baltimore: Johns Hopkins University Press, 2001, 107–25.

Ansaldi, Waldo. "La forja de un dictador: El caso de Juan Manuel de Rosas." In *Dictaduras y dictadores,* edited by Julio Labastida Martin del Campo. Mexico: Siglo XXI, 1986, 27–90.

Applebome, Peter. *Dixie Rising: How the South is shaping America.* New York: Times Books, 1996.

Aptheker, Herbert. *American Negro Slave Revolts.* New York: International Publishers, 1993.

Barich, Bill. "La Frontera." In *Immigration to the U.S.,* edited by Robert Emmet Long. New York: H.W Wilson Company, 1992, 50–71.

Barley, John. "Corruption and Democratic Governability in Latin America: Issues of Types, Arenas, Perceptions, and Linkages." Accessed March 27, 2007. http://pdba.georgetown.edu/security/referencematerials_Bailey.pdf.

Barre, Marie-Chantal. *Ideologías indigenistas y movimientos indios*. Mexico City: Siglo XXI, 1983.

Barthes, Roland. *Mythologies*. Translated by Annette Lavers. New York: The Noonday Press, 1972.

Bartley, Numan V., and Hugh D. Graham. *Southern Politics and the Second Reconstruction*. Baltimore: Johns Hopkins Press, 1975.

Beecher Stowe, Harriet. *Uncle Tom's Cabin*. Edited with an Introduction and Notes by Henry Louis Gates, Jr. and Hollis Robbins. New York: W. W. Norton, 2007.

Beers, Henry Putney. *French and Spanish Records of Louisiana*. Baton Rouge: Louisiana State University Press, 1989.

Belsie, Lament and Kris Axtman. "Post-Katrina, New Orleans coming back more Hispanic." Accessed April 5, 2007. http://www.csmonitor.com/2006/0612/p01s03-ussc.html.

Berlin, Ira. "Time, Space, and the Evolution of Afro-American Society on British Mainland North America." In *The Slavery Reader*, edited by Gad Heuman and James Walvin. New York: Routledge, 2003, 122–53.

Bernand, Carmen. "Imperialismos ibéricos." In *El libro negro del colonialismo*, edited by Mark Ferro. Madrid: La Esfera de los libros, 2005, 165–213.

Berryman, Phillip. *Liberation Theology*. London: I.B. Tauris and Co., 1987.

Biggar, Jeanne C. "Population Change and Social Adaptation in the South, Past and Future." In *The South moves into its future: studies in the analysis and prediction of social change*, edited by Joseph S. Hines. Tuscaloosa: University of Alabama Press, 1991, 13–31.

Black, Earl. "Southern Governors and Political Change: Campaign Stances on Racial Segregation and Economic Development." *The Journal of Politics* 33 (1971): 703–34.

Boeckelman, Keith, William Arp III, and Bernard Tenadot. "Messenger or Message? David Duke in the Louisiana Legislature." In *David Duke and the politics of Race in the South*, edited by Charles S. Bullock III, Keith Gaddie, and John C. Kucenski. Nashville: Vanderbilt University Press, 1995, 23–34.

Bouvier, Leon F., and Lindsey Grant. *How Many Americans?: Population, Immigration, and the Environment*. San Francisco: Sierra Club, 1994.

Boyd, Julian P., ed. *The Papers of Thomas Jefferson, v. 8*. Princeton, NJ: Princeton University Press, 1953.

Bullock, Charles S. III and Mark J. Rozell. "Southern Politics at Century's End." In *The New Politics of the Old South. An Introduction to Southern Politics*, edited by Charles S. Bullock III and Mark J. Rozell.Lanham, MD: Rowman and Littlefield, 1998, 3–21.

Carleton, William G. "The Southern Politician—1900 and 1950." *Journal of Politics* 13 (1951): 215–31.

Carter, Dan T. "From the Old South to the New: Another Look at the Theme of Change and Continuity." In *From the Old South to the New: Essays on the Transitional South*, edited by Walter J. Fraser, Jr. and Winfred B. Moore, Jr.. Westport, CT: Greenwood Press, 1981, 23–32.

Cash, W.J. *The Mind of the South*. New York: Vintage Books, 1964.

Cevallos, Diego. "Latin American Immigrants Harmed by Katrina." Accessed on April 5, 2007. http://www.louisianaweekly.com/weekly/news/articlegate.pl?20050912j.

Chambers, Veronica, Ana Figueroa, Pat Wingert, and Julie Weingarten. "Latino America." *Newsweek* July 12, 1999: 48–51.

Channing, Steven A. "Slavery and Confederate Nationalism." In *From the Old South to the New: Essays on the Transitional South*, edited by Walter J. Fraser, Jr. and Winfred B. Moore, Jr. Westport, CT: Greenwood Press, 1981, 219–26.

Chavez, Linda. "Hispanic Children and Their Families." In *The Latino Condition*, edited by Richard Delgado and Jean Stefancic. New York, NY: NYU P, 1998, 106–9.

Chehabi, H.E. and Juan L. Linz, eds. *Sultanistic Regimes*. Baltimore: University of Johns Hopkins Press, 1998.

Chen, Michelle. "Legal Fight over Harsh Illegal Immigration Law Moves Forward." Accessed April 4, 2007. http://newstandardnews.net/content/index.cfm/items/3628.

Clayton, Lawrence A., Vernon James Knight, Jr., and Edward C. Moore. *The DeSoto Chronicles*. Tuscaloosa, AL: University of Alabama Press, 1993.

Cleaner, Harry. "Introduction." Accessed March 29, 2007. http://lanic.utexas.edu/project/zapatistas/introduction.html.

Cobb, James C. "Beyond the 'Y'all Wall': The American South Goes Global." In *Globalization and the American South*, edited by James C. Cobb and William Stueck. Athens, GA: University of Georgia Press, 2005, 1–18.

———. *Redefining Southern Culture*. Athens, GA: University of Georgia Press, 1999.

Cochran, Augustus B. *Democrcacy Heading South. National Politics in the Shadow of Dixie*. Lawrence, KS: University Press of Kansas, 2001.

Coclanis, Peter. "Globalization before Globalization: The South and the World to 1950." In *Globalization and the American South*, edited by James C. Cobb and William Stueck. Athens, GA: University of Georgia Press, 2005, 19–35.

Cohn, Deborah N. *History and Memory in the Two Souths*. Nashville: Vanderbilt University Press, 1999.

Coker, William S. *The Financial History of Pensacolás Spanish Presidios 1698–1763*. Pensacola, FL: The Pensacola Historical Society, 1979.

Coquery-Vidovitch, Catherine. "El postulado de la superioridad blanca y de la inferioridad negra." In *El libro negro del colonialismo*, edited by Marc Ferro. Madrid: LaEsfera de Los Libros, 2005, 771–820.

Cortes, Natalie. "Latinos woefully underrepresented in US media, panelists say." October 8, 2001. Accessed October 23, 2003. http://www.freedomforum.org/templates/document.asp?documentID=15096.

Crabtree, John. "The Collapse of *Fujimorismo*: Authoritarianism and Its Limits." *Bulletin of Latin American Research* 20 (2001): 287–303.

Crocker, Christopher. "The Southern Way of Death." In *The Not So Solid South*, edited by J. Kenneth Morland. Athens, GA: University of Georgia Press, 1971, 114–29.

Cuadros, Paul. "Hispanics Targeted for Hate in the New South." Accessed September 10, 1999. http://www.latinolink.com/commentary/opinion/0305his3e.php3

Dahbour, Omar, and Micheline R. Ishay. *The Nationalism Reader*. Atlantic Highlands, NJ: Humanities Press, 1995.

Dale, Jack G., Susan Andreatta, and Elizabeth Freeman. "Language and the Immigrant Worker Experience in Rural North Carolina Communities." In *Latino Workers in the Contemporary South*, edited by Arthur D. Murphy, Colleen Blanchard and Jennifer A. Hill. Athens, GA: University of Georgia Press, 2002, 93–104.

Dalrymple, Mary. "Dixie's Dead, Long Live the South." Accessed August 3, 2003. http://research.unc.edu/endeavors/spr97.

Daly Heyck, Denis Lynn, eds. *Barrios and borderlands: cultures of Latinos and Latinas in the United States*. New York: Routledge Press, 1994.

Daniel, Pete. *Standing at the Crossroads: Southern Life in the Twentieth Century*. Baltimore, MD: Johns Hopkins University Press, 1986.

Daniels, Jonathan. *A Southerner Discovers the South*. New York: Da Capo Press, 1970.

Davis, David Brion. (1969a). "The Comparative Approach to American History: Slavery." In *Slavery in the New World*, edited by Laura Fraser and Eugene D. Genovese. Englewood Cliffs, NJ: Prentice Hall, 1969, 60–68.

———. "A Comparison of British America and Latin America." (1969b). In *Slavery in the New World*, edited by Laura Fraser and Eugene D. Genovese. Englewood Cliffs, NJ: Prentice Hall, 1969, 69–83.

Davis, Thomas J. *Race Relations in America*. Westport, CT: Greenwood Press, 2006.

Delgado, Richard and Jean Stefancic, eds. *The Latino/a Condition: A Critical Reader*. New York: New York University Press, 1998.

Delgado-Gaitan, Concha and Henry Trueba. *Crossing Cultural Borders: Education for Immigrant Families in America*. London, New York: Falmer Press, 1991.

Derby, Lauren. "The Dictator's Seduction: Gender and State Spectacle During the Trujillo Regime." *Callaloo* 23 (2000): 1112–46.

———. "In the Shadow of the State: The Politics of Denunciation and Panegyric during the Trujillo Regime in the Dominican Republic, 1940–1958." *Hispanic American Historical Review* 83 (2003): 295–344.

Diamond, Jared. *Collapse. How Societies Choose to Fail or Succeed*. New York: Penguin, 2005.

Díaz, Junot. "Interview." *New York Magazine* September 9, 1999: 28–32.

Donato, Katherine M., Carl L. Bankston, and Dawn T. Robison. "Immigration and the Organization of the Onshore Oil Industry: Southern Louisiana in the late 1990s." In *Latino Workers in the Contemporary South*, edited by Arthur D. Murphy, Colleen Blanchard and Jennifer A. Hill. Athens, GA: University of Georgia Press, 2002, 105–13.

Douglass, Frederick. "An Appeal to Congress for Impartial Suffrage." *Atlantic Monthly* 19 (1867): 112–17.

———. *Narrative of the Life of Frederick Douglass. An American Slave*. New York: Signet, 1968.

———. "Reconstruction." *Atlantic Monthly* 18 (1866): 761–65.

Duchon, Deborah A. and Arthur D. Murphy. "Introduction: From *Patrones* and *Caciques* to Good Ole Boys." In *Latino Workers in the Contemporary South*, edited by Arthur D. Murphy, Colleen Blanchard and Jennifer A. Hill. Athens, GA: University of Georgia Press, 2002, 1–9.

Dunn, John M. *The Relocation of the Native American Indian*. San Diego, CA: Lucent Books, 1995.

Eckes, Alfred. "The South and Economic Globalization, 1950 to the Future." In *Globalization and the American South*, edited by James C. Cobb and William Stueck. Athens, GA: University of Georgia Press, 2005, 36–65.

Elkins, Stanley. "Slavery in Capitalist and Non-capitalist cultures." In *Slavery in the New World*, edited by Laura Fraser and Eugene D. Genovese. Englewood Cliffs, NJ: Prentice Hall, 1969, 8–26.

Ellacuría, Ignacio. "Liberación." In *Conceptos fundamentales del cristianismo*, edited by Casiano Floristán and Juan José Tamayo. Madrid: Trotta, 1993, 690–710.

Elliott, Euel and Gregory S. Thielemann. "The White Knight Faces to Black: David Duke in the 1992 Presidential Campaign." In *David Duke and the politics of Race in the South*, edited by Charles S. Bullock III, Keith Gaddie, and John C. Kucenski. Nashville, TN: Vanderbilt University Press, 1995, 146–58.

Engstrom, James D. "Industry and Immigration to Dalton, GA." In *Latino Workers in the Contemporary South*, edited by Arthur D. Murphy, Colleen Blanchard and Jennifer A. Hill. Athens, GA: University of Georgia Press, 2002, 44–56.

Estrada. Larry J. "U.S.-Mexico Border." In *Immigration in America Today. An Encyclopedia*, edited by James Loucky, Jeanne Armstrong, and Larry J. Estrada. Westport, CT: Greenwood Press, 2006, 340–44.

Fernandez-Shaw, Carlos M. *The Hispanic Presence in North America*. New York: Facts on File, 1999.

Ferro, Mark. "Sobre la trata y la esclavitud." In *El libro negro del colonialismo*, edited by Mark Ferro. Madrid: La Esfera de los libros, 2005, 125–44.

Fishman, Sterling. "The Rise of Hitler as Beer Hall Orator." *Review of Politics* 26 (1964): 250–52.

Fitz, Earl E. "In Quest of 'Nuestras Américas' or Inter-American Studies and the Dislocation of the Traditional 'American' Paradigm or (with apologies to José Martí and Stanley Kubrick) How I Learned to Stop Worrying and Love Academic Change." *Ameriquests* 1 (2004). Accessed September 24, 2007. http://ejournals.library.vanderbilt.edu/ameriquests/printarticle.php?id=14&layout=html.

———. "Inter-American Studies as an Emerging Field: The Future of a Discipline." Accessed March 27, 2007. http://sitemason.vanderbilt.edu/files/b/bqYe9W/Fitz.pdf.

Flores, Juan. "Interview." *New York Magazine* September 9, 1999: 28–32.

Fox, Geoffrey. *Hispanic Nation: culture, politics, and the constructing of identity*. Tucson, AZ: University of Arizona Press, 1997.

Fraga, Luis, Herman Gallegos, Gerald P. López, Mary Louise Pratt, Renato Rosaldo, José Saldivar, Ramon Saldivar, and Guadalupe Valdés. "Still Looking for America. Beyond the Latino National Political Survey." In *The Latino Condition*, edited by Richard Delgado and Jean Stefancic. New York: New York University Press, 1998, 240–45.

Fry, Joseph A. *Dixie Looks Abroad. The South and U.S. Foreign Relations, 1789–1973.* Baton Rouge: Louisiana State University Press, 2002.

Fuentes, Carlos. *The Crystal Frontier.* Translated by Alfred MacAdam. New York: Harcourt Brace and Company, 1997.

Garcia, Alma M. *The Mexican Americans.* Westport, CT: Greenwood Press, 2002.

Garcia, Ismael. *Dignidad: ethics through Hispanic eyes.* Nashville: Abingdon Press, 1997.

García Lorca, Federico. *Poet in New York.* Translated by Greg Simon and Steven F. White. New York: The Noonday Press, 1998.

Garza, Rodolfo O. de la and Louis DeSipio. *Awash in the mainstream: Latino politics in the 1996 elections.* Charlottesville, VA: University Press of Virginia, 1996.

Gerster, Patrick, and Nicholas Cords. "The Northern Origins of Southern Mythology." *The Journal of Southern History* 42 (1977): 567–82.

Gibson, Ian. *Federico García Lorca. A Life.* New York: Pantheon Books, 1989.

Gimenez, Marta E. "Latino Politics—Class Struggles: Reflections on the Future of Latino Politics." In *Latino Social Movements: Historical and Theoretical Perspectives*, edited by Rodolfo D. Torres and George Katsiaficas. New York: Routledge Press, 1999, 165–80.

Ginés, Montserrat. *The Southern Inheritance of Don Quixote.* Baton Rouge: Louisiana State University Press, 2000.

Gonzalez, Juan. "Interview." *New York Magazine* September 9, 1999: 28–32.

Goodwin, Paul B., Jr. *Global Studies. Latin America.* Dubuque, IA: McGraw-Hill/Contemporary Learning Series, 2007.

Goodwyn, Lawrence. "Hierarchy and Democracy: The Paradox of Southern Experience." In *From the Old South to the New: Essays on the Transitional South*, edited by Walter J. Fraser, Jr. and Winfred B. Moore, Jr.. Westport, CT: Greenwood Press, 1981, 227–39.

Goodwyn Jones, Anne. "Women Writers and the Myths of Southern Womanhood." In *The History of Southern Women's Literature*, edited by Carolyn Perry and Mary Louise Weaks. Baton Rouge: Louisiana State University Press, 2002, 275–89.

Gossett, Thomas F. *Race. The History of an Idea in America.* New York: Oxford University Press, 1997.

Gould, Jeffrey L. "'For an Organized Nicaragua': Somoza and the Labor Movement." *Journal of Latin American Studies* 19 (353–87).

Grady, Henry W. *The New South.* New York: Robert Bouner's Sons, 1890.

Grantham, Dewey. "Henry Grady." *American National Biography Online.* Accessed March 22, 2007. http://www.anl.org/articles/16/16-00647.html.

Gray, Richard. "Negotiating Differences: Southern Culture(s) Now." In *Dixie Debates. Perspectives on Southern Cultures,* edited by Richard H. King and Helen Taylor. New York: New York University Press, 1996, 218–27.

Graylee, G. Jack. "Tom Watson Disciple of 'Jeffersonian Democracý." In *The Oratory of Southern Demagogues,* edited by Cal M. Logue and Howard Dorgan. Baton Rouge: Louisiana State University Press, 1981, 84–108.

Griffin, Larry J. "Why Was the South a Problem to America?" In *The South as an American Problem,* edited by Larry J. Griffin and Don H. Doyle. Athens, GA: University of Georgia Press, 1995, 10–32.

Griffler, Keith P. *Front Line of Freedom.* Lexington, KY: University Press of Kentucky, 2004.

Griggs, Alan. "Frank G. Clement." Accessed March 5, 2007. http://tennesseeen cylopedia.net/imagegallery.php?EntryID=C107.

Guibert, Rita. *Seven Voices. Seven Latin American Writers Talk to Rita Guibert.* Translated by Frances Partridge. New York: Alfred A. Knopf Publishers, 1973.

Guthey, Greig. "Mexican Places in Southern Spaces: Globalization, Work, and Daily Life in and around the North Georgia Poultry Industry." In *Latino Workers in the Contemporary South,* edited by Arthur D. Murphy, Colleen Blanchard and Jennifer A. Hill. Athens, GA: University of Georgia Press, 2002, 57–67.

Gutiérrez, David G., ed. *Between Two Worlds: Mexican Immigrants in the United States.* Wilmington, DE: Scholarly Resources, 1996.

Hagedorn, Anne. *Beyond the River. The Untold Story of the Heroes of the Underground Railroad.* New York: Simon and Schuster, 2004.

Harris, Marvin. "The Myth of the Friendly Master." In *Slavery in the New World,* edited by Laura Fraser and Eugene D. Genovese. Englewood Cliffs, NJ: Prentice Hall, 1969, 38–47.

Haubegger, Christy. "The Legacy of Generation Ñ. Latino America." *Newsweek* July 12,1999: 61.

Hendrix, Jerry A. "Theodore G. Bilbo. Evangelist of Racial Purity." In *The Oratory of Southern Demagogues,* edited by Cal M. Logue and Howard Dorgan. Baton Rouge: Louisiana State University Press, 1981, 150–72.

Hernández, Ambar. "Top 25 Recruitment Programs" (2002). Accessed October 20, 2003. http://www.hispaniconline.com/magazine/2002/may/Career/

Hevesi, Dennis. "Duke Forgiven His Past by Out-of-State Donors." *New York Times* November 5, 1991. A21.

Heyck, Dennis Lynn Daly. "Introduction: Latinos, Past and Present." In *Barrios and Borderlands,* edited by Dennis Lynn Daly Heyck. New York: Routledge, 1994, 1–15.

Heyman, Josiah. "Border Control." In *Immigration in America Today. An Encyclopedia,* edited by James Loucky, Jeanne Armstrong, and Larry J. Estrada. Westport, CT: Greenwood Press, 2006, 39–45.

Hill, Carole E. "Contemporary Issues in Anthropological Studies of the American South." In *Cultural Diversity in the U.S. South: Anthropological Contributions to a Region in Transition,* edited by Carole E. Hill and Patricia D. Beaver. Athens, GA: University of Georgia Press, 1998, 12–31.

Hill, Carole E. and Patricia D. Beaver, eds. *Cultural Diversity in the U.S. South: Anthropological Contributions to a Region in Transition.* Athens, GA: U of Georgia P, 1998.

Himes, Joseph S. "Introduction: Background of Recent Changes in the South." In *The South Moves into Its Future: Studies in the Analysis and Prediction of Social Change,* edited by Joseph S. Himes. Tuscaloosa, AL: University of Alabama Press, 1991, 1–9.

Hispanic Online. "Top 25 Recruitment Programs" (2000). Retrieved October 20, 2003. http://www.hispaniconline.com/res&res/toplists/t25recr_2000.html

———. "Top 25 Recruitment Programs" (2001). Retrieved October 20, 2003. http://www.hispaniconline.com/res&res/toplists/top25recr_2001.html

———. "Top 25 Recruitment Programs" (2002). Retrieved October 20, 2003. http://www.hispaniconline.com/magazine/2002/may/Career/

Hochschild, Jennifer L. *Facing Up to the American Dream: Race, Class, and the Soul of the Nation.* Princeton, NJ: Princeton University Press, 1996.

Hoffman, Lisa. "Hispanics criticize hurricane disaster response." Accessed April 5, 2007. http://www.shns.com/shns/g-index2.cfm?.

Hoffman, Paul E. "Lucas Vásquez de Ayllóńs Discovery and Colony." In *The Forgotten Centuries. Indians and Europeans in the American South 1521–1704,* edited by Charles Hudson and Carmen Chaves Tesser. Athens, GA: University of Georgia Press, 1994, 36–49.

Hornor, Louise L, ed. *Hispanic Americans: a statistical sourcebook.* Palo Alto, CA: Information Publications, 1999.

Hudson, J. Blaine. *Encyclopedia of the Underground Railroad.* Jefferson, NC: McFarland and Company, 2006.

Hudson, Charles M. "The Hernando de Soto Expedition." In *Forgotten centuries: Indians and Europeans in the American South,* edited by Charles M. Hudson and Carmen Chaves Tesser. Athens, GA: University of Georgia Press, 1993, 74–103.

———. "Introduction." In *Forgotten Centuries: Indians and Europeans in the American South,* edited by Charles M. Hudson and Carmen Chaves Tesser. Athens, GA: University of Georgia Press, 1993, 1–14.

Hudson, Charles M and Carmen Chaves Tesser, eds. *Forgotten Centuries: Indians and Europeans in the American South.* Athens, GA: University of Georgia Press, 1993.

Huntington, Samuel P. "Entrevista." *El Pais* 20 Jun 2004. Supplement "Domingo," pp. 6–7.

———. "The Hispanic Challenge." *Foreign Policy* 141 (2004): 30–45.

———. *Who Are We? The Challenges to America's National Identity.* New York: Simon and Schuster, 2004.

Jefferson, Thomas. *The Papers of Thomas Jefferson, vol. 8.* Edited by Julian P. Boyd. Princeton: Princeton University Press, 1953.

Jones, Eric C. and Robert E. Rhoades. "Comparative Perspectives on International Migration: Illegals or ´Guest Workers´ in the American South?". In *Latino Workers in the Contemporary South*, edited by Arthur D. Murphy, Colleen Blanchard and Jennifer A. Hill. Athens, GA: University of Georgia Press, 2002, 23–35.

Jordan, Winthrop D. "Modern Tensions and the Origins of American Slavery." In *The Slavery Reader*, edited by Gad Heuman and James Walvin. New York: Routledge, 2003, 112–21.

Kanellos, Nicolas. "An Overview of Hispanic Literature in the United States." In *Herencia. The Anthology of Hispanic Literature in the United States*, edited by Nicolás Kanellos. Oxford: Oxford University Press, 2002, 1–32.

———. *Thirty Million Strong: Reclaiming the HISPANIC Image in American Culture.* Golden, CO: Fulcrum Publications, 1998.

Kaplan, Robert D. *An Empire Wilderness. Travels into the Heart of America.* New York: Vintage, 1998.

Kasarda, John D., Holly L. Hughes and Michael D. Irwin. "Demographic and Economic Restructuring in the South." In *The South Moves into its Future: Studies in the Analysis and Prediction of Social Change*, edited by Joseph S. Himes. Tuscaloosa: University of Alabama Press, 1991, 32–68.

Key, V.O. *Southern Politics in State and Nation.* New York: Vintage, 1949.

King, Ronald F., Douglas D. Rose, and Matthew Crozat. "The Downfall of David Duke? Duke, Republicans, and the Structure of Elections in Louisiana." In *David Duke and the Politics of Race in the South*, edited by Charles S. Bullock III, Keith Gaddie, and John C. Kucenski. Nashville: Vanderbilt University Press, 1995, 127–45.

Klein, Herbert S. *Slavery in the Americas.* Chicago: Elephant Paperbacks, 1989.

Klein, Naomi. "The Threat of Hope in Latin America." Accessed March 27, 2007. http://www.thenation.com/doc/20051121/klein.

Kochhar, Rakesh, Robert Suso, and Sonya Tagoya. "The New Latino South: The Context and Consequences of Rapid Growth." Accessed March 2, 2007. http://pewhispanic.org/files/reports/50.pdf

Kristeva, Julia. *Strangers to ourselves.* Translated by Leon Roudiez. New York: Columbia University Press, 1991.

Kuzenski, John C. "David Duke and the Nonpartisan Primary." In *David Duke and the politics of Race in the South*, edited by Charles S. Bullock III, Keith Gaddie, and John C. Kucenski. Nashville: Vanderbilt University Press, 1995, 3–22.

Lambert, Peter. "A decade of electoral democracy: continuity, change and crisis in Paraguay." *Bulletin of Latin American Research* 19 (2000): 379–96.

Leland, John and Veronica Chambers. "Generation Ñ. Latino America." *Newsweek* September 9, 1999: 52–8.

Lind, Michael. *The Next American Nation: The New Nationalism and the Fourth American Revolution.* New York: Free Press, 1995.

Logue, Cal M. "The Coercive Campaign Prophecy of Gene Talmadge, 1926–46." In *The Oratory of Southern Demagogues*, edited by Cal M. Logue and Howard Dorgan. Baton Rouge: Louisiana State University Press, 1981, 204–29.

Logue, Cal M. and Howard Dorgan. "The Demagogue." In *The Oratory of Southern Demagogues*, edited by Cal M. Logue and Howard Dorgan. Baton Rouge: Louisiana State University Press, 1981, 1–11.

Loucky, James. "Racism." In *Immigration in America Today. An Encyclopedia*, edited by James Loucky, Jeanne Armstrong, and Larry J. Estrada. Westport, CT: Greenwood Press, 2006, 269–73.

Lumpkin, Katherine Du Pre. *The Making of a Southerner*. New York: Knopf, 1947.

Manning, Carol S. "Southern Women Writers and the Beginning of the Renaissance." In *The History of Southern Women's Literature*, edited by Carolyn Perry and Mary Louise Weaks. Baton Rouge: Louisiana State University Press, 2002, 242–50.

Martí, José. *Marti on the USA*. Selected and Translated, with an Introduction by Luis A. Baralt. Carbondale: Southern Illinois University Press, 1966.

Martin, Ken. "Neutrality and the Alliance with the Confederate States of America." Accessed April 19, 2007. http://cherokeehistory.com/confed.html.

Martin Alcoff, Linda. "Is Latina/o Identity a Racial Identity?" In *Hispanics/Latinos in the United States*, edited by Jorge J.E. Gracia and Pablo De Greiff. New York: Routledge, 2000, 23–44.

Maysilles, Duncan. "Hoke Smith." Accessed March 4, 2007. http://www.georgiaencyclopedia.org/nge/Article.jsp?id=h-2121.

McPeek Villatoro, Marcos. "Latino Southerners: A New Form of Mestizaje." In *Cultural Diversity in the U.S. South: Anthropological Contributions to a Region in Transition*, edited by Carole E. Hill and Patricia D. Beaver. Athens, GA: University of Georgia Press, 1998, 104–14.

McWilliams, Tennant S. *The New South Faces the World. Foreign Affairs and the Southern Sense of Self, 1877–1950*. Baton Rouge: Louisiana State University Press, 1988.

MDC, Inc. *The State of the South 1998*. Chapel Hill, NC: MDC Inc., 1998.

———. *The State of the South 2002*. Chapel Hill, NC: MDC, Inc., 2002.

———. *The State of the South 2004*. Chapel Hill, NC: MDC, Inc., 2004.

———. *The State of the South 2007*. Chapel Hill, NC: MDC, Inc., 2007.

Meier, Matt. S. and Margo Gutiérrez. *The Mexican American Experience. An Encyclopedia*. Westport, CT: Greenwood Press, 2003.

Mejía, Thelma. "A Murky Transparency Law." Accessed April 10, 2007. http://www.globalpolicy.org/nations/launder/regions/2007/0222 transparency.htm.

Melville, Margarita B. "'Hispanic' Ethnicity, Race and Class." In *Handbook of Hispanic Cultures in the United States*, edited by Thomas Weaver, 85–106. Houston: Arte Público Press, 1993.

Mencken, H.L. "The Sahara of the Bozart." In *The American Scene*, selected and edited, and with an introduction and commentary by Huntington Cairns. New York: Knopf, 1965. 157–68.

Mendieta, Eduardo. "The Making of New Peoples. Hispanizing Race." In *Hispanics/Latinos in the United States*, edited by Jorge J. E. Gracia and Pablo De Greiff. New York: Routledge, 2000, 45–59.

Michie, Allan A. and Frank Rhylick. *Dixie Demagogues*. New York: The Vanguard Press, 1939.

Middleton, Richard. *Colonial America. A History, 1565–1776*. 3rd ed. Oxford: Blackwell Publications, 1992.

Mignolo, Walter D. "The Larger Picture: Hispanics/Latinos (& Latino Studies) in the Colonial Horizon of Modernity." In *Hispanics/Latinos in the United States*, edited by Jorge J. E. Gracia and Pablo De Greiff. New York: Routledge, 2000, 99–124.

Miller, Randall. M. "The Development of the Modern Urban South: An Historical Overview." In *Shadows of the Sunbelt. Essays on Ethnicity, Race, and the Urban South*, edited by Randall M. Miller and George E. Pozzetta. Boca Raton, FL: Florida Atlantic University Press, 1989, 1–20.

Miller, Randall M. and George E. Pozzetta, eds. *Shadows of the Sunbelt. Essays on Ethnicity, Race, and the Urban South*. Boca Raton, FL: Florida Atlantic University Press, 1989.

Mohl, Raymond A. "Globalization, Latinization and the *Nuevo* New South." In *Globalization and the American South*, edited by James C. Cobb and William Stueck. Athens, GA: University of Georgia Press, 2005, 66–99.

Moore, Lindsay. "Magical Realism." Retrieved January 20, 2005. http://www.english.emory.edu/Bahri/MagicalRealism.html.

Morales, Beatriz. "Latino Religion, Ritual and Culture." In *Handbook of Hispanic Cultures in the United States*, edited by Thomas Weaver. Houston: Arte Público Press, 1993, 191–208.

Moya, Paula M. L. "Cultural Particularity versus Universal Humanity. The value of being *asimilao*." In *Hispanics/Latinos in the United States*, edited by Jorge J. E. Gracia and Pablo De Greiff. New York: Routledge, 2000, 77–97.

Muñiz, Brenda. "In the Eye of the Storm: How the Government and Private Response to Hurricane Katrina Failed Latinos." Accessed April 10, 2007. http://www.nclr.org/content/publications/download/36812.

Naipaul, V.S. *A Turn in the South*. New York: Alfred A. Knopf, 1989.

National Hispanic Leadership Agenda. *Congressional Scorecard 107th Congress. First and Second Sessions*. Retrieved October 23, 2003. http://www.nclr.org/policy/scorecard2003/NHLA_Scorecard.pdf.

Newby, I. A. *The South. A History*. New York: Holt, Rinehart, and Winston, 1978.

N'diaye, Pap. "Los esclavos del sur de los Estados Unidos." In *El libro negro del colonialismo*, edited by Mark Ferro. Madrid: La Esfera de los libros, 2005, 147–60.

Oboler, Suzanne. "Hispanics? That's What They Call Us." In *The Latino Condition*, edited by Richard Delgado and Jean Stefancic New York, NY: New York University Press, 1998, 3–5.

O'Connor, Flannery. "The Displaced Person." In *The Complete Stories*. New York: Farrar, Strauss and Giroux, 1971, 194–235.

Odum, Howard W. *Southern Regions of the United States*. New York: Agathon Press, 1969.

Odum, Howard W. and Gary B. Johnson. *The Negro and His Songs*. Chapel Hill: The University of North Carolina Press, 1925.

Office of Minority Health. "Hispanics in the United States: An Insight into Group Characteristics." Retrieved November 23, 2004. http://www.omhrc.gov/haa/HAA2pg/AboutHAA1a.htm.

Oquendo, Angel R. "Re-imagining the Latino/a Race." In *The Latino Condition*, edited by Richard Delgado and Jean Stefancic. New York: New York University Press, 1998, 60–71.

Ortiz Cofer, Judith. *The Latin Deli*. Athens, GA: University of Georgia Press, 1993.

Ortuño Martínez, Manuel. "España-Estados Unidos. Fronteras imposibles." *La Aventura de la Historia* 5 (2003): 44–48.

Page, Walter Hines. *The Rebuilding of Old Commonwealths*. New York: Doubleday, Page and Co., 1902.

Parent, Wayne. "Race and Republican Resurgence in the South: Success in Black and White?" In *David Duke and the politics of Race in the South*, edited by Charles S. Bullock III, Keith Gaddie, and John C. Kucenski. Nashville: Vanderbilt University Press, 1995.

Parish, Peter J. *Slavery. History and Historians*. New York: Harper and Row, 1989.

Pearson, Edward A. "A Countryside Full of Flames." In *The Slavery Reader*, edited by Gad Heuman and James Walvin. New York: Routledge, 2003, 569–93.

Peña, Richard. "Interview." *New York* 32.34 (1999): 28–32.

Petras, James. "The Centrality of Peasant Movements in Latin America: Achievements and Objections." Accessed March 27, 2007. http://www.greens.org/s-r/38/38-10.html.

Pew Hispanic Center. "Latinos and the 2006 Mid-term Election." Accessed April 5, 2007. http://Pewhispanic.org/files/factsheets/26.pdf.

Poloni-Simard, Jacques. "La América española: una colonización de antiguo régimen." In *El libro negro del colonialismo*, edited by Mark Ferro. Madrid: La Esfera de los libros, 2005, 216–46.

Porter, Eduardo. "The Surging Hispanic Economy." Retrieved on February 18, 2004. http://www.wsjclassroomedition.com/archive.

Posada, Alonso de. *Alonso de Posada Report, 1686*. Translated by Alfred Barnaby Thomas. Pensacola: The Perdido Bay Press, 1982.

Posada-Carbó, Eduardo. "Electoral Juggling: A Comparative History of the Corruption of Suffrage in Latin America, 1830–1930." *Journal of Latin American History* 32 (2000): 611–44.

Pozzetta, George E. "Migration to the Urban South: An Unfinished Agenda." In *Shadows of the Sunbelt. Essays on Ethnicity, Race, and the Urban South*, edited by Randall M. Miller and George E. Pozzetta. Boca Raton, FL: Florida Atlantic University Press, 1989, 193–206.

President's Advisory Commission on Educational Excellence for Hispanic Americans. *Our Nation on the Fault Line: Hispanic American Education*.

Washington, DC: President's Advisory Commission on Educational Excellence for Hispanic Americans, 1996.

Public Broadcasting System. "Wilson—A Portrait. Legislative Victories." Retrieved March 16, 2006. http://www.pbs.org/wgbh/amex/wilson/portrait/wp_legislate_02.html.

Radelat, Ana. "An Avalanche of Aid. Hispanic workers flood the Gulf Coast." Accessed April 10, 2007. http://www.hispaniconline.com/magazine/2005/december/Panorama/journal2.html.

Ramos, Jorge. *The Other Face of America.* Translated By Patricia J. Duncan. New York: Rayo, 2002.

Ratzinger, Joseph Cardinal with Vittorio Messori. *The Ratzinger Report. An Exclusive Interview on the State of the Church.* Translated by Salvator Attanasio and Graham Harrison. San Francisco, CA: Ignatius Press, 1985.

Reed, John Shelton. *The Enduring South: Subcultural Persistence in Mass Society.* Chapel Hill: The University of North Carolina Press, 1986.

———. *One South: An Ethnic Approach to Regional Culture.* Baton Rouge: Louisiana State University Press, 1982.

Roberts, Diane. "Living Southern in *Southern Living.*" In *Dixie Debates. Perspectives on Southern Cultures,* edited by Richard H. King and Helen Taylor. New York: New York University Press, 1996, 85–98.

Rodgers, William Warm, Robert David Ward, Leah Rawls Atkins and Wayne Flynt. *Alabama. The History of a Deep South State.* Tuscaloosa, AL: University of Alabama Press, 1994.

Rodríguez, Gloria. *Raising nuestros niños: bringing up Latino children in a bicultural world.* New York: Fireside, 1999.

Rodríguez, Gregory. *The Emerging Latino Middle Class.* Los Angeles: Pepperdine University Institute for Public Policy, 1996.

Rodríguez, Richard. "'Blaxicans' and Other Reinvented Americans." *The Chronicle Review* B10–11. Retrieved October 1, 2003. http://chronicle.com/weekly/v50/i03/03b01001.htm.

Rodriguez, S. "Hispanics in the U. S.: An insight into group characteristics." *Department of Health and Human Services.* Retrieved May 5, 1999. http://www.hhs.gov/about/heo/hgen.html.

Rodríguez, Yolanda. "Gangs get a grip on Latinos." *Atlanta Journal-Constitution* December 29, 1999. F1, F5.

Rose, Willie Lee, editor. *A Documentary History of Slavery in North America.* New York: Oxford University Press, 1976.

Rouquié, Alain. "Dictadores, militares y legitimidad en America Latina." Translated by Mario R. dos Santos. In *Dictaduras y dictadores,* edited by Julio Labastida Martin del Campo. Mexico City: Siglo XXI, 1986. 10–26.

Said, Edward W. *Culture and Imperialism.* New York: Vintage, 1993.

Sale, Kirkpatrick. *Power Shift: The Rise of the Southern Rim and its Challenge to the Eastern Establishment.* New York: Random House, 1975.

Salinas, María Elena. "Latinos paid dearly after Katrina." Accessed April 5, 2007. http://www.santamariatimes.com/articles/2006/03/13/sections/ opinion/031306c.txt.

Salvatore, Ricardo D. "Repertoires of Coercion and Market Culture in Nineteenth-Century Buenos Aires Province." *International Review of Social History* 45 (2000): 409–48.

Shelby, Annette. "Jeff Davis of Arkansas." In *The Oratory of Southern Demagogues*, edited by Cal M. Logue and Howard Dorgan. Baton Rouge: Louisiana State University Press, 1981, 12–44.

Shorris, Earl. "Borderline Cases." In *Immigration to the U.S.*, edited by Robert Emmet Long. New York: H.W Wilson Company, 1992, 71–85.

Simâo, Paul. "Hispanics Flex New Muscle in Southern U.S." Retrieved August 2, 2003. http://www.puertorico-herald.org/issues/2002/vol6n27.

Skidmore, Thomas E. *Modern Latin America*. 5th ed. New York: Oxford University Press, 2001.

Smith, John David, editor. *Anti-Black Thought. 1863–1925. "The Negro Problem."* New York: Garland, 1993.

Smith, Jon and Deborah Cohn. "Introduction: Uncanny Hybridities." In *Look Away! The U.S. South in New World Studies*, edited by Jon Smith and Deborah Cohn. Durham, NC: Duke University Press, 2004, 1–24.

Smith, W. Thomas Jr. "An Influx of Hispanics Causing Growing Pains for the South." Retrieved September 10, 1999. http://www.latinolink.com/news/ us/0309sur.php3.

Spener, David. "Smuggling Migrants through South Texas: Challenges Posed by Operation Rio Grande." In *Global Human Smuggling. Comparative Perspectives,* edited by David Kyle and Rey Koslowski. Baltimore: Johns Hopkins University Press, 2001, 1029–65.

Stavans, Ilan. "Life in the Hyphen." In *The Latino Condition,* edited by Richard Delgado and Jean Stefancic. New York, NY: New York University Press, 1998, 32–36.

———. *The Hispanic Condition*. New York: HarperCollins Publishers, 1995.

Stephens, Gregory. "Monolingualism and Racialism as Curable Diseases: *Nuestra América* in the Transnational South." In *The American South in a Global World,* edited by James L. Peacock, Harry L. Watson, and Carrie R. Matthews. Chapel Hill, NC: The University of North Carolina Press, 2005, 205–22.

Still, William. *The Underground Rail Road*. Philadelphia: Porter and Coates Publishers, 1872.

Stoll, David. *Rigoberta Menchú and the Story of All Poor Guatemalans*. Boulder, CO: Westview Press, 1999.

Strickland, William M. "James Kimble Vardaman. Manipulation Through Myths in Mississippi." In *The Oratory of Southern Demagogues*, edited by Cal M. Logue and Howard Dorgan. Baton Rouge: Louisiana State University Press, 1981, 66–82.

Studstill, John D. and Laura Nieto-Studstill. "Hospitality and Hostility: Latin Immigrants in Southern Georgia." In *Latino Workers in the Contemporary*

South, edited by Arthur D. Murphy, Colleen Blanchard and Jennifer A. Hill. Athens, GA: University of Georgia Press, 2002, 68–81.

Sublette, Ned. *Cuba and Its Music*. Chicago: Chicago Review Press, 2004.

Swing, Raymond Gram. *Forerunners of American Fascism*. Freeport, NY: Books for Libraries Press, 1969.

Tannenbaum, Frank. "Slavery, the Negro, and Racial Prejudice." In *Slavery in the New World*, edited by Laura Fraser and Eugene D. Genovese. Englewood Cliffs, NJ: Prentice Hall, 1969, 3–7.

Thompson, Ann. "Putting Down Roots." *Company* 17 (2000): 13–16.

Tindall, George Brown. *Natives and newcomers: ethnic Southerners and Southern ethnics*. Athens, GA: University of Georgia Press, 1995.

Todorov, Tzvetan. *The Conquest of America*. Translated by Richard Howard. Norman, OK: University of Oklahoma Press, 1999.

Torres, Rodolfo D. and George Katsiaficas, eds. *Latino social movements: historical and theoretical perspectives*. New York: Routledge, 1999.

Torres, Sonia. *Nosotros in USA*. Rio de Janeiro: Jorge Zahar Editor, 2001.

Tredoux, Gavan. "Review of *Rigoberta Menchú and the Story of All Poor Guatemalans*, by David Stoll." Accessed March 22, 2007. http://www.cycad.com/cgi-bin/pinc/apr2000/books/gt_menchu.html.

Trueba, Enrique (Henry). *Latinos unidos: From Cultural Diversity to the Politics of Solidarity*. Lanham, MD: Rowman & Littlefield, 1999.

Tsunokai, Glenn T. "Stereotypes." In *Immigration in America Today. An Encyclopedia*, edited by James Loucky, Jeanne Armstrong, and Larry J. Estrada. Westport, CT: Greenwood Press, 2006, 316–20.

Tujibikile, Muamba. *La resistencia cultural del negro en América Latina: lógica ancestral y celebración de la vida*. San José, Costa Rica: DEI, 1990.

United States Conference of Catholic Bishops. "Demographics." Retrieved November 6, 2003. http://www.usccb.org/hispanicaffairs/demo.htm.

———. *Hispanic Ministry at the Turn of the New Millenium*. (Conducted by Rev. Raúl Gómez and Dr. Manuel Vásquez.) Washington: Accessed September 5, 2007. http://usccb.org/hispanicaffairs/studygomez.shtml.

Urrea, Luis Alberto. *Across the Wire. Life and Hard Times on the Mexican Border*. New York: Random House, 1993.

———. *By the Lake of Sleeping Children. The Secret Life of the Mexican Border*. New York: Anchor Books, 1996.

———. *The Devil's Highway*. New York: Little, Brown and Company, 2004.

Vaca, Nicolas C. *The Presumed Alliance. The Unspoken Conflict Between Latinos and Blacks and What It Means for America*. New York: Rayo Publishers, 2004.

Valdivia Ortiz de Zarate, Veronica. "Terrorism and Political Violence during the Pinochet Years: Chile, 1973–1989." *Radical History Review* 85 (2003): 182–90.

Walker, Alice. *In Search of our Mother's Gardens: Womanist Prose*. San Diego: Harcourt Brace Jovanovich, 1983.

Warner, Judith. "Enslavement." In *Immigration in America Today. An Encyclopedia*, edited by James Loucky, Jeanne Armstrong, and Larry J. Estrada. Westport, CT: Greenwood Press, 2006, 92–97.

Weddle, Robert S. *The French Thorn: Rival Explorers in the Spanish Sea, 1682–1762.* Tuscaloosa, AL: University of Alabama Press, 1993.

Wei, Shang-Jin. "Local Corruption and global Capital Flows." *Brookings Papers on Economic Activity* 2000.2 (2000): 303–54.

Wexler, Laura. "A Possible Dream." Accessed March 7, 2007. http://www.uga.edu/gm/399/FeatPos.html.

White, O. Kendall and Daryl White. *Religion in the Contemporary South: Diversity, Community, and Identity.* Athens, GA: University of Georgia Press, 1995.

Wilson, Heidi and Jeanne Armstrong. "Unauthorized immigration." In *Immigration in America Today. An Encyclopedia,* edited by James Loucky, Jeanne Armstrong, and Larry J. Estrada. Westport, CT: Greenwood Press, 2006, 332–47.

Wilson, John K. *Newt Gingrich. Capital Crimes and Misdemeanors.* Monroe, Maine: Common Courage Press, 1996.

Wilson, Robin. "Anthropologist Challenges Veracity of Multicultural Icon." Accessed April 4, 2007. http://chronicle.com/weekly/v45/i19/19a00101.htm.

Wolfe, Thomas. *Look Homeward, Angel.* New York: Simon and Schuster, 1995.

Wyatt Brown, Bertram. *The Shaping of Southern Culture: Honor, Grace, and War.* Chapel Hill, NC: The University of North Carolina Press, 2001.

Yale-Loehr, Stephen and Ted Chiappari. "Immigration: Cities and States Rush in Where Congress Fears to Tread." Accessed March 20, 2007. http://millermayer.com/new/nylj_locallaw.html.

Yarrington, Doug. "Cattle, Corruption, Venezuelan State Formation During the Regime of Juan Vicente Gomez, 1908–35." *Latin American Research Review* 38 (2003): 9–33.

Index

About the Author

JOSÉ MARÍA MANTERO is Associate Professor of Spanish in the Department of Modern Languages at Xavier University. He has published a monograph on the Argentinean writer Marta Traba, *La voz política de Marta Traba* (1995), an anthology of recent Nicaraguan poetry, *Neuvos poetas de Nicaragua (Antología)* (2004), and numerous journal articles on Latin American literature that center on the creation of a national identity through poetry and autobiographical texts such as testimonials or memoirs. He has presented at conferences in the United States, Spain, Nicaragua, Panama, Belize, and Guatemala, and currently continues to research Spanish and Latin American literature, particularly texts that have contributed to the mythification and the formation of a national identity.